Cultural Legacies of Slavery
in Modern Spain

SUNY series in Latin American and Iberian Thought and Culture
―――――――
Rosemary G. Feal, editor
Jorge J. E. Gracia, founding editor

Cultural Legacies of Slavery in Modern Spain

Edited by

AKIKO TSUCHIYA and
AURÉLIE VIALETTE

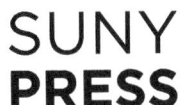

Cover art: Unknown, painting of the sailing vessel, La Amistad, off Culloden Point, Long Island, New York, 1839.

Published by State University of New York Press, Albany

© 2025 State University of New York

All rights reserved

Printed in the United States of America

No part of this book may be used or reproduced in any manner whatsoever without written permission. No part of this book may be stored in a retrieval system or transmitted in any form or by any means including electronic, electrostatic, magnetic tape, mechanical, photocopying, recording, or otherwise without the prior permission in writing of the publisher.

Links to third-party websites are provided as a convenience and for informational purposes only. They do not constitute an endorsement or an approval of any of the products, services, or opinions of the organization, companies, or individuals. SUNY Press bears no responsibility for the accuracy, legality, or content of a URL, the external website, or for that of subsequent websites.

For information, contact State University of New York Press, Albany, NY
www.sunypress.edu

Library of Congress Cataloging-in-Publication Data

Names: Tsuchiya, Akiko, 1959– editor. | Vialette, Aurélie, editor.
Title: Cultural legacies of slavery in modern Spain edited by Akiko Tsuchiya and Aurélie Vialette.
Description: Albany : State University of New York Press, [2025] | Series: SUNY series in Latin American and Iberian thought and culture | Includes bibliographical references and index.
Identifiers: LCCN 2024025623 | ISBN 9798855800845 (hardcover : alk. paper) | ISBN 9798855800852 (ebook) | ISBN 9798855800838 (pbk. : alk. paper)
Subjects: LCSH: Slavery—Spain—History. | Slave trade—Spain—History. | Spain—Social conditions. | Spain—Race relations. | Spain—Ethnic relations.
Classification: LCC HT1216 .C85 2025 | DDC 306.3/620946—dc23/eng/20240913
LC record available at https://lccn.loc.gov/2024025623

To what end does one conjure the ghost of slavery, if not to incite the hopes of transforming the present?

—Saidiya Hartman, *Lose Your Mother*

Contents

Acknowledgments   xi

Introduction   1
   Akiko Tsuchiya and Aurélie Vialette

Part 1
The Legacies of Slavery in the Archive

Chapter 1
The *Houseboys* of Fernando Poo: Domestic Service in Spanish
Colonial Africa   21
   Benita Sampedro Vizcaya

Chapter 2
Echoes of the Spanish Slave Trade in Nineteenth-Century London   49
   Kirsty Hooper

Chapter 3
Cosmetic of the Archive: An Autopsy of Slave Trader Antonio
López y López and the General Tobacco Company in
the Philippines   73
   Aurélie Vialette

Chapter 4
From Slavery to Anti-Black Racism: Racial Ideas from Cuba
to Catalonia   95
   *Martín Rodrigo-Alharilla and Juliana Nalerio, translated
   by María Cristina Urruela*

Part 2
Confronting the Legacies of Slavery in Cultural Memory Sites

Chapter 5
Confronting the Legacies of Slavery and Colonialism in Public Spaces: Debates around Racist and Colonial Monuments in Modern Catalonia 121
   Akiko Tsuchiya

Chapter 6
Spain and the Year of Toppled Statues of Enslavers and Colonizers: The Examples of Madrid and Cádiz 153
   Ulrike Schmieder

Chapter 7
Memorialized Blackness: The Case of the Museo Atlántico 191
   Jeffrey K. Coleman

Chapter 8
Public Memory Policies in Spain: How Is the Colonial Past Addressed? 209
   Oriol López Badell and Celeste Muñoz Martínez, interviewed by Akiko Tsuchiya and Aurélie Vialette, translated by María Cristina Urruela

Part 3
Interpreting the Legacies of Slavery in Literature, Music, and Visual Culture

Chapter 9
Pedro Blanco, the Accursed Slave Driver: Literature and Historical Memory of Slavery in Spain 223
   Gustau Nerín, translated by María Cristina Urruela

Chapter 10
Searching for Cayetana's Daughter: From Goya to Carmen Posadas 243
   Rosalía Cornejo-Parriego

Chapter 11
The Urgency of a Black Iberian Thought 273
*Tania Safura Adam, interviewed by Akiko Tsuchiya
and Aurélie Vialette, translated by María Cristina Urruela*

Chapter 12
On Making Art from Hidden Places 281
*Yinka Esi Graves, interviewed by Akiko Tsuchiya
and Aurélie Vialette*

Chapter 13
Hispano-tropicalism: Flamencology and the Denial of
   Black Presence in Spain 291
Miguel Ángel Rosales, translated by María Cristina Urruela

Contributors 301

Index 309

Acknowledgments

We began conceptualizing this project shortly before the pandemic. The process of completing this volume during these exceptional times has been an incredibly long road, considering the personal and professional challenges faced by many of us while trying to bring our projects to fruition. We thank all the contributors of the volume for their patience, perseverance, and collegiality. The conversations that took place virtually—many of them, across the Atlantic—have cemented our solidarity and shared commitment to bring to light the lives, histories, and stories of enslaved individuals that have been silenced and to reckon collectively with the legacies of these past injustices in the present moment.

We would like to thank the Center for the Humanities at Washington University in St. Louis for providing us with a Collaborative Research Seed Grant to carry out the research for this book, and the Center for the Study of Race, Ethnicity, and Equity (CRE²) for granting Akiko much-needed release time to complete the project. We are indebted to María Cristina Urruela for her superb translations of the essays originally written in Spanish.

Akiko is appreciative of the many friends and colleagues who have engaged her in conversations about this project, assisted her in locating materials, and offered her support, encouragement, and the opportunity to share her ideas during the conceptualization and elaboration of this volume. These individuals include Alex Alonso-Nogueira, Julia Chang, Luisa Elena Delgado, Pura Fernández, Teresa Fuentes, Helena González, Rebecca Ingram, Ying Ko, Jo Labanyi, María Xesús Lama López, Oriol López Badell, Gabrielle Miller, Gustau Nerín, Martín Rodrigo-Alharilla, Erika Rodríguez, Elzbieta Sklodowska, Lisa Surwillo and, especially, Aurélie Vialette. She is also grateful for the invaluable feedback she received from the director and the other faculty fellows at the Center for the Study of Race, Ethnicity,

xii | Acknowledgments

and Equity on her chapter of this project during the tenure of her CRE² Fellowship. Her thanks also go to James Colomina, Jordi Guixé, and Lázaro Lima for granting her permission to use their photos in her chapter of the volume.

Aurélie is grateful for the conversations and advice of many colleagues and friends during the years spent preparing this volume; some of them invited her to present the chapter included here or read previous drafts, which helped conceptualize general ideas for the project as well. Among them are Mireia Bo Gudiol (Arxiu Nacional de Catalunya), Pura Fernández, Daniela Flesler, Alex Gil, María Xesús Lama López, Cristina Lee, Daniel Levy, Annick Louis, Martín Rodrigo-Alharilla, Bécquer Seguín, Ann Stoler, Jesús R. Velasco, and Carlos Varón. I am forever grateful to Akiko Tsuchiya for her wonderful collaboration and friendship.

Finally, without the interest and unflagging support of our wonderful editor, Rebecca Colesworthy, this volume would not have come to fruition. We thank her for having faith in this project.

Introduction

Akiko Tsuchiya and Aurélie Vialette

> History is not the past. It is the present. We carry our own history with us. We are our history. If we pretend otherwise, we are literally criminals.
>
> —James Baldwin, *I Am Not Your Negro*

> I, too, live in the time of slavery, by which I mean I am living in the future created by it.
>
> —Saidiya Hartman, *Lose Your Mother*

Education about the history of slavery has been under attack in the United States, particularly in Republican states such as Texas and Florida. In these states, the government has made concerted efforts to silence references to slavery in education. At present, slavery is not taught in primary schools as part of the social studies curriculum, with the justification that the topic would make the students feel "uncomfortable" and should therefore be avoided. In 2015 a social studies textbook approved by the Texas Board of Education referred to enslaved Africans as "workers" (López). Initiatives, such as *The New York Times*' Pulitzer Prize–winning 1619 Project, which explains how slavery and Black Americans shaped the US, are being banned. As recently as 2022, Texas education officials proposed to change the term "slavery" to "involuntary relocation" in school textbooks. Although the proposal was not approved by the State Board of Education, Texas is not alone: Idaho, Louisiana, New Hampshire, and Tennessee have introduced bills that would "ban teaching about the enduring legacies of slavery and segregationist past, or that any state or the country is inherently racist or sexist" (Romero). In this social and political climate, research on slavery and its legacies is urgent. Slavery is part of a global system of racial exploitation, whose repercussions we cannot forget. As Joan Scott has affirmed, we cannot assume that "the past is past" (54); the "ghosts" of slavery haunt "all subsequent American history" (58). This observation applies equally to all other nations, including Spain, involved in the crimes of slavery and the slave trade. As this book will show, to acknowledge the continuing influence of the past on the present is a first step toward historical accountability and to fighting systemic racism in our contemporary world.

A critical approach toward the collective memory of a nation, which connects the past to the present, is, therefore, crucial to understanding and confronting the global legacies of slavery. Drawing on the idea of Maurice Halbwachs, Ana Lucia Araujo argues how "collective memory becomes public when it is transformed into a political instrument to build, assert, and reinforce identities of these groups . . . it is about the way the past of a group is lived again in the present" (*Politics of Memory* 1). She goes on to explain that collective memory, while representing a continuing legacy from the past, "is not homogeneous but conflictual" (*Politics of Memory* 1) and, especially, in the case of a traumatic past, such as that of the Atlantic slave trade, the collective memory of the subaltern group has frequently been erased and invisibilized in the public space due to their social, political, and economic exclusion. This is hardly surprising in the case of societies that benefited economically and politically from their participation in the slave trade—and from the slave workforce itself. As Araujo notes, what progress has been made in the past few decades in raising the public consciousness of slavery and its legacies—on American, European and African soil—often took the form of local, smaller-scale initiatives launched by anti-racist and historical memory organizations.[1] At the same time, major cultural projects, such as museums, monuments, and slavery routes (with the UNESCO slave route project constituting a prime example)[2] have played an important role in bringing out the collective memory of slavery into the public space for a long-overdue reckoning (Araujo, *Politics of Memory* 3–6).

In her *Slavery in the Age of Memory*, Araujo scrutinizes the ways in which representations of the public memory of slavery—through museums, monuments, statues, place names, and other sites of memory—have become "a permanent battleground" (69), as (racialized) sites of competing narratives about a nation's slaving past. As Pierre Nora has suggested, memory is an intentional, performative act that actively produces a connection to the present through its attachment to memory sites; collective memory is brought into consciousness by drawing meaning from those sites, through the act of commemoration (22–23). Therefore, what is at stake in the battle over collective memory is how we interpret history and represent it in the public arena, inevitably through the social, political, and cultural frameworks of the present. While Araujo studies the manifestations of the public memory of slavery in nations such as Great Britain, France, the Netherlands, and the US, which have led the way in engaging critically with the legacies of slavery, Spain is conspicuously absent from her work, for a good reason.[3] In spite of the progress that Spain's historical memory movement has made in confronting the legacies of the Franco dictatorship, particularly following the passage of the Law of Historical Memory (2007), there has been a dearth of government-supported memory programs and initiatives aimed to reckon specifically with the legacies of colonialism and slavery.[4] In fact, as Iñaki Tofiño has observed, despite the close links between Spanish colonialism and the Franco dictatorship, even the recently approved Law of Democratic Memory (2022),[5] presumably an improved version of the 2007 law, remains silent on the colonial question.

Since the turn of the twenty-first century, the field of modern Iberian studies has produced a steady stream of publications on the Spanish empire and its colonial legacies, of which slavery is a significant aspect.[6] That is, our discipline has finally taken the "imperial turn"—defined by Antoinette Burton as the "accelerated attention to the impact of histories of imperialism on metropolitan societies" (2)—forcing a recognition of the legacies of Spain's colonial past and its continued influence on the present. In more recent years, the emergence and expansion of the field of transatlantic studies have offered new perspectives on "the study of the cultures of Iberia as they transformed themselves and others in their Atlantic crossings," addressing issues such as "colonial and postcolonial legacies, genocides, circulations, appropriations, and expropriations" (Enjuto-Rangel et al 9).[7] As Michelle Murray has noted, foregrounding the history of slavery in the Iberian Atlantic forces us to confront Spain's role in the global processes of slavery and forced migration (349).

At the same time, it is understandable that much of the vast scholarship on slavery's impact in the Hispanic world has centered on Latin America (Ana Lucia Araujo, Manuel Barcia, Alex Borucki, Alejandro de la Fuente, William Van Norman, etc.) and on the early modern period in Spain (Emily Berquist, Carmen Fracchia, José Miguel López García,

Aurelia Martín Casares, Enriqueta Vila Vilar). Moreover, scholarly writings on slavery and its legacies in modern (post-eighteenth-century) Spain have been authored largely by historians, such as Martín Rodrigo-Alharilla, Josep Fradera, Christopher Schmidt-Nowara, and Michael Zeuske, to cite a few of the pioneering researchers in the field.[8] Michael Zeuske, the first scholar to systematically employ the concept of the "Hidden Atlantic," has challenged the common misperception, particularly among those focused on the Anglo-Atlantic world, that the nineteenth century was the "Age of Abolition." In fact, he demonstrated that it was a period of a booming (illegal) slave trade by the Spaniards, particularly to Cuba, which became one of "the most important locations of the Second Slavery in the context of global history" (Zeuske 104). Arguing that previous accounts failed to consider the transcultural dimensions of the slave trade, he coined the term "the Hidden Atlantic" to refer to the transatlantic space of exchange—particularly, between the Americas and Africa—in which the slave-trafficking system became established as a lucrative business in the nineteenth century, more specifically after 1808.

The marginalization and concealment of the "Hidden Atlantic" as a site of slavery and slave trade, from the early modern years to the nineteenth century, have undoubtedly contributed to the general lack of representation of the Iberian Atlantic in the contemporary period, particularly in Spain (Zeuske 105). Nevertheless, the social and economic impact of slavery endured in the Hispanic world long after the nineteenth century, when it was finally abolished in 1886 in Cuba, the last of the Spanish colonies in the Americas to do so. Beyond the more obvious, enduring social and economic repercussions of slavery, which have already been well documented by historians, its "hidden" legacies also reverberated over many centuries in the cultural arena not only in the colonies but also in the metropolis, where both the central Spanish state and regional governments have failed to reckon fully with the role that slavery played in the development of industrial sectors. Granted, the political institutions of Spain have been slow to confront the legacies of colonialism and slavery, as evinced by the lack of sustained memory programs on the national level addressing these issues and by the continued presence of monuments commemorating figures linked to slavery and colonialism. Yet this problem has taken on a special urgency for Iberian studies scholars and cultural activists alike in the past decade, given the growing impact of the global racial justice movements in the Spanish national context.

In the field of Iberian literary and cultural studies, Lisa Surwillo's pioneering study, *Monsters by Trade: Slave Traffickers in Modern Spanish Literature and Culture* (2014), was the first book to focus on the role that the slave trader played in the literature and cultural life of modern Spain; and the contributors to the volume *Mujeres esclavas y abolicionistas en la España de los siglos XVI al XIX* (2014), edited by Aurelia Martín Casares and Rocío Periáñez Gómez, scrutinized the writings of abolitionist women, as well as representations of enslaved women in literature and the visual arts in Spain. Art historian Carmen Fracchia's *"Black but Human": Slavery and Visual Arts in Hapsburg Spain, 1480–1700* (2019) is a groundbreaking study of the visual representations of enslaved and formerly enslaved Africans in Spain in the early modern period, as is Nick Jones's *Staging* Habla de negros*: Radical Performances of the African Diaspora in Early Modern Spain*, which elucidates the ways in which *habla de negros* language in early modern Spanish theater empowered Black Africans and enabled their resistance to white supremacy.[9] While our book builds on the work of these previous scholars, our anthology considers the manifestations of the legacies of slavery within a broader cultural context that includes literature and the visual arts, the mass media (magazines and radio programs), monuments and memorials, museums, tourist routes, historical archives, memory initiatives, and the increasingly vocal anti-racist, social justice, and immigrant advocacy movements in the Spanish state.

In sum, the contributors to this volume collectively address the question of how culture—understood in the broadest possible sense—produced in the Iberian Peninsula or in its overseas territories, from the nineteenth century to the present, both reflected and shaped ways of understanding the history and the heritage of a nation sustained on colonialism, slavery, and labor exploitation. On the one hand, our goal is to create an archive of cultural memory sites of slavery and its aftermath, and, as Aurélie Vialette suggests in her work, to investigate what is hidden behind these cultural forms and symbols—what untold stories they might hold about those of African descent in Spain, whose history and stories have long been suppressed ("Cosmetic of the Archive"). On the other, beyond the creation of this "archive," we ask how the recovery of those hidden stories might transform our vision and understanding of the Afro-descendant community's place in the national history of Spain, as well as in the global history of transatlantic crossings and forced migrations. Our contributors include literary critics, historians, anthropologists, colonial studies scholars, filmmakers, cultural practitioners, and grass-roots activists engaged in broader historical memory initiatives. To date, there is no book-length study, of similar interdisciplinary breadth, representing such a rich diversity of voices that addresses the legacies of slavery in the modern Iberian world in a sustained fashion.

The topic of our book could not be timelier. In Spain, cultural practitioners, artists, academics, and grass-roots activists have shed light on the legacies of slavery through cultural, urban, as well as academic initiatives. Yet these inquiries have created discomfort for some politicians and the general public, who have resisted coming to terms with their nation's past slavery practices, let alone seeking reparations. The EUROM report shows that only in Catalonia and the Basque Country have there been isolated initiatives to implement materials pertaining to colonialism and slavery into the educational curriculum in the Spanish state (Muñoz and López 18–19). One could argue that, in most of the Spanish state, with some exceptions,[10] there is still great resistance to decolonial and antiracist initiatives, on the part of many sectors of society across the political spectrum that continue to remain nostalgic for an imperial past. Moreover, many members of the bourgeoisie, especially in Catalonia, who in all likelihood fear the discovery of their own ancestors' implication in the slave trade, have naturally taken a defensive position when the society's slaving past is being publicly addressed (Palà).[11] Debates in Catalonia have been particularly lively after a documentary *Negrers: La Catalunya esclavista* (*Slavers: Catalonia and the Slave Trade*), directed by Jordi Portals and produced by Abacus, was released in February 2023 by TV3 on the Catalan public television's program *Sense ficció* (*Without Fiction*). The film reveals that Catalonia, its bourgeoisie, and its numerous ports had ties to slavery, showing how Catalonia enriched itself through slave trafficking and labor. It exposes how Catalonia's industrial revolution and its Modernist movement were financed by capital obtained from the slave trade.[12] The promotional video, released a few days before the film, underscores Catalan society's denial of its colonial and slaving past and signals a wish to change how history is transmitted to citizens: it affirms "aquesta tradició és la que s'ha de trencar" (1:24) ("this tradition is the one to be broken"). Catalan nationalists' reaction to this film, particularly those of the Assemblea Nacional Catalana (ANC) and the Front Nacional de Catalunya (FNC), on social media has been virulent. On Twitter, in response to a post by TV3's official Twitter account, while some users were enthusiastic about the film's reckoning with history, affirming the need to make amends for past injustices, others continued to deny Catalonia's slaving past. Some among the latter group maintained that slavery was a common practice at the time or that Catalans themselves had suffered slavery in the past—a statement devoid of historical accuracy.[13] This denial of an uncomfortable historical truth has contributed to effacing the legacies of slavery from public debate for more than a century.

Historian Celeste Muñoz Martínez, interviewed for this book, has written on this topic in "De memòries, distorsions i conflictes: El passat esclavista i colonial català en el punt de mira" ("Of Memories, Distortions, and Conflicts: The Catalan Slaving and Colonial Past in the Spotlight"). She and Alba Valenciano-Mañé show how slavery has been silenced in Catalonia through "distorsió històrica" ("historical distortion"). They explain that historical distortion occurs when the past is erased due to an overly reductive or universalizing representation of historical events: for example, by presenting a homogenizing vision of the colonial process across different national or historical contexts, or by underplaying the harm done to specific populations in historical narratives on colonialism and slavery. Their analysis dovetails with Araujo's account of the heterogeneous and conflictive aspects of collective memory mentioned earlier. In addition, their text underscores the importance of local grass-roots initiatives to awaken public consciousness about the history of slavery and its legacy. Local memory, for Muñoz and Valenciano-Mañé, needs to incorporate a critical approach to the colonial past.

A public function sponsored by the Office of Democratic Memory, titled *La Barcelona incòmoda: Jornades de debat sobre memòria i espai públic* (*Uncomfortable Barcelona: Debates on Memory and Public Space*), which took place in 2022 at a conference in Barcelona, exemplified this critical approach. This event centered on the city, its symbols, and its uncomfortable history: "Uns símbols que, amb la seva presència, a voltes han legitimat el franquisme, el colonialisme, l'esclavatge; i han silenciat l'altra Barcelona: la de les memòries subalterns obligades a ser oblidades, les sotmeses, amagades" ("Symbols that, with their presence, have sometimes legitimized Francoism, colonialism, slavery, and have silenced the other Barcelona: that of the subaltern memories that are forced to be forgotten, the ones that are hidden, the ones that have been hidden"; *La Barcelona incòmoda* 2). For Jordi Guixé, the Director of European Observatory on Memories (EUROM),[14] uncomfortable memories make room for choices: citizens should be able to choose if they want to represent, explain, and commemorate symbols in the public spaces of their cities ("La Barcelona incòmoda—taula de conclusions" 10:30). Following Guixé, Tania Safura Adam (whose interview is included in this book) has asked pertinent questions regarding cities, urban space, and history. To whom does the city belong? Whom does it represent? What does it mean to democratize public space? ("La Barcelona incòmoda—taula de conclusions" 24:26). In all these interventions, fundamental questions concerning collective representation and memory are at the center of debate, addressing the invisibility of Black people, women, and working classes in the use we make of urban space. In addition, the "misrepresentation" of history of the above-mentioned communities in urban spaces further exacerbates discrimination against them.

In response to these problems, many local (grass-roots) initiatives have emerged in Spain, in order to revise historical narratives of the past and to increase their visibility in the urban space.[15] The important anti-racist group SOS Racisme, as well as the collective Tanquem els CIE (Campaign to Close Down Internment Centers for Foreigners), which has campaigned to close down detention centers for immigrants, have intervened actively in the public space to protest racist and colonial monuments, and to expose institutional racism, by connecting the nation's racist and colonial past to present-day immigration policies and practices that continue to uphold racism and discrimination.[16] In March 2022, Canal Historia, which produces documentaries on historical issues of relevance to the public, broadcast the series *Encadenados*, centered on the history and legacies of slavery in Spain and its colonies, with the participation of prominent experts on slavery, some of whom are contributors to our volume. The first episode of the documentary brings to light the historical context for the enslavement of Afro-descendants in Spain and its colonies, also highlighting efforts to reckon with this past. For example, the documentary features Barcelona's slavery route, one of the public history initiatives promoted by EUROM, to address the prominent role that Catalan and Spanish entrepreneurs played in the slave trade in the nineteenth century, after it was legally banned.[17] Series such as these are crucial to bringing to the attention of the general Spanish public "el pasado esclavista de España [que] ha permanecido oculto entre los libros de historia" ("the slaving past of Spain that has remained hidden in history books"; *Encadenados*, episode 1).

In addition to the scholarly essays in this volume, we include other forms of contribution, such as interviews and creative writings, to reflect the diversity of perspectives from which the question of the legacies of slavery has been addressed in contemporary Spain. The inclusion of authors from outside of the academy is crucial to representing the broad range of important work that is being done "on the ground" by the cultural practitioners themselves, who "carry our own history with us," as James Baldwin affirmed. Among them are interviews with journalist and cultural critic Tania Safura Adam, founder of *Radio Africa*, *Radio Africa Magazine*, and the research project *España Negra*; Flamenco dancer and theorist Yinka Esi Graves, who, in her choreographic work, explores Flamenco from an African diasporic perspective; and Oriol López Badell and Celeste Muñoz, key players in EUROM, led by the University of Barcelona Solidarity Foundation, and engaged in promoting human rights. Additionally, López Badell, through his work in the Knowing History Association (an NGO established in Barcelona in 2008 to promote democratic memory), created and led the first guided historical tour of sites linked to colonialism and slavery in Barcelona. Finally, we include a creative essay by filmmaker Miguel Ángel Rosales, who in 2016 directed *Gurumbé: Canciones de tu memoria negra*, a documentary about African slavery in the Iberian Peninsula and its cultural influences, particularly on Flamenco.

More concretely, *Cultural Legacies of Slavery* consists of three parts. Part 1, "The Legacies of Slavery in the Archive," focuses on the role that the institution of the archive has played in both concealing and exposing the long-lasting impact of the transatlantic slave trade, by mapping the global networks of slave traffickers, previously hidden in archives. Part 1 opens with Benita Sampedro Vizcaya's essay, "The *Houseboys* of Fernando Poo: Domestic Service in Spanish Colonial Africa," in which the role of the Black body and Black labor is the subject. Her work reconstructs the social history of domestic workers, the economic and political structures that governed their work, and the discursive mechanisms through which the transition from a post-emancipation era to a pre-independence one was made possible. It also resituates domestic work and servants' narratives at the center of twentieth-century written traditions in Spanish colonial Africa.

The archive is also the cornerstone of the other chapters of Part 1. Kirsty Hooper's essay, "Echoes of the Spanish Slave Trade in Nineteenth-Century London" (chapter 2), sheds light on the activities of Spanish merchant families with extensive connections to the slave trade, who established their homes and offices in London during the nineteenth century. She draws on archival materials—among them, church and civil records, school registers, newspapers, and government papers—to reconstruct these families' activities, how they obscured their involvement in the Spanish slave trade, and to trace their cultural and material legacies in London, a city deeply opposed to Spain's persistent involvement in the trading of humans. For her part, Aurélie Vialette, in "Cosmetic of the Archive: An Autopsy of Slave Trader Antonio López y López and the General Tobacco Company in the Philippines" (chapter 3), delves into the archives of slave trader Antonio López y López, who founded the Compañía General de Tabacos de Filipinas. Her study reveals the intricate web of global networks of the slave trade in the nineteenth century and shows how archives can become manipulative tools to conceal and erase the role of the slave trade in sustaining multinational businesses.

Colonial slavery, especially that affecting persons of African descent, has been one of the principal sources of racism in modern Spain. Relying on archival sources, Martín Rodrigo-Alharilla and Juliana Nalerio trace the evolution of racial thought in the nineteenth and early twentieth century. Their chapter, "From Slavery to Anti-Black Racism: Racial Ideas from Cuba to Catalonia," centers on Catalonia as a case study of this circum-Atlantic reality, referring to Cuba, which is the true point of departure for their analysis of a past that has impacted how the legacies of slavery are confronted in the present. They show how the Atlantic slave trade, on the one hand, as well as the institution of slavery on the American continent, on the other, left a profound mark on the racial ideas, concepts, and categories populating both Anglophone and Hispanophone colloquial language, as well as on legal and cultural lexical traditions.

Part 2, "Confronting the Legacies of Slavery in Cultural Memory Sites," focuses on recent cultural initiatives and activism—including the dismantling of racist and colonial monuments, museum exhibits, public history initiatives such as slavery routes, and anti-racist cultural activism—that seek to refigure memory sites of slavery and colonialism in Spain, transforming them into spaces for critical reflection on the past. Chapter 5, "Confronting the Legacies of Slavery and Colonialism in Public Spaces: Debates around Racist and Colonial Monuments in Modern Catalonia," by Akiko Tsuchiya, focuses on two monuments—the Antonio López y López and Columbus monuments—related to colonialism and slavery that have become objects of public controversy in Barcelona over the years. She analyzes the significance of political and cultural initiatives that have been launched around these monuments to protest colonialism and transform the ways in which communities experience history in public spaces. She underscores the particular importance of initiatives that call attention to the connection between the past and the present, prompting the public to reflect on the ways in which the nation's racist and colonial history continues to shape society in the present. Along similar lines in chapter 6, Ulrike Schmieder centers her study, "Spain and the Year of Toppled Statues of Enslavers and Colonizers: The Examples of Madrid and Cádiz," on fallen statues of enslavers to address the question of why confronting the legacies of slavery is so difficult in Spain. She analyzes these memory sites and their connection to history, while also drawing on interviews conducted with those engaged in the politics of memory in academia, museums, local politics, arts, the Afro-Spanish movement, and the Afro-Cuban diaspora in Spain since 2017. The article discusses the lacunae of memory with respect to the enslavement of Africans in Spanish civil society and the gaps in knowledge, even in post-colonial activism, and reflects on its reasons.

For its part, the museum is another cultural memory site, full of cruel paradoxes in its representations of the legacies of the transatlantic slave trade. Chapter 7, "Memorialized Blackness: The Case of the Museo Atlántico," by Jeffrey K. Coleman, examines the role of the Museo Atlántico in Lanzarote (Canary Islands), which has served as a space for memorializing the deaths of African migrants in the Atlantic, while evoking a parallel to the transatlantic slave trade. His analysis considers the dual purpose of the museum as a space to memorialize and erase Blackness. Coleman argues that, despite the museum's mission to create social awareness around the humanitarian crisis of contemporary migrants, its location, ecological aesthetic, and general inaccessibility obfuscate and undermine its purpose of commemorating Black life/death, participating ultimately in the objectification of Black bodies that so often pervades the media.

An interview with Oriol López Badell and Celeste Muñoz Martínez in chapter 8 closes the second part. In "Public Memory Policies in Spain: How is the Colonial Past Addressed?" we ask López Badell and Muñoz Martínez to explain the absence of an institutional politics of memory addressing Spain's colonial past, as well as the public history initiatives that have been launched in Barcelona to respond to this absence and to raise public consciousness about this issue. They contextualize these initiatives within the larger historical memory movement in Spain, since the passage of the Laws of Historical and Democratic Memories, and within global movements such as Black Lives Matter. Part 2 is central to this book in that the authors study monuments, statues, museums, and activist interventions, communicating the urgency of raising awareness about the impact of slavery on the society and cultural institutions of Spain. In addition, these chapters call for the need to open spaces for critical reflection on Spain's colonial history.

The third part of the book, "Interpreting the Legacies of Slavery in Literature, Music, and Visual Culture," considers the representations of slavery—and of its hidden legacies—in the works of literary authors, filmmakers, and other cultural producers from the nineteenth century to the present. In chapter 9, "Pedro Blanco, the Accursed Slave Driver: Literature and Historical Memory of Slavery in Spain," Gustau Nerín carries out a comparative study of historical and fictional representations of another famous Spanish slave trader, Pedro Blanco. Drawing on literary representations of Blanco, Nerín complicates the stereotypical portrayal of the slave trader as the embodiment of evil, by bringing to light the social recognition granted to him. Through scrutiny of the ambiguity of these representations, Nerín's contribution allows us to understand Spain's ambivalence in remembering the figure of the slave trader. Rosalía Cornejo-Parriego's study in chapter 10, "Searching for Cayetana's Daughter: From Goya to Carmen Posadas," focuses on the representation of enslaved Black children in Western art, specifically on that of an eighteenth-century child in Spain named María de la Luz, whom the thirteenth Duchess of Alba adopted and emancipated. The essay aims to analyze the depiction of the child in various visual and literary texts, as well as the discourses surrounding her representation. María de la Luz appears prominently in two of Goya's artworks during the eighteenth century, as well as in a poem dedicated to her by the *ilustrado* Manuel José Quintana. Finally, in 2016, she is featured in Carmen Posadas's novel *La hija de Cayetana*. By examining the representation of the little girl in these works, the essay explores the commodification of Black bodies among the Enlightened European elites, the persistence of Africanist and Orientalizing practices, and the white savior narrative associated with the enduring discourse about Spain's exceptionalism in relation to slavery and colonialism.

Part 3 also includes the contributions of cultural practitioners, whose work helps us to understand the legacies of slavery in contemporary Spain in visual culture, literature, and dance. Our interview in chapter 11 with Tania Safura Adam, the founder of *Radio Africa*, *Radio Africa Magazine* and the leading member of the research group *España Negra*, shows "The Urgency of a Black Iberian Thought." Adam explains her efforts to "displace the center" by thinking through music, photography, and art. Her aim is to experiment with other epistemologies to better understand society and Blackness, in particular, in Spain. In her work she underscores how the Black person becomes a subject—instead of being relegated to the status of object. She problematizes commonly used terms, such as *decolonization* or *activism*, and argues for understanding Blackness as a political project. The last interview included in this volume is that of Yinka Esi Graves, a choreographer and Flamenco dancer, whose work explores Flamenco dance as an embodied performative expression that affirms the African roots of this genre and brings the experiences of Afro-diasporic people(s) to life. Her most recent work, *The Disappearing Act*, which premiered in the summer of 2023, represents a powerful gesture of making space for the freedom of people of African descent, despite the violence of being erased and made invisible in Spain throughout history. The performance, in her view, connects her individual experiences as a Black person living and working in Spain with the collective historical reality of Afro-diasporic communities, which continue to endure the legacies of slavery in the present day; at the same time, this creative art form offers the possibility of retelling this history on her own terms. We close the volume with filmmaker Miguel Ángel Rosales's creative essay in chapter 13, "Hispano-tropicalism: Flamencology and the Denial of Black Presence in Spain." The director of the documentary film *Gurumbé: Afro-Andalusian Memories* (2016) challenges the widely accepted Eurocentric "origin stories" of this genre: these accounts have erased the African origins of Flamenco, as well as the colonial system of slavery that gave rise to this form of musical expression. The point of Rosales's essay is to reclaim the presence and legacies of Afro-descendants in the creation of this art form. However, beyond introducing *Gurumbé* to those readers who have not yet viewed the documentary—which, in itself, would be a meritorious objective—Rosales's essay reframes his cinematic work from a broader cultural and theoretical perspective. His essay serves as a critical reflection—"creative archaeology," as he calls it—on his approach to uncovering the African traces of Flamenco, the new discoveries and connections made in this process, and the limits of the hegemonic cultural frameworks through which Flamenco has previously been imagined. His essay, therefore, serves as a valuable complement to his documentary work, furthering our understanding of the critical thinking behind its production.

All these contributions together, in the three sections of the book, demonstrate the impact of slavery in the cultural realm, beyond the nineteenth century when the practice was finally abolished in the Hispanic world. Culture has been crucial to shaping social attitudes, structures, and institutions, and to producing narratives about identities of social groups and defining power dynamics between them. At the same time, culture has served as a space for representing that which was often left unspoken or concealed in public discourse; as such, it has the potential to challenge and reshape dominant social narratives. As many of our contributors have shown, narratives about slavery are far from monolithic; as members of the Afro-diasporic community in Spain assert their voices through diverse forms of cultural production, these narratives have the potential to shift accepted versions of history written by the colonizers and the role of Afro-descendants in it. By transforming culture into a space of critical reflection on the legacies of slavery, we hope to achieve a deeper understanding of colonialism and its consequences in the contemporary culture of the Iberian Peninsula.

Notes

1. There has, of course, been tremendous resistance to such recent efforts internationally, as Araujo and others have shown, a prime example being the "presentist" critique of the *1619 Project* by the right-wing in the US (Araujo, "Political Uses"). The use of the "presentist" argument elsewhere, including in Spain when the slave trader Antonio López y López's statue was dismantled in March of 2018 (Caballé), merits analysis. The question is whether historians can apply present-day assumptions and standards to study the past. In the context of US history, accusations of presentism have often been used in defense of America's founders, for example when Thomas Jefferson was discovered to have fathered children with Sally Hemings, whom he had enslaved. While to interpret the past entirely in presentist terms is limiting, the assumption that current historical understanding remains unconnected to the institutions of the past is equally problematic. It is certainly not the case that opposition to slavery and racism is a phenomenon that arose in the present, nor is it true that only present-day insights enabled this opposition (Tsuchiya, "Monuments and Public Memory" 496n20).

2. The UNESCO site explains its objectives as follows: "Since its launch in 1994, the UNESCO 'Routes of Enslaved Peoples: Resistance, Liberty and Heritage' Project has contributed to the production of innovative knowledge, the development of high-level scientific networks and the support of memory initiatives on the theme of slavery, its abolition and the resistance it generated. At the international level, the project has thus played a major role in 'breaking' the silence surrounding the history of slavery and placing this tragedy that has shaped the modern world in the universal memory" (www.unesco.org/en/routes-enslaved-peoples). The website includes a section on "Cultural expressions and slave trade abolition" (ich.unesco.org/en/slave-trade-abolition-00505).

3. Among the most notable examples of such critical engagement are museums and monuments entirely dedicated to the history and memory of slavery, such as the International Slavery Museum in Liverpool, the Abolition of Slavery Memorial in Nantes, and the National Museum of African American History and Culture in Washington DC. French and British port towns (Nantes, Bordeaux, La Rochelle/London, Bristol, Lancaster) have galleries in historical and maritime museums dedicated to their involvement in the slave trade and Atlantic slavery.

In a much more recent essay ("Political Uses"), Araujo does include Spain among the list of countries that have launched a public debate about the transatlantic slave past and the European colonization of Africa; however, the specific situation of Spain is not discussed in this work.

4. Oriol López Badell and Celeste Muñoz, in the interview included in this volume, provide an explanation for the lack of an institutional politics of memory in Spain until very recently. See also Rodrigo y Alharilla (*Del olvido* 8–9). However, this is not to suggest that government-supported memory policies alone are always effective in fomenting the public's reckoning with difficult historical truths. As Huyssen has noted, given the proliferation of communication platforms easily accessible to the public in present times, dangerous forms of historical revisionism can easily proliferate on social media, thus undermining the original intentions of public memory discourse (Guixé, Interview 41).

5. The Law of Democratic Memory promotes a politics of memory, whose objectives are to bring about truth, justice, and reparation, through the recognition of the victims of violence and persecution between the beginning of the Spanish Civil War and the approval of the 1978 Constitution.

6. Book-length studies published since 2000 that address representations of imperialism in modern Iberian literatures and cultures include Alda Blanco's *Cultura y conciencia imperial en la España del siglo XIX* (2012), Mary Coffey's *Ghosts of Colonies Past and Present: Spanish Imperialism in the Fiction of Benito Pérez Galdós*, Michael Iarocci's *Properties of Modernity: Romantic Spain, Modern Europe, and the Legacies of Empire* (2006), Javier Krauel's *Imperial Emotions: Cultural Responses to Myths of Empire in Fin-de-siècle Spain* (2013), Susan Martin-Márquez's *Disorientations: Spanish Colonialism in Africa and the Performance of Identity* (2008), Lisa Surwillo's *Monsters by Trade: Slave Traffickers in Modern Spanish Literature and Culture* (2014), Michael Ugarte's *Africans in Europe: The Culture of Exile and Emigration from Equatorial Guinea to Spain* (2010), Akiko Tsuchiya and William Acree's *Empire's End: Transnational Connections in the Hispanic World* (2016), and Michelle Murray and Akiko Tsuchiya's *Unsettling Colonialism: Gender and Race in the Nineteenth-Century Global Hispanic World* (2019).

7. Another foundational text that addresses the memory of the slave trade is Gilroy's *Black Atlantic*, which examines how slavery shaped modern Black identity and consciousness in a transatlantic African diasporic context that transcends national and cultural borders. Gilroy's objective is to "explore how residual traces of [slave society's] necessarily painful expression" and "racial terror" (73) marked modern Black cultural consciousness and led to unique forms of aesthetic expression, mostly in the Anglophone world. Following the path opened by groundbreaking studies such as Gilroy's, we center on the legacies that slavery and the slave trade have left on cultural practices and institutions in the modern Iberian world, which is yet to be studied from this perspective. While some of the chapters, particularly in part 1, carry out original historiographic work based on archives, the main focus

of the volume is to analyze the *cultural memory* of slavery, as manifested in various forms of aesthetic expression, cultural institutions, and public memory initiatives.

8. Granted, some of these scholars lean more toward cultural history.

9. See also Fra-Molinero's earlier work on the representation of the African diaspora in Golden Age theater.

10. However, there are decolonial agendas being pursued in some Iberian territories, such as the Canary Islands and Galicia. We thank Benita Sampedro Vizcaya for this observation.

11. Prominent Catalan families, such as the Goytisolos, the Güell, and Artur Mas, were among those implicated in the slave trade.

12. It is important to note that historians, such as Martín Rodrigo y Alharilla and Josep María Fradera, have already uncovered documentary evidence of the Catalan bourgeoisie's involvement in the slave trade and have not only published their findings in works of historical scholarship, but have made this information more broadly available through their appearance in public functions and interviews with the press. However, it is not surprising that this TV program has provoked such great controversy, since given the medium of diffusion, it has the potential to have a much more widespread impact on the general public than a written text.

13. Among the many available threads on Twitter, one can consult twitter.com/Authenticindepe/status/1626306950123102208 and TV3's official twitter account twitter.com/tv3cat/status/1625487522758262786.

14. For a statement on EUROM's mission, see their website (europeanmemories.net/about-us/#mission).

15. The final report of the Trans-Atlantic Redress Network, coordinated by two of our contributors, Celeste Muñoz Martínez and Oriol López Badell, includes a summary of present-day protest movements in response to Spanish colonialism, slavery, and racism (hate crimes), as well as a list of initiatives by organizations promoting visibility on these issues and advocating for reparations.

16. See Tsuchiya's chapter in this volume.

17. On this particular initiative, see the interview with López Badell and Muñoz Martínez in this volume.

Works Cited

Araujo, Ana Lucia. *Politics of Memory: Making Slavery Visible in the Public Space*. Routledge, 2012.

———. *Slavery in the Age of Memory: Engaging the Past*. Bloomsbury, 2020.

Araujo, Ana Lucia, and Ynaê Lopes dos Santos. "Political Uses of the Past: Public Memory of Slavery and Colonialism." *Práticas da História*, no. 15, 2022, pp. 15–21.

La Barcelona incòmoda: Jornades de debat sobre memòria i espai públic. Conference program, 11 May 2022, Presó Model, Barcelona. Ajuntament de Barcelona.

ajuntament.barcelona.cat/memoriademocratica/wp-content/uploads/2022/04/la-barcelona-incòmoda.pdf.
"La Barcelona incòmoda—taula de conclusions." *YouTube*, uploaded by Barcelona Cultura, 11 May 2022, www.youtube.com/watch?v=GstYAO6DkAc.
Blanco, Alda. *Cultura y conciencia imperial en la España del siglo XIX*. U de Valencia, 2012.
Burton, Antoinette, editor. *After the Imperial Turn: Thinking with and through the Nation*. Duke UP, 2003.
Caballé, Anna. "Dos homes i un nomenclàtor." *El País*, 24 Feb. 2016.
Coffey, Mary. *Ghosts of Colonies Past and Present: Spanish Imperialism in the Fiction of Benito Pérez Galdós*. Liverpool UP, 2020.
Encadenados. Canal Historia, March 2022.
Enjuto-Rangel, Cecilia, et al, editors. *Transatlantic Studies: Latin America, Iberia, and Africa*. Liverpool UP, 2019.
European Observatory on Memories (EUROM). europeanmemories.net/about-us/#mission. Accessed 12 July 2023.
Fracchia, Carmen. *"Black but Human": Slavery and Visual Arts in Hapsburg Spain, 1480–1700*. Oxford UP, 2019.
Fra Molinero, Baltasar. *La imagen del negro en el teatro del Siglo de Oro*. Siglo XXI, 1995.
Gilroy, Paul. *The Black Atlantic: Modernity and Double Consciousness*. Harvard UP, 1993.
Guixé, Jordi. "Interview with Andreas Huyssen: Trumpism as a Social Movement Is a New Form of Fascism." *Observing Memories*, no. 6, Dec. 2022, pp. 34–41.
Hartman, Saidiya. *Lose Your Mother: A Journey along the Atlantic Slave Route*. Farrar, Straus and Giroux, 2008.
Iarocci, Michael. *Properties of Modernity: Romantic Spain, Modern Europe, and the Legacies of Empire*. Vanderbilt UP, 2006.
Jones, Nicholas R. *Staging* Habla de negros: *Radical Performances of the African Diaspora in Early Modern Spain*. Penn State UP, 2019.
Krauel, Javier. *Imperial Emotions: Cultural Responses to Myths of Empire in Fin-de-Siècle Spain*. Liverpool UP, 2013.
López, Brian. "State Education Board Members Push Back on Proposal to Use 'Involuntary Relocation' to Describe Slavery." *Texas Tribune*, 30 June 2022.
Martín Casares, Aurelia, and Rocío Periáñez Gómez. *Mujeres esclavas y abolicionistas en la España de los siglos XVI al XIX*. Iberoamericana Vervuert, 2014.
Martin-Márquez, Susan. *Disorientations: Spanish Colonialism in Africa and the Performance of Identity*. Yale UP, 2008.
Muñoz, Celeste, and Oriol López, coordinators. *Trans-Atlantic Racial Redress Network: Spanish Case: Final Findings Report*. EUROM, 2022. europeanmemories.net/eurom-new/wp-content/uploads/sites/19/2022/06/Redress-Network-2022-Spanish-Case.pdf.
Muñoz Martínez, Celeste, and Alba Valenciano-Mañé. "De memòries, distorsions i conflictes: El passat esclavista i colonial català en el punt de mira." *Catarsi*,

26 Apr. 2023. catarsimagazin.cat/de-memories-distorsions-i-conflictes-el-passat-esclavista-i-colonial-catala-en-el-punt-de-mira/.

Murray, N. Michelle. "Coerced Migration and Sex Trafficking: Transoceanic Circuits of Enslavement." *Transatlantic Studies: Latin America, Iberia, and Africa*, edited by Cecilia Enjuto-Rangel et al., Liverpool UP, 2019, pp. 348–60.

Murray, N. Michelle, and Akiko Tsuchiya. *Unsettling Colonialism: Gender and Race in the Nineteenth-Century Global Hispanic World*. SUNY P, 2019.

"'Negrers. La Catalunya esclavista' a Sense Ficció." *Facebook*, uploaded by Sense ficció, 10 Feb. 2023, www.facebook.com/watch/?v=728885632273368.

Nora, Pierre. *Les lieux de mémoire*. Gallimard, 1984.

Palà, Roger, "Qui són els descendents dels esclavistes catalans?" *El Crític*, 3 Apr. 2023. www.elcritic.cat/investigacio/qui-son-els-descendents-dels-esclavistes-catalans-161415.

Peck, Raoul, director. *I Am Not Your Negro*. Magnolia Pictures, 2018.

Portals, Jordi, director. *Negrers: La Catalunya esclavista*. Abacus, Feb. 2023.

Rodrigo y Alharilla, Martín. *Del olvido a la memoria: La esclavitud en la España contemporánea*. Icaria, 2022.

Romero, Simon. "Texas Pushes to Obscure the State's History of Slavery and Racism." *New York Times*, 20 May 2021.

Rosales, Miguel Ángel, director. *Gurumbé: Canciones de tu memoria negra*. Intermedia Producciones, 2016.

Scott, Joan Wallach. *On the Judgment of History*. Columbia UP, 2020.

Surwillo, Lisa. *Monsters by Trade: Slave Traffickers in Modern Spanish Literature and Culture*. Stanford UP, 2014.

Tofiño, Iñaki. "Memoria histórica y colonialismo." *CTXT: Contexto y Acción*, no. 285, 2022.

Tsuchiya, Akiko. "Monuments and Public Memory: Antonio López y López, Slavery, and the Cuban-Catalan Connection." *Nineteenth-Century Contexts*, vol. 41, no. 5, 2019, pp. 479–500.

Tsuchiya, Akiko, and William Acree. *Empire's End: Transnational Connections in the Hispanic World*. Vanderbilt UP, 2016.

TV3. "Al segle XIX, desenes de milers d'esclaus africans van ser venuts a Cuba per negrers catalans. Aquesta nit en parlem a @senseficcio, a les 22.05. #Esclavisme TV3." @som3cat, Twitter, 14 Feb. 2023, 8:30 a.m., twitter.com/tv3cat/status/1625487522758262786?lang=en.

Ugarte, Michael. *Africans in Europe: The Culture of Exile and Emigration from Equatorial Guinea to Spain*. U of Illinois P, 2010.

Zeuske, Michael. "Out of the Americas: Slave Traders and the Hidden Atlantic in the Nineteenth Century." *Atlantic Studies*, vol. 15, no. 1, 2018, pp. 103–35.

Part 1

The Legacies of Slavery in the Archive

Chapter 1

The *Houseboys* of Fernando Poo
Domestic Service in Spanish Colonial Africa

BENITA SAMPEDRO VIZCAYA[1]

> Our ancestors used to say you must escape when the water is still only up to the knees.
>
> —Ferdinand Oyono, *Houseboy*

> Examining archives is to be interested in that which life has left behind, to be interested in debt.
>
> —Achille Mbembe, "The Power of the Archive and Its Limits"

Domestic servants—commonly referred to as *boys* or *houseboys* in local Pidgin English[2]—were an essential feature in the households of both European settlers and local African elites in twentieth-century colonial Fernando Poo, as in the rest of colonial West Africa. They became part and parcel of the social structure that supported the plantation economies and the flourishing colonial infrastructure of the expanding urban centers and coastal cities. Skilled and unskilled workers, typically male, moved across the region—including Nigeria, Liberia, Sierra Leone, Cameroon, Gabon, and Equatorial Guinea—to support domestic life in new colonial towns, and were part of these towns' economies. Domestic workers, serving as *houseboys*, cooks, cook assistants, laundrymen, *motoboys*,[3] or other home employees, were only indirectly involved in the labor circuit of contracted *braceros* for plantation work, but both their labor and their urban presence were pivotal in supporting colonial enterprises and colonial dynamics. Despite their generic designation, the activities of *houseboys* also transcended the space of the private sphere; they were often employed in settler or local African family businesses as shop assistants, porters, and apprentices, as well as in a variety of other positions within the colonial service industry. In the case of the island of Fernando Poo (today Bioko), and its two major urban centers of San Carlos (today Luba) and Santa Isabel (today Malabo), *houseboys'* presence is well documented from the late nineteenth century until the territory gained independence from Spanish colonial rule in 1968.

Sources for documenting the traces of these domestic workers' histories, voices, images, experiences, claims, and movements include colonial administrative files, especially immigration records and labor contracts, council or court proceedings and depositions, consular officers' labor inspection reports, and records from the Policía Gubernativa. We can also find glimpses of these workers' actions and existence in settlers' accounts, narratives by missionaries, merchants, planters or colonial agents, family albums and photographic records, news clippings, literary production by African authors, and rare autobiographical sketches and diary entries.[4] However, as Florence Bernault has put it in "Suitcases and the Poetics of Oddities: Writing History from Disorderly Archives," in order to draft a minimally comprehensive portrait of domestic service workers operating in the labor enclave island of Fernando Poo, from the post-emancipation period to the country's independence, and to understand broader patterns, we need to rely on the incomplete, fragmented traces of their historical presence, and on clusters of meaning. Like Bernault's, my own research on this subject has "meandered between heterogenous finds, whose evidence is often transnational and multi-sited, scattered in various deposits across the world" (Bernault 276). Yet, for the purposes of this reflection, I will first be outlining a succinct genealogy of how this specific category of domestic employment was coded and institutionalized within the Spanish colonial labor system, and I will then be engaging with two unique written sources which provide a glance of *houseboys'* endeavors, trials, and claims in twentieth-century Fernando Poo.

The first of these sources is a surprisingly understudied narrative by the Fernandino writer Daniel Jones Mathama,[5] born in the city of San Carlos on the island of Fernando Poo: *Una lanza por el Boabí*, published in Barcelona in 1962, and generally cited in anthologies and literary histories as one of the earliest written expressions by an author from Equatorial Guinea. To date, it has been frequently referenced in passing, but rarely engaged with in a consistent way; due to this neglect, a new edition has yet to be released, and no translation of the book has been published.[6] In fact, *Una lanza por el Boabí* has been dismissed in assessments of the national literary canon, under the claim that it was considered an example of the "literature of consent," depicting an allegedly assimilationist agenda unapologetically aligned with colonial interests.[7] Its author has also been deauthorized by other critics, who read Jones Mathama's perspective in this book as that of a foreigner interpreting his native country's reality.[8] However, in revisiting the literary archive and the colonial library, I have argued elsewhere that we can never underestimate the importance of works published by African authors under a colonial context.[9] I read such texts, critically excluded by contemporary academics, as being more crucial than ever, not least because of their potentially interventionist intent, and by virtue of their engagement with colonialism.

The second source under analysis is an unusual archival finding from the Spanish colonial administration's records: the handwritten fragments of the personal diary and notebook annotations by a young Nigerian transnational worker, named Linus N. Gheme, who came for employment to Fernando Poo in 1961 and was hired in the city of San Carlos. These handwritten pages are part of a larger legal file compiled by the colonial Policía Gubernativa in Santa Isabel in 1962. The folder includes police reports, a deposition, cross-correspondence with the local Nigerian Consular Officer regarding migrant workers' background checks and political activities, the handwritten pages of Linus N. Gheme, and the Spanish Governor's final verdict on the case opened against him. Coming respectively from the realm of the literary and the judicial, the two sources under scrutiny are very different textual artifacts, and yet *houseboys* are, in both cases, central figures in the struggle for representation. They both situate servants and service relationships in a concrete geographic, social, political, legal, and economic setting in Fernando Poo, and they share a vivid description of *houseboys'* personal and professional experiences and interactions.

Master/mistress-servant relationships were, to a large extent, defined by, and constituted through, the use of various forms of violence within the domestic domain; this reflection will nonetheless turn its attention instead to the forms of servants' agency in these dynamics. The following questions will inform our inquiry: From small, everyday autonomous gestures to more overt actions spread across the city's households, how do we read servants' protestations and acts of defiance in these sources? And how do we account for their transformative potential in the service relationship?

Transnational Workers in Colonial Fernando Poo

The hiring of local porters, cooks, servants, guides, and interpreters was already a well-established practice for Europeans traveling across the African continent between the 1840s and 1880s, including explorers leading a geographic or scientific expedition, those serving in a military or administrative capacity, and missionaries. With the consolidation of European colonial societies toward the end of the nineteenth century, domestic servants in this post-abolition era occupied themselves with the personal needs of their employers, albeit in a relationship of mutual interdependency.[10] *Houseboys*, in this sense, were not just mere appendages of the household; they were, in fact, indispensable, both in the realm of labor and in terms of social and economic interactions, mediating the home and the outer space, and as markers of their masters' social status. The role they had—and the place they occupied—within colonial family and social structures necessarily evolved over time. Significant legal and political changes impacting labor relations (from recruiting to hiring and contracting), as well as shifts in family dynamics and new forms of domestic labor, took place between the late nineteenth and the mid-twentieth century. Regulations were articulated under the successive *reglamentos de trabajo* or labor codes, as well as through the terms of regional labor networks and intergovernmental agreements. The legal, social, and professional standing of these workers corresponded to that of a post-emancipation political culture, but due primarily to the way in which colonial labor markets functioned, the labor regime under which *houseboys* operated was somewhat reminiscent of the imagery and rhetorical modes of modern semi-slavery.[11] This was, for instance, the case in the linguistic terminology and verbal economy used to refer to this professional category. In this regard, Anne M. Menke suggests the implicit association between the *houseboy* and a household possession: "the '*boy*' is a commodity," she argues, pointing as well to their in-between status, as "neither child nor man . . . a member of neither community, yet present and all-knowing in both" (13). Nonetheless, the practices which were deployed to organize domestic work, from the point of recruitment to that of maintaining the boundaries of intimacy and loyalty, played a crucial role in the making and constant reworking of master/mistress-servant relationship.

In Fernando Poo, domestic work was officially codified as a semi-professional category of apprenticeships from the moment in which the Spanish administration took colonial control of the island, in 1858, with the appointment of the first governor. Historians who have engaged with this period, including Dolores García Cantús (*Fernando Poo: Una aventura colonial española en el África Occidental, 1778–1900*), who traced the record of labor legislations issued through the nineteenth century, and Enrique Martino (*Touts and Despots*), who has followed the steps of the migrant and labor networks across the Gulf of Biafra (the region that supplied the majority of plantation and domestic workers to Fernando Poo), provide us with the genealogy. As Martino argues, "Long before slavery was abolished in Cuba and Puerto Rico, the Spanish General of the first fleet, and first *Gobernador* Carlos de Chacón, signed an order saying no one was or could be a slave on the island; initially purely on paper, Chacón converted a variety of 'domestic servants,' who were mostly underage quasi-slaves, into five-years 'apprenticeships' inscribed in a governmental register of deeds and contracts" (35).

It became important for colonial authorities to regulate servants, who began to be regarded as employees as a result of the legal changes in contractual terms that defined the modern form of employment at the end of the nineteenth century. Regulations were both a symptom of historical change in the immediate post-emancipation era, and a statement of intentions to delineate boundaries. Through the twentieth century, various labor codes were approved, and different recruitment strategies put into motion: a new civic order was being implemented through legislative and juridical systems. This impacted not only incoming plantation workers—numerically the majority of migrant laborers into Fernando Poo—but also those to be employed in domestic service. Although locally defined, the hiring of *houseboys* and other domestic employees for settlers' homes and the homes of the local elite was neither purely domestic nor local, but rather a transnational enterprise. It was thus inscribed in a much larger dynamics of labor networks spanning the West Central African region, encompassing colonial labor provisions and legislation, migration, and mobility within the domestic service industry. Sometimes, in response to the high demand, it also transcended the boundaries of the regulated market, as Enrique Martino contends: "Panya [local pidgin rendering for Spain] was the largest labour smuggling and trafficking network in colonial West Africa, bringing tens of thousands of migrants to long and obligatory contracts on Fernando Pó" ("*Panya*: Economies of Deception" 91). *Houseboys*, like most fieldworkers, were brought into Fernando Poo from Cameroon, Gabon, Ivory Coast, Sierra Leone, Liberia and, especially, Nigeria.

Despite local administrative regulations, a form of bondage was implicitly part of this larger regional economy of transnational workers. Most of them either migrated across the region in search of work, or were licitly (and sometimes illicitly) recruited, brought to Fernando Poo, and assigned to a household with a contract that essentially subjected them to a regime of temporary paid semi-servitude. The contraband trade in domestic workers was a lucrative (if illegal) practice, and it is indicative of the fact that there was a ready market for young men below the age of sixteen—considered under-age for plantation work—to be employed as house servants. Recruiters resorted to coercion and deception, including making false promises, to entice them into these jobs: "the sweet-tongued recruiter convinced his victim that Fernando Po was a haven of wealth easily extracted from apprenticeships, shop-assistantships and domestic stewardships . . . latched on to people who were already on the move, redirecting the desire of migrant labourers and often leading them to thwarted hopes and an unwilling fate on Fernando Po's plantations" (Martino, *Touts: Recruiting Indentured Labor* 133). Examples of this layer of deception, belying the façade of legality, abound in the colonial administrative documentation. For instance, a report from the Nigerian Foreign Office on "Labour Conditions in Spanish Guinea" dated February 28, 1941, states, "One recruiter recently arrived with 30 labourers and of these 10 were refused permission by Spanish Medical authorities to engage in farm work, as being too young. I understand that many of these *boys* agree to come to Fernando Poo on the understanding that they will be apprenticed to some trade. The majority are obliged to accept domestic service" ("Recruitment of Labour for Island of Fernando Po"). In short, landing overseas in a domestic service position was not always the worker's choice, even when the transaction was in compliance with labor legislation.

The vulnerabilities associated with the type of employment as a domestic servant, and the typically young age of these workers, were sometimes coupled with a certain conception of freedom, and a sense of autonomy and decision-making. Rev. Henry Roe, a member of the British Primitive Methodist Church, who arrived at Fernando Poo in the year 1870, addressed the issue of hiring domestic workers on the island in the late nineteenth century in his ethnographic book *West African Scenes* (1874). He provided—from a settler missionary perspective—reflections on different aspects of this practice, including workers' frequent place of origin, attitudes, and expectations. He described how the Krumen, an ethnic group inhabiting the coastal areas of Liberia and Ivory Coast, were willing to seek employment one thousand miles away from home, including in Fernando Poo, both as *houseboys* and as plantation workers, and reports a perceived dichotomy between slavery and freely performing "even the most slavish work":

> The Krumen are spread all along the West African coast, and engage themselves to do all sorts of toil, such as rowing boats, paddling canoes, cutting forest wood, carrying water, clearing ground, cooking food, and, in fact, anything their masters dictate. They could never be forced into slavery, and say they would rather be killed, or kill themselves, than be slaves; yet they will cheerfully do all manner of drudgery—yea, even the most slavish work—so long as they are free and fed and paid. They hire themselves at so much per month for one or two years, then return to their country with their wages converted into goods. (44)

In the 1870s, there were approximately two hundred Krumen contracted in Fernando Poo and Roe further describes some of the employers' attitudes toward their *houseboys*, effectively depicting a culture in many respects reminiscent of the labor regimes, and master-servant relations, of the pre-emancipation period: "Their names are generally bestowed by their masters, and are often the most fantastic and absurd, such as Sunday, Monday, Friday, Telegraph, Bottler of Beer, Tin Pan, Black Will, Yellow Will &c. If their names make a white man laugh, they stick all the more closely to them, and refuse to change" (44–45). The passage exemplifies the use of rhetorical and discursive codes informed by planter and missionary ideology, in which infantilization and disrespect toward domestic service employees formed part of the colonial behavior. Meanwhile, regarding the workers themselves, we glimpse in the above quotations the capacity for resilience and adaptability in the social acceptance of these imposed nicknames, and the sense of freedom, decision-making, and a certain degree of autonomy. Despite the challenges ingrained in the position, working abroad as a West Central African migrant laborer could offer opportunities for individual, family, and community accomplishment, and mobility was a sign of independence and self-determination. Robin P. Chapdelaine, who has conducted research on Nigerian migrant labor networks into Fernando Poo from a gender perspective, indicates that women, too, gained access to economic and social upward mobility through migration: "The Spanish Labor Office recruited Nigerian men and encouraged them to bring their wives so that they could provide men some 'comfort' while in the colony for the duration of their contracts. Women—legitimate and fictitious wives, traders, and prostitutes—saw this opportunity as a way to improve their autonomy and money-earning capacities" (1). Moreover, Ndubueze L. Mbah, in his study of labor migration dynamics between Nigeria, Fernando Poo, and Gabon, concludes that "women used documentary and social forgeries to exploit fissures in colonial rule and create autonomous spaces of mobility and economic opportunity" (1). In this sense, some aspects of the Spanish labor codes evidently contributed, if unintentionally, to the concretization of new forms of freedom. In reading from other archives, of visual material, Jürg Scheneider (2018) and Erin Haney (2014) have persuasively argued that photography, a genre that emerged precisely at the cusp of post-emancipation Atlantic societies, offered a propitious means to record these new opportunities in labor migration and mobility patterns across the region, of transnational workers employed in domestic service in urban colonial contexts, including Fernando Poo.[12]

Daniel Jones Mathama's *Una lanza por el Boabí* (1962)

There is no literary equivalent in Spanish to the semi-fictional epistolary narrative *Houseboy* by Cameroonian writer Ferdinand Oyono. *Houseboy,* originally published in French in 1956 as *Une vie de boy,* narrates—through a series of diary entries in an exercise book—the life story of a young man, Toundi Ondoua, who has been in the domestic service industry in French Cameroon during the 1950s. Toward the end of his life, he crosses the border into Spanish Guinea reminiscing on the travails and perils of being a domestic servant under colonial rule.

Unlike Ferdinand Oyono's novel, Daniel Jones Mathama's *Una lanza por el Boabí* (1962)—a semi-fictional and semi-autobiographical book, depicting family life and social relationships in colonial San Carlos in the 1920s and 1930s—is not a narrative fully focused on domestic service and *houseboys'* lives or experiences; nor is it told from the point of view of a first-person *houseboy* narrator. However, labor relations and labor struggles within the confines of the domestic, in the growing urban and multi-ethnic community of San Carlos, are central to the story. Transnational workers, including the numerous domestic employees serving at the households of both white settlers and especially the local Fernandino elite, which dominated the city over this period, are a critical feature of that social fabric.

The title of the book invokes the figure of the Boabí, a patriarchal character who is the highest authority in the city of San Carlos. The Boabí at the center of the text is, in fact, an alter ego of the historical Maximiliano Cipriano Jones (1870–1944), the author's father and a member of the Fernandino community (fig. 1.1). Arguably, he was the richest plantation owner, business investor, and financier in Fernando Poo by the 1920s and '30s, and certainly the most authoritative representative of the island's local population. His political and economic clout was unquestioned by the Spanish colonial authorities, and he can partially be credited with bringing

Figure 1.1. Portrait of Maximiliano Cipriano Jones, San Carlos, circa 1920. *Source:* Private collection, Family Archive Trinidad Morgades Besari-Laida Memba Ikuga, Malabo-Barcelona. Used with permission.

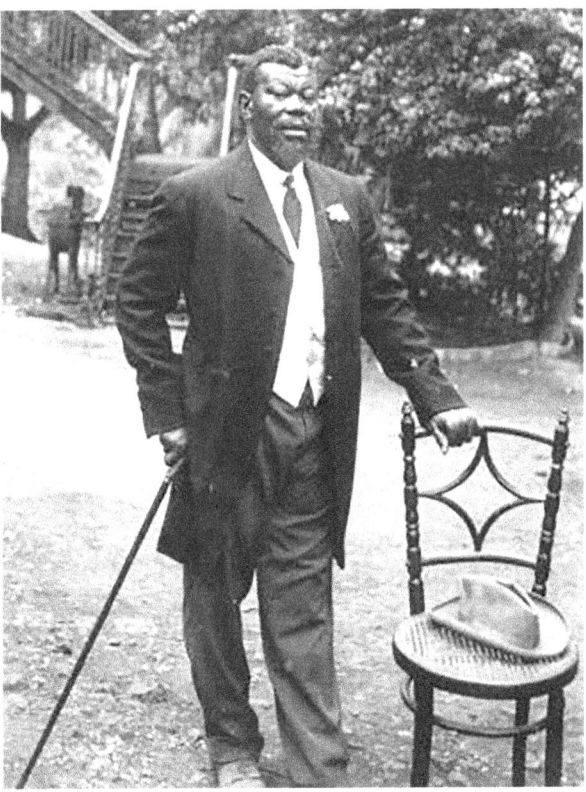

electricity to the island. He was, in short, a figure who evokes what Frederick Cooper and Ann Laura Stoler have termed the "tensions of empire," whereby competing agendas for using power, and competing strategies for maintaining control, often collided: "He was Claretians' providence, lending them his boat, helping to build churches, etc. In 1900 he opened a printer's shop in Santa Isabel. In 1910 he advised the Spanish troops in their repression of the Bubi revolt against forced labor. In 1920 he was the only African among the ten largest planters of the island. Thanks to him the first thermal power station was built in Santa Isabel in 1925" (Liniger-Goumaz 222). According to Mayca de Castro, Daniel Jones Mathama conceived *Una lanza por el Boabí* as a tribute to his father ("African Anticolonial Narratives" 137). The nickname *Boabí* was also the name that Maximiliano Cipriano Jones gave to a new boat he acquired in 1921, an event that the periodical *La Guinea Española*, published in Fernando Poo by the Claretian missionaries, considered worthy of inclusion in the current events section of the June 10th issue of that year.[13] The boat enhanced his monopoly in the maritime transport of people and goods between the urban centers of San Carlos (on the southern part of the island) and Santa Isabel (on the northern tip) in the decades before an efficient road network was created.

The book's first-person narrator and protagonist, Gue, is the alter ego of Daniel Jones Mathama himself, "el menor de los hijos reconocidos por Maximiliano Jones" ("the last recognized son of Maximiliano Cipriano Jones"; Ndongo-Bidyogo and Ngom 455). He is depicted as a resident of the city of San Carlos: "Gue, is born in the opening pages of the text and subsequently proceeds through a series of coming-of-age experiences that allow the narrator to explore various local landscapes and customs" (Lifshey, "And So the Worm Turns" 112). In the last chapter of *Una lanza por el Boabí*, Gue finally departs for Europe to pursue a university education after a two-year stay in Lagos where he attends a grammar school. While in Lagos, he will reside with his older sister, married to a prestigious lawyer.[14]

In this life trajectory, *houseboys* play a pivotal role. Gue becomes a semi-orphan at a very young age; his mother dies when he is only five years old, and he spends his crucial formative years under the watchful eyes of Inba,[15] a *houseboy* of noble origins, the descendant of a respectable clan from Cameroon. Inba is one of "small massa's" caregivers, since the Boabí is constantly traveling around from one property to the next; he becomes his best friend and his confidant, until Gue's father appoints him as foreman at Cotton House, another of his plantation and sawmill properties. For young Gue, Inba is a heroic figure; he also becomes a tragic one, crushed by a log at the sawmill when he tries to rescue two small children from the plantation workers, leaving Gue devastated and in a certain sense amplifying his orphanhood, depriving him of a quasi-parental figure.

Numerous other *houseboys* and domestic employees are also part of the Boabí's service staff. Gue inhabits a domestic world populated by servants, with many of whom—including Lawani, the stable *boy* from Nigeria—he maintained close interactions:

> En casa del Boabí vivían otros muchachos mayores que Gue. Eran los *boys* del Boabí, que se encargaban del trabajo doméstico de la enorme mansión. Entre ellos estaba Siloji, *small boy* (muchacho pequeño) debido a su corta estatura y poco desarrollo; Miuoa, Mayaro, Besu, Mariano y otros. Todos tenían sus quehaceres en la casa y no había ninguno que no fuese un redomado pillo, con más astucia que un zorro, pero todos se sentían orgullosos de pertenecer a la servidumbre del Boabí . . . Siloji y Mariano eran los encargados de preparar y de servir la mesa. (Jones Mathama 85)

> Other *boys* older than Gue lived in the Boabí's house. They were the Boabí's *boys*, responsible for the domestic work of the enormous mansion. Among them was Siloji, a *small boy* due to his short stature and poor development; Miuoa, Mayaro, Besu, Mariano, and others. Each had their chores in the house and there was not one who was not an outright rogue, with more cunning than a fox, but they all felt proud to belong to the service staff of the Boabí . . . Siloji and Mariano were in charge of preparing and serving the table.

While they are ubiquitous in the family life story as articulated by Gue, their representation is dependent on the figure of the Boabí: it is "contingent upon inhabiting the domestic world of the master and less on their own," as Prabhat Kumar has argued, analyzing servants' lives in literary traditions elsewhere (184). It is correspondingly suffused with the prejudices ("outright rogue," "more cunning than a fox") and ideological assumptions inflected by class arrogance ("they all felt proud to belong to the service staff of the Boabí") deriving from the narrator's privileged status.

Yet, read from another angle, these servants' attitudes also point in the direction of complex registers of agency and resistance. A vignette from *Una lanza por el Boabí*'s opening chapters describes a form of supplementary income for *houseboys*, working as human porters on rainy days in the swampy coastal city of San Carlos, traversed by a river, as well as these workers' interactions and negotiations with the local settler community. They are depicted as having the capacity to manage their own economies, by establishing a price for their services commensurate to the service provided, and the requirement of advance payment, as a risk control mechanism to protect themselves from the evasion of payment by clients:

> Tiempo atrás, una lluvia así significaba una ganancia para los ociosos *boys*, pues los vecinos de San Carlos que querían ir de visita, y no mojarse los pies, pagaban de quince a veinte céntimos a los *boys* que aguardaban a las puertas de las casas de la ciudad siempre que llovía. Eran unos chicos fuertes que no se preocupaban del peso de su cliente. Pero si tenían que transportar su humana carga a mucha distancia, entonces cobraban hasta cuarenta y cincuenta céntimos. El agua llegaba a veces hasta más arriba de las rodillas de los *boys*. En ocasiones solía ocurrir que algunos granujas de hombres blancos se dejaban transportar al lugar indicado y, una vez allí, se negaban a abonar lo estipulado o solo pagaban la mitad. En vista de esto, los *boys* a su vez se negaron a transportar a ningún blanco sin haber cobrado por anticipado. (54)

> Long ago, a rain like this meant a profit for the idle *boys*, because the residents of San Carlos who wanted to visit, and not get their feet wet, paid fifteen to twenty cents to the *boys* who waited at the doors of the houses of the city whenever it rained. They were strong young men, who didn't care about their client's weight. But if they had to carry their human burden a long distance, they would charge up to forty or fifty cents. The water sometimes reached above the knees of the *boys*. Sometimes it used to happen that some white scoundrels let themselves be carried to the indicated place and, once they got there, refused to pay the agreed amount, or only paid half. In view of this, the *boys* in turn refused to transport any white people without payment in advance.

The story continues by descending from the general into the particular, with an anecdotal episode that further illustrates the *houseboys'* agency at work: "Pero cierto día en que las calles se desbordaron tanto que el agua llegaba casi a la cintura de los *boys*, un blanco que casi pesaba cien kilos quiso que uno de aquellos le llevase a toda prisa a una casa distante unos trescientos metros" ("But one day when the streets overflowed so much that the water reached almost to the waist of the *boys*, a white man who weighed almost a hundred kilos wanted one of them to take him in a hurry to a distant house some three hundred meters away"; 54). The client is left as agreed at his destination, at the top of the landing of the staircase, but decides to compensate the porter *boy* with only half of the prearranged remuneration. The *boy* then takes justice into his own hands and makes a decisive gesture against abuse and exploitation:

> Entonces el *boy* le agarró por la chaqueta y le tiró en medio de la calle, llena de agua y barro. Se armó un gran alboroto y algunos europeos buscaron al muchacho para castigarle, pero este se refugió en la casa del Boabí, contándole lo sucedido, y aquellos europeos poco escrupulosos tuvieron que desistir de sus propósitos. Desde entonces el Boabí prohibió esta clase de servicios, y tanto blancos como negros tuvieron que proveerse de altas botas de goma para cruzar las calles en un día de lluvia en San Carlos. (55)

> Then the *boy* grabbed him by the jacket and threw him in the middle of the street, full of water and mud. A great uproar broke out and some Europeans looked for the *boy* in order to punish him, but he took refuge in the Boabí's house, telling him what had happened, and those unscrupulous Europeans had to give up their plans. Since then, the Boabí prohibited this kind of services, and both whites and blacks had to provide themselves with high rubber boots to cross the streets on a rainy day in San Carlos.

The narrator resolves the conflict between worker and white settler through the intervention of the Boabí, who rules that such subservient labor practices must be immediately eliminated. But the episode also signals a moment in which power dynamics within colonial society are shifting. Workers' prerogatives and tolerance levels have reached a new dimension, and the post-emancipation labor paradigm has been replaced by a pre-independence one, not necessarily through a direct, confrontational challenge to colonial rule or colonial authority but rather through a commitment to a sense of justice. This commitment is embodied in the novel by the paternal figure of the Boabí who throughout the narrative assumes a role as de facto mediator within the local community, and between the community and the colonial authorities.

On another occasion, early in the text, he is pinpointed as the lightning rod for social tensions: "Tanto fue el abuso y los actos de violencia, que los nativos elevaron sus quejas al hombre más influyente en toda la isla, o sea, el gran boabí" ("So much was the abuse and acts of violence, that the natives raised their complaints to the most influential man on the entire island, that is, the great boabí"; 16). And he imposes justice not only in situations of major social unrest, but also in regard to more mundane conflicts and labor disputes. Almost daily, "otros iban a exponer sus pequeños o grandes problemas ante el Boabí para que les ayudara a resolverlos" ("others would go to expose their small or big problems to the Boabí so that he would help them solve them"; 87). In critical circumstances of pressing urgency, even the colonial officers called on the authority of the Boabí to reestablish order, or to impose public measures among the local population that they themselves were incapable of enforcing. One such instance took place in the aftermath of World War I, when a smallpox epidemic spread over Fernando Poo and, paired up with a cholera surge, threatened with quickly decimating the population.[16] Daniel Jones Mathama's book relates how the residents, including the plantation workers, resisted the governor's mandate of enforced vaccination: "Se difundió el pánico de tal modo que el gobernador general tuvo que solicitar la intervención del Boabí para apaciguar los ánimos" ("Panic spread to such a degree that the governor general had to request the intervention of the Boabí to calm people down"; 96).

Published six years after Ferdinand Oyono's *Houseboy*, *Una lanza por el Boabí* belongs to the same tradition of emerging literary expressions by West Central African authors still immersed in a colonial context. Rather than opting for an explicitly anticolonial literary approach, both books articulate far more complex and nuanced positions, which in fact anticipate the end of post-emancipation subjugation and colonial abuse, especially in terms of labor relations. As Adam Lifshey has also stated, "*Una lanza por el Boabí*, of course, is not a call to arms amid an era of militant decolonization movements in Africa, but neither is it a sycophantic and wholesale submission to

European dominance" ("And So the Worm Turns" 116). Within this frame, domestic servants are actively mobilized in both texts—*Una lanza por el Boabí* and *Une vie de boy*—and brought forward to the center of political imagination; they are ubiquitous in the narrative plots, becoming part of this recasting of the domestic and public orders. It is in this sense that Daniel Jones Mathama's book succeeds at keeping a simultaneous focus on the everyday and the episodic, the domestic and the social, the individual family account and the political and economic structure in which it is inserted.

Linus N. Gheme's Notebooks

Although employment as a plantation worker and as domestic worker were legally two distinct categories, regulated by separate labor codes, the risk of slippage and overlap was always latent. This was the labor situation against which a twenty-two-year-old transnational worker from the Eastern region of Nigeria, Linus N. Gheme, protested vigorously, and which he reported through official channels in Fernando Poo in 1962—the same year in which *Una lanza por el Boabí* was published. His notebook and diary entries, dating from the time of his employment in 1961 to 1962, serve as a compelling example of migrant workers' actions and negotiation of expectations.

Linus N. Gheme (also known in the documentation as Monde Obongue) was an English-speaking Nigerian, professionally self-defined as a "steward," who had arrived from the port city of Calabar on November 17, 1961. Within a week of his arrival, he had been contracted for the household of Portuguese planter Antonio Dionisio dos Santos, in the Barrio las Palmas of the city of San Carlos. He thus found himself on Fernando Poo at a time when the island was still under full colonial occupation and when the plantation economy continued to thrive. But as a transnational worker, he brought with him a distinctive political sensibility. Gheme was evidently very aware that decolonization processes were underway; Nigeria had already celebrated its independence on October 1, 1960.[17] It was not long before he made his views heard. In an undated handwritten note, filed at the local Nigerian Consular Office, he requested his right to representation: "Sir, I have the honour and due respect in forwarding this my humble note. I am a free born independent Nigerian and has spent almost four months in this island. I therefore need your most kind assistance. Yours obediently servant, Linus Gheme" ("Expediente 622"). In March 1962, he followed up with a handwritten complaint against his employer, reporting that he had been initially contracted as a domestic worker but was subsequently required to perform plantation work, "cutting timber logs," a role which represented, in his view, a totally different professional category, turning him into "another figure," as indeed it was, in legal parlance (see fig. 1.2):

Figure 1.2. Letter by Linus N. Gheme to the Nigerian Consular Office in Fernando Poo. *Source:* Spain, Ministerio de Cultura, Archivo General de la Administración, Sección África, Box 81/08803.

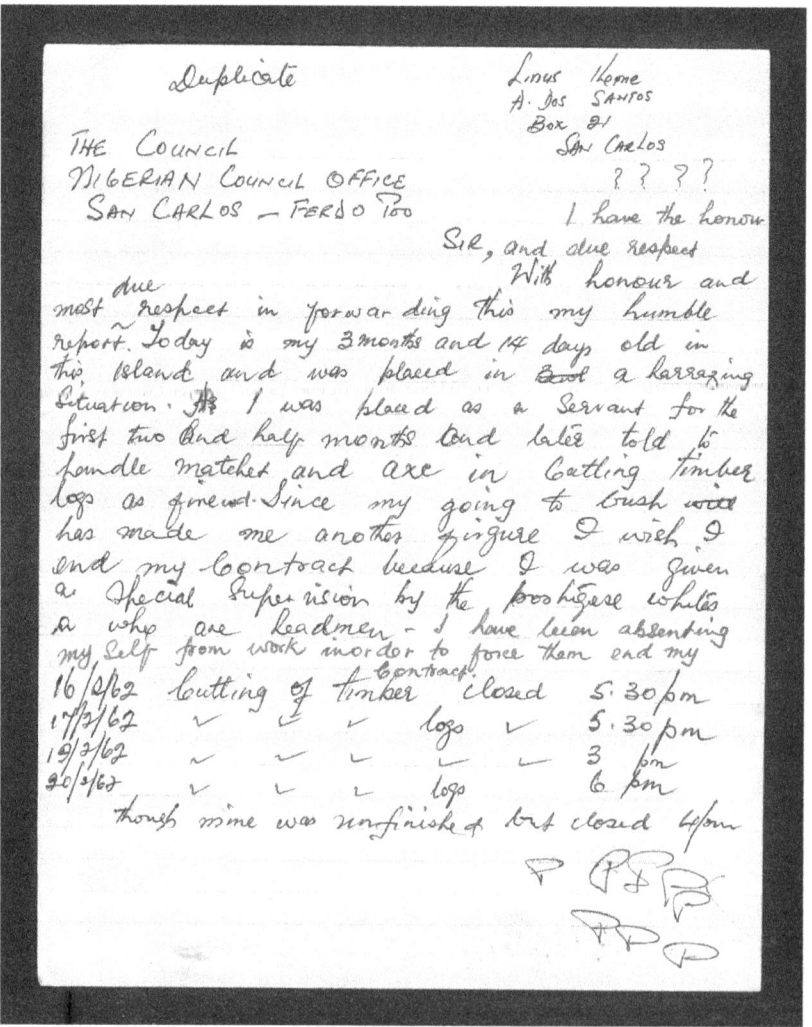

> I have the honour Sir, and due respect . . . in forwarding this my humble report. Today is my 3 months and 14 days old in this island and was placed in a harraging [sic] situation. I was placed as a servant for the first two and half months and later told to handle matchet and axe in cutting timber logs as firewood. Since my going to bush has made me another figure I wish I end my contract, because I was given as special supervision by the Portuguese whites . . . I have been absenting myself from work in order to force them end my contract. ("Expediente 622")

We learn of Linus N. Gheme precisely because he was on a list of migrant workers in Fernando Poo being investigated for their political activities. His case is part of a file of administrative proceedings compiled between February and May 1962 by the Policía Gubernativa. He was arrested in Santa Isabel one night in early April, in a dancing club called Life, accused of having come to the Spanish colony from Nigeria as a secret agent, "con el fin de ver la conducta que seguían los españoles con los nigerianos" ("in order to see how the Spaniards behaved toward the Nigerians"; "Expediente 622"). In March he had quit his job and left San Carlos to present the formal complaint (fig. 1.2) at the Nigerian Consulate. Upon his arrest, the authorities confiscated his personal archive, which included private correspondence, letters addressed to the Nigerian Consulate, a notebook filled with transcriptions of newspaper clippings, lists of books that he brought with him to Fernando Poo, book commentaries, a reflection on the celebrations of Nigerian Independence Day, diary entries dated prior and post arrival to Fernando Poo, and numerous labor-related notations pertaining to his employment in San Carlos, under the heading of "Personal record of events." These ranged from entries to document that a payment was received, to reports of warnings that he should refrain from drinking, false accusations from coworkers, and penalties imposed by "boss Mr. dos Santos," including "two days in jail house" and, more disturbing to him, being driven away from the servant work to be "sent to bush" (fig. 1.3).

Keeping a journal, affirming oneself as a lettered individual and a political subject, was a double-edged feature under colonial rule. His ability to document labor experiences imbued Linus N. Gheme with a sense of authority and allowed him to present his case at the legal level; it eventually allowed him to return to his native country free of charges, other than the expulsion from Fernando Poo. But it was also a factor that gave rise to suspicion and police investigation, to the point of including him in a

Figure 1.3. Personal record of events by Linus N. Gheme. *Source:* Spain, Ministerio de Cultura, Archivo General de la Administración, Sección África, Box 81/08803.

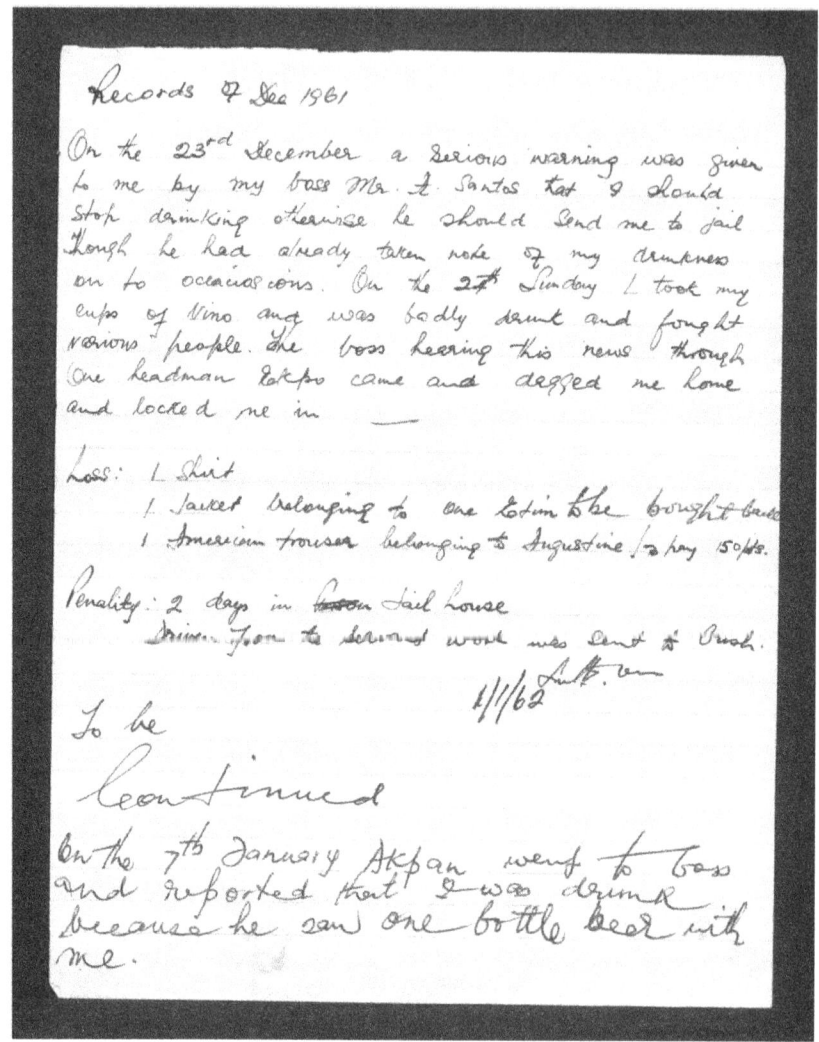

file of "dangerous individuals" ("Expediente 622"). The assessment of his confiscated writings prompted the colonial authorities to determine that "el detenido es un individuo poseído de inquietudes políticas avanzadas" ("the detainee is an individual possessed of advanced political concerns"), recommending "que se procediera al interrogatorio del mismo" ("that he should be interrogated"; "Expediente 622").[18]

An oral hearing, the legal transcription of which is part of the police file, was conducted on April 5, 1962. Legal depositions, testimonies, and witness accounts are, of course, always highly mediated sources: intervened by many layers of mediation, translation, interpretation, transcription and summarizing, they are shaped by the format, the reasons motivating the inquiry, and the power dynamics involved in the questioning, compounded by race or social differentials. Yet such testimonies can also reveal complex forms of agency by subordinate sectors of society. Even when their arguments are not persuasive enough to change a verdict, they register useful data that allows for a reconstruction, even if partial, fragmentary, and circumstantial, of their social and community interactions, employment conditions, and the materiality of their livelihoods and daily experiences. The law, Nitin Sinha and Nitin Varma have argued, "has a long, complex and wide-ranging influence in shaping the nature of master–servant relationships and the making of domestic order and authority" (16).

In the case of Linus N. Gheme, there is an oscillation between acceptance of the accusations against him, on the one hand, and assertive elaboration of arguments in his defense, on the other. Ultimately, through his oral hearing, the Policía Gubernativa was enabling his self-articulation within the realm of the law, revealing an unexpected complexity in the dynamics between servant and colonial authorities. Gheme's case speaks to a range of issues concerning wages, contract agreements, workers' duties, employers' responsibilities, but also regarding codified labor figures ("it made me a different figure, he claimed"; "Expediente 622"), forms of punishment, resistance mechanisms, and eventual manifestations of freedom. His case hints at a transition toward the emerging late colonial legal discourse featuring the employee as the initiator in the breaking of a contract. It was Gheme himself who initiated the process through an act of defiance against the arbitrariness of domestic service demands and punishments: "I have been absenting myself from work in order to force them end my contract," he acknowledged in his complaint ("Expediente 622"; fig. 1.2). Legal interventions concerning wages, and conflicting forms of interpreting notions of servitude, are common in twentieth-century colonial historiography, but other dynamics in the master-servant relationship, including the perceived politization of the working subject, are newer to this period. *Houseboys* and other domestic servants in late colonial Fernando Poo were not always passive victims or voiceless subjects. The acts of reading, writing, and record-keeping speak not only to the issue of agency but also to notions of selfhood, including modes of presenting oneself. This is what Linus N. Gheme does in the neatly crafted application letter he submits to the Nigerian Consular Office in Santa Isabel on March 27, 1962, requesting employment as a "messenger in your office" ("Notebook"; fig. 1.4).

Figure 1.4. Job application letter by Linus N. Gheme. *Source:* Spain, Ministerio de Cultura, Archivo General de la Administración, Sección África, Box 81/08803.

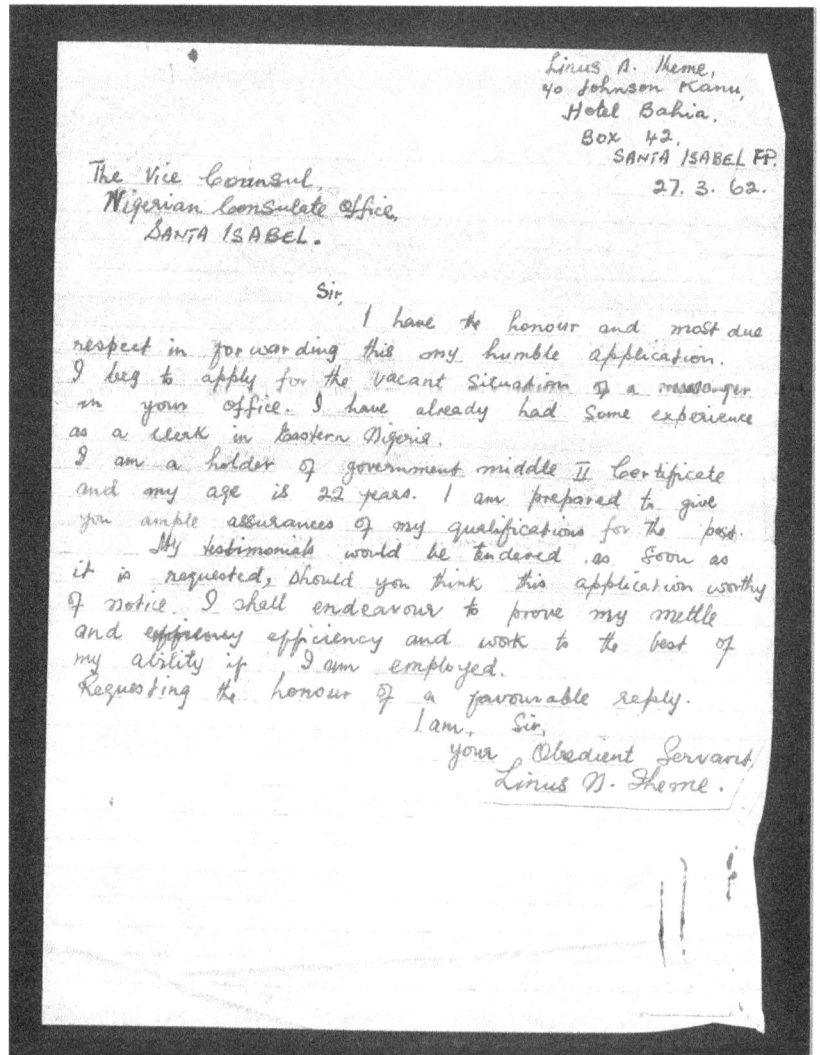

Certainly, Gheme's defense against the accusations and punishments deployed against him (including home prison and relocation from home to fieldwork), and his overt challenge to the employer's mandates, failed to bend the will of the colonial Spanish authorities; on May 3, 1962, Governor General Francisco Núñez Rodríguez signed Linus N. Gheme's expulsion from Fernando Poo and his enforced return to Nigeria. This effectively curtailed his ability to further pursue professional mobility in Fernando Poo, including through the position for which he had applied at the Consulate Office. However, his diary and letter-writing exercise operate as an individual initiative of documenting and generating archival matter. Collecting evidence served the author well in contesting authority and leaving an exploitative labor situation; diary writing created the space for the emergence of the author as claimant of his own history; it also allowed for the reenactment of events.

These diary pages and notations, the "Personal record of events," offer us traces of the constituent violence preserved in the conceptual and material entity of the colonial archive. Undusting these traces allows for the interpretation of new forms of agency, resistance, assertions of personhood, freedom of mobility, and employability within the *houseboy* sector. After all, "examining archives is to be interested in that which life has left behind, to be interested in debt" (Mbembe 25).

Conclusion

Despite their ubiquity, *houseboys* and other categories of employees in domestic service in colonial West Central Africa—and in colonial Fernando Poo in particular—have frequently been left out of historical narratives. They occupied a complex social position between subjugation and dependency; in the face of their submission, they also sensed the empowerment afforded to them by the very indispensability of the services they provided. We still know little regarding the physical, material, and emotional conditions of their employment, and of their transnational experiences across the region, but we can use the productive power of both the archive and the literary canon to advance meaningful conversations. Bringing servants to the center stage in the study of colonialism is one step in that direction.

This essay has therefore partially been conceived as an archival practice of sorts: in this attempt at drafting the social history of these servants, partly biographical, partly structural, and partly discursive, I have deployed a combination of methodologies, from close-contextual reading to reading against the grain, merging literary and administrative sources to present a non-uniform, discontinuous, but related account of *houseboys*' lives, simultaneously documenting the growing presence of the colonial government's control, which replaced a more direct local form of authority and corrective justice by the local elites. Paradoxically, the increased vigilance by colonial authorities, and the augmented bureaucracy, opened new opportunities for colonial subjects (including domestic employees) to manifest their identities and voice their claims in police, administrative, and judicial records, be that in the form of interrogations, oral hearings, complaints, petitions, or a variety of other written and non-written processes.

The two case studies that prompted this reflection, both dating to 1962, illustrate the variety of registers in which servants, in this concrete place and time, narrate and are narrated, allowing us to document the transition from a post-emancipation era to a pre-independence one. From newly freed workers on the move to transnational workers exercising their right to mobility, employment, and personhood, they became active participants in the dynamics of colonial status. These two sources put pressure on the boundaries of the written canon as conventionally established, inserting servants, and narratives about domestic service, into the writing tradition of twentieth-century Fernando Poo.

Notes

1. I am deeply indebted to Enrique Martino for many intellectual exchanges on labor networks in West Central Africa and colonial Fernando Poo, and for his bibliographical and archival suggestions; I am also deeply grateful to Dolores García Cantús and to Ibrahim K. Sundiata, whose pioneering work on the subject continues to be a necessary reference and a source of inspiration. My own work on this and other related subjects would not be the same without the stimulating conversations and sharp critical reading of José F. Siale Djangany. I am finally appreciative of the academic support provided by Susan Martin-Márquez and Lisa Surwillo throughout the research and writing of this and other projects.

2. They were generally referred to as either *boys* or *houseboys*, both by European settlers in colloquial conversation and in all period documentation; the Spanish term *marmitones* was also used for cook-assistants. I italicize the terms all throughout the essay in an attempt to establish critical distance from this terminology, as it is loaded with colonialist implications.

3. *Motoboy* was a Pidgin English term which typically referred, in this context, to the driver's assistant.

4. In a separate essay (Sampedro Vizcaya, "*Houseboys*"), I have engaged with the representation of *houseboys*, and domestic labor practices in Spanish settlers' homes in colonial West Africa, through the use of photographic archival sources both from private and institutional collections.

5. The Fernandinos are a multiethnic migrant social group whose families descend from English-speaking freed enslaved individuals, mainly from Sierra Leone and Liberia, and who settled on Fernando Poo from the mid-nineteenth century onwards. They quickly became a powerful local African elite on the island. For a study of their social, economic, and political status, including the leading role of Maximiliano Cipriano Jones, see especially Ibrahim K. Sundiata ("The Fernandinos"; *From Slaving to Neoslavery*) and Jesús Ramírez Copeiro del Villar (*Objetivo África*).

6. Among the few studies, Adam Lifshey published in 2007 an article on this narrative, arguing that "Jones Mathama's failures at metropolitan mimicry, both of ideology and form, are the true success of his novel and the reason why it should be read" (108). An expanded version of this article was included as one of the chapters of his book monograph *The Magellan Fallacy* (2012). More recently, Mayca de Castro has dedicated one chapter of her doctoral dissertation to *Una lanza por el Boabí*, and in a subsequent essay she has engaged with the complexities of anticolonial narratives written by African authors during the colonial period.

7. Mbare Ngom, followed by several other literary scholars, has claimed that "Mathama Jones' novel fervently celebrates the colonial situation, and it is strongly critical of the natives. It is part of what has been called 'literature of consent'" (n.p.). His assessment might be based on the way the native Bubi population is portrayed in the narrative, as opposed to the local Fernandino elite, who enjoyed social and economic prestige, were generally cosmopolitan, and had a different relationship to Europe.

8. This is the position sustained, for instance, by Marvin Lewis and by Michael Ugarte.

9. "It is in this category that I want to 'undust' . . . Daniel Jones Mathama's *Una lanza por el boabí* . . . For such observers, Jones Mathama's novel . . . is not even worth studying, by virtue of its allegedly pro-colonial sentiments. As if touched by a tradition of academic interventionism that has come to dominate the construction and reconstruction of the colonial library through the circuits of academic power and knowledge, such exercises do not seem to favor openness and inclusiveness. On the contrary, to bracket these texts within the rubric of literature of consent . . . has the effect of prolonging the colonizing project, and perhaps even, although maybe unintentionally, may be read as a postcolonial academic attempt to legitimize the colonizing project itself. Besides the pragmatic reasons for their inclusion in an autochthonous archive as part of a genealogy . . . the exclusion of these novels is limiting and interventionist in regard to that archive" (Sampedro Vizcaya, "Rethinking the Archive" 354–55).

10. As Anne M. Menke has stated, "Domestic servants were uniquely placed in the colonial world, privy to the most intimate details of the lives of their oppressors" (12).

11. Enrique Martino has argued that in early independent Nigeria, the concept of "modern slavery" was primarily associated with the ongoing existence of colonial labor regimes, including in the Spanish colonial island of Fernando Poo, which was the main destination for contracted Nigerian plantation and domestic workers. He observes that it was the economic conditions of colonialism that regulated the labor and hiring practices at the root of "modern slavery," and not the persistence of slavery proper or the slave trade: "from deception and entrapment of unsuspecting migrants in a new territory, to harshly enforced debt bondage, and penal sanction for non-fulfilment of contracts and other local legislation" ("When 'Modern Slavery' Meant Colonial Rule," n.p.).

12. See also Sampedro Vizcaya, "*Houseboys*."

13. "Con el vapor alemán 'Wigberto' Don Maximiliano C. Jones ha recibido una bonita lancha automóvil, llamada Boabi: tiene de largo 16 metros, de ancho 2,80, puntal 1,70 y cala 1,20; podrá cargar hasta 15 toneladas. La nueva lancha significa un nuevo adelanto que ciertamente se dejarán sentir para beneficio del público en la ampliación de los servicios marítimos. Felicitamos cordialísimamente a su propietario Don Maximiliano C. Jones y hacemos votos por la prosperidad de la nueva embarcación" ("With the German steamer *Wigberto*, Don Maximiliano C. Jones has received a beautiful motorboat, called Boabi: It is 16 meters long, 2.80 wide, 1.70 high, and 1.20 deep; it will be able to load up to 15 tons. The new boat means a new advance that will certainly redound to the benefit of the public in the expansion of maritime services. We cordially congratulate its owner Don Maximiliano C. Jones, and we hope that the new boat will flourish" *Guinea Española*, June 10, 1921, p. 172).

14. According to Mayca de Castro, who in turn summarizes the biographical note provided by Ndongo-Bidyogo and Mbaré Ngom, "Jones Mathama studied at Oxford University, spoke three languages (*Pidgin*, English, and Spanish) and, in 1931, moved to Barcelona to study medicine. There he founded an English academy, which, during Franco's regime, became one of the most prestigious among the Catalan bourgeoisie" (*Empatía y violencia* 134).

15. The narrative alternates between the spelling of Inba and Imba; similarly, Boabí is written both with and without capitalization.

16. The author's preoccupation with (and knowledge of) public health issues, illnesses, treatments, and medical and pharmacological practices occupy a significant portion of most chapters throughout the narrative.

17. All the documents related to Linus N. Gheme, and cited or reproduced in this article, including his handwritten "Notebook" and the Policía Gubernativa investigation records, come from the Spanish Archivo General de la Administración, Sección África, Caja 81/08803, and are part of the "Expediente 622." Henceforth, "Expediente 622" or "Notebook." Among the pages of his "Notebook," we find

some notations on how, and where, he spent the Nigerian independence celebrations of October 1, 1960, and 1961.

18. Letter signed by the governor and addressed to the Policía Gubernativa.

Works Cited

Bernault, Florence. "Suitcases and the Poetics of Oddities: Writing History from Disorderly Archives." *History in Africa*, vol. 42, no. 1, 2015, pp. 269–77.

Castro, Mayca de. "African Anticolonial Narratives in Perspective: The Case of *A Spear for the Boabí* (Daniel Jones Mathama, 1962)." *The Africas in the World and the World in the Africas: African Literatures and Comparativism*, edited by Sandra Sousa and Nazir Ahmed Can. Quod Manet Press, 2022, pp. 123–54.

———. *Empatía y violencia: Perspectivas transdisciplinares para leer el pasado colonial español en Guinea Ecuatorial durante el siglo XX*. 2020. U de Granada, doctoral dissertation.

Chapdelaine, Robin P. "Marriage Certificates and Walker Cards: Nigerian Migrant Labor, Wives, and Prostitutes in Colonial Fernando Pó." *African Economic History*, vol. 48, no. 2, 2020, pp. 1–36.

Cooper, Frederick, and Ann Laura Stoler, editors. *Tensions of Empire: Colonial Cultures in a Bourgeois World*. U of California P, 1997.

Copeiro del Villar, Jesús Ramírez. *Objetivo África: Crónica de la Guinea Española en la II Guerra Mundial*. Imprenta Jiménez S. L., 2004.

"Expediente 622." Spain, Ministerio de Cultura, Archivo General de la Administración, Sección África, Caja 81/08803.

García Cantús, Dolores. *Fernando Poo: Una aventura colonial española en el África Occidental, 1778–1900*. 2004. U de Valencia, doctoral dissertation.

Gheme, Linus N. [also referred to as Monde Obongue]. "Notebook." Spain, Ministerio de Cultura, Archivo General de la Administración, Sección África, Caja 81/08803.

Guinea Española: Revista quincenal (1903–1969).

Haney, Erin. "Going to Sea: Photographic Publics of the Free and Newly Freed." *Visual Anthropology*, vol. 27, 2014, pp. 362–78.

Jones Mathama, Daniel. *Una lanza por el Boabí*. Tip. Cat. Casals S. L., 1962.

Kumar, Prabhat. "Representing Servant Lives in the Household and Beyond." *Servants' Pasts: Late-Eighteenth to Twentieth-Century South Asia*, vol. 2, edited by Nitin Sinha and Nitin Varma, Orient BlackSwan, 2019, pp. 183–216.

Lewis, Marvin. *Equatorial Guinean Literature in its National and Transnational Contexts*. U of Missouri P, 2007.

Lifshey, Adam. *The Magellan Fallacy: Globalization and the Emergence of Asian and African Literature in Spanish*. U of Michigan P, 2012.

———. "And So the Worm Turns: The Impossibility of Imperial Imitation in *Una lanza por el Boabí* by Daniel Jones Mathama." *Chasqui: Revista de literatura latinoamericana*, vol. 36, no. 1, 2007, pp. 108–20.

Liniger-Goumaz, Max. *Historical Dictionary of Equatorial Guinea*. The Scarecrow P, 1988.

Martino, Enrique. "*Panya*: Economies of Deception and the Discontinuities of Indentured Labour Recruitment and the Slave Trade, Nigeria and Fernando Pó, 1890s–1940s." *African Economic History*, vol. 44, 2016, pp. 91–129.

———. *Touts: Recruiting Indentured Labor in the Gulf of Guinea*. De Gruyter Oldenbourg, 2022.

———. *Touts and Despots: Recruiting Assemblages of Contract Labour in Fernando Pó and the Gulf of Guinea, 1858–1979*. 2016. Humboldt-U zu Berlin, doctoral dissertation.

———. "When 'Modern Slavery' Meant Colonial Rule: Nigeria and Panya (Fernando Po) in the 1960s." *The Republic: A Journal of Nigerian Affairs*, June–July 2021.

Mbah, Ndubueze L. "'Wives Wishing to Join their Husbands': Colonial Forgery, Gender Legibility, and Labor Migration in West Africa." *History in Africa*, 2022, pp. 1–41.

Mbembe, Achille. "The Power of the Archive and its Limits." *Refiguring the Archive*, edited by Carolyn Hamilton et al., Palgrave Macmillan, 2002, pp. 19–27.

Menke, Anne M. "'*Boy!*': The Hinge of Colonial Double Talk." *Studies in 20th Century Literature*, vol. 15, no. 1, 1991, pp. 11–28.

Nigerian Foreign Office. "Recruitment of Labour for Island of Fernando Po. February 28, 1941." The National Archives of Nigeria. 371/26908. Also reproduced in www.opensourceguinea.org/2014/03/MichieLabourConditionsin SpanishGuinea.htmlhttp://www.opensourceguinea.org/2014/03/MichieLabour ConditionsinSpanishGuinea.html.

Ndongo-Bidyogo, Donato, and Mbaré Ngom. *Literatura de Guinea Ecuatorial (Antología)*. Sial Ediciones, 2000.

Ngom, Mbare. "The Missing Link: African Hispanism at the Dawn of the Millenium." *Journal of Iberian and Latin American Literary and Cultural Studies*, vol. 1, no. 1, 2001.

Oyono, Ferdinand. *Houseboy*. Waveland P, 2012.

Roe, Rev. Henry. *West African Scenes: Being Descriptions of Fernando Po, its Climate, Productions and Tribes: The Cause and Cure of Sickness; with Missionary Work, Trials, and Encouragements*. Elliott Stock, 1874.

Sampedro Vizcaya, Benita. "*Houseboys*: Domestic Labour Practices in Spanish Settlers' Homes in Colonial West Africa." *Bulletin of Spanish Visual Studies*, vol. 6, no. 2, 2022, pp. 175–96.

———. "Rethinking the Archive and the Colonial Library: Equatorial Guinea." *Journal of Spanish Cultural Studies*, vol. 9, no. 3, 2008, pp. 341–63.

Schneider, Jürg. "African Photography in the Atlantic Visualscape: Moving Photographers—Circulating Images." *Global Photographies: Memory, History, Archives*, edited by Sissy Helff and Stefanie Michels, Transcript, 2018, pp. 19–38.

Sinha, Nitin, and Nitin Varma, editors. *Servants' Pasts: Late-Eighteenth to Twentieth-Century South Asia*. Vol. 2. Orient BlackSwan, 2019.

Sundiata, Ibrahim K. *The Fernandinos: Labor and Community in Santa Isabel de Fernando Poo, 1827–1931*. 1972. Northwestern U, PhD dissertation.

———. *From Slaving to Neoslavery: The Bight of Biafra and Fernando Po in the Era of Abolition, 1827–1930*. U of Wisconsin P, 1996.

Ugarte, Michael. *Africans in Europe: The Culture of Exile and Emigration from Equatorial Guinea to Spain*. U of Illinois P, 2010.

Chapter 2

Echoes of the Spanish Slave Trade in Nineteenth-Century London

KIRSTY HOOPER[1]

Nineteenth-century London was home to hundreds of Spanish families and dozens of Spanish businesses, many with extensive connections to the slave trade. While Britain had famously legislated for the end of its own involvement in slavery in 1807 and was now vociferously in favor of its worldwide abolition, Spain's colonial economy depended on slave labor for much of the century. As David R Murray has written, "Britain's abolitionist campaign against the Spanish slave trade . . . challenged the basic assumptions of Spanish colonial policy" (x). Jesús Sanjurjo notes that within Britain's campaign for worldwide abolition, "the importance of Spain as a main antagonist was key" (12). How did the Spaniards who migrated to Victorian London, including those from the slaving islands of Cuba and Puerto Rico, navigate this conflict? In their pivotal study of the nineteenth-century Cuban colonial elite, *Hacer las Américas*, Ángel Bahamonde and José Cayuela outline a process they call "*britanización económica*" whereby elite Spanish and Cuban business families, aware that slavery was coming to an end and that they would no longer be able to extract wealth from the slaving economy, redirected their financial dealings from Cuban sugar and slavery to London property and finance. Bahamonde and Cayuela note in passing that this economic process "sólo se vio acompañado en casos contados . . . de un proceso paralelo de *britanización social*" ("was only accompanied in a handful of cases . . . by a parallel process of *britanización social*"; 71),[2] that is, of adaptation and integration into British society.

This essay explores the different means of exploiting the strategy of *britanización social* employed by three Spanish merchant families with extensive slave trade connections who arrived in London at three different touchpoints in Spain's nineteenth-century colonial journey. The Zuluetas of Cádiz arrived with the liberal exile of 1823, acquired denizenship in 1836, and were ennobled as Condes de Torre Diaz in 1845. During their first twenty years in London, the Zuluetas would have seen Spain's place in the British imagination shift radically. They arrived amid the "massive emotional investment" (Howarth ix) of the joint struggle against Napoleon that ensured a warm welcome for the liberal exiles. Within twenty years, patience with the exiles was running out, partly thanks to the rise of the French-inspired Romantic view of Spain as "Europe's other, a land of wild and exotic landscapes peopled by Moors, gypsies, and brigands" (Hooper 13). Alonso Jiménez from New Castile via Havana left Cuba against the turbulent political backdrop of the mid-1850s. He migrated first to Paris and then to London in 1861, where he was naturalized in 1864, and ennobled as Marqués de la Granja de San Saturnino in 1873. His presence in London coincided with rising British interest in Spain as a focus for economic investment (above all in the form of mining and railway concessions), which began in the 1850s and 1860s, was facilitated by the Spanish Republic's lifting of protectionist trade policies during the 1870s, and would continue until the First World War (Hooper 24–30). The Cabreras of Ponce, Puerto Rico, arrived within months of the end of unfree labor on the island in 1876 and were naturalized in 1885. While the Zuluetas have been the subject of some scholarly attention (Riddell; Sherwood), studies of the nineteenth-century Spanish slave trade and its legacy in London have mentioned the Jiménez and Cabrera families only in passing, if at all.

This essay employs a range of largely unexplored primary sources to reconstruct each family's London life and legacy, with particular attention to their strategic use of *britanización social* to obscure their participation in the Spanish slave trade. It argues that all three families resisted straightforward *britanización*: that is, none simply discarded their Spanish (or Hispanic) identity for a British one. Rather, they employed a range of strategies to navigate the tension between their presence in a strongly abolitionist city and their continued economic and emotional investment in a Spanish colonial economy still heavily dependent on slave labor. The essay explores how each family employed a variety of identities, from Catholic philanthropist to noble patriot to Caribbean gentleman, as a means of strategically developing diverse models for being visibly "Spanish" in the British capital while gradually obscuring their involvement in the Spanish slave trade. Nonetheless, as we will see, both material and archival traces persist, allowing us to locate echoes of the Spanish slave trade in nineteenth- and even twenty-first-century London.

The Zuluetas: Cádiz, Courtrooms, and Catholicism

On a cold October day in 1823, the Spanish politician and businessman Pedro Juan de Zulueta arrived in London aboard the schooner *Susan & Maria* ("Mirror"; "Spanish Exiles"; *Lloyd's* 1824). Zulueta, born in Cádiz in 1784 to a wealthy merchant family of Basque origin, was a prominent member of the Cádiz business community and had recently served in the Spanish liberal government of 1820 to 1823. When the government collapsed in October 1823, the Zuluetas joined the wave of liberal exiles heading for the sympathetic city of London. The widowed Pedro Juan was accompanied to London by his sons, three of whom would settle with him in London: Pedro José (1809–1882), Mariano (c. 1817–1888), and José Servando (c. 1821–1874). He left behind a large transatlantic business more than half a century in the making, largely built upon Spain's slaving economy. Zulueta's legacy would be definitively shaped by his decision to settle in London, a city hugely sympathetic to Spanish refugees, but hostile to both Roman Catholicism and the slave trade.

Zulueta swiftly reestablished his business in London. By 1826, he occupied an office at 5 Jeffreys Square in the City of London, where his fellow tenants included the merchant and linguist John Bowring, who had recently translated and published *Ancient Poetry and Romances of Spain*, and who would bankrupt himself in 1827 trying to finance a revolution in Greece (*Post Office London Directory for 1826* 47, 464). Contemporary newspapers record frequent, large cargoes of Spanish commodities such as wine, wheat, olive oil, lemons, nuts, aniseed, almonds, and grapes arriving under the Zulueta name from diverse Spanish Mediterranean and Atlantic ports. By 1828, the company was so valuable that Lloyd's of London insured it for £200k—approximately £14 million in today's money ("Insured").

Meanwhile, by 1829 ("Denization" 1831), the family had settled in Camberwell, renting 5 Andover Place, advertised for rent in December 1827 as "an excellent substantial Leasehold brick-built Residence and walled garden" situated "in the most preferable part of Camberwell Grove . . . opposite the park" ("Sales"). Their next-door neighbor in Andover Place was the broker Abraham Mocatta, of the extensive Sephardi family.

Although they remained closely involved in Spain's political and economic life, the Zuluetas were clear about their desire to stay in England; indeed, for the younger sons it was the only home they had known. Within five years of arriving in the country, Pedro Juan had decided to apply for permanent residence for himself and his sons, through the system of denizenship; he began his application in February 1829 with a letter to the Home Secretary, Sir Robert Peel ("Denization" 1831). The stakes for the family's future were high. As Pedro Juan explained in his letter of application, because he was "Alien Born," he was prevented either from signing a lease on his Camberwell townhouse or from investing in landed property, "which will afford a safe and permanent provision to his children" ("Denization" 1831). The family quickly discovered that becoming British was not a straightforward process; this first attempt, supported by fellow exile General Alava and Peninsular War veteran Lord Somerset, appears to have petered out before reaching a conclusion, although the reasons why are unclear. The second attempt, begun in 1835 with the support of Foreign Secretary Viscount Palmerston and Pedro Juan's friend Mendizábal, was successful, and in May 1836, all five Zuluetas were finally granted their letters of denizenship ("Denization" 1836).

The success of the Zuluetas' second attempt at achieving denizenship may well lie in their strategic decision to forge new connections with leading figures in the Anglo-Iberian mercantile establishment. In 1834, Pedro Juan and his fellow exile Juan Álvarez y Mendizábal were among the founding partners of a new shipping company, the Peninsular Steam Navigation Company. One of their first acts was to send Pedro José to Cádiz for a spell as the new company's local agent. The company's owner, Brodie McGhie Willcox, was very well connected in the Iberian Peninsula, having recently supported both the Spanish and Portuguese monarchies in the two countries' respective Carlist and Civil Wars. Not only did this give him political leverage, but it made him an attractive ally for the Zuluetas in both professional and personal terms. In 1836, six months after achieving denizenship, Pedro José married Willcox's daughter Sophia in the Anglican parish church of Christ Church Marylebone. It is hard not to make the connection between the

Zuluetas' achievement of denizenship and Pedro José's marriage into the heart of the Anglo-Iberian mercantile establishment. In 1837, the fledgling shipping line, with Willcox and the Zuluetas at the helm, was awarded the lucrative government contract for delivering mail to the Iberian Peninsula. Today, it is better known as P&O.

While the Zuluetas were strategically positioning themselves during the 1830s as key nodes in the Anglo-Iberian mercantile establishment, they also remained embedded in Spain's slaving economy. Marika Sherwood notes that the Colonial Office had been aware "since at least 1835, and perhaps before" of their role as London bankers for the notorious slave trader Pedro Blanco (61). Hugh Thomas records that during the 1830s Pedro Juan employed his "nephew" (in reality a distant relative) Julian de Zulueta as his agent in Cuba. As Thomas notes, Julian would go on to become "the slaver-planter par excellence of Cuba" (646). Notably, he ascribes Julian's involvement in the slave trade directly to his relationship with the London Zuluetas, writing that Julian "became interested in slaves . . . because of the interest of [his] uncle, Pedro Juan Zulueta de Ceballos, a successful London merchant" (646). The Zuluetas' continued participation in Spain's slaving economy had the potential to disrupt their progress into British mercantile and social networks. The conflict came to a head in 1841, when a British Commissioner, Dr. Madden, sent a report to the House of Commons that named the Zuluetas as active participants in the African slave trade. Madden recorded that the Zuluetas' ship the *Augusta* had been captured off the coat of West Africa with cargo on board that could only be intended for shipping slaves. A witness told the Select Committee investigating the case that "Zulueta, the gentleman in London . . . is a name well known on the coast in connection with the slave trade" (Zulueta 380).

The Zuluetas roundly rejected this accusation. In July 1842, Pedro José, now a director of his father-in-law's Peninsular Steam Navigation Company, gave evidence to the Select Committee, denying further witness allegations that Zulueta & Co. "have aided and abetted the slave trade for a number of years, by acting as the agents of slave dealers," namely Pedro Martínez and Pedro Blanco (House of Commons 555). This appearance would open the door to Pedro José's arrest in August 1843, and his notorious trial at the Old Bailey on a charge of slave trading from which he was, even more notoriously, acquitted. The crux of the case, which has been fully discussed elsewhere (Riddell; Sherwood; Zulueta), was not whether the *Augusta* was used in slave trading, since the evidence on that count was irrefutable, but whether the Zuluetas had knowledge of its use in slave trading. Pedro José's defense was that the company had sold the ship (to Blanco) and shipped the cargo (to Martínez) but had no knowledge of their intention to use either for slave trading. As Riddell observes, "it is safe to say that [Zulueta's] evidence was received with incredulity in several quarters, including The British and Foreign Anti-Slavery Society" (574).

By the time of Pedro José's high-profile appearance at the Old Bailey, the Zulueta family had been in England for two decades but had enjoyed the stability of denizenship for less than half that time. It was therefore imperative for Pedro José not only to refute the allegations against his company, but in doing so to construct a credible narrative to minimize both his foreign origins and the taint of slavery. As he explained in the story of his arrest, "thus it happened, that he who had left his home, his wife, and his children in the morning, with as assured a conscience as any of you can do, returned about ten o'clock in the evening a prisoner, with the possibility of a sentence of transportation hanging over his head, as ignorant of his accuser, of the facts deposed to against him, as if he had fallen into the hands of the Inquisition" (Zulueta xi). In comparing himself to a victim of the Inquisition, Zulueta cannily sought to place himself on the right side of one of the key British tropes of Spanish brutality. Given the somewhat shaky nature not only of the family's status as British residents, but more particularly of the evidence in his defense, it is not entirely surprising that Pedro José sought to rebrand himself, via family and business connections, as a member of the British establishment: "a merchant, to all practical purposes a British merchant, the junior member of a firm of unquestioned respectability" (ix).

The trial proved a watershed in the Zuluetas' strategic employment of their freshly acquired Anglo-Spanish identity as a means of obscuring their engagement in Spain's slaving economy. As the trial receded into the background, they rapidly extended their professional and social networks in London, a strategy boosted in November 1846 when Queen Isabel II appointed Pedro Juan I Conde de Torre Diaz and Senator of Spain. A widely syndicated item in the British national and regional press reported the honor, describing Pedro Juan as "the eminent Spanish merchant" and recording excitedly that "he has left England for Madrid" ("Fashionable World"; "Miscellany"). Pedro Juan now became one of the leading Spanish diplomatic figures in London, welcoming visiting dignitaries such as the Duchess of Nemours and Duke de Montpensier on their flight from Paris in 1848 ("Arrival"), or the Duke's wife, Infanta Luisa Fernanda, who visited London in 1852. The family's preeminence in London Spanish circles was consolidated when "his Excellency Count de Torre Diaz, Senator of Spain, Chevalier de Zuluetta [sic] and Madame de Zulueta" topped the guest list for the levée hosted by the Infanta at the Spanish Legation in Mansfield Street ("Political").

The family's rise to the top of Anglo-Spanish high society was reflected in the new home they moved into in 1850, a vast and elegant mansion at 21 Devonshire Place, Marylebone, that would quickly become a focal point for Anglo-Spanish and colonial networks. Between 1804 and 1840, it had been home to the banker Sir Thomas Baring, whose son Thomas is recorded as landowner in 1850 ("St Marylebone"), and whose company, like the Zuluetas, provided banking services to the notorious slave trader Pedro Blanco (Sherwood 61). The Zuluetas now became even more active and visible in British business and philanthropic initiatives at both a national and a local level. For example, in April 1851 Pedro Juan joined a committee of "members of Parliament and mercantile men of high standing" in an unsuccessful attempt to promote the formation of Tribunals of Commerce as an informal alternative to the courts for resolving commercial disputes ("Money Market"). Three months later, he attended a dinner for subscribers to the maintenance fund for his local hospital, St Mary's in Paddington ("St Mary's"). Pedro Juan retired from the family business in January 1853, leaving Pedro José and younger son Mariano in charge ("Partnerships"). He died on August 11, 1855, and was buried at Chelsea's All Souls Catholic Cemetery, leaving his four sons his fortune in England of £45,000, equivalent to £3.6 million today ("Will").

The second generation of London Zuluetas continued to redefine what it meant to be visibly Spanish in London, in ways that decisively erased not only the memory of Pedro José's 1843 trial, but also their role in Spain's slaving economy. Pedro Juan was succeeded as II Conde de Torre Diaz and Senator of Spain by Pedro José, who also inherited the Devonshire Place house, which the family would retain until after World War I. After Pedro José was formally presented to Queen Victoria at St James's Palace in May 1856 ("Her Majesty's Levée"), followed a year later by his wife and daughter ("Royal Drawing Room"), the Count and Countess de Torre Diaz would become regulars at both Spanish and British court functions and philanthropic events. Alongside their place at Court, they became leading figures in London's rapidly expanding Roman Catholic high society. This had emerged with the new freedoms permitted to Catholics by the Catholic Relief Act of 1829, which ended centuries of formal discrimination against Catholics in England. The Zulueta family home in Devonshire Place was ten minutes' walk from the Roman Catholic church of St. James Spanish Place, which had long been associated with the nearby Spanish Embassy, and the Zuluetas were active in parish philanthropy. They were also heavily involved in the reestablishment of Catholic rite and philanthropy at a national level ("Feast"; "Great"), were close to Cardinal Wiseman, the first Catholic Archbishop of Westminster, and had strong connections within England's Catholic aristocracy, notably the Petre family—a relationship cemented by the marriage in 1873 of Pedro José's heir Brodie Manuel with Constance, granddaughter of the 11th Baron Petre.

The distinctively Anglo-Spanish Catholic space carved out by the Zulueta family went beyond the Church itself. The family was closely involved with the Jesuit-run Beaumont College in Old Windsor, which opened in 1861. Thanks in part to the support of the Zuluetas, the college would become a popular destination for Spanish and Cuban students, as traced by Bernardo Rodríguez Caparrini in his series of archival studies. In 1865, Pedro José sent his youngest son Francisco to Beaumont; Rodríguez Caparrini records that he was popular among his fellow students, who called him "Zoo," and talented at both music and academics, passing the University of London's Matriculation Examination in July 1871 ([2007] 18–19). He would be admitted as a Jesuit novice two months later ([2007] 20). Francisco's parents had a presence at the college, attending formal dinners and events alongside other prominent parents, such as the Condes de Morella; in his son's penultimate year, Pedro José was invited to present the awards at the college's annual prizegiving ("Annual"). Other members of the extended Zulueta family would follow Francisco to Beaumont, including cousins from Havana, and, after the Spanish Revolution of 1868, from Cádiz (Rodríguez Caparrini [2011] 157–168). The family connection with the college would continue for at least another generation, as Pedro José's children sent their own sons to study there. Beaumont's curriculum married intensive religious instruction with a characteristically British classical education and plenty of music, drama, and sport. As such, the college was instrumental in normalizing the presence in England of scions of Spanish and Cuban slaving families, forging a new generation of Anglo-Spanish Catholics able to move comfortably in Anglo, Spanish, and colonial social and business circles.

When Pedro José de Zulueta, II Conde de Torre Diaz, died at Devonshire Place on 3 March 1882 at the age of 72, he left an estate valued at £35,543 10s 4d, equivalent to £2.3 million today (Public Record Office, "De Zulueta"). Over sixty years in London, he and his father had created a network of Anglo-Spanish social and cultural spaces, shaped as much by their devotion to Britain's re-emerging Catholic community as by their continued emotional and economic investment in their Spanish homeland. As the first Anglo-Spanish merchant family to operate in the top echelons of both the Spanish and English public spheres, they not only forged a fresh model for being visibly "Spanish" in the British capital but also erased from public memory any echo of that notorious trial for slave trading forty years earlier.

The Jiménez Family: Cuba, Cigars, and Civic Service

Alonso Jiménez Cantero arrived in London forty years later and to far less fanfare than the Zuluetas. Born in 1809 in the remote New Castilian village of Casas-Ibáñez ("Birth"), he emigrated to Havana as a young man in around 1831. There, in partnership with Ramón Herrera, he became an import/export merchant and financier, investing heavily in sugar plantations and slave voyages (Bahamonde and Cayuela 113). Jiménez was part of the large pro-Spanish business community on the island; in 1844, he was one of the signatories to a strongly worded letter to Queen Isabel supporting General O'Donnell, who had just violently suppressed a planned slave uprising ("Señora"). Jiménez and Herrera firmly embedded themselves in Cuba's Spanish establishment, becoming brothers-in-law on marrying Susana and Manuela Marcos y Diaz, daughters of a prominent businessman. Jiménez and Susana went on to have at least six children: Susana (1843–aft. 1893); Pedro (1844–1919); Ricardo (1846–1904), Matilde (c. 1850–aft. 1916), Arturo (1856–1877), and Manuel (1860–1875).[3]

Jiménez y Herrera operated in Havana and Matanzas until at least 1850. However, while Herrera remained in Cuba and became a wealthy shipowner, Jiménez had his eyes on a larger stage. Sometime between 1846 and 1856, he moved his family to Paris ("Poder"), and then in around 1861 to London, where he swiftly applied for naturalization ("Naturalisation Papers: Jimenez"). The papers, submitted in October 1864, give his address as 141 Westbourne Terrace and state that he has resided in London for three years. While the family does not appear on the 1861 census, the *Post Office London Directory* records them at Westbourne Terrace from 1862, listed under "Mrs Gemenes" from 1862 to 1865, and "Alonso Jimenez, Esq." from 1866. The grand, four-story, white stucco end terrace a few minutes' walk north of Hyde Park, built circa 1840, was located on a prestigious and very cosmopolitan street, with a high proportion of foreign residents. The family quickly settled in London. Son Ricardo attended Baylis House Roman Catholic School in Slough, where he embraced British life, joining Twickenham Rowing Club ("Twickenham") and playing for the school cricket team ("Cricket").

Jiménez's first decade in London was both professionally and personally successful, and he became one of the public faces of the Cuban import trade. From 1860 to 1866, probably working with a younger, Cuba-based relative, he operated as Jiménez y Sobrino, bringing in-demand Havana cigars, cotton, and lead to England and sending diverse goods in the opposite direction. The 1862 *Post Office London Directory* records the company at 23 Rood Lane in the City, although port records suggest most of their imports arrived via the northern gateway of Liverpool. When the partnership was dissolved in January 1866, Jiménez carried on the business in his own name ("City"), moving headquarters from Rood Lane to 116 Fenchurch St. and opening a second office in the northern industrial city of Manchester (Slater 95). From 1868, Jiménez was London agent for Julian Alvarez & Co. cigars, of Havana, leading a nationwide campaign to protect their "Henry Clay" brand from counterfeit competition (e.g., "Henry Clay"). Socially, he was active in the Tobacco Trade Benevolent Association, stewarding their Tenth Anniversary Dinner at Cannon St. Hotel on 15 June 1870 ("Tobacco Trade"). By 1870, his company was worth around 80 million reales, with offices on two continents and three transoceanic ships (Bahamonde and Cayuela 116). In January 1871, Jiménez took his eldest sons Alonso and Ricardo into partnership, renaming the company A. Jimenez and Sons ("Monetary"). The 1871 census, taken in April of that year, records Alonso and Susana in a new, larger home at 8 Westbourne St. with sons "Alphonse," Ricardo, and Manuel, daughter Susana with her husband and children, and five resident servants, including a Spanish chef and a French nursemaid.

Even as the family adapted to the British way of life, Jiménez remained strongly committed to his homeland. The Spanish Revolution of 1868 and the changes brought by the socially and economically liberal Republic created opportunities for him to play an important role, informed by his interests in Cuba. When the growing unhappiness of Cuban planters with Spanish rule led in 1868 to the outbreak of the Ten Years' War, the first of three anti-colonial wars eventually leading to Cuban independence, Jiménez was firmly on the side of the Spanish government. In 1869, as Spanish military repression on the island intensified, he was one of the two biggest donors to a subscription opened by the Spanish consul in London "destinada a auxiliar los heroicos esfuerzos de nuestros hermanos de Cuba" ("destined to aid the heroic efforts of our Cuban brothers"), according to one Spanish newspaper ("A Instancia"), and aimed at "la conservación de la isla de Cuba" ("the preservation of the island of Cuba") according to another ("Ayer"). His donation of £500 (approx. £31,000 today) was more than a quarter of the total raised.

Against this background of political and economic upheaval, the company began to follow a new trajectory, diversifying its earlier mercantile activity into the world of finance. They opened an office in Madrid in 1870, which Bahamonde and Cayuela suggest was part of a strategy that "tendría como objetivo planificar una política de inversiones de alcance nacional" ("would aim to plan an investment policy on a national scale"; 116). Jiménez's involvement in Spanish affairs only intensified after the election of King Amadeo in November 1870 and the assassination shortly afterwards of the man who had made Amadeo's election possible, General Juan Prim. In March 1871, Jiménez donated the substantial sum of 5000 reales to the subscription raised by *La Iberia* newspaper to build a statue to the memory of "nuestro querido y malogrado amigo" ("our dear departed friend") Prim, who as Capitán General of Puerto Rico in 1847 to 1848 had instigated the notorious "Código negro" that brutally repressed not only the island's enslaved people, but all Puerto Ricans with even a hint of African blood ("El señor don Alonso"; Morales Carrión; Carlo Altieri 107). On January 8th, 1873, "teniendo en consideración las especiales circunstancias que concurren en D. Alonso Jiménez y Cantero, y queriendo darle una prueba de Mi aprecio" ("taking into consideration the special circumstances of D. Alonso Jiménez y Cantero, and wishing to give him a token of My appreciation"), Amadeo named Jiménez Marqués de la Granja de San Saturnino ("Ministerio").

Throughout the 1870s and 1880s, the now-Marqués continued to shift his business away from Cuba and commerce, and toward "una nueva forma de producción patrimonial basada en prácticas rentistas" ("a new form of patrimonial production based on rentier practices"; Bahamonde and Cayuela 117), simultaneously expanding his public profile as a philanthropist and committed royalist. In February 1878, he celebrated the marriage of Spain's new king by funding a mass in his native village of Casas-Ibáñez, organized by his brother Marcelino. The celebration included a "gran comida" and alms of between one and ten reales for the village's twenty-two prisoners, its poor, and "cuantos se presentaran en demanda de socorros" ("all who come forward requesting help"). In the event, so many people showed up from the surrounding villages that three pairs of guards had to be placed at the church door to protect the almsgivers ("El Excmo"). Jiménez was always among the largest donors to charitable subscriptions set up by London's Spanish business community, for example to support victims of the floods in southern Spain in October 1879, when he sent 20,000 reales to be used for reconstruction ("El señor Marqués"), or in 1885, when along with Zulueta, the Marqués de Misa, and the Duke of Wellington, he was one of the four largest donors to a subscription for earthquake victims ("La suscrición"). In 1888, Spain's Queen Regent issued a Real Orden thanking Jiménez for his 25,000 pesetas donation to build a new school at Casas-Ibáñez ("Fomento") and tasking a high-level civil servant with an inspection to ensure best use of the funds ("Ilmo. Sr."). Fewer records survive of Jiménez's philanthropy in London, although in August 1879 he ostentatiously presented London Zoo with a Spanish imperial eagle (Zoological Society of London 375).

Although he worked closely with them on philanthropic and diplomatic events, such as the London mass for Spain's late King Alfonso XII in 1885, Jiménez did not so visibly inhabit the same high-level royal and religious spaces as the Zuluetas. Where the two families did coincide was in seeing the potential of the transnational Catholic space of Beaumont College as a means of integrating their children into British social and professional networks. Having initially followed his brother Ricardo to Baylis House, the third Jiménez son, Arturo, took a by now well-established path for the sons of Cuban and Spanish merchants in England when he enrolled at Beaumont in May 1869. Here, as Rodríguez Caparrini shows, he joined a number of students from prominent Anglo-Spanish and Anglo-Cuban families, including the Zulueta cousins Francisco (son of Pedro José, of London), Salvador (son of Julian, of Havana), and another Salvador, son of Antonio, of Cádiz ([2011] 156, 159, 165–66). After Arturo left Beaumont in the summer of 1871, however, he diverged from his peers when instead of taking up a mercantile position, he matriculated as an undergraduate at Hertford College, Oxford. Here, he embraced English student life; active in athletics and cricket, he spent the summer of 1875 playing golf and refereeing swimming tournaments at the seaside resort of Westward Ho! It must have been a terrible shock when the fit young man died of pericardial effusion, a buildup of fluid around the heart, at the age of just 21 (Rodríguez Caparrini 204).

The surviving Jiménez children followed divided paths, with the sons integrating into British life while their sisters settled abroad. Eldest son and heir Pedro was the only one to marry outside conventional mercantile networks; in 1875, he married Alice, daughter of the English composer Lewis Henry Lavenu, settling in Putney and later, after Alice's early death, in Mayfair. Susana married French merchant Henri de Nard at Westminster French Chapel in 1865 and relocated to her husband's native Paris. Their remaining siblings both married into families whose fortunes also originated in the Spanish colonial slave economy. Matilde married Tenerife-born Francisco de Lecuona, who had made his fortune in Havana and who briefly joined the family business before his early death in 1880. She and her children settled in Lecuona's native Santa Cruz and appear to have maintained few links with England. The only sibling whose legacy remains visible in London today was Ricardo, who, in Paris in 1872, married Isabel González Solar y Ureta, part of Havana's powerful Solar slave-owning family (Bahamonde and Cayuela 96, 114). Ricardo and Isabel made their home in Wimbledon, South London, where they were early parishioners of the new Roman Catholic church of the Sacred Heart, donating an altar with a statue of St. Joseph that remains in the Church today (Millward 5). When Ricardo died in June 1904, the local newspaper headlined his obituary "Death of a Prominent Catholic" and did not mention his origins other than to note that his company, "Messrs A Jaiemez [sic]," was a "Spanish merchant" house ("Death"). Although the Jiménez family home in Wimbledon has been demolished, one of their greenhouses, together with some of their "exotic trees," can still be seen in the Copse Hill Conservation Area (Merton Council).

Alonso Jiménez, the Marqués de la Granja de San Saturnino, died at his Bayswater home on February 17, 1893, aged 83. Jiménez left two wills, one for his Cuban and Spanish property, and the other for his property in Britain. The latter amounted to £91,000 (£7.5 million), including £16,000 (£1.3 million) each for his two daughters, while the family home at 28 Pembridge Square went to his eldest son, Pedro Alonso ("Wills"). Jiménez was buried in the family tomb, "an extraordinarily tall Gothic mausoleum," at St. Mary's Catholic Cemetery in Kensal Green (Mausolea). As II Marqués, Pedro would continue his father's public work. Just eight months later, he and Brodie Manuel Zulueta, the III Count de Torre Diaz, headed up the Santander Disaster Relief Fund, formed in London to raise funds for the victims and survivors of a dynamite explosion in that Spanish port town ("Santander"). Within just one generation, the Jiménez family had decisively left behind not only their social origins in rural Castile, but also their economic origins in the Cuban slave trade. Their achievement in rewriting their own history is crystallized in a twenty-first-century English local government document analyzing the area where traces of Ricardo and Isabel's family home can still be seen, which records them as "relatives of the Spanish Royal family named Jiminez [*sic*]" (Merton Council).

The Cabreras: Puerto Rico, Plantations, and Protestantism

Our final family, the Cabreras, followed an entirely different strategy from their predecessors when they migrated from Puerto Rico to London late in 1876. Their decision to move to London was a direct result of the abolition of slavery and subsequent end to unfree labor in Puerto Rico, and the subsequent desire to find alternative sources of finance for the island's slaveowners. Gustavo Cabrera Rosaly was born in Ponce, Puerto Rico, in 1843, the son and heir of plantation owner José Emeterio Cabrera and Jerónima Rosaly ("José Emeterio Cabrera"). Unlike the Zulueta and Jiménez families, the Cabreras actually owned enslaved people who worked their four plantations in the province of Juana Diaz. José Emeterio was wealthy enough to travel abroad to seek treatment for an illness in Paris, where he died on December 11, 1860 ("Solicitud"). After his father's death, Gustavo Cabrera and his brothers, operating as Cabrera Hermanos, took on the plantations and the family's enslaved workers; Andrés Ramos Mattei records that by 1869, they owned a total of 161 enslaved people, of whom 94 worked at the largest plantation, Boca Chica (378).

Cabrera became a prominent figure in Ponce, standing for election to the Corregimiento de la Villa de Ponce in 1868 (he came fourth) and subsequently acting as *regidor*, election secretary, and *concejal* for Ponce ("Corregimiento"; "Villa"; "Acta"). Sometime around 1870 or 1871, he married Emily Henna, from a prominent Anglo–Puerto Rican family. Her father, Joseph Henna, was a pharmacist born in Plymouth, England, who had migrated to Ponce and married Maria del Rosario Pérez. The Hennas were among the founders of Ponce's Protestant community, which, as Luis Martínez-Fernández notes, "emerged in 1869 as the first ever in Spanish colonial territory," a direct response to the Spanish Republic's new religious tolerance decree (265, 272). This connection may well have shaped the Cabrera family's approach to life in Britain.

Cabrera was closely involved in negotiations as Puerto Rico moved slowly toward abolition. Christopher Schmidt-Nowara quotes a letter Cabrera wrote to the abolitionist José Julián Acosta, in which he suggests that many in Ponce had reconciled themselves to abolition, recognizing not only the new political currents of the September Revolution, but also the validity of the abolitionist alternative articulated by Acosta and others since the 1850s. He signs off by warning Acosta that "concerning slavery, you should <u>sweeten</u> [azucararan] it a bit by making it gradual and giving us five to ten years" (136). In the end, Cabrera and his fellow slaveowners got their wish. Slavery in Puerto Rico was abolished in 1873, while unfree labor continued until 1876. The island's former slaveowners were issued with *bonos* or vouchers intended to compensate them for their losses, but the island's government struggled with liquidity and was unable to make payments promptly. Within months of the end of unfree labor, Cabrera had moved his family to London.

Cabrera's new base in London placed him at the heart of efforts to identify alternative funds for Ponce's former slaveowners. Cabrera was closely linked with Ponce's powerful Sociedad de Agricultura, whose members, according to Ángel Martínez Soto, held around forty-three percent of all *bonos* (187). Mistrusting the government's ability to honor the *bonos*, the Sociedad looked to Europe for alternate sources of funding. A proposal tendered by Spanish politician Tomás Sáenz Hermua and the Union Générale de Paris, which one historian describes as "mysterious," may have involved investing £20,000 in a London bank in exchange for "4/5 partes de las cédulas de esclavos" (Santiago de Curet 28). Was stewarding this connection part of Cabrera's role? While the negotiations were slow and met several setbacks, the Sociedad's president expressed his continued confidence in Cabrera's London mission in a speech in October 1877:

> no debe considerarse la operación como fracasada, pues, ya sea modificando las bases del convenio celebrado con el Sr Hermua en 8 de agosto del año próximo pasado . . . ya sea utilizando los trabajos que en igual sentido practica en Londres nuestro representante en aquella metrópoli Don Gustavo Cabrera, es de esperarse que el éxito más feliz corone nuestros esfuerzos. ("Sociedad")

> the operation should not be considered a failure, since, whether by modifying the bases of the agreement concluded with Sr Hermua on 8 August of last year . . . or by using the work that our representative in London is doing in the same direction, it is to be hoped that the happiest success will crown our efforts.

Cabrera obviously made some progress; at the end of December 1877, he was elected a Corresponding Member of the Society ("Nombramientos"). It is not clear, however, whether he was involved in Union Générale's acquisition in London of 1.5 million Mexican pesos, which arrived in Ponce in July 1879 (Martínez Soto 188). He certainly remained involved in Puerto Rican matters. Although he was resident in London until his death in 1906, he and his brothers Guillermo and Enrique maintained ownership of Boca Chica, placing their uncle Carlos Cabrera in charge of the plantation's day-to-day management ("Real").

The Cabrera family emigrated to England sometime after September 2, 1876, when daughter Maud was born in Ponce. Their first recorded address in London, in the 1877 *Post Office London Directory*, was 61 Redcliffe Rd., Kensington. This elegant four-story terrace was a short walk from Brompton Cemetery and in the same street as that of Cabrera's new business partner Miguel Ventura, who had moved into number 18 with his family a year earlier. Ventura was an Italian-Dominican cigar merchant who was in London by 1871, and in 1874 became the city's Consul for the Dominican Republic. We don't know whether the two men knew each other before Cabrera's arrival in London, but by 1878, they had set up business as Ventura & Cabrera, merchants, at 18 Coleman St. in the City (*Post Office London Directory for 1878*). The partnership would survive until January 1889 ("London Gazette").

During the Ventura & Cabrera period, the Cabreras established themselves comfortably in London. Unlike the Zulueta and, to a lesser extent, the Jiménez families, they did not form part of the city's Spanish Catholic networks; in fact, they seem to have had only limited involvement even in the city's Protestant religious life. Unsurprisingly, given Emily's family background, their two youngest children were baptized in Church of England parish churches in Kensington, a few minutes' walk from the family home: Maud on January 5, 1879, at St. John, World's End, in Blantyre St., and William on March 28, 1880, at St. Jude, Courtfield Gardens. By March 1880 the family had moved a short walk from Redcliffe Road to Philbeach Gardens, a curving terrace of substantial, newly built four-floor townhouses backing onto three acres of communal gardens. The 1881 census records Gustavo, described as a "West India Merchant," with wife Emily and children Gustavo Jr. (9), Mary (6), and Maud (4), all born in "Porto Rico," and William (1), born in Kensington. The family had three live-in servants: a Danish nurse and two general servants, one Scottish and one Jamaican. They obviously saw their future in the city, and in January 1885, the British

Government approved Cabrera's application for naturalization, under the Anglicized name Gustavus Cabrera ("Naturalisation Certificate").

When it came to integrating their children into British life, the Cabreras followed a different, and arguably more profitable, strategy than their Spanish Catholic predecessors, sending their children to secular English schools. Both boys boarded at the prestigious Cheltenham College, Gustavo from May 1884 to December 1888, and William from January 1894 to December 1897 (Hunter 494, 576). The Cheltenham connection seems especially to have shaped Gustavo's life. A keen musician and sportsman, he regularly performed on cello with the school orchestra, appearing on programs for at least five years after he left. He also played for the Old Cheltonians football team from 1889 to 1891 and was remembered in the team's "Birthday Book" as late as 1901. Maud also attended boarding school, appearing on the 1891 census, age fourteen, at "The Cliff" Ladies' College in Eastbourne, where "Instruction is given in English subjects, Foreign Languages, Music, Singing, &c" ("The Cliff"). In fact, the very British seaside resort of Eastbourne, on the southern coast of England, was the family's favorite summer destination. Gustavo Junior is recorded taking part in sports events at the city's Devonshire Park as early as 1882, when he came second in the U12 100 Yards Race ("Devonshire Park"). In 1894, at the same venue, he even reached the second round of the Gentleman's Doubles in the South of England Lawn Tennis Tournament ("Lawn Tennis").

After the dissolution of Ventura & Cabrera in 1889, Cabrera set up on his own as Gustavus Cabrera, drug exporter and merchant, with an office at 5 Laurence Pountney Hill in the City. Sometime between 1885 and 1890, the family moved a few doors along Philbeach Gardens, from number 101 to number 74, an even larger red-brick terraced townhouse, newly built in the second wave of the street's construction. The 1891 census records "Gus" and Emily, with nineteen-year-old Gustavus, now a clerk, sixteen-year-old Mary, and three servants: a London-born cook, a Swiss housemaid, and a Swiss manservant. Ten years later, the 1901 census shows the three youngest children still at home and unmarried, while the three live-in servants, reflecting the family's own trajectory, are all now English.

In 1902, Cabrera retired, leaving the business to his son Gustavo, who celebrated by getting himself arrested twice for speeding, racing friends at over 19 miles an hour in Surrey and Lincolnshire ("Furious"). Shortly after retiring, Cabrera took a trip home to Ponce, returning in February 1903 via New York. The family were active in upper-middle-class English social circles, largely erasing the Hispanic dimension of their identity from public view. Emblematic of their success was Maud's appearance in 1902 in an amateur charity production of the Anglo-Spanish-themed musical *Florodora* where, paradoxically in a chorus made up of five English and five Spanish characters, she was cast as English ("Popular Opera"). The following year, she and Mary attended a fancy-dress ball and champagne supper at Atholl Hydropathic Hotel in Pitlochry, where Maud wore "harvest dinner dress" and Mary, like countless of her Scottish and English peers, appeared in the costume of a "Spanish dancer" ("Atholl").

When Cabrera died at 53 Barkston Gardens, South Kensington, on March 10, 1906, he left his family more than £25,000, or nearly £2 million in today's money (Public Record Office, "Cabrera"). Unlike his father forty-six years earlier, Cabrera's body was not returned to the family pantheon in Ponce, but rests in a new family grave at Brompton Cemetery in London, where Emily and Gustavo would eventually join him ("Brompton"). As the family's resting place demonstrates, the Cabreras differed from their Zulueta and Jiménez predecessors in remaining outside both London's well-established Anglo-Spanish high society and the city's Roman Catholic elite. Their Anglo-Hispanic Protestant background, aided by the boys' Cheltenham education, facilitated the family's swift absorption into upper-middle-class British social circles. Although they retained ownership of Boca Chica, the Cabrera children all made their lives in England, settling outside London in the elegant south coast resorts of Eastbourne, Folkestone, and Worthing. To all intents and purposes, the Cabreras succeeded completely in erasing both their Puerto Rican identity and their very recent slave-owning history, the latter of which seems to have vanished (at least publicly) into thin air.

Conclusion

Each of the three families we have looked at in this essay made their fortune in Spain's colonial slave economy. Each arrived in London at a different touchpoint of Spain's nineteenth-century colonial journey, and each exploited different strategies of *britanización social* to carve out a space within London's British, Spanish, and colonial mercantile and social networks. The Zuluetas were the pioneers, in every sense. Pedro José's trial provided an opportunity to create a public narrative that left no space for open discussions of Anglo-Spanish slaving activity, instead using ennoblement and Catholic philanthropy to forge a distinctively Anglo-Spanish, Catholic identity. The Jiménez family was less upper class, less overtly Catholic, and more civic-minded. They participated in Anglo-Spanish mercantile and philanthropic activities alongside the Zuluetas and sent their sons to the same schools, but with a more direct commercial flavor, given their involvement in the nationwide branding of Cuban tobacco. They are emblematic of the "new mercantile aristocracy" ennobled by Amadeo I to try and shore up support (and funds) for his faltering reign. In the rather different case of the Cabreras, the distinctively Puerto Rican elements of the family's identity, partly diminished by their Protestantism, seem to have given way irretrievably to the characteristic pull of the British upper middle class. As far as their British public image was concerned, all three families seem to have succeeded entirely in obscuring their slaving origins; nonetheless, both archival and material traces persist, allowing us to locate echoes of the Spanish slave trade not only in nineteenth-, but also in twenty-first-century London.

Notes

1. The research for this essay was undertaken as part of the Leverhulme Trust Major Research Fellowship *Hispanic London: Culture, Commerce and Community in the Nineteenth-Century City*. I am immensely grateful to the Leverhulme Trust for their support.

2. All translations from Spanish are my own.

3. Some published information about the Jiménez children is inconsistent with available documentation. Bahamonde and Cayuela refer to a son called Carlos, who managed the Jiménez affairs in Madrid from 1851 (114–15), although since Alonso and Susana were married only in 1841, this is unlikely to have been a son of their marriage. They also record that son Ricardo had set up his own company in Havana in 1852 and moved to London to work for a British firm in 1858 (115), but since Ricardo was born only in 1846, this is likely a misidentification. Alonso's will, dated 1890, references only four living children: two sons and two daughters (sons Arturo and Manuel having died in the 1870s).

Works Cited

"A instancia de los españoles residentes en Londres . . ." *Boletín de comercio*, 25 Oct. 1869, p. 3.

"Acta de Escrutinio General." *Gazeta de Puerto Rico*, 26 Mar. 1870, p. 1.

"Annual Athletic Sports at Beaumont College." *Windsor and Eton Express*, 23 Apr. 1870, p. 4.

"Arrival of the Duchess de Nemours and the Duke de Montpensier." *Morning Post*, 2 Mar. 1848, p. 5.
"Atholl Hydropathic Fancy Dress Ball." *Dundee Courier*, 7 Sept. 1903, p. 5.
"Ayer publicó la *Gaceta*." *La Discusión*, 18 Feb. 1870, p. 2.
Bahamonde, Ángel, and José Cayuela. *Hacer las Américas: Las elites coloniales españolas en el siglo XIX*. Alianza, 1992.
"Birth of Alonso Felix Jiménez Cantero." Casas-Ibáñez (Albacete)—Various Parish Record Indexes, 1809, Libro X: image 1136. *FamilySearch*, www.familysearch.org.
Bowring, John. *Ancient Poetry and Romances of Spain*. Taylor and Hessey, 1824.
Brompton Cemetery Burial Register. "No. 167625. Gustavus CABRERA, 15 Mar. 1906"; "No. 188745. Emily Victoria Agatha CABRERA, 19 Oct. 1938"; "No. 193875, Gustave CABRERA, 30 Nov. 1945." *The Royal Parks*, portal.royalparks.org.uk.
Carlo Altieri, Gerardo A. "Derecho y esclavitud en el Puerto Rico del siglo XIX." *Cuadernos intercambio sobre Centroamérica y el Caribe*. vol. 6, no. 7, 2009, pp. 91–128.
"City." *London Evening Standard*, 4 Jan. 1866, p. 2.
"The Cliff, Eastbourne" [advertisement]. *Gentlewoman*, 5 Sept. 1891, p. 3.
"Corregimiento de la Villa de Ponce." *Gazeta de Puerto Rico*, 19 Nov. 1868, p. 4.
"Cricket." *Windsor & Eton Express*, 7 May 1864, p. 3.
"Death of a Prominent Catholic." *Wimbledon News*, 11 June 1904, p. 1.
"Denization Papers: de Zulueta, Pedro, from Spain." 1831. Home Office: Denization and Naturalization Papers and Correspondence, HO 1/10/22, The National Archives, London, England.
"Denization Papers: de Zulueta, Peter John, from Spain." 1836. Home Office: Denization and Naturalization Papers and Correspondence, HO 1/11/13, The National Archives, London, England.
"Devonshire Park, Eastbourne." *Field*, 26 Aug. 1882, p. 48.
"El Excmo. Señor marqués de la Granja de San Saturnino." *La Época*, 20 Feb. 1878, p. 4.
"Fashionable World." *Morning Post*, 24 Nov. 1846, p. 3.
"The Feast of SS Peter and Paul . . ." *Dublin Weekly Nation*, 19 July 1856, p. 12.
"Fomento." *La Correspondencia de España*, 12 May 1888, pp. 3.
"Furious Motoring." *Sheffield Daily Telegraph*, 17 Aug. 1903, p. 7.
"Great Catholic Meeting at St James's Hall, London." *Glasgow Free Press*, 18 June 1859, pp. 2–3.
"Henry Clay Cigars." *Clerkenwell News*, 28 Feb. 1868, p. 1.
"Her Majesty's Levée." *Globe*, 8 May 1856, p. 4.
Home Office. *England and Wales Census*. 1841–1921.
Hooper, Kirsty. *The Edwardians and the Making of a Modern Spanish Obsession*. Liverpool UP, 2020.

House of Commons. *British Parliamentary Papers: Report from the Select Committee on the West Coast of Africa, together with Minutes of Evidence, Appendix and Index*. Part II. Irish UP, 1968.

Howarth, David. *The Invention of Spain: Cultural Relations Between Britain and Spain, 1770–1870*. Manchester UP, 2007.

Hunter, A[ndrew] A[lexander], editor. *Cheltenham College Register: 1841–1910*. G Bell and Sons, 1911.

"Ilmo. Sr.: El banquero español . . ." *La Unión: Periódico de primera enseñanza*, 20 May 1888, p. 5.

"Insured: Messrs Zulueta and Co., 5 Jefferies Square, St Mary Axe, merchants." Records of Sun Fire Office, Policy Register, 4 Sept. 1827. MS 11936/513/1065394; 1065395, London Metropolitan Archive, London, England.

"José Emeterio Cabrera pide legitimación de su esposa." 1850. Archivo Histórico Nacional, PARES. ES.28079.AHN/16/Ultramar, 2028, Exp. 16.

"Lawn Tennis." *Manchester Courier*, 15 Sept. 1894, p. 6

Lloyd's Register of Shipping for 1824. London, CF Seyfang, 1824.

"London Gazette—Jan. 1. Partnerships Dissolved." *Lloyd's List*, 2 Jan. 1889, p. 5.

Martínez-Fernández, Luis. "Marriage, Protestantism, and Religious Conflict in Nineteenth-Century Puerto Rico." *Journal of Religious History*, vol. 24, no. 3, 2000, pp. 263–78.

Martínez Soto, Ángel P. "Entre la Corona y la colonia: Los orígenes de la Banca Comercial en Puerto Rico, 1877–1888." *Revista del Centro de Investigaciones Históricas*, vol. 22, 2013, p. 173–215.

The Mausolea and Monuments Trust. *Jimenez Mausoleum*. N.d. www.mmtrust.org.uk/view.php?name=245.

Merton Council. *Copse Hill Character Assessment*, part 2. N.d. www.merton.gov.uk/system/files?file=0177_copse_hill_character_assessment_pt2.pdf.

Millward, Richard. *Sacred Heart Church Wimbledon: A History Guide*. N.d. www.sacredheartwimbledon.org.uk.

"Ministerio de Gracia y Justicia." *Gaceta de Madrid*, 9 Jan. 1873, p. 1.

"Mirror of Fashion: The Spanish Deputy Zulueta has arrived in London." *Morning Chronicle*, 1 Nov. 1823, p. 3.

"Miscellany: Original and Select." *Bell's Weekly Messenger*, 16 Jan. 1847, p. 4.

"Monetary and Mercantile Affairs." *London Evening Standard*, 3 Jan. 1871, p. 2.

"The Money Market." *Morning Advertiser*, 17 Apr. 1851, pp. 4–5.

Morales Carrión, Arturo. "El año 1848 en Puerto Rico: Aspectos del mando de Prim." *Revista de Occidente*, vol. 147, June 1975, pp. 211–42.

Murray, David R. *Odious Commerce: Britain, Spain, and the Abolition of the Cuban Slave Trade*. Cambridge UP, 1980.

"Naturalisation Certificate: Gustavus Cabrera. From Spain." 19 Jan. 1885. Home Office: Immigration and Nationality Department, HO 334/12/4234, The National Archives, London, England.

"Naturalisation Papers: Jimenez, Alonso, from Spain." 1864. Home Office: Denization and Naturalization Papers and Correspondence, HO 1/117/4534, The National Archives, London, England.

"Nombramientos." *Boletín mercantil de Puerto Rico*, 7 Dec. 1877, p. 3.

"Partnerships Dissolved." *Liverpool Mercury*, 4 Jan. 1853, p. 7.

"Poder para testar de Susana Marcos." 5 Oct. 1857. Registros del Consulado de Paris, ES 28079 AHPM 2.4767.1.T.0032017.f.170, Archivo Histórico de Protocolos de Madrid, Madrid, Spain.

"Political and Fashionable Re-Unions: The Spanish Legation." *Morning Advertiser*, 5 June 1852, p. 5.

"The Popular Opera 'Florodora' . . ." *The Queen*, 28 June 1902, p. 108.

Post Office London Directory. London, various publishers, 1801–2003.

Public Record Office. "Cabrera, Gustavus." *England and Wales, National Probate Calendar (Index of Wills and Administrations)*, 1906, Cabaud–Dyson, p. 1.

Public Record Office. "De Zulueta y Madariaga, Pedro Joseph." *England and Wales, National Probate Calendar (Index of Wills and Administrations)*, 1882, Dabell–Ezard, p. 143.

Ramos Mattei, Andrés. "The Plantations of the Southern Coast of Puerto Rico: 1880–1910." *Social and Economic Studies*, vol. 37, no. 1–2, Mar.–June 1998, pp. 365–404.

"Real Decreto—Riegos del rio 'Jacaguas.'" *Gazeta de Puerto Rico*, 4 Apr. 1878, p. 2.

Riddell, William Renwick. "A Notable Trial for Slave-Trading." *Journal of Criminal Law and Criminology*, vol. 20, no. 4, Feb. 1930, pp. 572–77.

Rodríguez Caparrini, Bernardo. "Alumnos españoles en el internado jesuita de Beaumont (Old Windsor, Inglaterra), 1861–1868." *Archivum Historicum Societatis Iesu*, vol. 76, no. 151, 2007, pp. 3–37.

———. "Alumnos españoles en el internado jesuita de Beaumont (Old Windsor, Inglaterra), 1869–1874." *Archivum Historicum Societatis Iesu*, vol. 80, no. 159, 2011, pp. 151–250.

"Royal Drawing Room." *London Daily News*, 8 June 1857, pp. 4–5.

"Sales by Auction." *Public Ledger*, 6 December 1827, pp. 1.

Sanjurjo, Jesús. *In the Blood of Our Brothers: Abolitionism and the End of the Slave Trade in Spain's Atlantic Empire, 1800–1870*. U of Alabama P, 2021.

"Santander Disaster Relief Fund." *The Observer* [London, England], 19 Nov. 1893, p. 1.

Santiago de Curet, Annie. *Crédito, moneda y bancos en Puerto Rico durante el siglo XIX*. U de Puerto Rico, 1989.

Schmidt-Nowara, Christopher. *Empire and Antislavery: Spain, Cuba, and Puerto Rico, 1833–1874*. U of Pittsburgh P, 1999.

"El señor don Alonso Jiménez y Cantero . . ." *La Iberia*, 11 Mar. 1871, p. 1.

"El señor marqués . . ." *La Correspondencia de España*, 9 Nov. 1879, p. 3.

"Señora . . ." *El Heraldo*, 30 July 1844, p. 4.

Sherwood, Marika. "Britain, the Slave Trade and Slavery, 1808–1843." *Race & Class*, vol. 46, no. 2, 2004, pp. 54–77.

Slater, Isaac. *Slater's Royal National Commercial Directory of Cumberland, Lancashire, and Westmoreland.* Manchester, Isaac Slater, 1869.

"Sociedad de Agricultura." *Boletín mercantil de Puerto Rico*, 7 Oct. 1877, p. 3.

"Solicitud de traslado de restos mortales." 1861. Archivo Histórico Nacional, PARES. ES.28079.AHN/16//ULTRAMAR, 5082, Exp. 43.

"The Spanish Exiles." *Morning Chronicle*, 10 November 1823, pp. 2.

"St Marylebone, Devonshire Place, Pedro Zulueta / Sir Thos Baring." 1850. Folio 11, Westminster Rate Books 1634–1900. *Find My Past*, www.findmypast.co.uk.

"St Mary's Hospital." *Morning Post*, 12 July 1851, p. 1.

"La suscrición abierta . . ." *La Correspondencia de España*, 8 Jan. 1885, p. 2.

Thomas, Hugh. *The Slave Trade: The Story of the Atlantic Slave Trade, 1440–1870.* Simon & Schuster, 2013.

"Tobacco Trade Benevolent Association." *London City Press*, 4 June 1870, p. 1.

"Twickenham." *Field*, 5 Mar. 1864, p. 9.

"Villa de Ponce." *Gazeta de Puerto Rico*, 23 Jan. 1869, p. 3.

"Will of Pedro Juan de Zulueta, Count de Torre Diaz, of No. 21 Devonshire Place, Middlesex." 25 Sept. 1855. PROB 11/2219/393, The National Archives, London, England.

"Wills and Bequests." *Illustrated London News*, 20 May 1893, p. 27.

Zoological Society of London. *List of the Vertebrated Animals Now or Lately Living in the Gardens of the Zoological Society of London.* London, Longman, Green for the ZSL, 1883.

Zulueta, Pedro de. *Trial of Pedro de Zulueta, Jun., on a Charge of Slave Trading, &c.* C Wood & Co., 1844.

Chapter 3

Cosmetic of the Archive

An Autopsy of Slave Trader Antonio López y López and the General Tobacco Company in the Philippines

AURÉLIE VIALETTE[1]

> One could not learn history from architecture any more than one could learn it from books. Statues, inscriptions, memorial stones, the names of streets—anything that might throw light upon the past had been systematically altered.
>
> —George Orwell, *1984*

George Orwell's *1984*, with its analysis of how power controls history and how the state domesticates both the future and memory, has never been more relevant than in the twenty-first century. Citizens have begun to recognize the necessity of investigating what is hidden behind the names of those who are memorialized in public spaces and national history. People no longer take received history for granted, instead asking what untold story might be contained in a given monument or who really were the generals, CEOs, and bankers singled out as great advocates of national values or as indispensable philanthropists. The historical narratives or commemorative plaques beneath the statues may not reveal the full story and we might have to dig farther, into the archives that preserve their secrets.

Modern monuments, according to Eelco Runia, are metonymical and do not provide an account of the events they purport to stand for, but rather render an absence in our own present. The particular absence I study in this chapter refers to that which has been hidden, both intentionally and unintentionally, in the archives that convey the business of slave traders. I concentrate on slave trader Antonio López y López's archive to ask fundamental questions about the construction of historical narratives and the legacies of slavery effaced by the archive's political use. Indeed, I name specific entrepreneurs, businesses, and banks that were part of an intricate web of global slave-trade networks in the nineteenth century, networks that participated in the commerce of tobacco in the Philippines. Their names are found all over the archive and, yet, this same archive conceals how they profited and generated capital from their participation in slavery.

In Spain, the specific question regarding slave traders and the more general question regarding the concealment of history in public spaces have been remarkably present in contemporary public debates. As Akiko Tsuchiya demonstrates in "Monuments and Public Memory," and in her contribution to this volume, urban structures and features in Spain, such as buildings, statues, monuments, and street names have been challenged by civic associations and activists who have asked their governments to revisit the way their cities have explicitly and implicitly praised dictatorial politicians or slave traders. She argues that "as in the case of Confederate monuments in the United States, López's memorialization is anything but innocent" (482). López y López's statue in Barcelona was removed in March 2018 as a consequence of the city's rising consciousness of and desire to make amends for its participation in the slave trade during the Spanish Empire (Rodrigo, *Un hombre* 9–29). At the base of the statue, erected in 1884, an inscription read "España ha perdido uno de los hombres que más grandes servicios le han prestado" ("Spain has lost one of the men who have rendered the greatest service to the country"). A laudatory poem by Jacint Verdaguer was inscribed on the pedestal. Yet López y López was one of the most important slave traders of the nineteenth century, which, in 1881, allowed him to create the Compañía General de Tabacos de Filipinas (CGTF), popularly known as the Tabacalera. There was, of course, no reference to the slave trade on the commemorative plaque, nor is there in his archive. This absence says much about the way our past is obscured in the monuments, understood broadly, that surround us. It also reveals the kind of physical urban archive that was built so that a specific version of the past could accompany future generations in the construction of the nation and provide a sense of harmonious historical continuity. Martín Rodrigo-Alharilla explains that the statue's removal triggered a debate in which those opposed to the change argued that López could not be called a "negrero" because there is no written record that proves he participated in the slave trade (*Un hombre* 11).

The archive of López y López's company, held at the Arxiu Nacional de Catalunya, is perfectly in tune with the sanitized version of the story that the monument sought to represent. It is clean, beautiful, and in all aspects perfectly legal. Its cleanliness is notable. There are boxes and boxes containing thousands of administrative documents: workers' contracts, payroll records, shipping status reports, correspondence, records of international bank accounts in New York, London, Paris, Barcelona, and Madrid, and administrative documents about the company's relationships with English, French, Spanish, and American banks, among others, all of them authorized by legal documents drawn up by the firm's numerous lawyers. And yet, in this perfectly shipshape archive, there is no sign anywhere of the slave trade or forced labor. Historians, such as Dale Tomich, have coined the concept of *second slavery* to talk about how slavery and nineteenth-century capitalism were compatible and complementary. Tomich insists on the "continuity of forms of forced labor in the historical development of the capitalist world-economy" (477). In addition, Martín Rodrigo-Alharilla has shown that the Tabacalera's regulations were extremely severe ("Del desestanco" 270). This, I would affirm, makes them resemble those of a penal institution.[2]

I argue that a hidden part of slavery is actively performed in the archive, what I call a "cosmetic of the archive." A cosmetic implies an intervention to restore, modify, or improve a condition, affecting above all the appearance or aesthetic of an object or person, more than their substance. The cosmetic of the archive is a dynamic intervention, and through it, we can better understand the intricacies of the erasure of slavery and its legacies—or the intent of doing away with it. It consists of the careful curation of data, numbers, and people and explains why researchers have had trouble finding evidence of the slave trade in the documents that are available today.[3] The archive reveals a crime scene, so to speak, and its investigation calls for a transversal reading of the data—a sort of autopsy of the archive. Through the cosmetic of the archive, we see the body of the slave trader presented as incorruptible. As if embalmed, it is physically dead but historically alive. The archive contains a lie that only an autopsy can recover. In the same vein, as with the removal of López's statue in 2018, we need a sort of archival coroner to exhume the lie. Martín Rodrigo-Alharilla could, in fact, be considered the first archival coroner of López y López. From his doctoral thesis *Empresa, política y sociedad en la restauración: El grupo comillas (1876–1914)* to his latest book, *Un hombre, mil negocios*, he leaves no doubt regarding the source of López's fortune and his involvement in the slave trade. He explores the numerous networks constructed by López, whose impacts are part of the legacies of slavery in modern Spain, as they have permanently infiltrated the socioeconomic structures of society. With the concept of cosmetics, we can understand better how the abuses of the nineteenth-century capitalist era were similar to the colonial slave abuses, yet disguised.

In what follows, I first point out the economic legacy of the Tabacalera, which supported Francisco Franco's dictatorship in the twentieth century, and second, I address the erasure of the past in the archive. I then discuss how to decipher clues and enigmas in archival documents such as those found in López y López's archive, and proceed to analyze the relevant networks, both of banking and of friends and family.

The Economic Legacies of Slavery in the Archive

My contribution to the many studies on López y López is an analysis of his business archive, which reveals a subterfuge: how a central figure of the slave trade revamped himself as a successful CEO in the documents for posterity. In this sense, slavery was the point of departure that generated the language and activity of capitalism. "Studying the ways profit and innovation can accompany violence and inequality is particularly important in the world of modern capitalism," says Caitlin Rosenthal (xiii), who goes on to explain how easy it is to overlook the connections between capitalism and slavery (xiv). The archive I am analyzing contains clues that make this connection comprehensible. It incorporates the structure of slavery and its legacies, that is, slave traders' names, their financial capital, their businesses, and their networks, to create one of Spain's most important businesses, the Compañía General de Tabacos de Filipinas. This business survived for a century. The economic legacies of slavery went as far as supporting dictator Francisco Franco's troops during the Spanish Civil War (1933–1936) with tobacco and money lending (fig. 3.1), hence contributing to the victory of the Nationalist troops and the establishment of a dictatorship in Spain.

Figure 3.1. "Distribución" ("Distribution") details the gifts the Compañía General de Tabacos de Filipinas made to Franco's troops during the Spanish Civil War (1936–1939). *Source:* Arxiu Nacional de Catalunya. Used with permission.

Figure 3.1 details the donations made to the different Nationalist armies during the war (in the south, north, and center of Spain), whereas figure 3.2 reveals the language used by the company to describe the Nationalist victory in 1939: "Nuestro glorioso ejército" ("Our glorious army"), "1939. Año de la Victoria" ("1939. The Year of Victory"). Among other things, we can see that the company gave money to the FET y de las JONS, Falange Española Tradicionalista y de las Juntas de Ofensiva Nacional Sindicalistas (Traditionalist Spanish Phalanx and of the Councils of the National Syndicalist Offensive). The FET y de las JONS, created in 1937, was the sole legal political party of the Francoist regime during the dictatorship. The archive reveals that the company, built by former slave traders, became a supporter of Spain's twentieth-century dictator.

Asking if archival documents are part of a complete or incomplete archive is unproductive. That is not the point. Nor is it the point to ask if the archives have been manipulated for, of course, they have been. They always are, and we should not try to find any absolute truth in them. Arlette Farge explained it beautifully when she affirmed, "L'archive ne dit peut-être pas la vérité, mais elle dit *de* la vérité" ("The archive perhaps does not speak the truth, but it speaks *some* truth"; 41). It is this insistence on *some*

Figure 3.2. "Donativos y suscripciones patrióticas" ("Patriotic donations and subscriptions") details the Tabacalera's donations to and support of Franco after he won the Spanish Civil War. Compañía General de Tabacos de Filipinas. MS. Arxiu Nacional de Catalunya. *Source:* Arxiu Nacional de Catalunya. Used with permission.

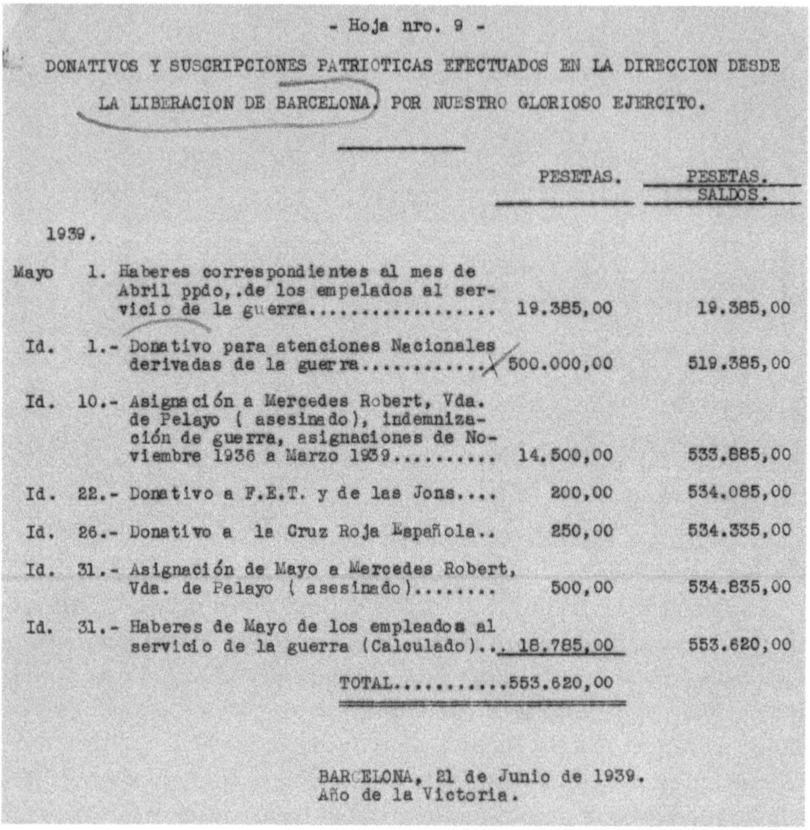

truth that is particularly compelling in Farge's theoretical approach to the archive. Indeed, when reading documents about a business born of slave-trade capital, we should focus on the particular moment in history when this archive began to be assembled and the kind of language with which it was populated, so to speak. Working on the Southeast Asian archives, Ann Stoler is probably one of the most prominent voices in archival studies. She combines an analysis of governance and ethnography to understand the colonial archives. If we understand the archive as she does, we realize the extent to which colonial archives are the result of state machines, and that "it is only now that we are seeing them in their own right, as technologies that reproduce those states themselves" (28). The historical distance that we now have in the twenty-first century allows us to perceive the extent of the cosmetic of the archive. The archive is an instrument of reproduction, yet it can also be considered, in equal measure, a production of those who inherit it, a product of the heirs (Fritzsche 3). The heirs of an archive can intervene, manipulate, and leave their traces on it, as I demonstrate forthwith.

Erasure of the Past

The role of the heirs in the construction of an archive such as the Compañía General de Tabacos de Filipinas is fundamental. The company was created in 1881 by Antonio López y López with Spanish and French capital: the Banque de Paris-Pays-Bas and the Crédito Mobiliario Español backed Banco Hispano Colonial's initiatives, which funded the Tabacalera (Rodrigo, "Del desestanco" 206–07). As established by historians, the Banco Hispano Colonial was composed of Catalan businessmen whose capital came from America and was linked to slave-trade networks in Cuba (Rodrigo, *Un hombre* 212–12; "From Slave Trade to Banking" 610).[4] The most important slave traders, such as Julián Zulueta and José Baró, were the two most important investors, after López, in the establishment of this bank in 1876, only five years before the creation of the CGTF. The particularity of the Tabacalera, and López y López's business activities in general, is that they were based on a network of family and trusted colleagues (Rodrigo, "Del desestanco" 208). The networks that the company built were international, as it had agencies and committees around the globe: in Paris, Madrid, London, New York, Naples, Liverpool, and Hamburg. The company sold tobacco all over the world, from Europe to the Russian Empire, Romania, Turkey, Tunisia, Asia, and Australia (Bastida et al. 12–13).

There is little written about the Tabacalera's economic aspects. The few studies that are available focus on López y López's personality and business achievements, although they recognize his involvement in the slave trade or, as some critics prefer to put it, that he made a fortune in Santiago de Cuba. That statement, decoded, indicates that he was part of the many networks of Spaniards who made a fortune with slavery. López y López and his collaborators, including Pedro de Sotolongo y Alcántara, José Ferrer y Vidal, and Eusebio Güell y Bacigalupi, among others, fought hard against abolition during their lifetimes and were pro-slavery to their deaths. The networks of which López y López was part, and the institutions he worked with or created, such as the Banco Hispano Colonial, used capital from the slave trade to function and prosper (Rodrigo, *Un hombre* 219).

Ramón Bastida, Antonio Somoza, and Josep Vallverdú's economic analysis of the Tabacalera in the period from 1881 to 1922 shows that the CGTF's account notebooks are very complex and detailed, especially compared to the epoch's standard. In their study, they affirm that the only way to understand this business initiative is to be cognizant of López y López's personality, and of his and his collaborators' economic, political, and financial connections. However, they never use the word *slavery* (26). Why? And why do they not even try to interpret the incongruities they identify in the archive, especially inconsistencies in the account notebooks, such as the lack of activity in all the "cuentas de tesorería/bancarias" ("treasury/bank accounts"; 21, 27), or the "valores pendientes" ("outstanding balances") accounts, which they describe as a "cajón de sastre" (22), a Spanish idiom meaning a jumble or a mess. These accounts, in their archival form, are sophisticated but hard to interpret because they contain heterogeneous documents—in this case, numbers coming from unknown sources. Researching these numbers is complicated, yet it seems timely and necessary, especially since researchers such as Michael Zeuske have underscored the difficulties of working with the slave-trade archive (*Amistad*, "Hidden Markets, Open Secrets"). It becomes clear, then, that we must investigate the archives and build a map of names, banking institutions, and ship crossings, to find and reveal what seems to have been concealed. Archival data, its organization, and its multiple connections can help undo some of the arguments presented by those who assert that we do not have proof of López's involvement in the slave trade. Martín Rodrigo-Alharilla has underscored in his latest book how such arguments are not limited to right-wing politicians and slavery deniers, but that they also circulate among Catalan intellectuals (Rodrigo, *Un hombre* 16).

What does it mean to work with a multinational company's archive containing documents that do not fully reflect the activities in which its founders and participants were involved? I have had a great time playing detective and finding clues, evidence, and concealed schemes involved in these business operations. But now, as a researcher, I read in these shrouded documents the dangers of a radical erasure of a specific historical reality. This reality must be made present. We also should question how the past is presented to us, how we relate to it, and how we are affected by it. In this case, the important distinction that Ann Stoler makes in *Along the Archival*

Grain is relevant. It is the distinction "between what was 'unwritten' because it would go without saying and 'everyone knew it,' what was unwritten because it could not yet be articulated, and what was unwritten because it could not be said" (3). It seems that in the case of López y López's activities and their subsequent traces in the archive, there is unwritten data, including López's participation in the slave trade, because this data was known to the participants. In addition, in the second half of the nineteenth century, slavery and its profits would not be revealed to the outside world so readily. Finally, historians point out that there was up to a fifty-year gap between the end of the slave trade by legislation and the end of slave labor in practice. The price of slaves, naturally, peaked after slavery was abolished (Engerman 225–32), which indicates that it hardly disappeared immediately.

In addition, while the African slave trade was legally abolished in most of the Spanish colonies, when we talk about slavery in Southeast Asia, we need to account for the war between Spain and pirates, in particular the Iranun and the Balangingi, South Pacific Muslim groups. The Iranun and Balangingi participated in the slave trade in Southeast Asia between Jolo, Canton, and London; they lived and worked in the Sulu archipelago and southwestern Mindanao. Spaniards captured Muslims. Some were sent to Cagayan and from there, according to James Warren, kept as slaves in the tobacco fields of the Isabela province (*Iranun and Balangingi* 366).[5] Warren explains, "The Spanish proponents of deportation and forced resettlement argued that Spanish progress in the Philippines and their 'manifest destiny' were dependent upon the removal of the Balangingi as 'savages' from the pathway of Spanish civilization" (366). Thus, the forcible resettlement of the Balangingi in Isabela served both the nation and the financial interests of the tobacco industry in the Philippines, of which the Tabacalera was part. The vocabulary of the African slave trade justified the use of forced labor through a moral and civilizational discourse. This discourse, in turn, helped to create the Spanish tobacco monopoly in the Philippines. Those Muslims slaves, as I decipher below, might be referred to as "migrants" in the Tabacalera archive.

Deciphering Documents: Clues and Enigmas

The Tabacalera archive is a palimpsest of sorts with different levels of meaning, and the vocabulary and language provide clues that reveal the Tabacalera's ties to slavery and forced labor. These archival clues can be seen as an example of what Stoler has called an "archiving-as-process," a proposal to consider archives "as condensed sites of epistemological and political anxiety rather than as skewed and biased sources" (20). Indeed, it does not make sense, as she says, to look at "archives-as-things" (20). This is doubly important when studying the traces or erasures of the slave trade in the archive.

The composition and vastness of the transatlantic slave trade archive and, more specifically, of the modern Hispanic archive has yielded more questions than answers. To begin with, the vocabulary used to describe the different roles in the Atlantic trade is confusing. For instance, according to Douglas R. Egerton, some planters in the US called slaveholders "businessmen" (208). Slaveholders around the world thought of slavery as part of good market practices. Participation in the trade led to wealth and power; it was just like "any other economic venture" (Egerton 208). Many historians have used this argument to minimize the role of slave traders in their historical accounts in the era before abolition. And today, the heirs of slave traders use this qualification to distance themselves from their family's past. In *Un hombre, mil negocios* Rodrigo-Alharilla gives the useful example of María del Mar Arnús, who from 1999 to 2018 published and asserted that López was not a slave trader but a businessman who gave Barcelona an international profile (12–15). However, as it happens, del Mar Arnús is the heir of Arnús Ferrer (1820–1890), a friend and business partner of López. This assertion makes it clear that the legacies of slavery are denied in plain sight, that historical data is transformed, and that facts are ignored to safeguard a family's reputation. Hence, the heirs' silence demonstrates a refusal to recognize the socioeconomic impact of the legacies of slavery in modern Spain, with some exceptions such as the Goytisolo family.[6] We can simultaneously consider these refusals as one of the many legacies of slavery, the comfortable silence about slavery allowing Spanish and, in this case, Catalan society to function without interrogating the roots of its prosperity. Indeed, nowadays, when looking at the legacy of slavery, the euphemizing business vocabulary deployed in the characterization of these slavery networks creates another obstacle to the recognition of what those slave traders are responsible for. The polemic around the removal of López's statue, with his defenders arguing that he was a patron of the arts and an important businessman, begins with the obfuscating vocabulary of slavery in the nineteenth-century archive.

Likewise, the word "migrant" is a slippery term that appears quite often in the slave-trade archives. Alessandro Stanziani has demonstrated that in the Indian Ocean world during the long nineteenth century, there was no clear-cut distinction between unfree slaves and indentured migrants (1). The fact that one finds the word *migrant* in the Tabacalera's archive leaves questions to be answered. In this case, the word is used to describe how workers or other individuals move from one plantation to another. The records of the traffic of migrants sent to work in Manila and other cities and colonies (such as San Antonio and Santa Isabel, north of Manila) are what most stand out in the Tabacalera archive. We know that there are migrants who come from Cuba (probably industrial cigar workers), various islands in the Philippines, and other parts of Asia. The archive leaves open the question of which migrants it refers to for each part of the world and for what type of (maybe exploitative) work they were brought to these plantations in the Philippines to do. Strangely, for such a meticulous archive, nothing is specified. Perhaps the word *migrant* is a euphemism here for slave, indentured immigrants, or forced labor.

In this case, the challenge is not to find or verify slave labor in the plantations but to understand the complexity of working with an archive in which the displacement of bodies is unclear. Workers coming from distinct territories were referred to with a diverse vocabulary: *workers* (the mentioned cigar workers from Cuba), *deportees*, *migrants*, and *settlers*. Margarita Cojuangco has worked with archival documents, as well as oral histories of Balangingi descendants, and explains that "the captured Balangingi were brought to Cagayan by force and ordered to work in the plantations as slaves" (138). The Tabacalera's manuscript archive (see fig. 3.3) mentions paying someone to transport migrants from Cagayan to the tobacco fields: "Gratificacion al conductor de los emigrantes" ("emigrant driver bonus") and "la 1ª expedición de emigrantes . . . Gastos de embarque de los mismos por Tomas Qurubín de Cavayan" ("first expedition of migrants . . . Shipping costs of the same to Tomas Qurubín of Cavayan"). Interestingly, Cojuangco mentions not only the lack of available data for the 1880s (when the Tabacalera was created) but also the certainty that slave labor persisted: "The period after 1869 to the mid-80's is a blank space as far as historical data is concerned. The next document found is dated 1885, describing the fate of the Balangingi in the Colonia Agrícola de Alcazar in barrio Sta. Isabel in Tumauini where they worked as tobacco planters. Again, this document supports the stories culled from the interviews of present-day Balangingi" (145). Cojuangco also adds that in the 1880s, those who worked in the fields were called "migrants" and violently punished, denied food, and whipped if they did not work enough (146). Even if the slave trade in the region had ended officially, migrants were treated as such until the Philippine

Figure 3.3. Colonia de San Antonio, Compañía General de Tabacos de Filipinas. Diary entry number 336, 1890. *Source:* Arxiu Nacional de Catalunya. Used with permission.

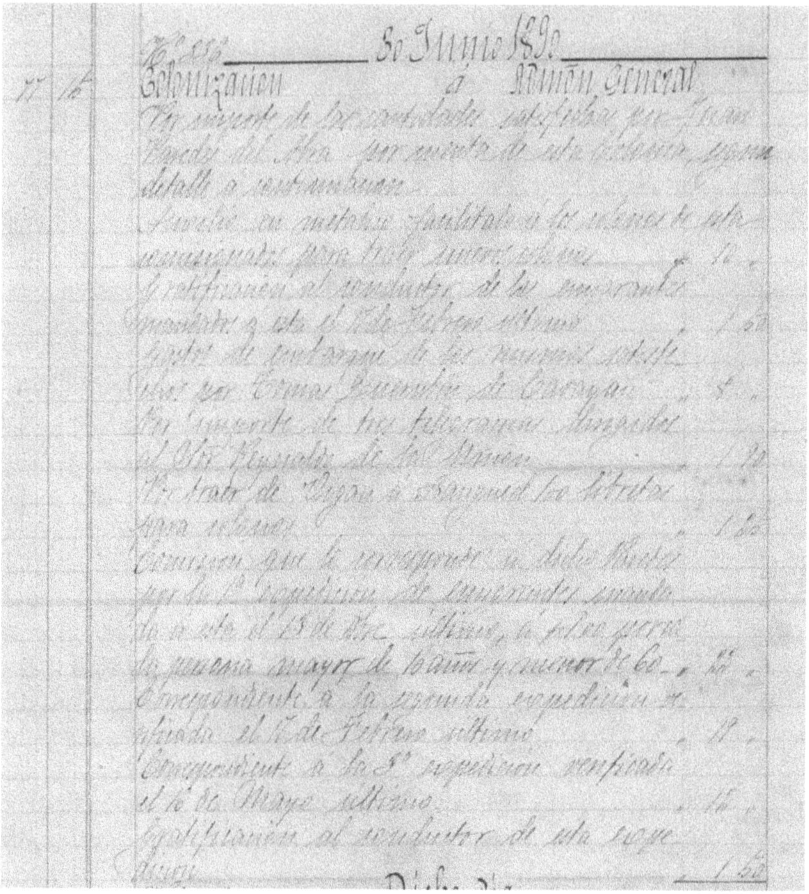

Revolution (1896). Cojuangco's research describes their repeated attempts, some successful, to escape from the plantations, further reinforcing their status as forced labor or slaves (150).

In the same document from López's archive describing the transport of migrants, we find that the word *settler* appears to refer to the movement of other workers. Indeed, settlers are paid to go to look for other settlers in other parts of the archipelago: "Auxilio en metalico facilitado á los colonos de esta comisionados para traer nuevos colonos" ("Cash aid provided to the settlers of this commission to bring in new settlers"). Furthermore, and as mentioned, the Philippines and Cuba exchanged workforces for tobacco plantations, and Cojuangco mentions that tobacco plantations were "owned by some enterprising Spanish businessmen," and that the Spanish government "helped with the importation of tobacco seeds from Cuba" (137). Indeed, the *Memoria* of the Tabacalera read at the Junta General Ordinaria of January 15, 1883, addresses the company's factories from pages 15 to 17 and states that tobacco workers were sent and "contratados" ("hired") from Cuba to the Philippines. The vocabulary used in López's manuscript archive corresponded to precise categories. I find that it shows the conceptual framework developed by Stoler when she explains the unwritten or unexplained data in the construction of archives in the past. The epistemological anxiety (20) she refers to is perceptible here in the precise nomenclature used to describe the different types of workers. Yet the use of this same nomenclature reveals how people of that era knew what each word connoted, without the necessity to explain further.

Banking and Friends and Family Networks

In the Tabacalera's *Acta de Constitución*, written on November 26, 1881, the first ten names of directors, founders, and stockholders that are mentioned are directly connected to the slave trade. The directors, founders, and stockholders of the Tabacalera were intimate friends of López y López (Pedro de Sotolongo y Alcántara, Eusebio Güell y Bacigalupi). Some had signed the manifesto against the abolition of slavery (José Ferrer y Vidal, Eusebio Güell y Bacigalupi), owned shipping companies (José Ferrer y Vidal, José Carreras y Xuriach, Angel Bernardo Pérez[7]), and acted as advisers at top banks such as Crédito Mercantil, Banco de Barcelona, Banco de España in Santander, and Banco Hispano Colonial.

This data is of utmost importance for understanding the impact of slavery after its abolition in the second half of the nineteenth century. Indeed, as Martín Rodrigo-Alharilla has analyzed, "in the nineteenth century, there was a certain chronological parallel between the ever-increasing incorporation of the Spanish into the slave trade and the construction of a modern banking system in Spain," with slave traders converting themselves into bankers when slavery was abolished ("From Slave Trade to Banking" 601). The legacies of slavery perdured in other business ventures because, as banal as it may seem, its champions did not change their ideology and continued to enjoy their privileges, take advantage of free labor, and discriminate against bodies they considered inferior. Tracing the connections and relationships found in the archives is not an easy task because many of the names of historical characters involved in banking networks are not cataloged in libraries, and the authorship of nineteenth-century administrative documents can be difficult to determine.

Kinship and ideological affinities are central to understanding these connections. I will illustrate this with two names connected to the slave trade to show the impact and necessity of such research: 1) Don Pedro de Sotolongo y Alcántara was an intimate friend of López y López and a slave trader in Cuba. He promoted the Asociación de Hacendados y Propietarios de Esclavos (Landowners' and Slave Owners's Association) in Cuba in 1873. Participants in this association were Juan A. Zulueta, Francisco F. Colomé, Nicolás Martínez Valdivieso, Pedro Sotolongo y Mamerto Pulido. 2) Eusebio Güell y Bacigalupi was López y López's son-in-law. He married López's daughter, Luisa Isabel López Bru, and was the son of Joan Güell, who signed the manifesto against the abolition of slavery and was a patron of the famous Catalan architect Antoni Gaudí. Eusebio Güell was also an adviser at Banco Hispano Colonial, Tabacalera, Compañía Trasatlántica Española, and Compañía de los Caminos de Hierro del Norte de España. These two examples afford us an understanding of the complex web of people and businesses involved with the institution of slavery and its aftermath, as well as the centrality of kinship in their lucrative business endeavors.

One aspect of kinship is, understandably, the role of gender. Lisa Surwillo has shown how the wives of López y López, Güell, and other businessmen signed the petition against the abolition of slavery in 1873 (4–5). According to Surwillo, these women insisted on their status as wives and mothers in the petition, accentuating "the dynastic and familial ties that bind Creole to *indiano*" and thus their belonging to both marriage and nation (7). And, indeed, these international networks functioned successfully because most of them were built on family relationships with strong ties to the nation. Daughters of slave traders were to marry other slave traders or their sons, who would later be able to continue the business. Kinship is a fundamental aspect to be explored for theorizing the slave-trade archive and understanding its global networks if we are to illuminate the hidden nature of contemporary legacies of slavery. One of the most important aspects of family and kinship when it comes to business is generational continuity, inheritance, and succession (Akhter 175–76), particularly because the use of family and kinship relations becomes a business resource (Alsos et al.

97). It was certainly the case in the nineteenth century, when, according to Josef Ehmer, "family was an important means of economic success" (187). Thus, the question of kinship and family is highly relevant in the context of the slave trade and its legacies. The private, so strongly attached to the values of family, becomes central to this type of institution.

When family, business, and empire converge, the archive must be read against the grain. Adele Perry, talking about empire, family, and archive in the nineteenth century, affirms, "all of these archives are profoundly shaped by the individuals who created them, the state and private enterprises they labored on behalf of, and by the people, institutions, and societies that preserved them" (3). The names of institutions that appear in López's archive underscore Perry's conception of the interconnectedness of people, institutions, and society. The main connection in the Tabacalera's archive is that of father and son. Claudio López Bru inherited his father's estate after his death. Martín Rodrigo-Alharilla shows how the son followed his father's steps in the organization of the company and gives the example of López Bru asking managers to disguise the high-interest loan that tied up workers because "it would look terrible" in the files ("Del desestanco" 213). This is an example of the cosmetic of the archive: the company needed to tie down its workers by incrementing their debt. These were exploitative measures, yet they could not be shown to investors in the archive.

For the creation of networks and their maintenance, López y López struck up alliances with people who were connected, in one way or another, to the slave trade. Joaquín Eizaguirre, Patricio Satrústegui, and Ángel B. Pérez were involved in Banco Hispano Colonial and the shipping company A. López y Cía., founded by López in 1857. López y López also collaborated with Samá Sotolongo y Cía. In fact, the first president of Banco Hispano Colonial was Antonio López y López himself and its first manager was *his friend*, slave trader Pedro Sotolongo (Rodrigo, "Familia, redes" 79). Many merchants' surnames associated with the Hispanic slave trade appear in the Tabacalera's archive to record exchanges between Cuba and the Philippines. One of them is Ramón de Larrinaga, a Basque businessman established in Liverpool, who founded the sailing company Olano, Larrinaga & Company with fellow Basque merchant José Antonio de Olano e Iriondo. This company would travel between Liverpool and Manila, sometimes routing through Havana. The name Larrinaga, like many other Basque surnames in the mid-nineteenth century, was associated with the Cuban slave trade, and Ramón de Larrinaga's father was a known merchant and slave trader in Cuba.[8] Another aspect to sort out is the association of certain surnames with specific ports and shipping routes. Ports were instrumental to the establishment of trade and commerce routes. The Tabacalera built itself into a global industry, closely linked to the geography of the archipelago, by establishing commercial ports on numerous islands. (Keep in mind that the Philippines comprises more than 7,000 islands.)

The manuscript archive of the Tabacalera recorded all ships, inventories, and workers' entries and exits from one archipelago port to another, from the Philippines to Spain, and the rest of the world, including the Spanish colonies in the Caribbean, such as Cuba and Puerto Rico. Manuscript diary entry 1 from 1882 records the steamships that arrived in Manila and indicates the fee the company paid the ships' captains.

Diary entry 409 (fig. 3.4) reads, "Vapor Isla de Mindanao viage nº 3 á Delegacion de la Compª Trasatlantica, Cadiz. R=175 que el acreedor ha entregado a José de Larrinaga, Capitán de dicho vapor segun recibo del mismo . . . 11 y 12 de Diciembre [1882]" ("Steam boat Mindanao Island trip nº 3 to the Delegation of the Transatlantic Company, Cadiz. R=175 that the creditor gave to José de Larrinaga, Captain of this boat according to the receipt of the same . . . 11 and 12 December [1882]"). Diary Entry

Figure 3.4. Diary entries 409 and 410 of the Tabacalera, San Antonio Colony, 1882. Compañía General de Tabacos de Filipinas. *Source:* Arxiu Nacional de Catalunya. Used with permission.

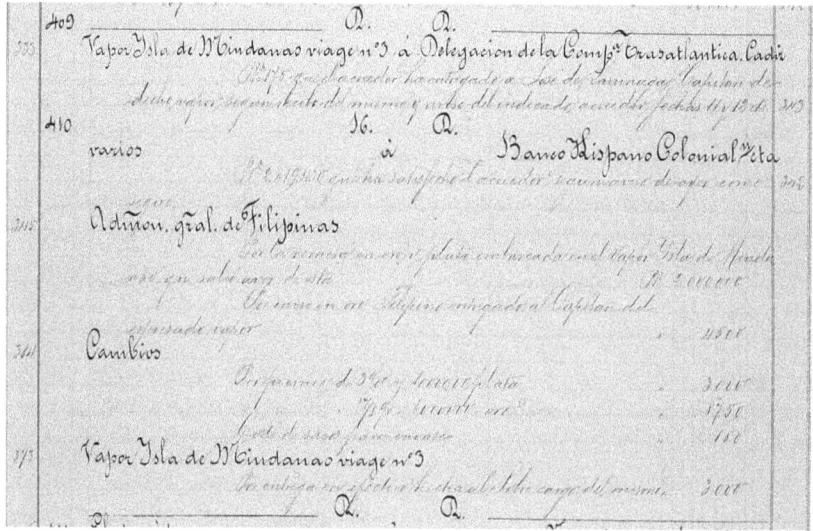

410, which documents that the company paid José de Larrinaga in gold and silver, does not indicate for which services the gold and silver were remitted. Later, Entry 413 shows that a ship went from Manila to Cuba and Puerto Rico (56). Hence, a fundamental question arises: How is it that these routes from Spain to the Philippines to Cuba and back could be completely separated from the slave trade and abuses of colonial power given the timeframe and people involved? David Eltis affirms, "The traffic in slaves was . . . the most 'international' of all business activities" (123). Slavery was officially abolished in Cuba in 1886, five years after the creation of the CGTF and four years after the recording of the aforementioned document.[9] The Atlantic slave trade was nevertheless illegal starting in 1821 (Rodrigo, *Un hombre* 17). It is difficult to believe that the Tabacalera would, almost miraculously, be exempt from any ties to the slave-trade market, especially given its exchanges between the Philippines and Cuba, where slave labor was common on tobacco estates in the 1880s (Morgan 243–44). As we have seen, Larrinaga, a slave trader in Cuba, regularly shipped goods from Cuba to the Philippines before the abolition of slavery.

The problems I encounter reading the Tabacalera archive are not exceptional. Transparency, as Stoler says, "is not what archival collections are known for" (8). Edward Ball, in "Retracing Slavery's Trail of Tears," points out that "so much of the vocabulary of slavery has been effaced from the language" and that, likewise, many records about individuals or journeys did not survive. He furthermore explains how ships would sometimes carry five to fifty slaves, who were oftentimes excluded from the ship's inventory. In addition, it is common knowledge that the traces of slavery were effaced from many nineteenth-century archives. Contemporary slave traders were well aware of how to proceed with their trade. Michael Zeuske, in *Amistad: A Hidden Network of Slavers and Merchants*, notes that documents that provide insights into the slave trade are difficult to find since records of illicit transactions were easy proof to use against slave merchants and were thus destroyed (133). Even if slavery was not illegal in the Hispanic world for most of the century, it was being attacked and abolished in many places around the world. One example is Britain's Slavery Abolition Act of 1833. From this moment on, the purchase of enslaved people became more expensive, making the slave trade more difficult.[10] Yet we must consider that the abolition of slavery did not mean the complete eradication of slave trafficking; Zeuske writes, "Slavery was considered systemic up to 1808 and thereafter it was considered to have been abolished. Actually, slavery was not abolished, but rather, a legal mechanism was implemented whereby the government 'abolished' slavery, but in fact it was not abolished at all. It was legally hidden—it became 'legally illegal,' so to speak—making slavery and slave trading in the Atlantic part of a 'Hidden Atlantic'" (*Amistad* 137).

Upper-class families received incentives to emancipate slaves. The abolitionist discourse implied a sort of silence about slavery, and the goal was to suppress its presence in the public sphere and, as such, implement a sort of "forgetting" of slavery. Zeuske, referring to the British slave traders, explains that this collective amnesia implied a marginalization and silencing of upper-class families' involvement and participation in the slave trade ("Hidden Markers" 240). This is exactly what happened in the case of López y López. It is not a surprise that the Banco Hispano Colonial was created at the moment when the business of trafficking enslaved people became more difficult. Slave traders' money was redirected through this banking network and the Banco Hispano Colonial was used to create new businesses, closely linked to the same companies, particularly those in shipping and tobacco, involved in the slave trade.

Conclusion

A distinct point of interest herein is what is *not* in the archive. Zeuske affirms that one must read carefully between the lines and that, as of 2015, "hardly any research [had] been done on the records of the Iberian nations" (*Amistad* 137). Theorists of the archive have pointed out that it is necessary to recognize the limits of archival recovery and the inability, at times, to reconstruct a reliable narrative (Raimon 258). Kenneth E. Foote states that "archives are sometimes said to be society's collective memory" (379), although it is also certain that, as he asserts, "bureaucracies and corporations may seek to control the flow of damaging information by destroying incriminating records" (384). Indeed, the brutality and inhumanity of the slave trade is something that some countries in Europe, among them Spain, have had difficulty confronting. The archive's concealment of this traumatic past is not unexpected. Instead, it poses an ethical imperative to uncover what has been intentionally covered over and forgotten in history. The revelation of such an obfuscation illustrates a national desire to *not* remember or remember *less* of a past that is troubling and shameful. In the words of Foote, "if the violence fails to exemplify an enduring value, there is a greater likelihood of the site, artifacts, and documentary record being effaced, either actively or passively" (385).

Even if we cannot definitively prove the involvement in the slave trade of some of the actors mentioned in this chapter, the fact that they were part of networks, including banks, businesses, and capital, built by slave traders, former slave traders, or anti-abolitionists tells us about the legacies of slavery, their durability, their permeability in the social fabric and, above all, how the economic and cultural structures of a city such as Barcelona have been built through the exploitation of Black bodies. In addition, if, as we have seen, kinship was fundamental in building the networks of slavery in the past, it is still used today to cover the legacies of slavery and to both deny and hide the participation of Spanish families in it. Arguments used in the nineteenth century, such as the text at the base of López's statue in Barcelona, are still proffered by family members in the twenty-first century.

I have shown how the Atlantic space's violent history has been carefully arranged in the archive. It presents a deliberately crafted memory of the Tabacalera, the major business in the Philippines in the nineteenth century, that rehabilitates its slave-trade participants. Moreover, their public image as fundamental figures in modern and contemporary Spain's economic, urban, and political development, be it in Barcelona, Madrid, Santander, Comillas, or almost anywhere we can imagine, has been passed down to and accepted by Spanish society. We do not have to look very hard for information to affirm the impact these great businessmen have had on the urban and economic structures of today's Spanish cities. But to understand their role in the transatlantic slave trade of the nineteenth century, we must grasp at clues and seek information, which is simply, and probably intentionally, not to be had.

Notes

1. This paper began as a presentation for the Archive Symposium at Columbia University in 2018, organized by Roland Béhard (Ecole Normale Supérieure, ULM), Annick Louis (EHESS, Université de Besançon), and Jesús R. Velasco (Yale University). I would like to thank Evelyn Cruise (Stony Brook University), Nicole Basile (Columbia University), and Lexie Cook (Durham University) for their suggestions and comments, as well as Ann Stoler, with whom I shared the session at the Symposium. I would also like to thank Bécquer Seguín, who invited me to Johns Hopkins to present on this topic. I am indebted to Akiko Tsuchiya for all the fundamental comments she has provided me when I was writing this chapter. Finally, Martín Rodrigo-Alharilla offered historical data and bibliography, for which I am very grateful.

2. The company attracted indebted families by saying that it would pay off their debts. In exchange, the families would work for the company and repay the original debt with the fruits of their labor. They were immigrants who were sought after because of their fragile economic situation. They immigrated to the agricultural colonies; they became colonists with an exclusive debt to the company. See Rodrigo ("Del desestanco") for more information.

3. For a discussion on how to find evidence of the slave trade in archival documents today, see Zeuske ("Hidden Markers") and Sanz Rozalén and Zeuske ("Towards a Microhistory of the Enslaved").

4. For a comprehensive list of names of slave traders involved in the creation of the Banco Hispano Colonial, see Rodrigo ("From Slave Trade to Banking" 610–14). For general information about the Banco Hispano Colonial, see Rodrigo ("Del desestanco" and *Los marqueses de Comillas*).

5. For more information on slavery and Southeast Asia, see James Warren (*The Sulu Zone 1768–1898*).

6. For more information, see Rodrigo (*Los Goytisolo*).

7. Bernardo Pérez was a slave trafficker in Cienfuegos.

8. See *Basques in the Philippines* by Marciano R. De Borja (93–95). De Borja does not mention slavery in his analysis of Basque merchants, particularly Ramón de Larrinaga and José Antonio de Olano. See Kirsty Hooper's chapter in this volume about Basque merchants.

9. On slavery in the Philippines see Hernández Hortigüela, "La esclavitud en las Islas Filipinas."

10. According to Eltis, "In 1850 and 1865, the Brazilian and Cuban governments respectively took serious action against the slave trade. . . . Between 1810 and 1900, almost every Atlantic potentate from King Bell of the Cameroons to the President of the United States signed literally hundreds of anti-slave trade treatises" (133–34).

Works Cited

Akhter, Naveed. "Kinship and the Family Business." *Theoretical Perspective on Family Businesses*, edited by Mattias Nordqvist et al., Elgaronline, 2015, pp. 175–90.

Alsos, Gry Agnete, et al. "Kinship and Business: How Entrepreneurial Households Facilitate Business Growth." *Entrepreneurship & Regional Development*, vol. 26, no. 1–2, 2014, pp. 97–122.

Ball, Edward. "Retracing Slavery's Trail of Tears." *Smithsonian Magazine*, Nov. 2015.

Bastida Vialcanet, Ramón, et al. "Estudio económico y contable de la Compañía General de Tabacos de Filipinas 1881–1922." *De Computis*, vol. 12, no. 22, 2015, pp. 7–36.

Borja, Marciano R. de. *Basques in the Philippines*. U of Nevada P, 2005.

Cojuangco, Margarita. *Kris of Valor: The Samal Balangini's Defiance and Diaspora*. Manisan Research and Publishing, 1993.
Compañía General de Tabacos de Filipinas. *Acta de Constitución*. 26 Nov. 1881. Arxiu Nacional de Catalunya.
———. Colonia de San Antonio. Diary, 1882. Arxiu Nacional de Catalunya.
———. Colonia de San Antonio. Diary number 4, 1889. Arxiu Nacional de Catalunya.
———. "Donativos y suscripciones patrióticas." Arxiu Nacional de Catalunya UC 03.02.02
———. *Memoria de la Compañía General de Tabacos de Filipinas leída en la Junta General Ordinaria de 15 de Enero de 1883*. Establecimiento Tipográfico de los Sucesores de N. Ramírez y Ca., 1883.
Egerton, Douglas R. "Markets without a Market Revolution: Southern Planters and Capitalism." *Journal of the Early Republic*, vol. 16, no. 2, 1996, pp. 207–21.
Ehmer, Josef. "Family and Business Among Master Artisans and Entrepreneurs: The Case of 19th-Century Vienna." *History of the Family*, vol. 6, no. 2, 2002, pp. 187–202.
Eltis, David. "Was Abolition of the American and British Slave Trade Significant in the Broader Atlantic Context?" *Humanitarian Intervention and Changing Labor Relations: The Long-term Consequences of the Abolition of the Slave Trade*, edited by Marcel van der Linden, Brill, 2011, pp. 117–39.
Engerman, Stanley L. "Slavery after the Abolition of the Slave Trade." *Humanitarian Intervention and Changing Labor Relations: The Long-term Consequences of the Abolition of the Slave Trade*, edited by Marcel van der Linden, Brill, 2011, pp. 223–43.
Farge, Arlette. *Le goût de l'archive*. Seuil, 1989.
Foote, Kenneth E. "To Remember and Forget: Archives, Memory, and Culture." *American Archivist*, vol. 53, 1990, pp. 378–92.
Fritzsche, Peter. "The Archive." *History & Memory*, vol. 17, no. 1–2, 2005, pp. 15–44.
Hernández Hortigüela, Juan. "La esclavitud en las Islas Filipinas." *Revista Filipina*, vol. 12, no. 4, Winter 2008–09. revista.carayanpress.com/esclavitud.html.
Morgan, William A. "Cuba Tobacco Slavery in the Nineteenth Century." *Tabaco e Escravos nos Impérios Ibéricos*, edited by Santiago de Luxán, Joao de Figueirôa-Rêgo, and Vicent Seanz, Cham, 2015, pp. 243–69.
Orwell, George. *1984*. Signet Classic, 1961.
Perry, Adele. *Colonial Relations: The Douglas-Connolly Family and the Nineteenth-Century Imperial World*. Cambridge UP, 2015.
Rodrigo y Alharilla, Martín. "Del desestanco del tabaco a la puesta en marcha de la Compañía General de Tacacos de Filipinas (1879–1890)." *Boletín Americanista*, vol. 59, 2009, pp. 199–221.
———. *Empresa, política y sociedad en la Restauración: El grupo Comillas (1876–1914)*. 2000. U Autònoma de Barcelona, PhD dissertation.

———. "Familia, redes y alianzas en la gran empresa española: El holding Comillas (1857–1890)." *Prohistoria*, vol. 10, no. 10, 2006, pp. 73–92.

———. *Los Goytisolo: Una próspera familia de indianos*. Marcial Pons, 2016.

———. *Un hombre, mil negocios: La controvertida historia de Antonio López, Marqués de Comillas*. Ariel, 2021.

———. *Los marqueses de Comillas, 1817–1925: Antonio y Claudio López*. LID, 2000.

———. "From Slave Trade to Banking in Nineteenth-Century Spain." *Comparativ*, vol. 30, no. 5–6, 2020, pp. 600–14.

Rosenthal, Caitlin. *Accounting for Slavery: Masters and Management*. Harvard UP, 2018.

Runia, Eelco. "Presence." *History and Theory*, vol. 45, 2006, pp. 1–29.

———. "Spots of Time." *History and Theory*, vol. 45, 2006, pp. 305–16.

Raimon, Eve Allegra. "Lost and Found: Making Claims on Archives." *Legacy: A Journal of American Women Writers*, vol. 27, no. 2, 2020, pp. 257–68.

Sanz Rozalén, Vicent, and Michael Zeuske. "Towards a Microhistory of the Enslaved: Global Considerations." *El tabaco y la esclavitud en la rearticulación imperial ibérica (s. xv–xx)*, edited by Santiago de Luxán Meléndez and João Figueirôa-Rêgo. Publicações do Cidehus, 2018. books.openedition.org/cidehus/6545.

Stanziani, Alessandro. *Sailors, Slaves, and Immigrants: Bondage in the Indian Ocean World, 1750–1914*. Palgrave McMillan, 2014.

Stoler, Ann Laura. *Along the Archival Grain: Epistemic Anxieties and Colonial Common Sense*. Princeton UP, 2008.

Surwillo, Lisa. "Enslaved by Liberalism: Spain after 1868." *Republics of Letters: A Journal for the Study of Knowledge, Politics, and the Arts*, vol. 3, no. 1, 2012, pp. 1–9.

Tomich, Dale. "The Second Slavery and World Capitalism: A Perspective for Historical Inquiry." *IRSH*, vol. 63, 2018, pp. 477–501.

Tsuchiya, Akiko. "Monuments and Public Memory: Antonio López y López, Slavery, and the Cuban-Catalan Connection." *Nineteenth-Century Contexts*, vol. 41, no. 5, 2019, pp. 479–500.

Warren, James Francis. *Iranun and Balangingi: Globalization, Maritime Raiding and the Birth of Ethnicity*. Singapore UP, 2002.

———. *The Sulu Zone 1768–1898: The Dynamics of External Trade, Slavery, and Ethnicity in the Transformation of a Southeast Asian Maritime State*. New Day Publishers, 1985.

Zeuske, Michael. *Amistad: A Hidden Network of Slavers and Merchants*. Translated by Steven Rendall, Markus Wiener, 2015.

———. "Hidden Markers, Open Secrets: On Naming, Race Marking and Race Making in Cuba." *New West Indian Guide/Nieuwe West-Indische Gids*, vol. 76, no. 3–4, 2002, pp. 235–66.

Chapter 4

From Slavery to Anti-Black Racism

Racial Ideas from Cuba to Catalonia

Martín Rodrigo-Alharilla and Juliana Nalerio,[1]
translated by María Cristina Urruela

The argument that we will present is that colonial slavery is a primary source for the racial ideas in anti-Black racism and white supremacy in modernity. The violent resettlement of Africans and Indians to America shaped modern racism. Though this was a vast reality, our analysis will center on a single case study, Catalonia and Cuba, the pearl in the Atlantic "modern" world. In this chapter, we limit our study of the origins of racism to particular historical moments from the exchange of popular and elite print culture between colonial Cuba and Catalonia, which reflect broader anti-Black and white supremacist institutions and practices. We exclude premodern peninsular racialist ideas that were antisemitic and anti-Muslim and premised on notions of "casta" or "nation" rather than "race." In our study, the colloquialisms in journalism and the novel or writ in legal and administrative literature reveal a distinctly modern form of racism that is fundamentally anti-Black and syncretic. We will examine the semantic field of *negro* and the collective noun *negrada* and the linguistic usage of the second term long after the slave trade and slavery were abolished in the nineteenth century. Our primary aim will be to critique the historical Black/white binary and perform an antiracist critique that stresses the tenuousness of race.

A White Atlantic?

The *white* Atlantic we critique is intended as foil to Paul Gilroy's study of *Black* Atlantic culture celebrating Black nationalism and modernism. That Atlantic was not counterculture to modernity. The ideology of white supremacy was modernity itself in the kingdoms, colonies, and eventually republics of the Atlantic world (e.g., Spain and most of Europe and the Americas excluding Haiti) and the central institution. The motor was not the genocide of enslaved Africans and Indians but the work camp, plantation, or *encomienda*, a world of violent labor extraction and dispossession from enslaved Africans and Indians to benefit whitening elites. The discursive field qualified necropolitical social and political interactions, as implicit and explicit racial ideas distinguished among new social groups and identities in the restructuring of the colonial system and in the racialization that went along with it. From the end of the eighteenth century until the twentieth century, relationships between Cuba and Catalonia were extensive (Martí; Junqueras; Cabré; Costa; Rodrigo, *Indians a Catalunya*) and covalent with networks developed in slavery. The Middle Passage and Atlantic slave markets shaped the Spanish empire and Atlantic world, with La Habana as the so-called *perla*.

Even as slavery was abolished in the nineteenth century, modern Spanish, American, and European racial categories continued to form based on the racial ideas that had upheld slavery as white supremacy. By the nineteenth century, colonial racial ideas had altered notions of belonging and nation on both sides of the Atlantic (Feros). Early in the century Catalans began seeing Cuba as a colony rather than an outpost of the Spanish crown. Liberal forces among Creole and mixed-race elites in America and the Haitian Revolution set the wars for independence in motion. It was in this context that race and racial ideas became more and not less important. Loyal *peninsulares* in Cuba and Catalan *Indianos* in Catalonia, both *arguably* "Americanos," looked to define themselves against the racialized Africans, Indians, and mestizos that were the "other Americans" (Van Deusen; Feros; Fuente). Slavery's racialized worldview amended nascent national belonging but always supported the notion that Catalans, like Spaniards and Europeans, were necessarily white and Christian.

Negro in Cuba-Catalonia

As Michael Zeuske states, "in Cuba, references to those actors close to the enslaved in the slave trade and in control of the enslaved in the workplace were based on the word 'Catalan.' Not 'Spanish' or 'Cuban' but 'Catalan.'" He makes clear that the signifier "'Catalan' in Cuba colloquially meant a 'miserly' or 'stingy' merchant often with the connotation of slave trader" (Zeuske, "Capitanes" 63–100). The existence of a Catalan colony in Cuba active in commerce and the agro-exporting sector of coffee and sugar is a well-documented fact. After visiting the Cuban capital in 1841, the Countess of Merlin wrote that there were no people but only slaves; and that among the masters were two classes, the proprietary nobility, and the merchant middle class. The latter, she remarked, were composed mostly of "Catalans" that arrived on the island without patrimony who wound up with great fortunes (Santa Cruz y Montalvo 73). The Frenchman Arthur Morelet found something similar in a monopoly of food items at the mercy of Catalans (67). In Cuba, many Catalans owned slaves who worked in sugar mills, coffee plantations, or simply in their homes. Moreover, several Catalans were dedicated to the transatlantic trade in enslaved Africans and Catalan involvement only increased after illegalization in the nineteenth century. All of them participated in the construction of Cuban plantation and slave-owning society, and Catalan slave traders, merchants, and plantation owners all contributed to the ubiquity of slavery in Cuba, an institution that dehumanized and reduced the enslaved to livestock, animals, and trade values.

A dangerous metonymy mechanically identified "negro" with slave status. There is no doubt that the process of identifying an entire "race" with slavery would form the basis for racist practices in Cuba at that time and in later times (Fuente). Consider that, in 1840, the Catalan Lorenzo Xiqués Gudumá undertook an inventory of his coffee plantation La Purísima Concepción, located between Havana and Matanzas, upon the death of his wife, Gertrudis Romagosa, who was also Catalan. Xiqués entrusted this inventory to another Catalan, Pablo María Serra. His inventory describes 141 enslaved people owned on the Xiqués estate: the eighty-seven born in Africa and the fifty-four born on the island. He writes with great detachment, "Ignacio Mina, about 38 years old, one-eyed, healthy and without blemishes," "Luis Carabalí, 41 years old, lazy at work and sickly" (Blanco 18). Following each name a second marker identifies their African origins vaguely and imprecisely: *carabalí, lucumí, mina, congo* or *conga, arará, gangá*. These entries and the form of María Serra's synthetic descriptions underscore the harshness of the institution of slavery. They are "somewhat sickly," "healthy and without defects," "sickly and somewhat demented," "with a chronic sore," "one-armed in the left arm and without defects," or "useless for being sickly." In combination with their age, each graphic description of their untreated illnesses and pain will justify the monetary value assigned to them by an appraiser (Blanco 18). The nature and language of the inventory reflects the dehumanization inherent in converting Africans to livestock and property. Whether born free in Africa or enslaved in Cuba, a child born to an enslaved mother was a slave. And yet, at no time in María Serra's official inventory does the word "slave" or "enslaved" appear; what appears is the word "negro" or "black." This evidences the racialization of slavery in nineteenth-century Cuba and the reduction almost by definition of any "negro" person to the status of slave, at least in colonial records and despite the existence of thousands of free Afro-descendants on the island (Piqueras and Balboa).

The Pre-history of Race: From Religious "Purity of Blood" to Racial "Purity"

Anti-Black racism is a syncretic amalgamation of Spanish, European, and American racial ideas. It developed with Atlantic slavery in the colonial context and later fed racial democracy. As Paul Gilroy points out, "racism does not, of course, move tidily and unchanged through time and history. It assumes new forms and articulates new antagonisms in different situations" (Gilroy, *There Ain't No Black* 11) like the British imperial context that he examines in *There Ain't No Black in The Union Jack*. The lack of comparable studies on the Spanish imperial context for anti-Black racism makes the problem of this chapter particularly unique. While erasing the historical dimension of racism and racial ideas certainly pushes racism "outside of history and into the realm of natural, inevitable events" (11), a mistake on all counts, ignoring the Spanish American context of anti-Black racism conflates the transnational history of white racism, enslavement, and anti-Blackness with the history of the African diaspora in modernity. It is time to parse the two.

While early modern Spanish racial ideas can be encapsulated in "blood purity" decrees that integrated theology and emergent biology from natural philosophy, by the eighteenth century the same blood purity laws that had expelled Jewish and Moorish subjects with "dirty blood" from fifteenth-century Spain were again in use. This time they bestowed "white" privileges on Spanish descendants in the Americas, substantiating difference along racial rather than religious lines. Blood purity, in the colonial context, established proof of Spanish blood as "white," that is, not of African or Indian descent. Conversely, the racial ideas behind concepts like "negrada," "negro," and "negrero" derive from the descriptions in animal husbandry and fed the pseudoscientific racist discourses at their height in the nineteenth century. The premise of animal husbandry to categorize the breed, race, and stock of an animal, when applied to negro "livestock," supported racist attitudes that African and Indian "negros" were an inferior "stock" and a distinctly racial rather than religious Other. In colonial notarial documents, the enslaved are described as "negros" and "self-moving goods," that is, as property that moves on its own like oxen and horses as opposed to real estate or real property. In Spain's nascent racial epistemology, African-descended "negros" were at the bottom of a hierarchy that also saw racialized mestizo Indians as laboring bodies that were arguably human. Mestizos or mulattos with African "blood"—as degraded and distinct from "pure," "white" Spanish descendants—had significantly less rights and privileges in colonial society. *Mestizaje*, or the idea of racial mixing, may have been unique to Spanish America but did not protect mestizos from racist practices. As Joshua Goode states, "Spanish racial theorists did exist in the late nineteenth and early twentieth centuries, when race and racial sciences were most in vogue in the rest of Europe. Spaniards devised their own racial identities using scientifically substantiated racial ideas" (19). Proto-scientific discourses in scientific racism used concepts of "caste," "color," "race," and "spirit" to distinguish between the human races (Cooley 19) once considered "the children of Adam and Eve" in premodern pre-contact theology, and the modern notion of race became prevalent.

The Post-Abolition Criminalization of Black Life

The identification of Blackness with criminality and delinquency continued even after abolition and is prevalent in the criminalization of Black life presently. In Cuba as in Spain and Europe, Lombrosian theory was widespread by the end of the nineteenth century (Goode 157–58), justifying the identification of criminality with "certain" qualities of certain "races" like negros and gypsies. In 1906, in a typical example of the racial thinking of the time, the Cuban anthropologist Fernando Ortiz published *Los brujos negros*, a work that, along with that of others like Israel Castellanos, perpetuated a form of scientific racism based on the idea that "negros" were an inferior race with innate criminal tendencies (Díaz Martínez 40). Moreover, after the War of Independence from Spain, white Cuban elites no longer need to join cause with Afro-Cubans against a common enemy, which led to the 1912 "Race War" on the island. After abolition *and* fighting for the Cuban republic, when Afro-descendant Cubans ceased to be slaves and became citizens, Blackness became synonymous with delinquency in Cuba. Díaz Martínez argues that, furthermore, after the War of Independence the establishment of the Cuban nation was superimposed on the racist, colonial conflation of "slave" with "negro" and successively "negro" with "delinquent." The same can be said for Catalan and Spanish society.

The Negro Stain

It should not be forgotten that the liberalization of the slave trade destined for the Spanish dominions in America, decreed by Charles IV in 1789, implied an increased number of African or Afro-descendant slaves in peninsular Spain (López García) and in Catalonia (Solà; Martín Corrales). At the end of the eighteenth century and at the onset of the nineteenth century, there existed even a small market of enslaved Africans in Barcelona. The city's press offers different testimonies about the presence of enslaved men and women, Africans or Afro-descendants, in Catalonia at the end of the eighteenth century and beginning of the nineteenth. Thus, for example, a confectioner from Arenys de Mar offered for sale in June of 1800 a slave that he owned. He published an ad in the *Diario de Barcelona*: "Sebastian Pages, confectioner of the Vila de Arenys, has for sale a negro person of 14 years of age, who knows well the Christian doctrine, and speaks Catalan and Spanish well" ("Sebastian Pages"). In that same period, the Catalan press also relayed the frequent escapes of enslaved people seeking the precious good of freedom. A wealthy merchant in the Catalan capital named Pedro Gil Babot was looking for a runaway slave in 1814, whom he described as "short, fat, bald" and "with a scar on his face" and "pox" (Babot 911–12). Years later, in 1834 and again in 1842, two press releases reported new escapes by slaves, also in Barcelona:

> Se suplica a la persona que haya encontrado un negrito de edad de 12 a 13 años, que se extravió en las inmediaciones de la Rambla, lo presente a D. Francisco Javier Armenta, que vive en la Rambla, frente del Correo, núm. 11, quien lo gratificará. ("Pérdidas")

The person who has found a little black boy aged 12 to 13 years, who went astray in the vicinity of the Rambla, is requested to present him to Mr. Francisco Javier Armenta, who lives on the Rambla, in front of the Post Office, No. 11, who will reward him.

Se nos ha dicho que se ha fugado una negra de la casa de su ama, y que el señor gefe político ha dispuesto que permaneciese interinamente en clase de depósito en casa del coronel D. Ramon Sánchez Soto, sita en la Ciudadela. Estamos a la mira para ver cuáles serán las ulteriores disposiciones de dicha autoridad. ("Se nos ha dicho")

We have been told that a negro woman has escaped from the house of her mistress, and that the political chief has ordered that she remain temporarily in a kind of deposit in the house of Colonel Ramon Sánchez Soto, located in the Citadel. We are watching to see what the further orders of said authority will be.

Though purportedly scarce, the presence of Africans or Afro-descendants in Catalonia is apparent.

There were, of course, also free people of African origin who sought work in Barcelona. The Catalan press offers different relevant testimonies, for example in 1835: "A *negrito* from Cadiz is looking for a job as a cook or to guide carriages; he is faithful and humble, and lives in the Mesón del Violín" ("Sirvientes"). We would like to draw attention to the indistinct use of the words *negro*, *negra*, *negrito*, or *negrita* to refer to both legally free and enslaved persons. At first, slaves were referred to as "negros" and when these same slaves or former slaves attained freedom they were still referred to by the same word: "negro." Although in legal terms, an enslaved "negro" person was not the same as a free "negro" person, the use of the same word (*negro/negra*) to refer to both the free and enslaved indicates that the social perception of one and the other would have been similar. The dominant perception was related to the color of the skin, the person's race. Thus, after abolition, the diminished legal status of an enslaved person was transferred to a free person because of the color of their skin. The stigma of slavery was encapsulated in the designation *negro* or *negra*, which could now refer indiscriminately to an enslaved or free person of African descent, forming one discredited social group regardless of whether they were legally enslaved or free. This reveals the discriminatory attitudes that defined negro men and women as unequal to whites. Despite achieving their freedom, whites had historically been masters and "negros" were necessarily treated as their subordinates even after abolition. The identification of "negro" with "slave" was transmitted as a stigma on former slaves who were now legally free people, even when they left Cuba and accompanied their former masters to Europe.

Racial Stigma and *Sin Otro Apellido* (SOA)

To illustrate, on December 5, 1869, the Catalan *indiano* Fidel Marqués Bolet, who had become rich in Santiago de Cuba, made his last will and testament on his deathbed in Barcelona. In one of the clauses of his last will and testament, he expressly considered a former slave who had traveled with him from Cuba to Catalonia. He states, "It is his will that if the negra Ceferina in his service should decide to return to the island of Cuba, the sum of 600 escudos shall be given to her of course" (*Joaquín Serra*). There is no doubt that his will expressed some goodwill toward "la negra Ceferina" but there is also no doubt that its writing helps us understand the stigma on former slaves. Ceferina was not the only person identified in his will only by a first name. The other person was "a slave servant named Juan" (*Joaquín Serra*) who resided in Santiago de Cuba and was at the service of the house and warehouse that Marqués Bolet had in Santiago de Cuba. Juan, the male slave residing in Santiago de Cuba, and Ceferina, a free woman residing in Barcelona, were identified only by their first names. The other beneficiaries of the will mentioned by the businessman and decedent (Pablo Camprubí, Antonio Ferrer, etc.) were identified with one or two last names (*Joaquín Serra*). In legal terms, the absence of surnames was a clear distinction that separated negros and mulattos from whites, a marker that served to stigmatize those whose skin implied African origins (the "slave servant named Juan" or "the negra Ceferina") regardless of whether they were free or not. The stigma of slavery was maintained even though Ceferina, or whoever was in the same situation, had achieved freedom, had a salaried job, and resided in a European city like Barcelona. Her label as a "negro" person, therefore, cast a shadow over her legal status to recall her condition as a former slave. The lack of a surname identified individuals who had previously been enslaved. Therefore, regardless of whether they were currently free or not, the stigma of the status of "slave" continued.

Thus, Ceferina or individuals in a similar situation who had achieved freedom, had a salaried job, and resided in a European city like Barcelona still suffered a diminished status in society. The lack of a surname was another indicator for racist whites.

Regarding the racial stigma of slavery, we would like to examine several examples from the Catalan capital. Barely seven weeks after the *indiano* Fidel Marqués drew up his will, the businessman Antonio López y López, the future Marquis of Comillas, did the same in the same capital. Among multiple bequests obtained from exploits in Cuba, the decedent stated, "I bequeath to D. Serafín Romeu de la Habana and his wife Dª Josefa Robato the two *negras* of my property that today they have in their house, understanding that if any of them dies before me this legacy will be for the remaining one that has survived me and if both were prematurely dead the two *negras* will belong to their unmarried daughters, one or more, that survive them." (*Ramón de Miquelerena, manual de 1870*). Nine years earlier in a former will, Antonio López had directed a gift "to the negro woman Eloísa two hundred duros" (*Ramón de Miquelerena, manual de 1861*), the equivalent of one thousand pesetas or about two hundred dollars in 2024 adjusted for inflation. We know that Eloísa López was then a free woman who received a salary for her work. She was the former wet nurse to the López family and had accompanied her former masters from Santiago de Cuba to Barcelona. Even so, he identifies her simply as "negra," using the same appellative with which he describes the two slaves in his property in Havana. The Blackness of the African Eloísa López underscored her former condition as an enslaved woman despite her status as a legally free person. In nineteenth- and twentieth-century Barcelona, describing the *negros* Ceferina or Eloísa by means of an appellative as paternalistic as it is stigmatizing reveals how the enslavement of Africans and Afro-descendants in America engendered racism in both the New and Old World. In other words, anti-Black racism, the stigma against African-descended and mixed-race descendants has its roots in the enslavement of millions of Africans in the early Americas. Although some maintain racism engendered slavery, we assert that the racist ideas permeating our institutions and legal system in the West have roots in the racial ideas from 350 years of Atlantic slavery (1518–1867). The end of the nineteenth-century development of "SOA" in Cuba, "sin otro apellido" or "without another surname," served to further stigmatize legally free people of color (Zeuske, "Sin otro apellido" 153–208). SOA functioned as a stigma to signify the inferiority and subalternity of that person. The status of persons without another surname depended, thus, on their genealogy. SOA functioned as a racial marker of "negro" or African or Afro-descendant free people. The genealogy implied in SOA transcended their status as free persons and prevented them from being equal to either Creoles or *peninsulares* of European descent.

Anti-Abolitionist *Indianas* and Religious Superiority

We will examine another set of racial ideas that traveled from the Caribbean to Catalonia. Having identified the metonymic identification between "slavery" and "blackness," it seems appropriate to highlight how the Catalan and white elite owners of slaves in Cuba and Puerto Rico were able to transfer their derogatory view of Africans and Afro-descendants to Catalonia. This vision sometimes described them as savages and other times as naive but considered them, always and in any case, inferior to whites and in need of their tutelage. On January 8 in 1873, an argument made by 238 women born on the islands of Cuba and Puerto Rico residing in "this capital," that is, in Barcelona, arrived to the Spanish president of the Council of Ministers. Addressing him, the American-born women of the Barcelona elite committed to writing their opposition to abolition in Puerto Rico (Surwillo 4–9). In their manifesto, the signers identify themselves as "Christians" who, having been born in Cuba or Puerto Rico, know "better without doubt" than the "men of State" the question of "the ill-named slavery." They argue that precisely because of their intimate ties to and knowledge of colonial slavery, their voices merit consideration. Affirming they do not want slavery, they continue in rhetorical interrogation: "Why should we want it if we are women and Catholics? We want even less that it be added to the barbarism of the unfortunates whom it is intended to favor, making of beautiful Cuba, of beautiful Puerto Rico, two tribes like the wretched Santo Domingo" (Archivo Histórico Nacional, *Ultramar*, 3554). Employing the specter and fear that whites harbored about free Blacks and revolution in Haiti, they claim abolition will be detrimental to Cuba and Puerto Rico, which will become like "wretched" Santo Domingo, neighbor to Haiti, and predominantly Black. The slaves' own misfortunes, they say, would also grow with the "burden" of freedom: "Put a gun in the hands of a child and he will be wounded by it. A child is the one who has always lived under guardianship and freedom is a deadly weapon for those who do not know how to use such a precious gift" (*Expediente*). The women's paternalism veils their belief in the natural inferiority of the untrustworthy negro needy of Catholic education from their masters and mistresses before sovereignty. Analogies between children and people of color, Indians, and Africans were common in the period. As a form of persuasive rhetoric employed to garner the sympathy of white readers, even the discourse of antislavery activists could refer to African and Indian "innocence" and need for "education" or "salvation" from whites (Stoddard).

The women of the Catalan bourgeoisie, born in Cuba or Puerto Rico, criticized, for the same reason, the abolitionists, whom they characterized as mere demagogues who spoke without knowledge of the cause: "Much is talked about and much talk is drivel . . . when dealing with this delicate question, because it lends itself so much to pompous and bombastic declamations. . . . But the truth is that those who most declaim against the ill-named slavery of the West Indies, philanthropists in appearance and 'two-faced' ['de double'] Catholics that treat their servants with more tyrannical contempt than the inhabitants of Cuba and Puerto Rico treat their so-called slaves" (*Expediente*). Decrying abolition and abolitionists, the women claim their religious superiority and reasonable—in their eyes—support for continued slavery. "Besides, Your Excellency," they continue, addressing Ruiz Zorrilla, "what convenient use do you want them [the slaves] to make of their freedom without any preparation, beings who by their natural instincts, by their condition and for other reasons known to all, do not know how to live except guided by the gentle yoke of advice and love of their masters, with whom they are identified?" (*Expediente*). In the opinion of the Barcelona *indiana* bourgeoisie, women born in the Spanish West Indies, abolition would only bring misfortune to the enslaved, whom they see as unfit for freedom and dependent on their masters. "Barbaric cruelty would be, therefore, not charity or even philanthropy, to throw so many thousands of our brethren into the pit of vice and crime." The "vice and crime" that free Blacks were predisposed to, according to the women's racist letter, was evident in that "slaves who graciously attained freedom" whether "by a lottery or other such means," they said, "lose themselves miserably by indulging in idleness and in the vices to which their natural inclination drags them with terrible force" (*Expediente*). These *indianas* were only willing to accept the individual manumission of slaves through self-purchase of freedom, whereby each slave paid his owner a ransom equivalent to his market value (*Expediente*).

The *Negrada* Herd

Negrada is synonymous with "slave-herd," meaning an amorphous collective of slaves in a "pack" or "herd," and is collective noun formed through the use of *-ada* as in *manada*. This profoundly racist piece of language, according to the current edition of the Royal Spanish Academy's *Dictionary of the Spanish Language*, is defined as "Set or meeting of negro slaves that constituted the endowment of a farm." The comparison of Black slaves to herds of farm animals is apparent. In nineteenth century Cuba it was common for *negrada* to be used as the synonym for an "endowment" on a sugar mill or coffee plantation. For example, in April 1833 the lieutenant governor of Matanzas denied rumors of clandestine slave disembarkations by slave ships on the shore of his jurisdiction coming from Africa (Estado, 8034, 20). A few months later, in September, it was the Captain General of Cuba himself, Mariano Ricafort, who would use this term, also in the same sense, when addressing the British Consul in Havana and informing them of recent slave rebellions. "In Banes, the *negradas* [slave-herds] of the estates of Dn. Francisco Aguirre rose up . . . the appropriate punishment will be applied to the guilty parties" (Archivo Histórico Nacional, Estado, 8015, 21). Several specific examples of the word *negrada* suggest that enslavers used the word to define any grouping of enslaved Africans, and not just the endowment of a farm. It had, by extension, a meaning equivalent to that of "herd of slaves" or "herd of Blacks," that is, as "herd" of pigs or "flock" of sheep. This is how it was used, for example, in the fall of 1817 by Francisco de Ornes. The captain of the slave ship *La Circasiana* signed a sea protest in Havana upon its arrival from the Gallinas region. Ornes stated that he had been forced to disembark the ship's boatswain, Juan Francisco Letón, in the Cape Verde archipelago. In addition to his "bad treatment" of the other crew members and the bad treatment of the "the slave-herds" he had also "disregarded the orders given" by the captain himself (*Protocolos*). More than fifty-six years later, in January of 1874, the Catalan Joaquín Bartra wrote from Havana to the ex-minister of overseas, also Catalan Víctor Balaguer. Bartra denounced the shameful way that many from the Iberian Peninsula had obtained great fortunes in Cuba, starting from extreme poverty. While many, he said, had started as mere clerks "behind stinking counters" to "earn their first hard currency," he added that later, "between their tricks and their savings from their salaries, [they] managed to gather an amount of money that they then used in the *negradas* and other fraudulent enterprises, which brought them huge profits" (Bartra). The word *negrada* appears in these two references not as a synonym of an "endowment" on an agrarian estate but as a word that refers to a shipment of enslaved Africans on slave ships to Cuba. The dictionary of the Royal Spanish Academy itself includes, in fact, a second meaning of the word, according to which in some Latin American countries *negrada* means, derogatorily and colloquially, any "group of people of black race" (*Diccionario de la lengua española*).

Evidently, the word *negrada* came from the slave trade and slavery in Spanish America. Its use survived, however, in both the Old and New Worlds. It is easy to find tokens of its use in the nineteenth and twentieth centuries in Catalonia. A few examples from journalistic language and theater include plays written and performed in Catalonia years after the end of the slave trade that employ language born in slavery, the institution that served to stigmatize "negros" as inferior beings. A play from 1891, authored by the Catalan playwright Josep Pin i Soler, entitled *La Sirena* (*The Mermaid*), is named after the slave ship that appears in it. It premiered in February of 1892 at the Teatro Catalán de Novedades in Barcelona. The characters travel through different scenarios, including an imaginary village on the Catalan coast (called Port Nou), a slave ship called *La Sirena* loaded with African captives across the Atlantic, and the fertile sugar cane fields in Cuba. In it, the English Navy chases the ship *La Sirena*. The Catalan sailors escape victorious when the English steamer fails mid-chase. After escaping the English, the captain of the ship, Pau Sendra, and his crew "unload the negro-herd in a hut next to Cárdenas" ("La Sirena"). The Barcelona weekly *La Tomasa* reported, even more extensively, on the premiere of *La Sirena*. The chronicler used the same word, *negrada*, to refer to the group of African captives unloaded on the island's northern coast. He emphasized how "the mulattoes" or "mulaticas," naked and enslaved, were, for the Catalan officers and sailors, mere sexual objects distributed in the same way as postcards and bottles of rum. A troubling combination of easy money, alcohol, and naked "mules" and cheap "mulatas" made Cuba a "good country," regardless of the whips the author wanted seen on stage:

> aixís es que en lo acte seguent ja está *la negrada* á salvo en un *bohío* de la hisenda de la mare de don Luisito.
> Surten majorals ab *jipi-japa*, y látigo y patillas, a més d'això *mulaticas*, fruita apetitosa i tints negres de debó, mitj despullats, que ballan y . . . . jugan i ab un xich més descarrilarían, perquè aixó de portar las cosas tan *al natural* en la escena, és molt escabrós.

> Allí se reparteixen tres cosas: las mulatas, lo rom y fins cartas pel correu: *¡oh, qué buen país!*
>
> Sembla que allí las mulatas
> son molt bonas y baratas
> y'ls mariners de Port-Nou
> s'en aprofitan bé prou. ("La Sirena"; emphasis added)

> by the next act the *black-herd* is safe in the hut in Luisito's Mother's hacienda.
> Overseers with straw Panama hats and whips come out, as well as *mulaticas,* appetizing fruit in shades of black frankly, half nude, dancing . . . and playing and, with a tad more, they'd go off track because this carrying on so "au naturel" on stage is very risky.
> Three things are distributed there: mulatas, rum, and finally, letters for the mail: oh what a good country!
>
> Looks like there the mulatas
> are very good and cheap
> and the sailors of Port Nou
> good that they take advantage. (emphasis added)

In 1892, it had been six years since slavery disappeared in Cuba, nineteen years since there had been slavery in Puerto Rico, and twenty-five years since the last ship carrying African captives arrived in Cuba. Yet the word "negrada" continued its use in literature and journalism. It would continue to appear well into the twentieth century, regardless of the ideological orientation of the newspaper in question. For example, the Republican newspaper *La Publicidad* defined as "*negradas insurgente,*" in 1895, the Cuban guerrillas who took up arms for the independence of Cuba (*Roselló 1*). In this context, the term *negrada insurgente* was used to discredit the political and military adversary of Spain on the island who they saw as the US benevolent to the "*negradas insurgentes.*"

Representing Anti-Black Racism in Catalan Culture

Anti-Black racism appeared in public discourses in Catalonia and Cuba in the nineteenth century but was also debated and refuted as today. The March

23, 1894, edition of *La Esquella de la Torratxa*, a satirical Republican and anti-clerical Barcelona newspaper, mocks the second Marquis of Comillas for his involvement in the slave trade as a slave trafficker and "negrero" ("negro-maker"). In it, the son of the slave trader Antonio López is followed by a line of racial caricatures of Black and Asian "negres" or slaves (so-called "coolies"). As per the caption, the Marqués is gathering Christian pilgrims and willing to pay the trip for "various negres . . . brought from distinct corners of the globe" ("La comedia"). In this 1894 satirical cartoon, the Catalan word *negres* refers both to people descended from Africa and Asia of differing races; *negre* or *negro* appears synonymous with being a racialized and subordinated Other and being a "slave." *L'Esquella de la Torratxa* implies that whites, too, are subservient to the Marqués as an institution, having been fooled into enslaving, brutalizing, and defrauding even themselves as "dumb" commodities and docile Christians. The white stockholders in the Marqués's slave-trading ventures are pictured below the "negres" painting themselves in Blackface to have the "pilgrimage" paid for, suggestive of their collective disposition to follow the Marqués and his money at any cost.

In 1897, under scientific pretexts, a group of 150 African men and women from the ancient kingdom of Ashanti ("Axanti") were exhibited in Barcelona next to the Plaça de Catalunya. The same group had been exhibited in Lyon and was being displayed across Europe as an exotic spectacle in the form of "ethnic exhibitions" germane to the period (López Sanz and Sánchez Durá). In Barcelona, the price of a ticket was somewhat expensive: one peseta. The July 28, 1897, morning edition of *El Diluvio* published a letter written by a resident of the Catalan capital describing the exhibition of the city's guests.

> Es claro quo todas las noches, á eso de las nuevo menos cuarto, empieza toda aquella negrada á chillar ó cantar, como ellos le llamarán, desconcertadamente, acompañados de una orquesta cuyos instrumentos no son otros que los que se usan para las cencerradas de mayor cuantía. . . . Y no pára aqui la cosa. Todos los vecinos . . . percibimos unos olores tan asquerosos y un humo tan denso, procedente de las cocinas improvisadas al aire libre por los negros aschantis. ("Un habitante")

> Clearly, every night, at about a quarter to nine all that *negro-herd* begins to shout or sing, as they call it, in an embarrassing manner, accompanied by an orchestra whose instruments are none other than those used for the biggest *cencerradas*. . . . And

> it does not stop there. All the neighbors . . . we perceive such disgusting smells and such dense smoke, coming from the kitchens improvised in the open air by the negro ashantis.

In the same city that hosted the strange encampment of Africans as spectacle and human zoo were those who rejected it with even more racial contempt. The author of the letter describes "a negrada" that did nothing but shriek when they thought they were singing ("as they would call it"). The contempt for the African "visitors" and their identification with a herd of cows is heightened by equating their instruments to cowbells (*cencerradas*), small, crude bells that cows and other livestock carry so that a herder can hear and find them. To finish, the Barcelona resident noted that the smells produced by their cooking in "open air kitchens" were "disgusting."

Few Catalan voices were critical of anti-Black racism in Catalan society. However, the modernist writer Santiago Rusiñol did address the ambivalent and racist relationship between Catalan society and Black people. In his work *Llibertat!* (*Liberty*, 1901), Jaumet Negre is a mulatto born in Cuba, who returns to Catalonia with his master. Negre is both adopted by a Catalan village and excluded from it. The values with which Negre is raised make him believe in the equality of citizens before the law, and that he could integrate in Catalan society if he were to marry the daughter of a neighbor. However, the idea of "miscegenation" is disgusting to these neighbors, who have Jaumet Negre expelled from his village and from Catalan society. In August of the same year *La Esquella de la Torratxa* ("En Jacmé Rusiñol") parodied Rusiñol as "Great Mister of Cau Ferrat / and painter of the favorites, who has now been declared *father* of <Liberty> / and defender of the negritos." In the cartoon, Rusiñol is depicted adjacent to a circle of dancing "negritos" as he holds up his work *Liberty*. A well-dressed, dignified "negro" atop the volume suggests that Rusiñol's work *Liberty* in his left hand is higher and mightier than the whip low-slung in his right—or that at least a proud Rusiñol thinks so (see fig. 4.1). As Jeffrey K. Coleman contends (1), with *Liberty*, Rusiñol staged one of the few cultural interventions critical of anti-Black racism in Catalan culture in 1901 at the turn of the century.

In contrast, many celebrated authors in the Generation of '98 and collaborators in the Catalan press continued to use the word *negrada* in a deeply derogatory and racist fashion. In 1925, the Havana correspondent for *La Veu de Catalunya* deplored the recent prohibition by the Cuban government, "of all this instrumentation—congas and maracas—and everything that sounds like African music . . . without the cadenced sound of the

Figure 4.1. La Esquella de la Torratxa. *Source:* Public domain.

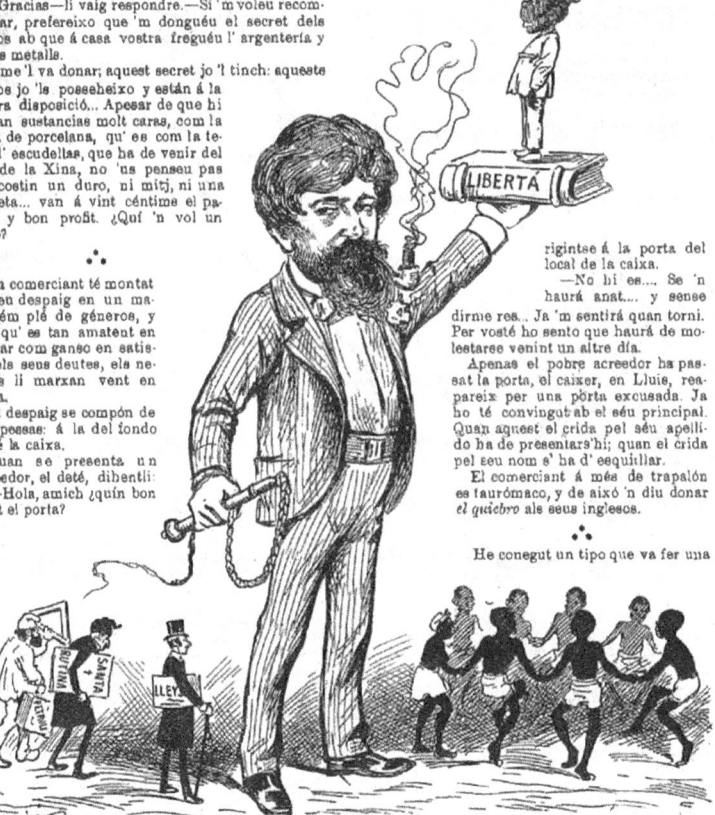

negrada playing to its own tune, it will lose all its color and its mood" ("De Cuba estant"). While *La Veu de Catalunya* was the unofficial mouthpiece of the Lliga Regionalista, other Catalanist media also continued using the term *negrada* in the 1920s. On January 7, 1928, *El Baix Penedés*, a weekly newspaper, published an autobiographical note by Josep Aixalá, "My slippers in 1881," written and dated in Havana, December 1927: "What the heck! I thought. Let me see the *negrada* with all its contortions, and for what it's missing . . . Never in my life have I experienced greater enjoyment." Furthermore, in February 1928 the Teatro Novedades hosted six performances of the "unprecedented and formidable . . . negro jazz" show entitled "Negro Follies," in which "40 negro artists," musicians, and dancers performed a show created because of the "New-York negro revue." It received negative reviews by the Catalan press, who, rejecting the artistic and musical legitimacy of those who performed this art, also rejected the human expression and creativity of this social group. The word *negrada* was still commonly used in the Barcelona press in the 1930s and with clear negative, racist connotations.

In August 1932, *El Diluvio* published a chronicle written on the island of Bioko, then Fernando Poo, by Luis Sáenz de Morales. It describes, among other things, the Miss Santa Isabel contest. Again, in a condescending manner, the same word, *negrada*, appears. "It is about choosing the prettiest negro woman in Santa Isabel. A few moments later, the whole island is watching the *negrada*." Another example is even more significant. One political adversary criticized by *El Diluvio* was the conservative, Catalanist leader Francesc Cambó. His decision to form a pact between the Lliga Catalana and the Confederación Española de Derechas Autónomas (CEDA) during the elections of February 1936 led to his public condemnation. In a letter against him, its author claims that "Cambó does not consider himself the head of a party, but the overseer of a negrada over which he has the right to everything" (Toll 179). It comes as no surprise, then, that Barcelona's *La Humanitat* and *El Diluvio* newspapers both with Republican orientations, publish notes by Celilio Gasóliba using the word *negrada* to describe the publication, in 1933, of a biographic novel about Pedro Blanco, the slave trader or *Pedro Blanco, el negrero*, by the Cuban journalist Lino Novás Calvo (Gasóliba, "Un gran libro"; "Un llibre dinamic"). (See Gustau Nerín's chapter in this volume, "Pedro Blanco, the Accursed Slave Driver: Literature and Historical Memory of Slavery in Spain.") In 1856 Pedro Blanco died in Barcelona, in the metropolis that acquired so much of its wealth from the colonies in the long nineteenth century.

Earlier, in January 1906, *Vida Marítima*, a decennial magazine based in the same metropolis, published an extensive article by Antonio María Manrique entitled "La presa de un negrero en Cuba" (The seizure of a slave ship in Cuba). This text describes the seizure of one of the last slave ships to reach the island, which Navy authorities took with its human cargo to the port of Nuevitas. There its African captives are freed and acquire the status of "emancipated." When referring to the large group of *emancipated* people the author chose, again, to describe them as a "negrada," although they were legally free, using the same synonym for "slave stock" (or "*dotación de esclavos*") on an estate (Roldán de Montaud 159–92).

Conclusions: Contemporary Culture and Anti-Blackness

Reflections on the activity of slave ships in Catalan literature or by the Catalan press overwhelmingly romanticized the activity of the sea and businessmen involved in the Atlantic slave trade, including the Catalan involvement. This was the case in the play *La Sirena* by Josep Pin i Soler that premiered in 1892. Far from morally questioning this activity, Catalan authors incorporated slave ships and "negradas" most casually. Enslaved African "negradas" appear as a backdrop in the literature and not as subjects of history or of their own histories but as objects of commerce. In this way, the Catalan, Cuban, and Spanish readerships of these cultural interventions continued to receive in the theater, press, and novel the same dehumanizing gaze on Black life typical of any racist slave society. This went on for years after the end of the slave trade and slavery in the Old and New World. Anti-Blackness became a social pathology.

On the cusp of the twenty-first century, the representation of people of color in Catalan culture is changing thanks to the work of cultural interventions by scholars, authors, political entities like SOS Racisme, and public figures like Desirée Bela-Lobeddé and other Afro-Spanish and Afro-Latina anti-racist activists in Barcelona, such as Tania Adam, or Lucía Asué Mbomío Rubio, a prominent Black writer, filmmaker, journalist, and TV reporter. US scholar Akiko Tsuchiya argues that the removal of the statue of the infamous slave trader the Marquis of Comillas from Barcelona in 2018 shows "that there is a desire, at least among some sectors of the population, to hear the stories of those who have been suppressed" (Tsuchiya 493). The level of public interest in historian Martín Rodrigo-Alharilla's *Un hombre, mil negocios: La controvertida historia de Antonio López, Marques de*

Comillas (2021), which garnered attention from *La Vanguardia, elDiario. es, El Periódico,* and a documentary series produced by *the BBC* and *TV3,* certainly implies the reality of public interest in understanding this legacy. Moreover, literature about the racial legacy of slavery is becoming curriculum in some secondary schools in Catalonia. Josep Lorman, former member of SOS Racisme, is the author of *Atlàntic* (2021), *La Venus negra* (2016), and *El fil del funàmbul* (2015). In his novels Lorman humanizes Black life in Catalonia. He cites the US literary genre of slave, neo-slave narrative, and especially Toni Morrison as influences in this work, as well as his research and lived experience with the Black community in coastal Mataró. Lorman's *El fil del funàmbul* is the coming-of-age story of a teenage Black girl adopted by a Catalan family. The novel confronts racial and historical tensions when the protagonist learns that she is slave-descended from Cuba and her adoptive parents are descendants of slave traders. In 2022, the play *Amèrica* by Sergi Pompermayer premiered in Barcelona. During a family dinner on September 11, the National Day of Catalonia, the slave-owning past of a bourgeois Catalan family surfaces when the oldest son brings his girlfriend to dinner and she is Black and Catalan. The play aims and succeeds at asking its spectators to reflect on the Catalan slave-owning past and the need to approach a historical reality that was voluntarily hidden or at least forgotten. Only after racist identifications of Blackness with slavery and criminality are addressed can future generations cultivate a present that is as different as informed by the past.

Notes

1. Translated from Spanish by María Cristina Urruela and from Catalan by the authors.

Works Cited

Aixalá, Josep. "Les meves sabates en 1881." *El Baix Penedés,* 7 Jan. 1928, p. 2.
Archivo Histórico Nacional, Estado, leg. 8015, doc. 21.
Archivo Histórico Nacional, Estado, leg. 8034.
Archivo Histórico Nacional, Ultramar, Cuba, Gobierno, leg. 3554.
Archivo Histórico Nacional, Ultramar, Cuba, Gobierno, leg. 8934, doc. 20.

Babot, Pedro Gil. *Diario de Barcelona*, 30 Nov. 1814, pp. 911–12.
Bartra, Joaquín. *Epistolario de Víctor Balaguer, 1874/612: Carta de Joaquín Bartra a Víctor Balaguer de 30 de enero de 1874.* Gentileza de Gwénaelle Colez. Biblioteca Museo Víctor Balaguer.
Blanco, Luis. *Escribanía de Luis Blanco.* Archivo Nacional de Cuba, legajo 428.
Cabré, Tate. *Catalunya a Cuba: Un amor que fa història.* Edicions 62, 2004.
"La comedia pelegrinesca." *La Esquella de la Torratxa*, 23 Mar. 1894, p. 181.
Coleman, Jeffrey K. "The Racial Limitations of Freedom in Santiago's Russinyol *Llibertat!*" *Catalan Review*, vol. 33, 2019, pp. 1.
Cooley, Mackenzie. *The Perfection of Nature: Animals, Breeding, and Race in the Renaissance.* U of Chicago P, 2022.
Costa, Lluís. *El nacionalisme cubà i Catalunya.* Publicacions de l'Abadia de Montserrat, 2006.
"De Cuba estant." *La Veu de Catalunya*, 20 Nov. 1925, evening ed., p. 3.
"Quien neceiste un negrito." *Diario de Barcelona*, 4 Mar. 1836, p. 516.
Díaz Martínez, Yolanda. *La Peligrosa Habana: Violencia y criminalidad a finales del siglo XIX.* Editoriales de Ciencias Sociales (Havana), 2005.
Diccionario de la lengua española. Real Academia Española, 2022. dle.rae.es.
"En Jacmé Rusiñol." *La Esquella de la Torratxa*, 30 Aug. 1901, p. 579.
Expediente general de esclavitud: Exposiciones pidiendo que no se lleve a cabo las reformas proyectadas en las Antillas. Archivo Histórico Nacional, Ultramar (Cuba, Gobierno), documento 30.
Feros, Antonio. *Speaking of Spain: The Evolution of Race and Nation in the Hispanic World.* Harvard UP, 2017.
Fuente, Alejandro de la. *A Nation for All: Race, Inequality, and Politics in Twentieth-Century Cuba.* U of North Carolina P, 2001.
Gasóliba, Cecilio. "Un gran libro español y un nefasto libro yanqui." *El Diluvio*, 5 Aug. 1933, p. 7.
———. "Un llibre dinamic." *La Humanitat*, 16 July 1933, suppl., p. 2.
Gilroy, Paul. *The Black Atlantic: Modernity and Double Consciousness.* Harvard UP, 1993.
———. *There Ain't No Black in the Union Jack: The Cultural Politics of Race and Nation.* Routledge, 1987.
Goode, Joshua. *Impurity of Blood: Defining Race in Spain, 1870–1930.* Louisiana State UP, 2009.
"Un habitante de los alrededores . . ." *El Diluvio*, 28 July 1897, p. 9.
Joaquín Serra, manual de 1869, tercera parte. 5 de diciembre de 1869. Archivo Histórico de Protocolos Notariales de Barcelona, fols. 3082–85.
Junqueras, Oriol. *Els catalans i Cuba.* Proa, 1998.
López García, José Miguel. *La esclavitud a finales del antiguo régimen: Madrid, 1701–1837: de moros de presa a negros de nación.* Alianza Editorial, 2020.

López Sanz, Hasan, and Sánchez Durá, Nicolás. *Let's Bring Blacks Home!: Imaginació colonial i formes d'aproximació gràfica dels negres d'Àfrica (1880–1968)*. Exhibition catalogue. Universitat de València, 2020.

Lorman, Josep. *El fil del funàmbul*. Barcanova, 2015.

———. *Atlàntic*. Columna Cat, 2021.

———. *La Venus negra*. Documenta Balear, 2016.

Manrique, Antonio María. "La presa de un negrero en Cuba." *La Vida Marítima*, 30 Jan. 1906, p. 45.

Martí, Carlos. *Los catalanes en América: Cuba*. Minerva, 1920.

Martín Corrales, Eloy. "La esclavitud negra en Cataluña entre los siglos XVI y XIX." *Negreros y esclavos: Barcelona y la esclavitud atlántica (siglos XVI–XIX)*, edited by Martín Rodrigo y Alharilla and Lizbeth J. Chaviano Pérez, Icaria, 2017, pp. 17–45.

Masriera, Artur. *Oliendo a brea: Hombres, naves, hechos y cosas de mar de la Cataluña ochocentista*. Editorial Políglota, 1926.

Morelet, Arthur. *Voyage dans l'Amèrique centrale, l'île de Cuba et le Yucatan*. Gide & J Baudry, 1857.

"Pérdidas." *Diario de Barcelona*, 6 Mar. 1834, p. 534.

Pin i Soler, Josep. *La Sirena: dramas en quatre actes y un cuadro*. Barcelona [s.n.], 1891 (Tipolit. de Lluis Tasso).

Piqueras, José Antonio, and Imilcy Balboa, editors. *Gente de color entre esclavos: Calidades raciales, esclavitud y ciudadanía en el Gran Caribe*. Comares, 2019.

Pompermayer, Sergi. *América*. La Villarroel, 2022.

Protocolos notariales de marina. 24 Nov. 1817. Archivo Nacional de Cuba, vol. 2, fols. 1197r–1199–1200r.

Ramón de Miquelerena, manual de 1861, primera parte. 6 de junio de 1861. Archivo Histórico de Protocolos Notariales de Barcelona.

Ramón de Miquelerena, manual de 1870, primera parte. 27 de enero de 1870. Archivo Histórico de Protocolos Notariales de Barcelona.

Rodrigo y Alharilla, Martín. *Un hombre, mil negocios: La controvertida historia de Antonio López, Marqués de Comillas*. Ariel, 2021.

———. *Indians a Catalunya: Capitals cubans en l'economia catalana*. Fundació Noguera, 2007.

Rodrigo y Alharilla, Martín, and Lizbeth Chaviano Pérez. *Negreros y esclavos: Barcelona y la esclavitud atlántica (siglos XVI–XIX)*. Icaria, 2017.

Roldán de Montaud, Inés. "En los borrosos confines de la libertad: El caso de los negros emancipados en Cuba, 1817–1870." *Revista de Indias*, vol. 71, no. 251, 2011, pp. 159–92.

Roselló, Francisco. "Españolismo" *La Publicidad*, 26 Sept. 1895, p. 1.

Rusiñol, Santiago. *Llibertat!: Comèdia en tres actes*. Tip. L'Avenç, 1901.

Sáenz de Morales, Luis. "Barcelona—Fernando Póo." *El Diluvio*, 17 Aug. 1932, p. 8.

Santa Cruz y Montalvo, María de las Mercedes. *Viaje a La Habana*. Imp. de la Sociedad Literaria y Tipográfica, 1844.
"Sebastian Pages, confitero . . ." *Diario de Barcelona*, 8 June 1800, p. 643.
"Se nos ha dicho . . ." *Diario de Barcelona*, 2 Nov. 1842, pp. 4180–81.
"La Sirena: Obra dramática d'espactacle per Francisco Soler y Rovirosa, ab lletra de Joseph Pin y Soler." *La Tomasa*, 4 Mar. 1892, pp. 134–35.
"Sirvientes." *Diario de Barcelona*, 7 Nov. 1835, p. 2514.
Solà, Àngels. "Tres notes entorn les actituds i valors de l'alta burgesia barcelonina a mitjan segle XIX." *Quaderns de l'Institut Català d'Antropologia*, no. 3–4, 1981, pp. 101–28.
Stoddard, Eve W. "A Serious Proposal for Slavery Reform: Sarah Scott's Sir George Ellison." *Eighteenth-Century Studies*, vol. 28, no. 4, 1995, pp. 379–96.
Surwillo, Lisa. "Enslaved by Liberalism: Spain after 1868." *Republics of Letters*, vol. 3, no. 1, 2012, pp. 1–9.
Toll, Gil. *"El Diluvio," la prensa y la Segunda República*. Icaria, 2021.
Tsuchiya, Akiko. "Monuments and Public Memory: Antonio López y López, Slavery, and the Cuban-Catalan Connection." *Nineteenth-Century Contexts*, vol. 41, no. 5, 2019, pp 479–500.
Van Deusen, N. E. *Global Indios: The Indigenous Struggle for Justice in Sixteenth-Century Spain*. Duke UP, 2015.
Wudermann, John G. F. *Notes on Cuba*. 1844.
Zeuske, Michael. "Capitanes y comerciantes catalanes de esclavos." *Negreros y esclavos: Barcelona y la esclavitud atlántica (siglos XVI–XIX)*, edited by Martín Rodrigo y Alharilla and Lizbeth Chaviano Pérez, Icaria, 2017, pp. 63100.
———. "'Sin otro apellido': Nombres esclavos, marcadores raciales e identidades en la transformación de la Colonia a la República, Cuba 1879–1940." *Tzintzun: Revista de Estudios Históricos*, no. 36, 2002, pp. 153–208.

Part 2

Confronting the Legacies of Slavery in Cultural Memory Sites

Chapter 5

Confronting the Legacies of Slavery and Colonialism in Public Spaces
Debates around Racist and Colonial Monuments in Modern Catalonia

Akiko Tsuchiya[1]

> Perhaps no one monument could be made to tell the whole truth of any subject which it might be designed to illustrate.
>
> —Frederick Douglass[2]

The general public is well aware by now that monuments and statues around the world have become sites of contested memory. Monuments typically commemorate a particular version of history and its players, evoking a common identity, or a "heritage" that a community presumably shares. This heritage, as Stuart Hall has argued, is bound up with the meaning of the nation: it is a "discursive practice . . . one of the ways in which the nation constructs for itself a sort of collective social memory" (5). Thus, public memory emerges as a product of "the struggle between social groups to gain cultural authority to selectively represent and narrate their pasts" (Rowlands and Tilley 502). We need only remember the battle waged by many southerners in the US to preserve the Confederate monuments as emblems of their heritage and regional pride, despite their association with slavery, Jim Crow, and resistance to the Civil Rights movements of the mid-twentieth century. That these monuments have come to represent the myth of the "Lost Cause," through which white southerners seek to uphold the ideology of white supremacy and to extend its legacies into the future, is a clear testament to the racialized nature of collective memory.[3] Yet the meaning of memory sites is always open to revision and contestation by subsequent generations, as shown by the toppling of monuments to racists and colonizers in recent years: previously accepted versions of collective memory, enshrined in public spaces, monuments, and place names for years, have the potential to undergo a shift with changes in historical and political circumstances. These public spaces holding one version of collective memory can thus be transformed into spaces of resistance, generating new political conversations and altering the ways in which a community understands its past.

Lisa Knauer and Daniel Walkowitz, in *Contested Histories in Public Spaces*, refer to memory sites as palimpsests, where the narratives of opposing sides struggle for control over the foundational "myth" that monuments and other historical sites represent.[4] The most cherished myths of a community—often tied to notions of national identity—are transformed into collective memory through the act of commemoration (Nora 12; Rowlands and Tilley 501). Yet, of greater importance, for these scholars, is to examine critically "how and when the myth gained currency, whose interests it serves, and what power relations are revealed or masked" (Knauer and Walkowitz 15). They go on to argue for the need to situate, within a broader historical context, the battles over memory sites, as the myths and narratives that nations have mobilized around memory sites—and the "heritage" they presumably represent—are not always monolithic (18). Rather, different institutions and communities within the nation can also reinforce, reshape, or undermine these narratives (18). Monuments, therefore, are not embodiments of History, in any objective sense, as many opposed to the dismantling of racist monuments have claimed,[5] but rather, sites of negotiation where disparate viewpoints of stakeholders who claim a right to determine their meaning vie for authority (Dell 24).[6]

In light of these theoretical reflections, this study focuses on the public debates around two principal monuments in Barcelona connected to slavery and colonialism: the first is the monument to the Cantabrian slave trader Antonio López y López; the second is the one dedicated to Columbus, which is much better known to the international community. This discussion needs to be considered in view of the fact that Catalonia was a region with strong connections to the illegal slave trade in the nineteenth century, where much of its economic, social, and cultural infrastructure has been built on capital that originated from this activity, as a number of historians have documented (Piqueras; Rodrigo y Alharilla and Chaviano Pérez). In an earlier study, I examined the controversies surrounding Barcelona's monument to the slave trader Antonio López y López, the Marquis of Comillas, between the time of its construction in 1883 and the final removal of the statue in March of 2018 ("Monuments"). While I would like to minimize covering the same ground as in my previous publication, a brief history of López's place in nineteenth-century Iberian transatlantic history, particularly his connection to the slave trade, is key to understanding the broader implications of the controversies that his statue has generated around the problem of memory and representation in the public space in Barcelona.

Antonio López y López (1817–1883), the Marquis of Comillas, was born in 1817 in the small town of Comillas in northern Spain, traveled to Cuba in his youth, and made his fortune through the slave trade. On his return to Spain in 1853, he settled in Barcelona and used this capital to build a vast industrial empire there, founding three major companies: the Transatlantic Shipping Company (1881, originally established in 1857 as Antonio López y Compañía), whose steamships were used in the colonial wars in Morocco (1859–60) and Cuba (1868–78); the Hispano-Colonial Bank (1876), which lent money to the Spanish government for the Cuban War; and the Philippine Tobacco Company (1881), Spain's first transnational company, also created with slave trade money. As historian Martín Rodrigo y Alharilla has shown, López became a pivotal figure not only in building Catalonia's economic infrastructure, but also in sustaining Spanish colonialism in Africa and Spanish America.[7] Yet many Catalans prefer to remember him as an economic benefactor of Catalonia and a patron of the arts, who left the nation with an important cultural patrimony, conveniently overlooking the ignominious origins of his fortune.

The case of López's statue in Barcelona illustrates not only the conflicting claims to history made by various "stakeholders" (to use Upton Dell's term) who have been engaged in the polemic over the years, but also the changes in the symbolic meaning of the statue. This is to say, while controversy around the statue and the public space where it stood has existed since the moment of its construction, historical and political factors that motivated the controversies have shifted over the years, thus transforming the public memory associated with the site. When the monument's construction began in September 1883, with the authorization of Barcelona's city council, the Spanish nation was facing the imminent loss of its last colonies overseas. In this context, the monument of the returned emigrant (the *indiano*) stood as a symbol of—and nostalgia for—empire, rather than of racial supremacy per se, as it would later come to represent. According to one press account of the time, a group of prominent merchants in Barcelona took the initiative to propose the construction of the statue, dedicated to López's memory, as a tribute for having established his business operations and "for having associated himself during his life with all of the businesses of true interest" for Catalonia and its capital (quoted in Aramburu-Zabala Higuera, 41–42). Barcelona's then mayor and the city council embraced this project wholeheartedly; and, in his speech on the occasion of the monument's inauguration, the mayor echoed King Alphonse XII's words praising the Marquis as "uno de los hombres a quienes más debía la patria" (one of the men to whom the country owed the most) ("Crónica" 6285).

The original monument was torn down on August 24, 1936, shortly after the outbreak of the Civil War, by the popular demand of the anarchists. According to press accounts, these individuals had left on the statue's pedestal a red and black flag symbolizing anarchism, along with an inscription renaming the city square as the Plaza of Captain Biardeau, "Martyr of Liberty," who had lost his life defending the Catalan state during the revolt of October 6, 1934 ("El monumento de Antonio López y López"). Catalan workers of the 1930s, who participated in the revolutionary general strike, were protesting against fascism and affirming the sovereignty of Catalonia. In this context López's statue became an iconic representation of the monarchy and of the economic elite identified with the rise of fascism, against which the Catalan working classes stood in defiance. An article published in the Republican newspaper *El Diluvio*, urging Barcelona's City Hall to take down the slave trader's statue, refers to López precisely as "el gran servidor de la dinastía alfonsina, la siniestra figura que mejor simboliza a las hordas negras del fascismo" ("the great servant of the Alfonsine dynasty, the sinister figure who best symbolizes the black hordes of fascism"; "Los insultos en pedestal," p. 2, quoted in Rodrigo y Alharilla, "Memories in Dispute," p. 371).[8] That eight years later (1944), during Francisco Franco's fascist dictatorship, the pro-Franco Barcelona City Council ordered the restoration of the statue is in itself an symbolic act with clear ideological implications (fig. 5.1).[9] This reconstructed statue remained in place in the neighborhood of Ciutat Vella at the bottom of Via Laietana, a major thoroughfare in Barcelona, by the seafront, until its final removal in 2018.

Confronting the Legacies of Slavery and Colonialism in Public Spaces | 125

Figure 5.1. Reconstructed monument to Antonio López y López (1944–2018). *Source:* Wikimedia Commons, by Jordiferrer—Own work, CC BY-SA 3.0.

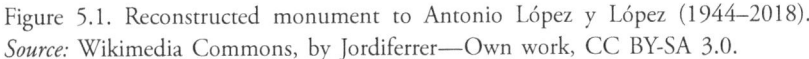

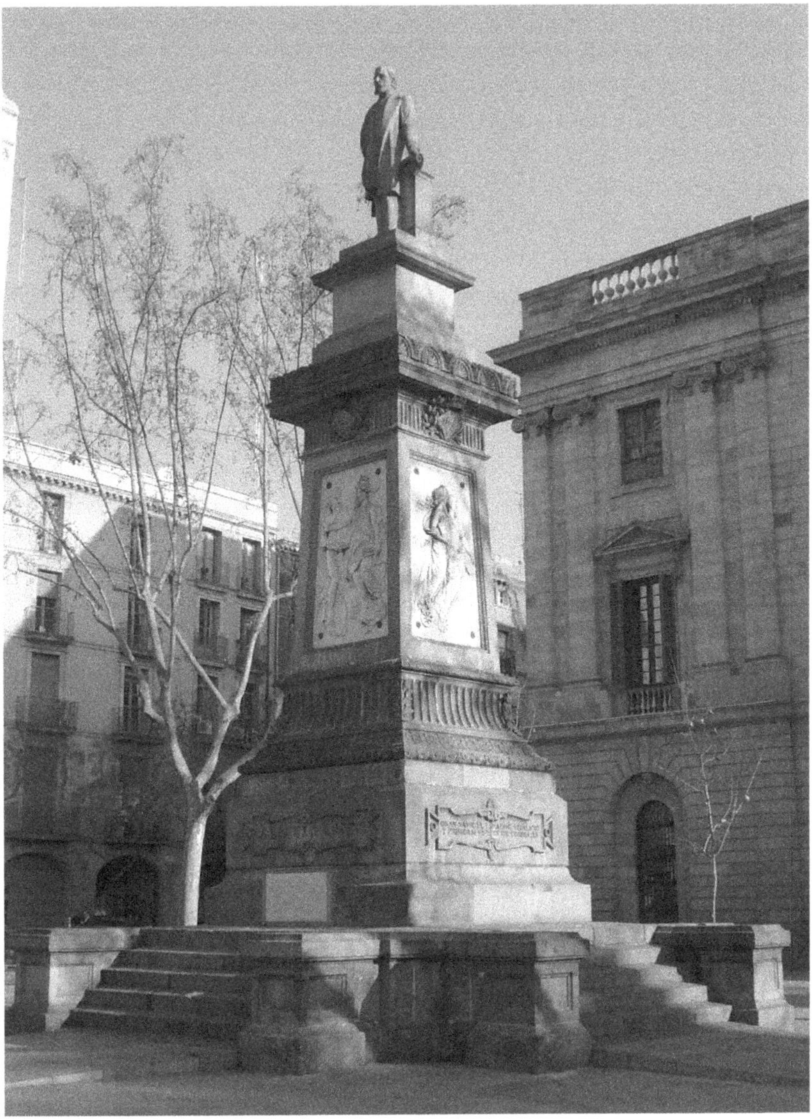

It took years (seventy-four to be exact) for the statue to be dismantled, even though various citizens' groups had been calling for its removal since the end of Franco's dictatorship in 1975 (Castillo). Since Franco's death, there have been a number of emblematic moments in national and global history that have led to a shift in public attitudes toward the López monument. The first was the emergence of the historical memory movement in Spain, which led to the passage of the Law of Historical Memory in 2007, under the Socialist government of Rodríguez Zapatero,[10] to recognize the rights of those who suffered persecution during the Spanish Civil War and the ensuing dictatorship, and to promote reparation and recovery of personal and family memory of these citizens. Article 15 of the Law of Historical Memory also mandated the removal of all public symbols and monuments commemorating the fascist dictatorship or its protagonists. Catalonia had passed its own version of the law two months earlier, to recover "democratic memory" (memoria.gencat.cat/ca/inici).

It is in the context of these laws that the movement to dismantle the slave trader's statue gained momentum. Since 2010, the labor unions CCOO and the UGT, as well as the anti-racist organization SOS Racisme, have been demanding the removal of López's statue. The election of grassroots activist Ada Colau as the first woman mayor of Barcelona in 2015 and the appointment of historian Ricard Vinyes as Commissioner of Memory Programs pushed the city forward in applying the laws of historical memory. The decision to dismantle López's statue was delayed another 3 years, due to the opposition of conservative political groups, but pressure by the Popular Unity Candidacy (CUP), the left-wing pro–Catalan independence party, led to a vote in the Barcelona City Council that recommended the removal of the statue in 2018. The statue was finally removed in March of 2018 (fig. 5.2); however, the pedestal remains in place to this day, displaying allegorical engravings celebrating López's various business ventures, as well as an inscription of King Alphonse XII's words glorifying the Marquis's "service to the nation." Moreover, Colau's promised "multi-consultation"[11] in June of 2018 to rename the plaza was significantly delayed, and it was not until June 2021 that the city finally announced its plans to change the name of the square to Plaça Idrissa Diallo, in memory of a Guinean immigrant who died in the Foreigner's Internment Center in Barcelona in January 2012 after being denied humanitarian aid. The official name change did not occur until March 25, 2022, 4 years after the statue had been removed (fig. 5.3).

What interests me beyond the removal of the statue—which, admittedly, was an important symbolic gesture on the part of Barcelona's city council—are the different public debates that have ensued, concerning the question of what should be done with the dismantled statue, if and how the square should be renamed, and how the public space itself might be recontextualized. Some press accounts have called attention to and criticized

Confronting the Legacies of Slavery and Colonialism in Public Spaces | 127

Figure 5.2. Pedestal of monument to Antonio López y López (front view). *Source:* Photo by the author.

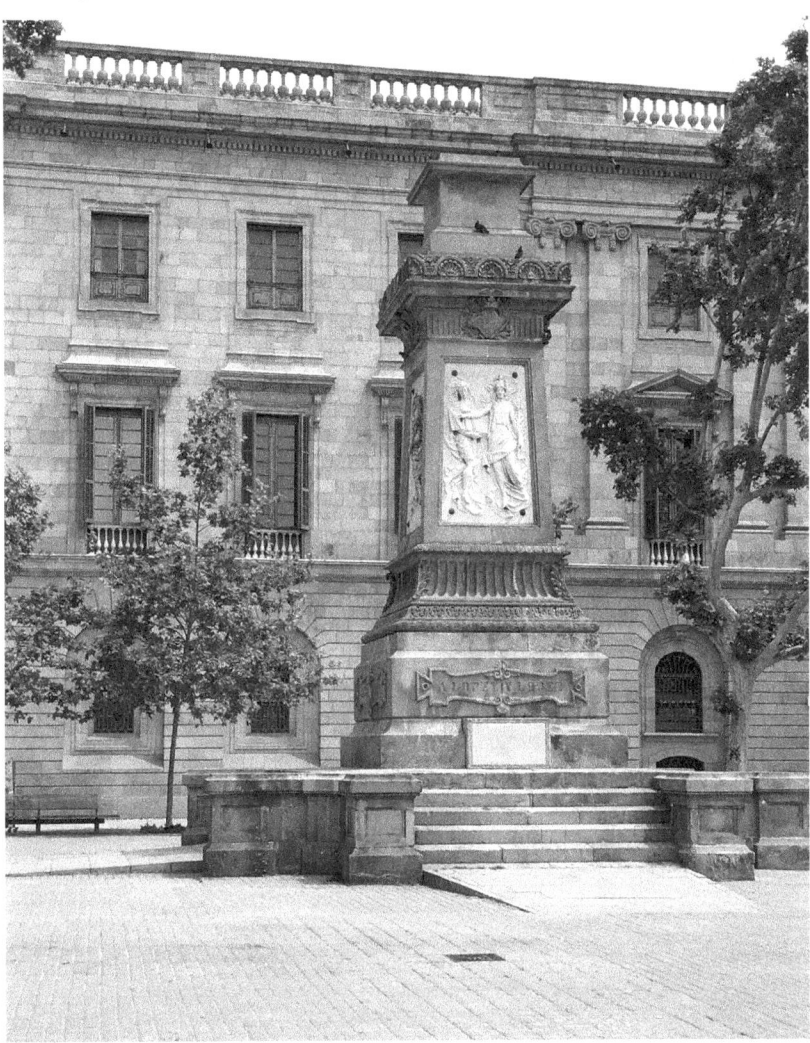

the extravagant public festivities—consisting of a circus, musical performances, and other forms of public spectacle—which the city organized on the occasion of the statue's removal and for which they spent 40,000 euros.[12] Defining this spectacle as a carefully orchestrated media event, Jordi Guixé Coromines, the Director of the European Observatory on Memories

Figure 5.3. Plaque for Idrissa Diallo Square, Barcelona, June 2022. *Source:* Photo by the author.

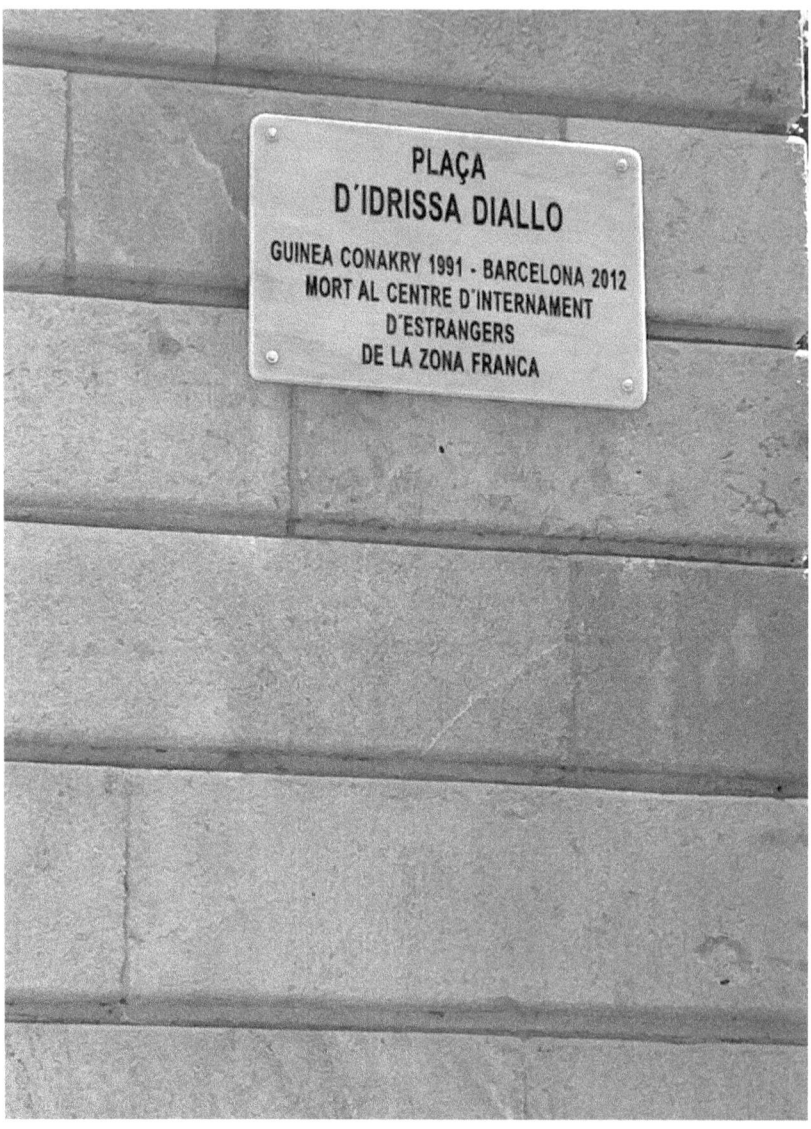

(EUROM),[13] and Núria Ricart ask if this was really an effective strategy for re-signifying the symbol of López's cultural patrimony for the general public, especially since, once dismantled, the statue was placed in a space of "public invisibility" in the museum warehouse (Guixé and Ricart 143–45).[14] At the same time, the images and inscriptions on the pedestal that remains standing on the plaza continue to prolong the legacies of the slave trader (158). At the base of the pedestal on what was the front side of the statue contains a segment of the Catalan national poet Jacinto Verdaguer's masterpiece *L'Atlàntida* (*Atlantis*) (1877), which, as Lisa Surwillo notes, "characterized *indianos* as the noble heirs of Columbus and Spain's glorious early empire" (150).[15] On the other side of the pedestal is an inscription from a telegram sent by King Alphonse XII on the occasion of the Marquis's death, reading, "Spain has lost one of the men who lent it greatest service." (fig. 5.4) The permanence of the pedestal, even after the disappearance of the visual marker of the slave trader's body from sight, symbolizes the impossibility of removing the foundations of colonialism from the European metropolis.[16]

As suggested earlier, the question of how to rename the square remained a source of controversy following the city's decision to dismantle

Figure 5.4. Text of Alfonso XII's telegram on back side of pedestal where Antonio López y López's statue once stood: "Spain has lost one of the men who lent it greatest service." *Source:* Photo by the author.

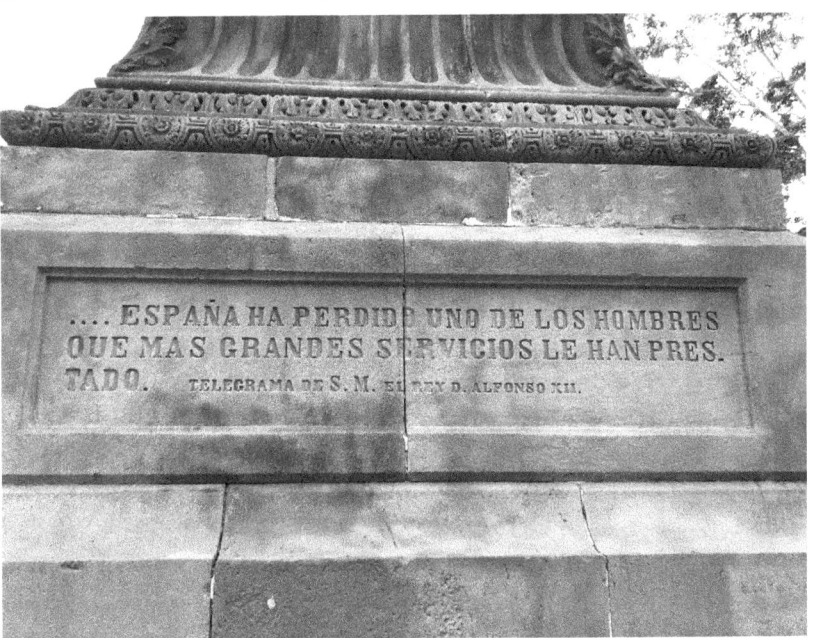

López's statue. One citizen's group proposed that the square be renamed Plaza de les Bullangues (Square of Popular Uprisings) to commemorate the popular uprisings against authoritarianism that took place between 1835 and 1843; others wanted the plaza to be renamed after the South African anti-apartheid leader Nelson Mandela. Another activist group (Tanquem els CIE), fighting to close detention centers for immigrants, petitioned to rename the square after the aforementioned Guinean immigrant, Idrissa Diallo. Finally, a Pan-Africanist group presented a petition to the city council to rename the plaza after the Haitian physician Alphonse Arcelin, who in 1991 led the protest against the "el negro de Banyoles" ("the black man of Banyoles") exhibit at the Darder Museum of Natural History.[17] While the first proposal highlighted the working-class struggle, so foundational to the narrative of post-industrial Barcelona, the second sought to commemorate a figure who became a symbol of the struggle against white supremacy and institutional racism, and an advocate for universal human rights. Yet some have problematized the proposed renaming of the square after Mandela as a way of deflecting the problem of colonial violence and racism away from the present time and national space of Catalonia, thus erasing its colonial past (Azarmandi and Hernández, "Colonial Redux" 16). The last two proposals, in contrast, demanded a recognition of the legacies of colonialism and slavery—and of racism against individuals of African descent—in the specific context of Catalonia.

In a broader sense, these debates call attention to the very nature of public memory, shaped by different sectors of society with their own stakes in the memory battle. Thus, we return to the question of who the stakeholders were in this controversy and what the stakes were. In 2014 Lisa Surwillo argued that the demands of the twenty-first-century union workers who campaigned for the removal of the statue largely privileged their working-class identity over the rights of enslaved individuals (166). In 2017 Mahdis Azarmandi and Roberto Hernández claimed, along the same lines, that the critique of the monument emerged not so much as a response to López's overt links to the slave trade as to the reconstruction of the monument in 1944 by Franco's fascist regime ("Colonial Redux" 10). Ada Colau's own public stand on the issue was that the statue's removal was a political act of reparation for the nation's colonial past and, more specifically, for the crime of slavery.[18] Yet some viewed Colau's decision to remove the statue and, subsequently, to rename the square where it stood as a "part of a broader political campaign to address Spain's fascist . . . past," rather than as a critique of its colonial past (Azarmandi and Hernández,

"Colonial Redux" 10; "Decolonizing Spain"). While an advocacy for worker's rights and the stand against fascism are not incompatible with the critique of colonialism and the legacies of slavery, the question is precisely which narrative has been privileged in different circumstances. In Catalonia, the issues of race and colonialism have often been subordinated to those of class and Catalan nationhood.

The city council's decision ultimately to rename the plaza after the Guinean Idrissa Diallo seemed to be a deliberate gesture to bring the contemporary issues of race and immigration to the forefront in the local context of the Catalan capital and to link them to the legacies of slavery in the public space.[19] In March 2022, the city placed two plaques in front of the pedestal to contextualize the monument, and to explain to the public the history of the plaza and the reason for the statue's removal, thus using the public space for pedagogical purposes (fig. 5.5).[20] If earlier in the century, the reclamation of the working class and anti-fascist activists propelled the demand to remove racist and colonial monuments, more

Figure 5.5. Plaque placed in front of the pedestal of the Antonio López y López statue explaining the history of the square. *Source:* Photo by the author.

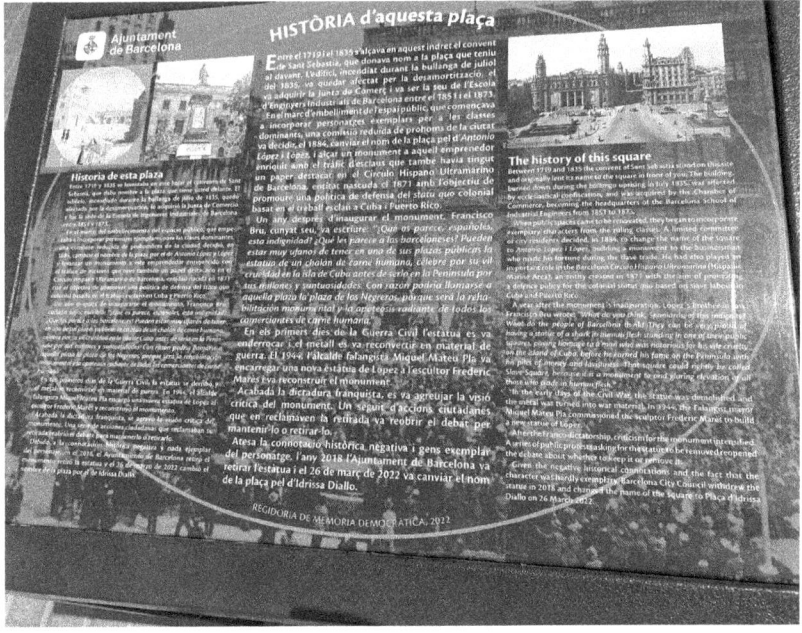

recently—as a consequence of the global impact of the Black Lives Matter movement—antiracist (SOS Racisme), Pan-Africanist (Federació Panafricanista de Catalunya), and immigrant advocacy groups (Tanquem els CIE), as well as a small group of decolonial artist-activists, have become more visible in the public space, protesting the silencing of the nation's colonial past. A number of compelling artistic initiatives have provoked reflection and dialogue around the commemorated figure, by recontextualizing it, by producing counternarratives to re-signify it. Back in 2014, art activists Daniela Ortiz (a Barcelona-based Peruvian immigrant) and Xose Quiroga García-Boente organized a photography and video exhibit, titled *Estat Nació*, for the Museum of Contemporary Art in Barcelona (MACBA); their objective was to "read the slave-based colonial past of Barcelona through its statues, commemorative plaques and buildings" to critique symbols of colonialism and the general historical amnesia in Catalonia about slavery and other forms of colonial exploitation in the Americas ("Estat Nació"). That the exhibit was hosted by a high-profile museum in the Catalan capital—and financed by the Government of Catalonia, the Barcelona City Council, and the Spanish Ministry of Culture—represented a significant step forward in the recognition of efforts to raise public consciousness about these issues.

There have been other more recent activist art interventions, using multiple media, in the public space of the slave trader's monument. Many of them represent what Andreas Huyssen has called "counter-monumental practices" that provoke the viewers to think differently about the figure on the pedestal, thus "undermining monumentalization itself" (40). In July 2018, an anti-racist collective creatively transformed the pedestal where López's statue once stood by painting the faces of African immigrants on its front façade, along with sign that included a brief explanation of the Marquis's crimes against humanity ("Making off 'Esclavitud sin Comillas' ").[21] Part of their activism consisted of producing a video to document their anti-racist cultural work and to disseminate it on social media.[22] The following year, Núria Ricart and Jordi Guixé published on the EUROM website their proposal for an "anti-slavery countermonument" to recontextualize the dismantled statue of the marquis. The statue would be placed in a glass tomb to be displayed on the plaza, submerged under the Mediterranean waters of the Port Vell, symbolically returning López to the same seas from which he had arrived having profited from the slave trade. In contrast to the dismantled statue, made invisible in the museum warehouse,[23] this project would allow the public to view the open tomb of the Marquis from every angle (fig. 5.6). Though the proposed exhibit never materialized, Ricart and Guixé

Figure 5.6. "L'Atlàntida: A Countermonument Proposal." *Source:* Courtesy of Núria Ricart and Jordi Guixé.

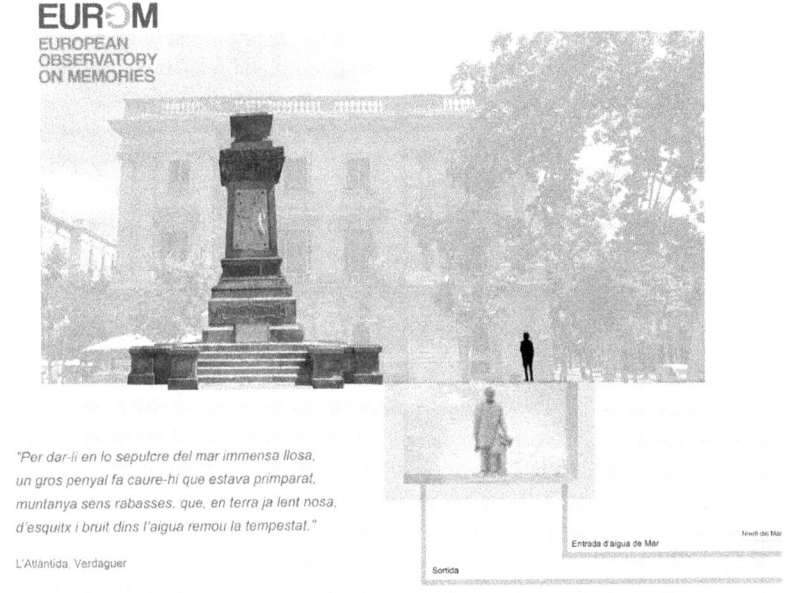

explained that it was meant to "dethrone the marquis, de-hierarchizing his statue," prompting the public to reflect on the connection between the past and the present (42).[24] Additionally, they proposed to establish an annual art competition to be held for the selection of a work—to replace the old statue—that would allow the public to think deeply about the problem of colonial memory and its transmission in the public space (43).

In January 2022, the French street artist James Colomina, known for making political statements through his public art, surprised the citizens of Barcelona by secretly installing a sculpture, titled "Humanity" (fig. 5.7), on the pedestal where López's statue once stood, to commemorate the anniversary of the official abolition of slavery in Spain. The sculpture consisted of two bright red figures of a teddy bear and a young man, presumably an immigrant, embracing. According to the artist, it was "a symbol of the positive relationship between men, regardless of skin color, sex, religion" ("Barcelona Gets Surprise"). Although the statue was erected without official permission, the city government allowed it to remain standing until

Figure 5.7. "Humanity." *Source:* Courtesy of James Colomina, www.james-colomina.com.

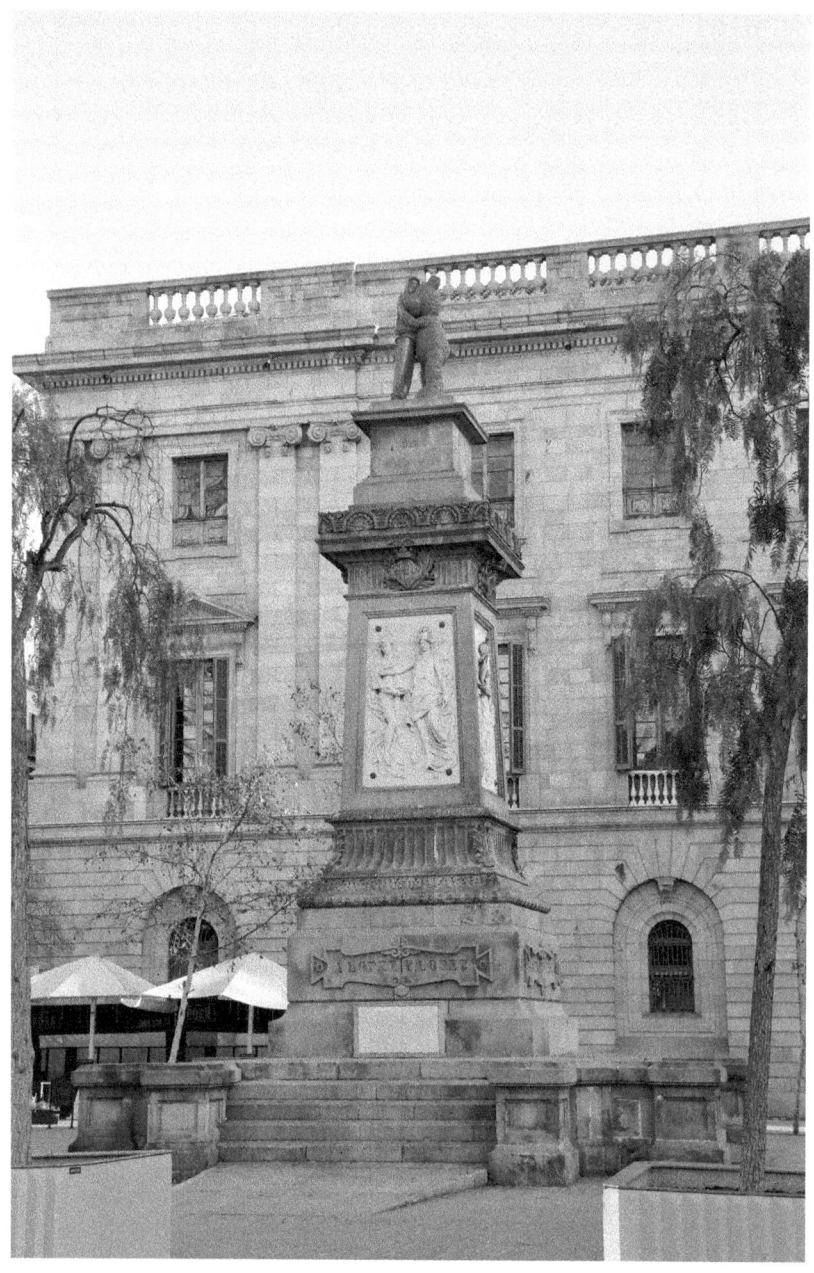

Confronting the Legacies of Slavery and Colonialism in Public Spaces | 135

mid-February and the name of the plaza was changed shortly thereafter to that of the Guinean immigrant (March 2022). And in summer of 2022, activists surrounded the base of the pedestal with silhouette images of immigrants, along with signs proclaiming the importance of Black lives and demanding the closure of the Immigrants' Detention Center (fig. 5.8).[25]

Figure 5.8. "Reconfigurando el legado de Antonio López y López" (2022). *Source:* Courtesy of Lázaro Lima.

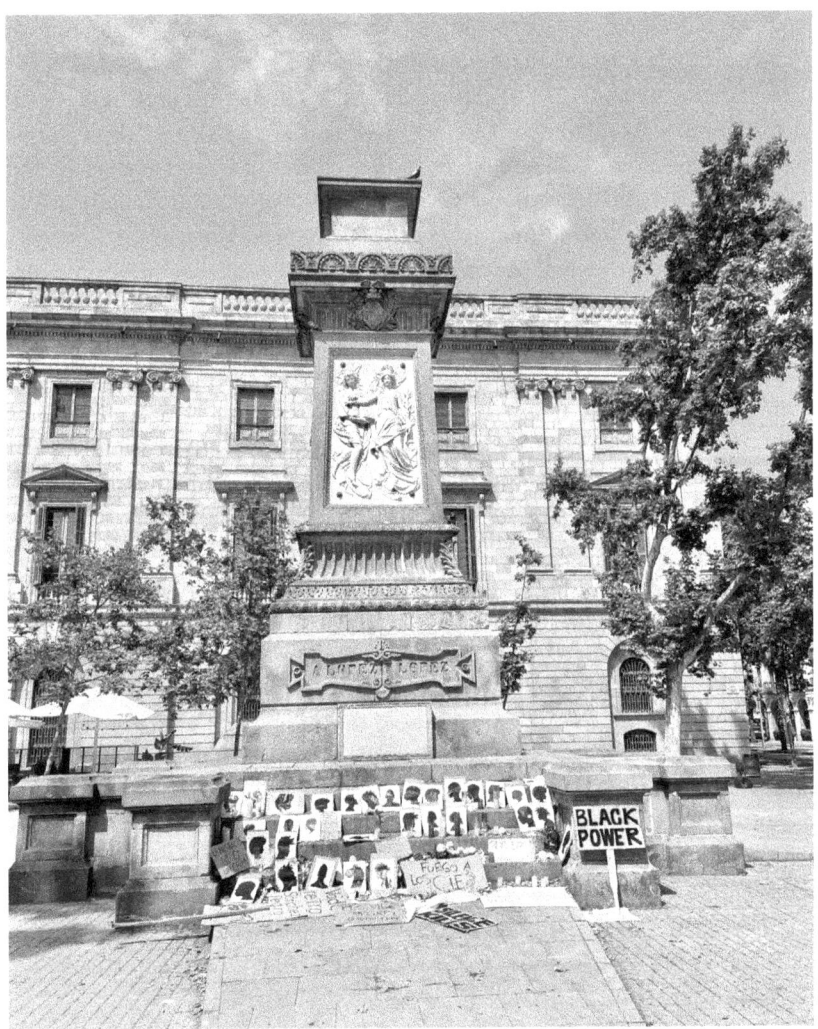

These artistic initiatives, together, have contributed not only to raising the community's awareness of past injustices by provoking reflections on the monument's relationship to history, but also to generating on-going public debates on the legacies of slavery and colonialism *in the present*. As Geoff Ward has stated in another context, while toppling racist icons and monuments is an important symbolic gesture, beyond that, there is also a need to "connect the conversation around symbols to systems to how the history of racism continues to shape society" ("Keynote Conversation").

The other major monument that has become the object of controversy in Barcelona, not surprisingly, is the one dedicated to Columbus, a colonizer who, as we know, established the foundations for slavery, of both indigenous and African populations. Erected by the port at the foot of the famous Ramblas, not far from the López monument, the Columbus monument was inaugurated on June 1, 1888, on the occasion of the Barcelona Universal Exposition (fig. 5.9). As a plaque placed visibly at the site shows, the Barcelona monument commemorated Columbus's first voyage to the Americas and the success of the Catholic monarchs' imperial enterprise; the colonizer reported to King Ferdinand and Queen Isabella in their Barcelona court on his return in April of 1493.[26] Yet, as historian Martín Rodrigo y Alharilla has shown, the timing of the Columbus statue initiative, which developed in parallel to the Universal Exposition—that is, from 1881 to 1888—was more than a mere coincidence ("Memories in Dispute" 364); it represented an extension of the Spanish imperial project in Catalonia.[27] Shortly after Barcelona's city council passed the resolution to build the monument in 1881, the commission in charge of the project held a competition for those wishing to submit designs for the monument. What is striking is the language used in the call for submissions, which claims Columbus as one of Catalonia's own, as one of the nation's "hijos predilectos" ("favorite sons/children"), thus reclaiming, by extension, Catalonia's specific place in the "discovery of the Americas" (*Concurso nacional libre*). For the Catalans who celebrated the construction of the Columbus monument in the 1880s, it came to symbolize the connection between the dream of the Medieval Catalan empire (Rodrigo y Alharilla, "Memories in Dispute" 367; Michonneau)[28] and the colonial ambitions of those in the nineteenth century who traveled to the Americas to seek fortune and who, on their return to the metropolis, invested their newfound capital in the emergent industrial economy of the region (Rodrigo y Alharilla, *Del olvido*; "Spanish Merchants").

Figure 5.9. Columbus monument, Barcelona, July 2023. *Source:* Wikimedia Commons, by RayAdvait, CC BY-SA 4.0.

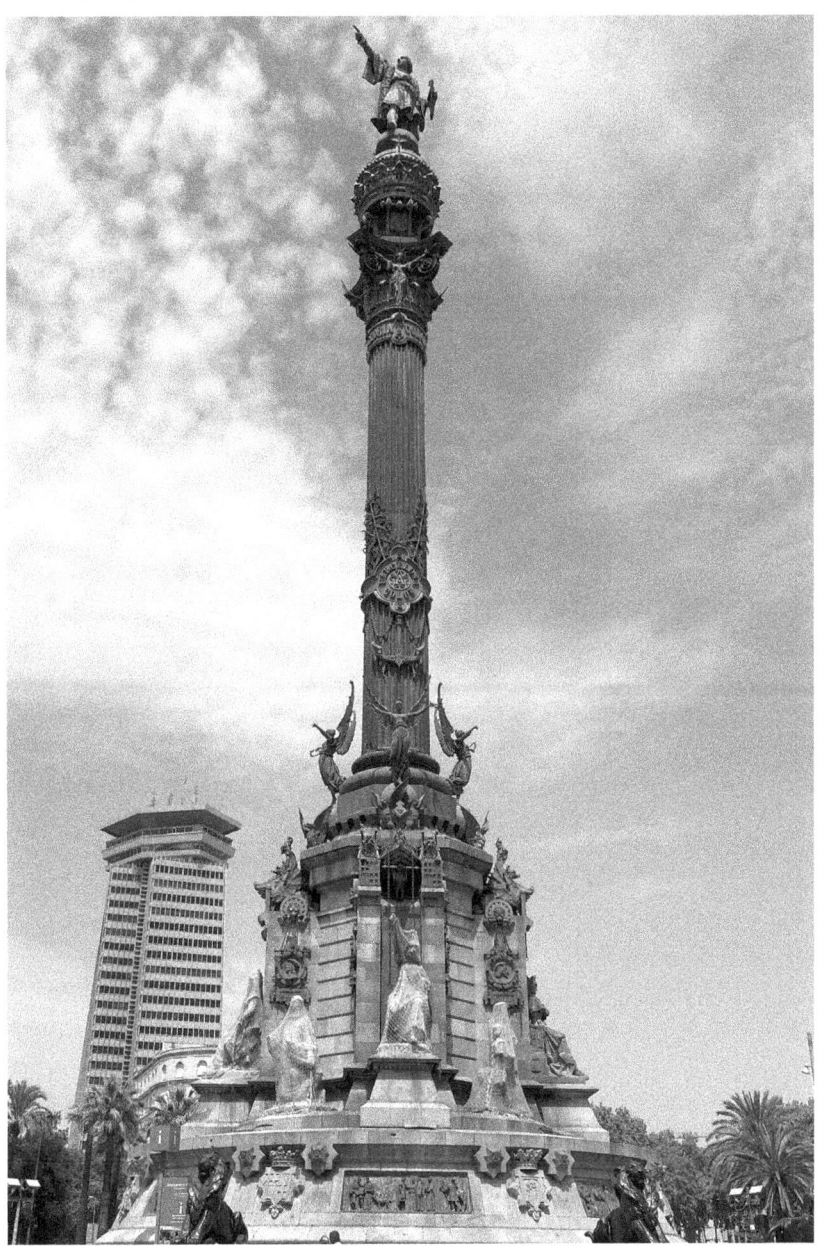

Entangled with the imperial implications of the Columbus monument was Barcelona's project of modernity. The 1888 Universal Exposition was a carefully orchestrated spectacle intended to inaugurate the city's entry into modernity as a European metropolis (Resina 15, 180–81). Thus, the monument represented a gateway to the transatlantic empire—and, hence, to modernity and progress. We know that in the Spanish state, as elsewhere, colonialism was seen as a condition for—and constitutive of—modernity (Blanco 46; Azarmandi, "Commemorating" 62). Furthermore, the monument was to complement the nineteenth-century urban planning projects to modernize the city and offer its visitors the opportunity to imagine the "'new America' of modern Spain," by symbolically reenacting Columbus's voyage of "discovery" (Michonneau 3).[29] The choice of location for the monument was in itself strategic, as it was to be constructed at the point of intersection of the city's major avenues at the time, including the world-famous Rambla, and it would be the first sight to greet those arriving at the port. At almost two hundred feet, it was the tallest monument in the world at the time of its construction. Given its size and complexity, the monument could not have been completed without the private financial contributions of wealthy industrialists, bankers, and the elite Catalan society, including Antonio López, his son Claudio, and his son-in-law Eusebi Güell, whose father Joan was a wealthy industrialist and President of the pro-slavery organization Círculo Hispano Ultramarino.

In view of this context, I turn to more contemporary responses to the Columbus monument in Barcelona to scrutinize the relationship between the politics of commemoration and national history. After the monument's completion in 1888, Catalonia ceased to participate in official Spanish commemorations of Columbus, even during the quarter centenary celebrations held in 1892 in other parts of Spain (Michonneau). While the city of Barcelona capitalized on the monument for touristic purposes,[30] transforming it into an icon of its capital, historian Stéphane Michonneau argues that it no longer had the same meaning as the other Columbus monuments inaugurated elsewhere in Spain, whose primary purpose was to exalt the monarchy and the religious Reconquest. He notes that celebrations of Columbus, on October 12, in Catalonia came about only with the revival of notions such as *Hispanidad* and *raza* in the years following the colonial loss of 1898.

The National Day of Spain, celebrated on October 12 of each year, was established in 1892, through the royal decree of Queen María Cristina of Habsburg, to commemorate Columbus's conquest of the Americas; originally called *Día de la Raza*, the holiday later came to be known as the *Día de la Hispanidad* when it was first celebrated in Madrid in 1935.[31] The notion of "race," particularly that of "Latin race," in Spain had much more to do with genealogy and with "purity of blood" than with biology or skin color, and it emerged from within a uniquely Spanish imperialist discourse (Gabilondo 797). In other words, the ideology of *Hispanidad*, or Pan-Hispanism as it came to be called, represented a colonizing gesture whereby the Spanish state sought to re-assimilate Spanish America into the former empire by claiming a spiritual or cultural unity among the Spanish-speaking world (Arbaiza 40; Loureiro 68). The national holiday subsequently became institutionalized in 1958 during the Franco dictatorship: his regime further exploited the myth of Hispanism to serve its National-Catholic agenda and exalt the fascist dictatorship. Most notably, the legacies of this ideology persisted beyond the end of the dictatorship. Following the transition to democracy, the Socialist government of Felipe González passed a law in 1987 to reaffirm October 12 as a national holiday, and in October 2022, the current President of Spain, Pedro Sánchez, also a Socialist, presided over the celebration, complete with the monarchs' presence, a full-fledged military procession, and a reception in the Royal Palace for prominent politicians and diplomats.

In Barcelona, while Ada Colau has refused to participate in the October 12 festivities, tweeting that it was a "celebration of genocide," the ideology of Hispanism has not completely disappeared in response to the national holiday. Conservative, anti-independence Catalans have taken to the streets to reclaim their national identity as Spaniards and to call for unity under the banner of the central Spanish state, echoing the discourse of Francoism. Decolonial art activist Daniela Ortiz claims that even Catalan nationalists, who favor independence from the Spanish state by which they believe themselves to be colonized,[32] have often turned a blind eye to Catalonia's own complicity in Spanish colonial history ("La 'inverosímil' conclusión"). During the celebration of the National Day of Catalonia on September 11, 2013, Ortiz and García-Boente filmed a video that shows her visiting sites in Barcelona related to slavery and colonialism.[33] When she arrives at the Ciutadella Park where the celebrants are congregated, she goes around and asks them whether they would vote in favor of dismantling the monument to Columbus, were there to be a referendum on this issue. The answers ranged from "no, it doesn't bother me," to "no, it's a symbol of Barcelona" to "no, it's a historical monument to the man who discovered America" to the incredulous response of "Why would we want to do that?" When Ortiz explained the reasons (namely, what Columbus symbolized for people who were victims of colonial violence) and noted that most Catalans wanted Francoist monuments removed, one person replied, "No, it's not the same thing because Franco was the dictator of Spain, there was a war and a lot of people died. Columbus is different." And when Ortiz quipped, "[D]uring colonization, nobody died?" her interlocutor replied, "But that was so many years ago." We can see where this conversation went.

The following year (2014), Ortiz produced another video ("Réplica") in which she is filmed kneeling in front of people who were gathered at the Plaça de Catalunya to celebrate the National Day of Spain, imitating the posture of an indigenous person kneeled before Father Bernardo Boil in a sculpture at the base of the pedestal of the Columbus monument (fig. 5.10). Ortiz included a text in the video urging her audience to reflect on the history of colonization and on the colonial symbols around them. The following year, on October 12, 2015, members of a radical, grassroots collective calling itself "Fuck the Fascism" protested the celebration through the performative gesture of symbolically "raping" the Columbus monument as a response to the colonizer's own violence.[34] Through their

Figure 5.10. Statue of Father Bernat Boil at the base of the Columbus monument, Barcelona, December 2007. *Source:* Wikimedia Commons, public domain.

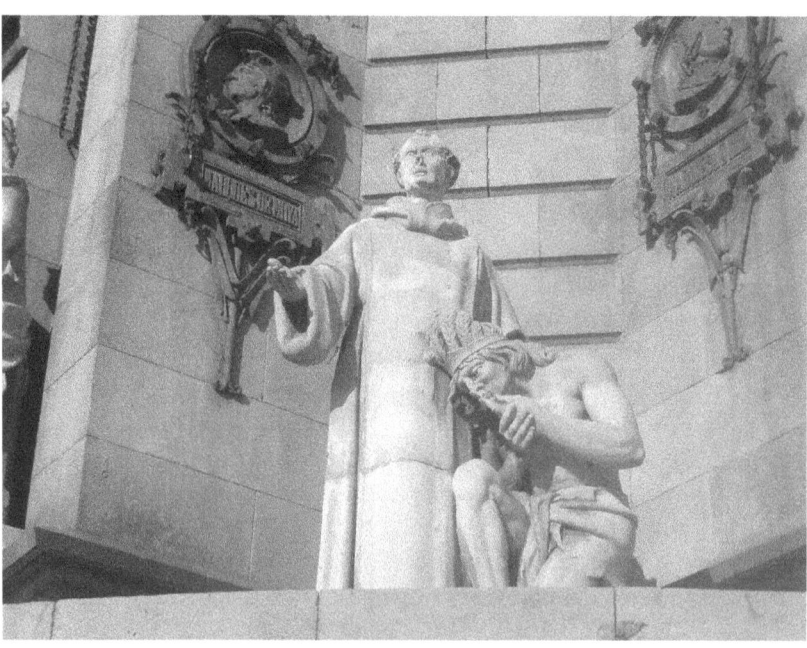

"performance," these activists transformed the act of rape, often employed as a trope for colonial violence (gendered masculine), into a palimpsestic counternarrative that challenged the status of the monument as a colonial symbol.[35] According to one of the organizers, the group has continued their protest yearly on October 12, covering the conqueror's figure with feces and with the blood of one of the performers.

Throughout the past decade, the Popular Unity Candidacy (CUP) has demanded that the Columbus statue be taken down. In 2016 the CUP first presented a petition to the City of Barcelona, asking not only that the Columbus statue be removed, along with that of Antonio López y López, and that the Spanish flag and other symbols of the monarchy be taken down from municipal buildings, but also that October 12 no longer be allowed to be celebrated. The CUP proposed to replace the monument and all the ornaments at the base of the column commemorating the conquest with a "symbol of American resistance against imperialism, oppression and indigenous (and Afro-American) segregation" ("La CUP pedirá"). Their petition was not approved. Yet again, in 2018, after the López statue was finally dismantled in March, the CUP renewed its demands to have the Columbus monument removed, this time by proposing to create a space to "place it at the service of the historical memory of the popular classes" ("La CUP vuelve a proponer"). This demand was conveniently timed to coincide with municipal workers' fight for better working conditions, but again, the CUP failed to get their demand met.

Most recently, in June 2020, amidst the global protests against racism, the public debate around this monument was revived yet once again. This time, Jéssica Albiach, the President of the left-wing coalition Catalonia in Common[36] (Ada Colau's own platform), agreed to remove the Columbus monument. Referring to racism against a Moroccan teen who died in custody in July 2019 at a juvenile center in Andalusia[37] and, more generally, against temporary African workers in Spain, she deliberately drew a connection between institutionalized racism of the present, codified by the Ley de Extranjería, and colonialism of the past ("Los comuns quieren"). However, hours later she backtracked on social media, stating that the sculpture needed to be contextualized in its present site. Only a few days later, Colau declared that she would not take down the monument, but that, instead, she would favor critically contextualizing it in some fashion, by placing a plaque or by organizing an exhibit around it. In her words: "this statue is an icon of the city of Barcelona, for better or for worse, with everything that it implies. . . . The statue of Columbus forms part of the critical memory of the city," but then she went on to add that it was necessary to continue debating with anti-racist groups and with experts on democratic memory, and to engage in a critical analysis of public art ("Ada Colau estudia"). As of this writing (June 2023), there has been no plaque or exhibit around the Columbus statue to contextualize it, as in the Idrissa Diallo Square, although every October 12, anti-racist and anti-colonial groups continue to come out to protest.

We can only speculate on the reasons for Colau's decision to preserve the Columbus monument while agreeing to take down that of Antonio López y López. What is, however, evident is that Catalan nationalist identity politics, as we have seen, have always been deeply entangled with colonialism. Columbus has been transformed into the icon of *catalanidad* (Catalan identity), much as it has always been a symbol of Spanish colonialism. A 2019 exhibit at the MACBA, titled "Undefined Territories: The Colonial Legacy in Art," included a series of works by diasporic artists of various geographical origins to critique colonialism, of which the work of the aforementioned artist Daniela Ortiz formed a part. Her work, which included a series of photographs, videos and a text, linked Columbus to Catalan national identity. In Ortiz's words, her work on Columbus was just one small part of her exhibit, the objective of which was to critique the role of colonial monuments in the construction of collective memory in Catalonia ("La 'inverosímil' conclusión"). Yet some members of the public, goaded on by the conservative anti-independence political party Ciudadanos, reacted to this project by accusing the artist of falsifying Catalan history, alluding to the absurd theory propagated by the nationalist revisionist thinker Jordi Bilbeny that Columbus was Catalan.[38] As the director of the MACBA notes, what Ortiz's critics did was to interpret quite literal-mindedly her ironic and, admittedly polemical, statement that "Columbus was an ambassador of the Generalitat" ("El supremacismo se instala").

In June of 2020, the TV program *Espejo público* (which broadcasts public interest news) interviewed Ortiz, asking her to explain why she felt Columbus monuments needed to be dismantled. She stressed, once again, the connection between the statue, as a colonial symbol, and present-day racist immigration policies in Catalonia. The presenter then interjected the comment that the statue did not offend her, to which the artist quipped back, "Of course, it's because you're white" (Riaño). This comment, along with Ortiz's statement that Spain was a racist country, provoked a strong public reaction and, from that day on, the Peruvian artist became the target of harassment on social media. Right-wing groups jumped on the bandwagon and threatened to denounce her to the government as a terrorist and, according to her, the Catalan left also joined in this defamation. By her account, she decided to leave the country, for the sake of her own and her son's safety, after having lived in Barcelona as an immigrant for 13 years (Mas de Xaxàs).

This incident shows the challenges of doing decolonial or antiracist cultural work in the Spanish state (and this includes Catalonia), of intervening in these public spaces that hold collective memory, to desacralize and divest colonial or racist monuments of taken-for-granted historical narratives that have long gone unchallenged. In fact, there has been quite a bit of pushback from reactionary groups against more recent efforts to force a reckoning of Catalonia's role in the slave trade. For example, the airing of the documentary *Negrers: La Catalunya esclavista*, broadcast on TV3 in February of 2023, was met with great resistance—and with attempts to revive imperial nostalgia, not only from among the conservative Spanish establishment but also from the Catalan left (Muñoz Martínez and Valenciano-Mañé). Yet art and cultural work, by refiguring these public symbols and spaces, offer a tremendous potential for revising our view of history. Although public debates about slavery and reparatory justice are long overdue in the Spanish state, it is significant that many anti-racist and immigrant advocacy groups at the local level, including Pan-Africanist organizations, are reclaiming the public spaces where colonial monuments have stood as symbols of power. The fact that the newly renamed Plaça Idrissa Diallo has become, as of late, a gathering place for anti-racist and pro-immigrant advocacy activists shows how space can quite literally transform memorial practice, turning symbols of power into sites of protest and resistance.[39] Art historian Sarah Beetham has said, "Statues themselves are not history. Statues are memory, important aspects of visual culture that can tell us things about historical moments and people who put them up. Anything that happens to those statues is itself adding other layers of history to them" ("Why Are So Many"). Or another way to put it is that memory is "living history" (De Nardi et al. 2). The trajectories of these monuments reflect how these layers of living history are continuously being revised, transforming memory sites into contested territories.

Notes

1. I am grateful to Helena González, Jordi Guixé, María Xesús Lama López, Oriol López Badell, Celeste Muñoz, Gustau Nerín, Martín Rodrigo-Alharilla, Ulrike Schmieder, Lisa Surwillo, and Aurélie Vialette for the conversations, exchanges, and

sharing of materials that helped me to formulate, develop, and nuance the ideas in this chapter. I thank Rebecca Ingram, Gabrielle Miller, Alex Alonso-Nogueira, and Lisa Surwillo for the opportunity to present my work at their respective universities, and the Center for the Study of Race, Ethnicity, and Equity (CRE²) at Washington University for the Fellowship that provided me with release time to complete this project. My colleagues at the CRE² provided helpful feedback on an earlier version of this study. Any views, findings, conclusions, or recommendations expressed in this publication do not necessarily reflect those of the CRE².

2. This quote is from a recently discovered letter by the famed abolitionist, which was originally published in the *National Republican* on the occasion of the construction of a statue dedicated to Abraham Lincoln in Lincoln Park in Washington, DC, in 1876. This controversial memorial depicts Lincoln standing beside a formerly enslaved African American man in shackles on his knees (White and Sandage).

3. Ana Lucia Araujo discusses, precisely, the racialized nature of collective memory in the context of atrocities, such as slavery (13). Memory, as she notes, is also "molded by class, age, and gender, and impacted not only by the actions of particular social actors but also by changes in national and international contexts" (38).

4. Knauer and Walkowitz's argument recalls Andreas Huyssen's concept of "urban palimpsest," that is, the idea that "city surfaces and structures [are] palimpsests, analogous to texts rewritten, erased, written over in light of political history and the demands of the present" (39).

5. For Araujo, those monuments are not "history," but rather "part of the realm of public memory, which in this context [the effort to reclaim Confederate symbols] is a reconstruction of the past that aims to fulfill the present-day political agenda of a specific group of white individuals who pretend to claim the legacy of those who fought to keep slavery alive" (89).

6. Núria Ricart Ulldemolins, in reference to the dismantling of Francoist monuments following the passage of the Memorial Democràtic in Catalonia, affirms that "la creación de la monumentalidad es una dinámica asociada a la representación simbólica en la lucha—siempre conflictiva—de legitimidades por la hegemonía del espacio y, por tanto, del debate y la esfera pública . . . los monumentos son agentes de los debates dicotómicos de legitimación/deslegitimación de ideas, referentes, ideologías" (the creation of monumentality is a dynamic associated with the always conflictive symbolic representation in the struggle for legitimacy of the hegemony of space and, therefore, of debate and the public sphere . . . monuments are agents of dichotomous debates to legitimize/delegitimize ideas, referents, ideologies) (143–44). All English translations of Spanish quotes are mine.

7. Thanks to Martín Rodrigo-Alharilla's groundbreaking work, there is ample historical evidence to document the origins of López y López's capital in the slave trade, his close ties with an extensive network of slave traffickers, and his anti-abolitionist activities. For the most comprehensive study of López's life and business activities, see Rodrigo y Alharilla (*Un hombre*; *Los Marqueses*).

Confronting the Legacies of Slavery and Colonialism in Public Spaces | 145

8. Different newspapers of the period naturally took different ideological positions in reaction to the events surrounding the controversial monument in honor of the slave trader. While the Republican *El Diluvio* openly denounced the monument and celebrated its removal by the anarchists, the more conservative *Diario de Barcelona* lauded the restoration of the statue to its "proper" place, both in ideological and aesthetic terms, condemning the "rojos" (Communists) who destroyed it in 1936 ("Visita a la Plaza").

9. The Catalan sculptor Frederic Marès restored the statue in 1944, based on the original model, but in stone, rather than in bronze. Notably, Marès also reconstructed the fallen statues of other prominent figures with links to slavery (Guixé 150), including the industrialist Joan Güell, whose son married López y López's daughter, and the statesman and politician General Juan Prim who, as captain general of Puerto Rico (1847–48), imposed extreme repressive measures against all individuals of African descent on the island.

10. The law was motivated by the work of organizations such as the Asociación para la Recuperación de la Memoria Histórica (ARMH), established in 2000, to recover the remains of victims of the Spanish Civil War and Franco's dictatorship and to seek justice for the victims of crimes against human rights, whose perpetrators were granted amnesty in 1977 through a vote of the parliament.

11. One of Colau's promises as a mayor was to encourage a more participatory democracy by establishing a process of consultation with the citizenry of Barcelona, whereby citizens would be able to petition to bring issues of importance to a vote in the City Council ("Aprovades les preguntes de la multiconsulta").

12. The López statue has been placed in the warehouse of the museum, along with the remains of an equestrian statue of Franco and other objects glorifying the dictatorship (Guixé and Ricart 145). For security reasons, this part of the museum is not open to the public, but my understanding is that limited access has been granted to researchers ("El López de Cuba").

13. The EUROM, established in 2012, is a transnational network of institutions and organizations committed to the promotion of memory initiatives.

14. Carrie Ruiz has raised a similar concern surrounding the removal of Francoist monuments after the passage of the 2007 Historical Memory Law: "the removal of the past visual representations has created a double void: a physical one because the plazas and avenues that contained the monuments have been left as empty spaces, and a historical one since all information about that past is omitted. The public sites where the removals have occurred are characterized by a deficiency of any narrative form referring to the past" (121).

15. That Verdaguer, as an employee of the Transatlantic Shipping Company, wrote the poem, dedicated to López, aboard his ship during the journey between Cuba and Spain adds another layer to the interconnection between colonialism and Catalan nationalism.

16. I thank Aurélie Vialette for raising this question.

17. For an account of this controversy, see Martin-Márquez (64–67).

18. In the words of Colau's Deputy Mayor, Gerardo Pisarello: "It's an act of reparation and of recognition. Colonialism and slavery are the worst products of the human species. . . . It's an act of reparation for all those who feel offended by these crimes against humanity. It's also an act of recognition of the Barcelona that we love, a free city" (Castillo).

19. It is, of course, important to move beyond the commemoration of Black death to grant Diallo (and other immigrants in his situation) greater humanity by focusing on the narratives of their lives. While I have been unable to locate information about Diallo's life, beyond the circumstances of his detention and mysterious death, his case is particularly significant in galvanizing activist interventions of human rights and immigrant advocacy organizations (such as Tanquem els CIE), due to the egregious nature of the repression and injustice suffered by the Guinean immigrant, who was denied "fundamental rights such as privacy, legal assistance, moral integrity and personal dignity" (Meyer). The proposal to rename the plaza after the Guinean immigrant, according to a spokesperson for Tanquem els CIE, was not merely to "seek symbolic reparation for Diallo's death, but also to commemorate the struggles and resistances of migrants and to break the tradition of honoring the Catalan slaving tradition through statues and plaques in the city of Barcelona" (text of the petition, translation mine, www.decidim.barcelona/initiatives/i-7?locale=es). Thus, the memorialization of Diallo through the renaming of the plaza, particularly in the wake of the global Black Lives Matter movement, humanizes the individual migrant, granting him new life as a symbol of migrants' struggle for rights, rather than merely relegating him to victim status. In the words of a member of Tanquem els CIE: "To name the plaza after Idrissa is a homage to him, to his family, to everyone who is victim of the racist policies of CIE, but not only honoring them as victims, but also as persons who have radical and revolutionary potential against an unjust system" (Díaz, translation mine). Diallo's case also inspired activist independent filmmaker Xavier Artigas to produce a documentary film, titled *Idrissa, Chronicle of an Ordinary Death* (2018), traveling with Guinean artist Nakany Kanté to Diallo's birthplace in Guinea to find his family and to serve as an advocate for them in their efforts to repatriate his body. The filmmaker's aim was to posthumously restore justice and dignity to Diallo, to assert his humanity in death (Marvena).

20. One of the plaques explains the history of the "Bullangues" as a part of the city's "democratic memory" initiative, commemorating those who participated in the rebellion to fight for a more democratic and egalitarian society.

21. The sign reads: "In the nineteenth century Antonio López y López, the Marquis of Comillas, became rich exploiting people, thanks to the racism and colonial practices of the period."

22. In their words: "La acción #EsclavitudSinComillas busca visibilizar cómo en pleno siglo XXI, en España, la Ley de Extranjería y el racismo institucional

permiten la explotación laboral de personas en beneficio del sistema capitalista-colonialista-patriarcal" ("The action *#EsclavitudSinComillas* seeks to make visible how, in the middle of the twenty-first century, the immigration law in Spain and institutional racism allow for labor exploitation to benefit the capitalist-colonial-patriarchal system"; "Making off 'Esclavitud sin Comillas' ").

23. Huyssen, likewise, favors "strategies of redressing and refunctioning monuments in order to provide lessons of learning about the past," rather than simply eliminating them. In his view, the toppling of a monument, while "purging a festering past," potentially runs the risk of eradicating history by making it invisible (Huyssen 40).

24. The proposal also included the suggestion to inscribe a different passage from Verdaguer's *L'Atlàntida* on the pavement next to the crystal tomb, to put the stone statue to rest, so to speak.

25. Press accounts seem to suggest that this act was organized by Tanquem els CIE to protest the structural violence that led to the deaths of immigrants at the border.

26. The Barcelona monument represented a culminating point in the construction of monuments to the colonizer that had been proliferating all over the world, since the end of the eighteenth century and, particularly, after 1860. Currently, there are about fourteen monuments dedicated to Columbus in the Spanish state, and at least eight monuments to Columbus were erected in rapid succession in Spain between 1888 and 1892, in anticipation of the fourth centenary of the "discovery" of America (Michonneau; Schmidt-Nowara 59). As Schmidt-Nowara notes, the wave of *colonofilia* overtook the Peninsula precisely when the Spanish empire was in crisis (55–59). Spanish efforts to reclaim Columbus as a national symbol emphasized the myth of fraternal harmony between Spain and the Americas, rather than the historical reality of his role as a plundering and bloodthirsty conqueror, as a way of strengthening the ties between the metropolis and the Caribbean colonies at a time when the end of Spain's empire in the Americas was imminent (Schmidt-Nowara 57).

27. Schmidt-Nowara maintains that "Barcelona's commemoration of Columbus linked the city to a glorious chapter in Spanish history . . . and reaffirmed the city's commitment to *la España ultramarina*" (63).

28. At the end of the Medieval period, Barcelona became the capital of a commercial empire that conquered and controlled most of the important regions of the Mediterranean, including Mallorca, Valencia, Ibiza, Sicily, Naples, Sardinia, and Athens. Catalonia was politically independent from Castile during this period.

29. Yet, as Azarmandi notes, "The framing of the statue through 'discovery' and 'voyage,' effectively, negates the violence of colonialism that the statue represents" ("Commemorating" 64).

30. For the ways in which the city continues to use the image of the Columbus monument to promote tourism and commerce, erasing the violence on which it was built, see Azarmandi ("Commemorating" 59–60; "Monumentos" 180).

31. This name was popularized by ultra-conservative intellectual Ramiro de Maeztu's essay "Defensa de la Hispanidad" (1934).

32. Historians and activists have rightly challenged the equalization of Catalan victims of Castilian rule with the colonization and enslavement of African and indigenous populations in the Americas (Azarmandi, "Monumentos" 181; Rubio; Schmieder and Zeuske 310).

33. This video is no longer available online.

34. I owe Azarmandi the reference to this event ("Monumentos" 175). In a personal communication, one of the organizers of Fuck the Fascism explains that the project is "una serie de cortometrajes de porno político re educativo filmados en diferentes ciudades y países, con el objetivo de exponer la verdadera historia oculta tras monumentos que glorifican genocidios, tiranía y esclavitud; mostrando la cara oculta de aquellos venerados héroes patrios que legaron grandes fortunas forjadas con robo, abuso y sangre" ("a series of political and educational pornographic shorts filmed in different cities and countries, with the objective of exposing the true hidden story behind monuments that glorify genocide, tyranny, and slavery; showing the hidden face of those venerated national heroes who bequeathed great fortunes made by theft, abuse and blood").

35. I thank Erika Rodríguez for this observation.

36. This municipal platform emerged in part from the 15-May movement in Spain, and advocates for social justice and a more participatory democracy. Prior to her election as mayor, Colau was an activist on behalf of those who were displaced by mortgage debt following the 2008 economic crisis.

37. The teen, Ilias Tahiri, was violently restrained by security guards, though footage of the incident showed that the youth offered no resistance.

38. Jordi Bilbeny was the founder of the pseudohistorical cultural foundation Institut Nova Història.

39. For a discussion of the connection between space and memorial practice in a different context, see Árvay and Foote. Judith Butler shows how the assembly of marginalized groups has a performative force, especially when it takes the form of bodies assembled in a public space (*Notes* 48). I thank Erika Rodríguez for this reference.

Works Cited

"Ada Colau estudia contextualizar la estatua de Colón, pero no retirarla." *El Periódico*, 15 June 2020.

"Aprovades les preguntes de la multiconsulta." *Ajuntament de Barcelona,* ajuntament.barcelona.cat/participaciociutadana/ca/noticia/aprovades-les-preguntes-per-a-la-multiconsulta-ciutadana_726363. Accessed 24 Feb. 2019.

Aramburu-Zabala Higuera, Miguel Ángel. "La imagen de Antonio López, primer marqués de Comillas." *Estudios de patrimonio*, no. 1, 2018, pp. 13–68.

Araujo, Ana Lucia, editor. *Slavery in the Age of Memory: Engaging the Past*. Bloomsbury Academic, 2021.

Arbaiza, Diana. *The Spirit of Hispanism: Commerce, Culture, and Identity Across the Atlantic, 1875–1936*. U of Notre Dame P, 2020.

Árvay, Anett, and Kenneth Foote. "The Spatiality of Memoryscapes, Public Memory, and Commemoration." *The Routledge Handbook of Memory and Place*, edited by Sarah De Nardi et al., Routledge, 2020, pp. 129–37.

Azarmandi, Mahdis. "Commemorating No-bodies—Christopher Columbus and the Violence of Social-Forgetting." *Somatechnics*, vol. 6, no. 1, 2016, pp. 56–71.

———. "Monumentos coloniales, migración y memoria en la Barcelona (post)colonial." *Rivista dell'Istituto di Storia dell'Europa Mediterranea*, no. 11, 2020, pp. 169–202.

Azarmandi, Mahdis, and Roberto D. Hernández. "Colonial Redux: When Re-naming Silences—Antonio López y López and Nelson Mandela." *Borderlands*, vol. 16, no. 1, 2017, pp. 1–27.

———. "Decolonizing Spain: Colonial Legacies and the Importance of Renaming." *Truthout*, 27 Sept. 2015, truthout.org/articles/decolonizing-spain-colonial-legacies-and-the-importance-of-renaming/.

"Barcelona Gets Surprise New Anti-racism Statue." *Catalan News*, 31 Jan. 2022.

Blanco, Alda. *Cultura y conciencia imperial en la España del siglo XIX*. U de València (Spain), 2012.

Butler, Judith. *Notes Toward a Performative Theory of Assembly*. Harvard UP, 2015.

Castillo Cerezuela, Queralt. "Adiós Antonio López, hola Idrissa Diallo." *El Salto*, 4 Mar. 2018, www.elsaltodiario.com/colonialismo/retirada-estatua-esclavista-antonio-lopez-barcelona.

"Los comuns quieren retirar el monumento a Colón de Barcelona." *Metrópoli Abierta*, 13 June 2020, metropoliabierta.elespanol.com/informacion-municipal/20200613/los-comuns-quieren-retirar-el-monumento-colon-de-barcelona/497450319_0.html.

Concurso nacional libre: Monumento a Cristóbal Colón, proyecto del arquitecto D. C. Buigas Monrabá. Barcelona: Talleres de la Renaixensa, 1882.

"Crónica." *La Vanguardia*, 25 Sept. 1883.

"La CUP pedirá la retirada del monumento a Colón en Barcelona." *El País*, 26 Sept. 2016.

"La CUP vuelve a proponer la retirada del monumento a Colón y repensar el espacio." *El Periódico*, 10 Dec. 2018.

Dell, Upton. *What Can and Can't Be Said: Race, Uplift, and Monument Building in the Contemporary South*. Yale UP, 2015.

De Nardi, Sarah, et al. "Introduction." *The Routledge Handbook of Memory and Place*, edited by Sarah De Nardi et al., Routledge, 2020, pp. 1–7.

Díaz, Sato. "Plaza Idrissa Diallo: Quitarle la plaza al negrero para dársela al esclavo." *Cuartopoder*, 4 Jan. 2018, www.cuartopoder.es/espana/2018/01/04/plaza-idrissa-diallo-barcelona-esclavo/.

"Estat Nació—Part 1." *MACBA*, www.macba.cat/en/art-artists/artists/ortiz-daniela-quiroga-xose/estat-nacio-part-1-exercici-1-historia-antoni-lopez. Accessed 15 Feb. 2023.

Gabilondo, Joseba. "Genealogía de la 'raza latina': Para una teoría Atlántica de las estructuras raciales hispanas." *Revista Iberoamericana*, vol. 75, no. 228, 2009, pp. 795–818.

Guixé, Jordi. "Interview with Andreas Huyssen: Trumpism as a Social Movement Is a New Form of Fascism." *Observing Memories*, no. 6, Dec. 2022, pp. 34–41.

Guixé Coromines, Jordi, and Núria Ricart Ulldemolins. "To López y López. The Fifth Assault. Inconvenient Memories in the Public Space." *Rivista dell'Istituto dei Storia dell'Europa Mediterranea*, no. 7, 2020, pp. 139–67.

Hall, Stuart. "Un-settling 'the Heritage,' Re-imagining the Post-Nation. Whose Heritage?" *Third Text* 13, vol. 49, 2000, pp. 3–13.

"Los insultos en pedestal." *El Diluvio*, 23 Aug. 1936.

"La 'inverosímil' conclusión de la catalanidad de Colón." *El País*, 8 Aug. 2019.

"Keynote Conversation: Toward Monumental Justice." *Vimeo*, uploaded by Pulitzer Arts Foundation, 20 July 2020, vimeo.com/441046412.

Knauer, Lisa Maya, and Daniel J. Walkowitz. "Introduction: Memory, Race, and the Nation in Public Spaces." *Contested Histories in Public Space*, edited by Daniel Walkowitz and Lisa Maya Knauer, Duke UP, 2009, pp. 1–27.

Ley de la Memoria Histórica (Ley 52/2007 de 26 de diciembre). *Ministerio de Política Territorial y Memoria Democrática*, 26 Dec. 2007, www.mpr.gob.es/memoria-democratica/normativa-y-otros-recusos/Paginas/ley-memoria-historica.aspx.

"El López de Cuba se queda, dice Barcelona a Cantabria." *La Vanguardia*, 10 March 2018.

Loureiro, Ángel. "Spanish Nationalism and the Ghost of Empire." *Journal of Spanish Cultural Studies*, vol. 4, no. 1, 2003, pp. 65–76.

"Making off 'Esclavitud sin Comillas.' Acción Fotográfica." *YouTube*, uploaded by SOS Racisme, 24 Oct. 2018, www.youtube.com/watch?v=3XObXf4MDcM.

Martin-Márquez, Susan. *Disorientations: Spanish Colonialism in Africa and the Performance of Identity*. Yale UP, 2008.

Marvena, Elisa. "Idrissa Diallo: From an Unmarked Grave to the Symbol of Migrant Struggle in Spain." *Global Voices*, 2 Mar. 2018, globalvoices.org/2018/03/02/idrissa-diallo-from-an-unmarked-grave-to-the-symbol-of-migrant-struggle-in-spain/.

Mas de Xaxàs, Xavier. "La artista Daniela Ortiz sale de España por una campaña de amenazas racistas." *La Vanguardia*, 2 Aug. 2020.

Memorial Democràtic. memoria.gencat.cat/ca/inici. Accessed 10 Feb. 2023.

Meyer, Willy. "Death of Idrissa Diallo in the Detention Centre for Foreigners (CIE) in Barcelona. Permanent violation of human rights, mistreatment and repression in Spanish Dentention Centres." Question to the Commission of the European Parliament, 12 Jan. 2012, www.europarl.europa.eu/doceo/document/E-7-2012-000333_EN.html.

Michonneau, Stéphane. "¿Por qué un monumento a Colón en Barcelona?" *Ajuntament de Barcelona*, Dec. 2017, ajuntament.barcelona.cat/memoriademocratica/wp-content/uploads/2017/12/Per-que-un-monument-de-Colom-a-Barcelona-Michonneau-%C3%A1-es-ES.pdf.

"El monumento de Antonio López y López destruido por el pueblo." *La Vanguardia*, 25 Aug. 1936.

Muñoz Martínez, Celeste, and Alba Valenciano-Mañé. "De memories, distorsions i conflictes: El passat esclavista i colonial català en el punt de mira." *Catarsi*, 26 Apr. 2023, catarsimagazin.cat/de-memories-distorsions-i-conflictes-el-passat-esclavista-i-colonial-catala-en-el-punt-de-mira/.

Nora, Pierre. "Between Memory and History: *Les Lieux de Mémoire*." *Representations*, no. 26, 1989, pp. 7–24.

Piqueras, José Antonio. *La esclavitud en las Españas: Un lazo transatlántico*. Catarata, 2017.

"Réplica." *YouTube*, uploaded by daniela ortiz,15 Oct. 2014, www.youtube.com/watch?v=9bQz4pPGg9k.

Resina, Joan Ramon. *Barcelona's Vocation of Modernity: Rise and Decline of an Urban Image*. Stanford UP, 2008.

Riaño, Peio H. "Daniela Ortiz: 'Conforme tu voz crece, la violencia contra ti también.'" *El País*, 5 Aug. 2020.

Ricart Ulldemolins, Núria. "Monumentos. Memoria y espacio público. 2007–2017." *Diez años de leyes y políticas de memoria (2007–2017)*, edited by Jordi Guixé et al., Catarata, 2019, pp. 143–58.

Ricart Ulldemolins, Núria, and Jordi Guixé Coromines. "Arte público y memoria: Sistemas de significado." *Geografía e Historia*, vol. 27, 2020, pp. 21–45.

Rodrigo y Alharilla, Martín, editor. *Del olvido a la memoria: La esclavitud en la España contemporánea*. Icaria, 2022.

———. *Un hombre, mil negocios: La controvertida historia de Antonio López, Marqués de Comillas*. Ariel, 2021.

———. *Los marqueses de Comillas 1817–1925: Antonio y Claudio López*. LID Editorial Empresarial, 2000.

———. "Memories in Dispute: Statues in Honour of Enslavers and Conquerors in Barcelona." *Comparativ*, vol. 31, 2021, 356–73.

———. "Spanish Merchants and the Slave Trade: From Legality to Illegality, 1814–1870." *Slavery and Antislavery in Spain's Atlantic Empire*, edited by Josep M. Fradera and Christopher Schmidt-Nowara, Berghahn Books, 2013, pp. 176–99.

Rodrigo y Alharilla, Martín, and Lizbeth Chaviano Pérez, editors. *Negreros y esclavos: Barcelona y la esclavitud atlántica (siglos XVI–XIX)*. Icaria, 2017.

Rowlands, Michael, and Christopher Tilley. "Monuments and Memorials." *Handbook of Material Culture*, edited by Christopher Tilley et al., Sage, 2006, pp. 500–15.

Rubio, Maria. "Por qué Catalunya nunca ha sido una colonia: así lo ven tres activistas descoloniales." *Público*, 29 Nov. 2019, www.publico.es/sociedad/catalunya-sido-colonia-ven-tres-activistas-decoloniales.html.

Ruiz, Carrie L. "Pieces from the Past: Contestation around Francoist Monuments in Modern-Day Spain." *Outrage: Art, Controversy, and Society*, edited by Richard Howells, Andrea Ritivoi and Judith Schachter, Palgrave McMillan, 2021, pp. 101–28.

Schmidt-Nowara, Christopher. "Columbus's Remains, Columbus in Chains: Commemoration and Its Discontents in Late Nineteenth-Century Spain and Cuba." *The Conquest of History: Spanish Colonialism and National Histories in the Nineteenth Century*, U of Pittsburgh P, 2006, pp. 53–95.

Schmieder, Ulrike, and Michael Zeuske. "Introduction. Falling Statues around the Atlantic: Colonizers, Enslavers, and White Abolitionists as Targets of Anti-Racist Activism and the Historical Background of Non-decolonized Memorial Cityscapes." *Comparativ*, vol. 31, no. 3–4, 2021, pp. 297–313.

"El supremacismo se instala en el Macba: Colón era catalán." *Crónica Global*, 4 Aug. 2019, cronicaglobal.elespanol.com/creacion/colon-catalan-macba_266250_102.html.

Surwillo, Lisa. *Monsters by Trade: Slave Traffickers in Modern Spanish Literature and Culture*. Stanford UP, 2014.

Tsuchiya, Akiko. "Monuments and Public Memory: Antonio López y López, Slavery, and the Cuban-Catalan Connection." *Nineteenth-Century Contexts*, vol. 41, no. 5, 2019, pp. 479–500.

"Visita a la Plaza Antonio López y apertura del nuevo tramo del Paseo de Colón." *La Vanguardia*, 26 Jan. 1944.

White, Jonathan W., and Scott Sandage. "What Frederick Douglass Had to Say About Monuments." *Smithsonian Magazine*, 30 June 2020.

"Why Are So Many Confederate and Columbus Statues Coming Down?" *YouTube*, uploaded by Inside Edition, 12 July 2020, www.youtube.com/watch?v=_7LiMKJUK9A.

Chapter 6

Spain and the Year of Toppled Statues of Enslavers and Colonizers
The Examples of Madrid and Cádiz

Ulrike Schmieder[1]

In 2020, the pandemic affected Afro-descendant persons more severely than other groups of people, for instance in the United States, Great Britain, France, and Brazil, due to their socioeconomic situation (housing that made social distancing and home-schooling difficult), their employment (work as manual workers with many client contacts), and the high incidence of preexisting medical conditions resulting from racialized social inequality and restricted access to medical care, as well as from being constant targets of racist attacks ranging from verbal abuse to murder (*Racial Discrimination*). After the killing of George Floyd in Minneapolis in May, 2020 became the year in which enslavers' and colonizers' monuments were removed by the Black Lives Matter movement or by sympathizing town councils, but it was also the year of violent counter-activism by white supremacists (Schmieder and Zeuske).

The research on the events of 2020 forms part of my project referring to the physical sites of memory of enslavement[2] such as museums and monuments and the material vestiges of the slavery past, in France and Spain, Martinique and Cuba. After having witnessed the silences and the mythical, distorted versions of the history of enslavement at many historical sites during my research on slavery and post-emancipation in Martinique and Cuba (Schmieder, *Nach der Sklaverei*), I extended the perspective to the legacies and memories of enslavement on both islands. The former colonial powers—France and Spain—were included in my research because material vestiges of slavery-based businesses, traces of enslavers and enslaved persons, deliberately forgotten, have resurfaced in both countries in the last three decades, a process worthy of being researched from a comparative perspective as well. Until now, studies on the sites and politics of memory have usually been carried out with reference to a single town, region, or country, or a single empire or linguistic space. Occasionally, comparisons have focused on the United Kingdom and France (Chivallon, *L'usage*; Hourcade), the United Kingdom and the Netherlands (Nimako and Small) in Europe, and the United States and Brazil in America (Araujo).

The remembrance of enslavement in museums and the public space from a de-colonial perspective has advanced slowly. Many sites historically connected to Atlantic slavery are not visible as such today and many places have not yet been identified. New memory regimes commemorating the enslaved as victims or resisters[3] coexist with memory regimes inherited from other historical periods. Monuments paying homage to enslavers, colonizers, and defenders of slavery remain in the public space. The attacks on statues occurred very selectively, sometimes intentionally (Rodrigo, *Memories in Dispute*), sometimes because the full history of enslavement is not known, for instance the role that European emperors, kings, and queens played in the traffic of African captives (Schmieder and Zeuske 305–309). Only a very small group of historians have devoted their research to this topic (Pettigrew in the UK, Diakité in France, López, Piqueras in Spain, Caldeira in Portugal). School curricula either did not address the topic at all or did not make it compulsory or approached it from a colonial-apologetic angle (for instance in Portugal, Ribeiro da Silva). Even in France, where the Taubira law prescribes the inclusion of the history of slavery, there are still gaps in teaching that history (Ledoux).

The research on sites of memory and oblivion includes documentation of memorial sites and research through oral history methods, participant observation in commemorative ceremonies, and the analysis of media debates. In the case of statues and monuments one has to decipher their visual narrative and textual message and analyze their visibility depending largely on their location and size. The interlocutors of the expert interviews in this oral history research were academics, particularly historians; artists and filmmakers engaged in the politics of memory with reference to enslavement; museum staff; and members of memorial associations of Antilleans and Africans.

Although Pierre Nora (*Les lieux de mémoire*) excluded overseas France from his definition of *lieux de mémoire* of French national identity, his basic idea is useful: a monument is not a site of memory because of its mere existence, but it becomes a site of memory through commemoration rituals taking place there (Nora, *Entre mémoire* 34–35). The toppling of a statue makes it a site of counter-memories that contest the original intention of the builders of the monument. The statue of Edward Colston, thrown into the river, retrieved, but not re-erected at the original site in a vertical position, but presented in a horizontal position, with the labeling of protesters in the M Shed Museum (temporarily), no longer commemorated the benefactor of the city of Bristol, but rather the trafficker of African captives who invested a part of his fortune in charity.

This chapter will refer to two Spanish cities (Cádiz and Madrid) whose involvement in enslavement in the Atlantic space is not as well-known as that of Barcelona, the "capital city of financial return" from Cuban plantation slavery (Rodrigo, *Barcelona*), where the statue of the notorious Cantabrian enslaver Antonio López was removed by the city in 2018. Cádiz, the most important Spanish port for human trafficking from African coasts in the eighteenth and nineteenth centuries (Chaviano, *Cádiz*), had been a place for the investment of profits from slavery (Cayuela and Bahamonde 135; Rodrigo, *From Slave Trade* 601–06) and a space where enslaved Africans lived from the fifteenth to the nineteenth centuries (Morgado, *Una Metrópoli esclavista*). Madrid, once a colonial metropolis, was the residential city of kings and queens who profited from the trade in African captives. Enslaved Africans were brought to Madrid (López, *La esclavitud*), and the colonialist and pro-slavery lobby influenced politics there (Schmidt-Nowara 144–150). Money from Cuban slavery flowed to the capital city (Cayuela and Bahamonde). Is there an awareness that Madrid and Cádiz had connections to the enslavement past and monuments related to that history? Most studies on the memories of slavery in Spanish towns focus on Barcelona (Tsuchiya; Rodrigo, *Memories in Dispute*; Guixé and Ricart; Azarmandi), some on Madrid or on Madrid and Catalonia (González et al.; Surwillo; Schmieder, "Sites of Memory"; "Lugares de memoria"). The non-remembrance of enslavement in Cádiz had been studied only by Schmieder

(*Orte des Erinnerns*, 2012). Has the memorial culture changed since then? Who are the protagonists of the concealment of enslavement and colonial crimes, who looks at this past with a critical, de-colonial intention?

Cádiz: Pride in a "Heroic" Colonial Past and an Almost Total Silence about Its Leading Role in the Enslavement of Africans

There are few studies about the entanglements of Cádiz, from 1717 to 1790 the seat of the Casa de Contratación, the institution governing the American trade, with the traffic in captured Africans to America, in the periods of the trade monopoly, the "legal" enslaving commerce (1789–1819) and illegal human trafficking (1820–1873). An early pioneering study referred to the Compañía Gaditana de Negros as the owner of an *asiento*, a monopoly contract for delivering African captives to Spanish America between 1765 and 1779 (Torres). The study by Arturo Morgado about the slavery of Africans in the city is known among historians, but the local media was not interested in the topic (Morgado, personal interview). A conference held in 2017 concerning Cádiz and enslavement (Cózar and Rodrigo) was mentioned in newspaper articles, as well as *La orca del Atlántico*, María del Carmen Cózar's book about the most important human trafficker in Cádiz, Pedro Martínez (José Antonio López). However, the media coverage and the public resonance of the topic are insignificant compared with the debates in Barcelona (Rodrigo, *Un hombre* 9–26).

The publications of Cózar ("Entre Cádiz" 233) and Martín Rodrigo ("Cádiz y el tráfico ilegal" 216; "From Slave Trade" 604–05) revealed the locations of the residences of enslavers Pedro Martínez (fig. 6.1), Antonio Vinent Vives, and Peter Harmony.

Lydia Pastrana ("El patrimonio" 233–38, personal interviews) recently identified more former residences and company seats of enslavers, of Antonio López, Pedro Juan de Zulueta, and Antonio de Zulueta, as did María Vázquez-Fariñas (210–19) with respect to the Abárzuza brothers. The related project directed by Martín Rodrigo, "Memories of Slavery and the Slave Trade in Contemporary Spain," involves mapping the traces of enslavers for each town investigated (Barcelona and smaller Catalan port towns, Madrid, Cádiz, Bilbao). In 2020 when the statues of enslavers were destroyed, this academic knowledge was not yet available to the public. Information about the Compañía Gaditana de Negros, the debate of the Cortes of 1812 on the abolition of slavery (Vila Vilar), and the presence of the enslaved in

Figure 6.1. Detail of former residence of enslaver Pedro Martínez in Cádiz, 29 calle Ancha, Sept. 2018. *Source:* Photo by the author.

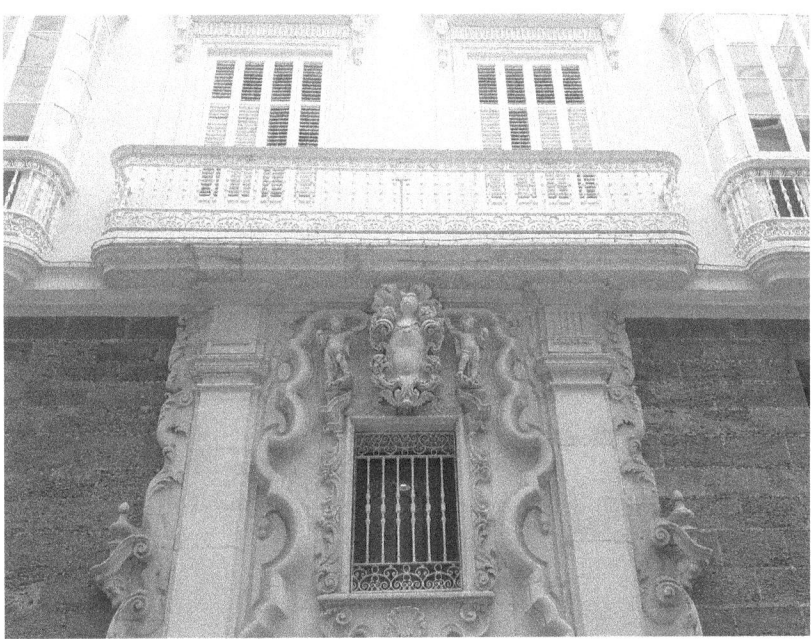

Cádiz was accessible. There is subliminal remembrance of the origins of the fortune in slavery of influential local families, like the Abárzuza. The Abárzuza Hermanos company in Havana trafficked in enslaved persons; the brothers José and Francisco maintained a base for this commerce in Sierra Leone. After their return to Cádiz in 1845 they continued this traffic and worked as bankers, insurers, and wine merchants. As late as 1860 they were transporting 1,250 captives from Angola to Cuba on the steamship *Quevedo* (Rodrigo, "Cádiz y el tráfico ilegal" 208–11). The Abárzuza family owned a bodega of sherry in El Puerto de Santa María till the 1960s (Soto) and they maintained their political influence in Cádiz.

The local museums, such as the Museo de Cádiz, Museo de las Cortes, and Centro Cultural El Doce ignore Cádiz's enslavement past completely. Instead, the role of Cádiz in the American trade, which produced the opulence of the eighteenth century and enabled the building of the giant Catedral de las Américas, is seen as something of which to be proud. In 2017, the tricentenary of the transfer of the Casa de Contratación from Seville to Cádiz was celebrated with great pomp without a hint of de-colonial thinking.

Colonial nostalgia marks the representation of a glorious, golden age past of commerce and the acquisition of scientific knowledge in the museums, the Ruta de los Cargadores a Indias—the touristic route of monopoly traders with America—and commemoration in the public space. A plaque on the main street, referring to "DISTINGUISHED PEOPLE FROM CADIZ IN XVIIITH CENTURY," reads: "Cadiz is the centre of the world thanks to the trading. A bridge between Europe and the Americas" (fig. 6.2).

The historian Fernando Osuna García from the Cultural Foundation of Cádiz points to the Compañía Gaditana de Negros when he shows the famous watchtower of Tavira, owned by the Marqueses de Recaño, cargadores a Indias, to visitors (Osuna). The permanent exhibition at the tower glorifies the trade with the Americas and fails to mention that the imported products were the result of a system of forced labor by indigenous peoples (silver, mercury) and by enslaved Africans (sugar, coffee, cacao, cotton) (MacCreery 38–48, 51–54). On Osuna's initiative, local slavery appeared in 2017 in a municipal cartoon exhibition for young people.[4]

What people in Cádiz could also have known in 2020 is the origin of the money of Claudio López Bru (1853–1925), who is honored with a giant monument from 1922. López Bru had been a benefactor of the town and the Church with money inherited from his father, Antonio López (1817–1883), whose trade in and ownership of enslaved Africans and speculation in Cuban plantations had been proven (Rodrigo, *Los marqueses* 18–25). Claudio López Bru had directed the Cádiz branch of the steamship company and managed his father's businesses. He inherited the nobility title of Marqués de Comillas and parts of the immense slavery-based fortune (Rodrigo, *Entre Barcelona*). He became president of the Banco Hispano Colonial, the Crédito Mercantil, the Compañia Trasatlántica, whose steamships connected Spain with its colonies, and the Compañía General de Tabacos de Filipinas. In Morocco various companies of the Comillas holding participated in the founding of the mining company Sociedad Española de Minas del Rif. In Equatorial Guinea, the Compañía Trasatlántica owned African workers on cocoa plantations who were subjugated to "neo-slavery" labor relations (Martino). Claudio López Bru followed his father in exploiting colonized populations and, like him, he did everything to prevent the impending loss of Cuba (Rodrigo, *Los Marqueses* 184–92, 203–12, 236–40, 308–16). He promoted a special Catholic social policy toward the new working class, and he supported the monarchist and clerical right. He founded and financed the Universidad Pontificia de Comillas. The Catholic Church even considered canonizing him (Rodrigo, *Los Marqueses* 269–92, 295). The pedestal of the memorial in Cádiz (a column with a bust of Claudio López and the genius of Christianity on its top,

Figure 6.2. Public commemorative plaque celebrating Cádiz as "bridge town between Europe and the Americas," Sept. 2018. *Source:* Photo by the author.

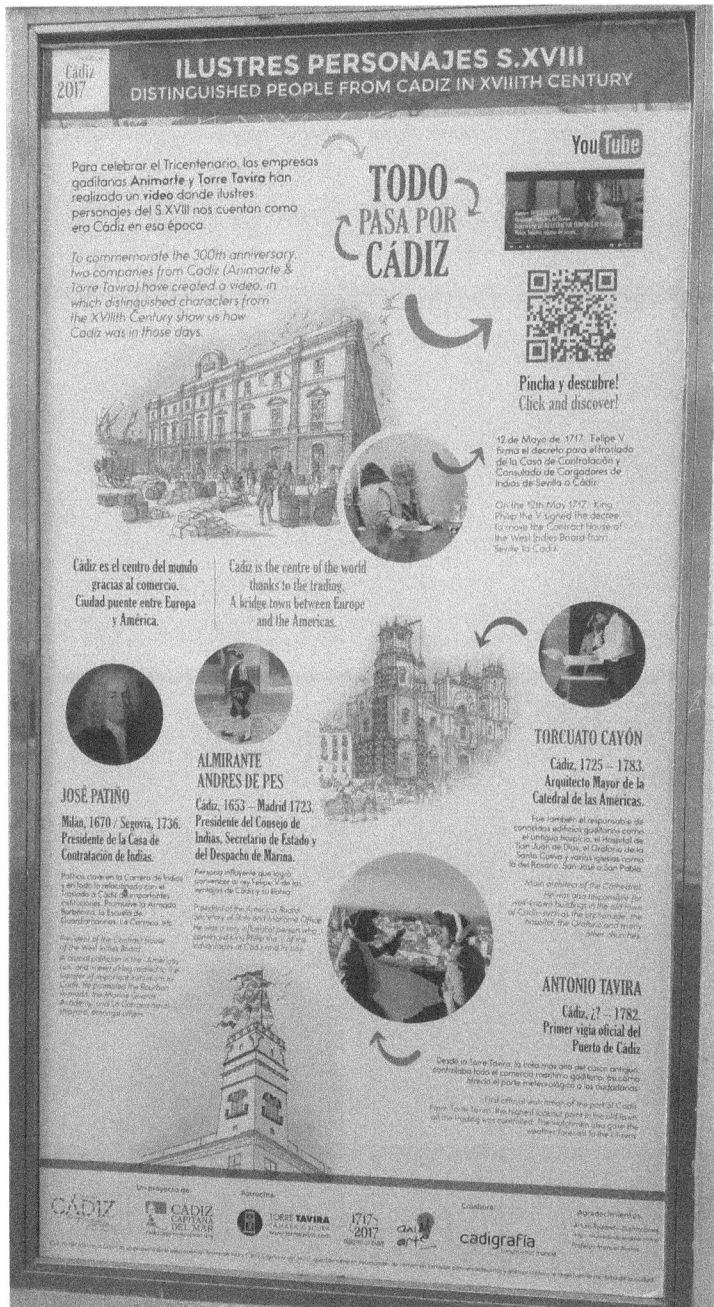

with allusions to seafaring) bears the inscription "HOMENAJE AL CONSTANTE PROPAGANDISTA DE LA UNION HISPANOAMERICANA" ("Homage to the constant propagandist of the Spanish-American Union"). The figures of a lion and a condor symbolize Europe and America (fig. 6.3).

Figure 6.3. Monument for Claudio López Bru, II Marqués de Comillas, in Cádiz, Sept. 2018. *Source:* Photo by the author.

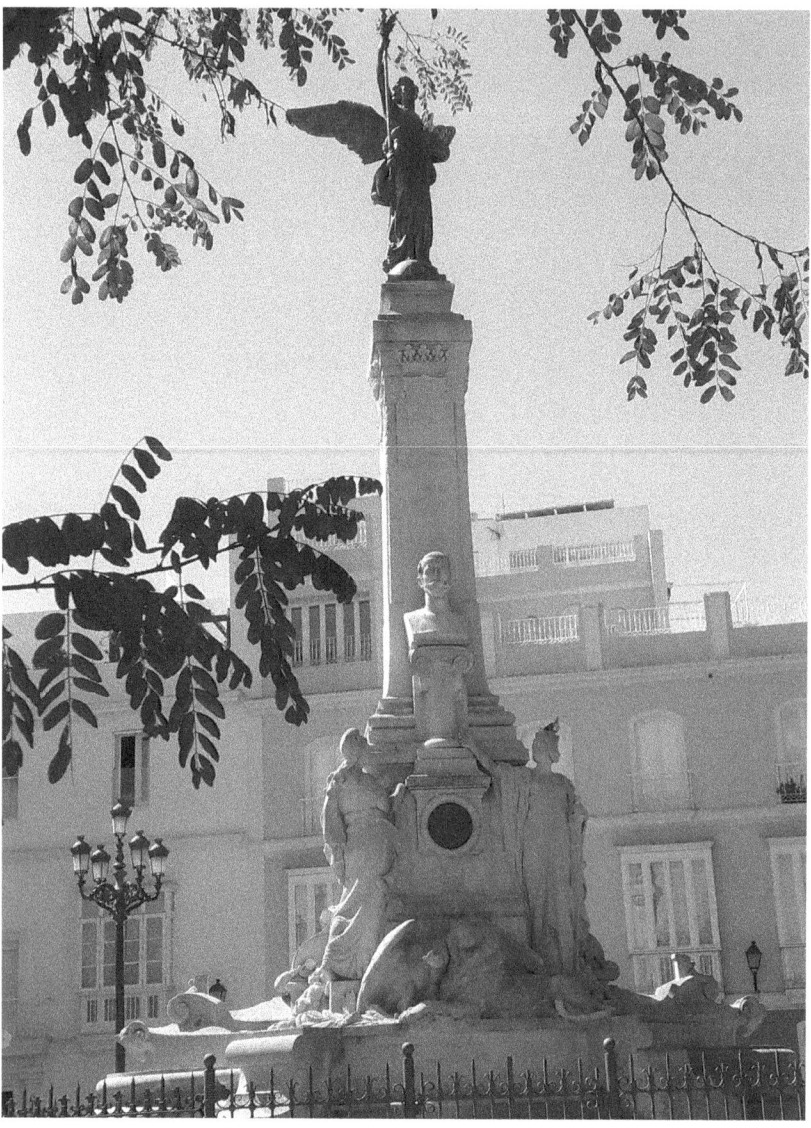

Nobody protested in 2020 against this monument, although it honors a profiteer from the traffic of African captives and slavery through heritage and propagates colonialist ideology. The most important local newspaper, *El Diario de Cádiz*, reported cursorily about the Black Lives Matter movement after the murder of George Floyd as part of US-American politics (Jordá). One journalist expressed his pride that in Cádiz monuments had not been vandalized and emphasized that statues of Spanish and American personalities coexisted peacefully in Cádiz. He enumerated all the monuments, but neither their connections to slavery via King Carlos III nor Claudio López were mentioned. Conflicts around statues honoring fascists were mentioned, with most readers commenting on that. One commentator referred to slavery in Cuba and Spanish colonialism in North Africa (Hidalgo). Only a report about the Black Lives Matter demonstration in front of the cathedral on 14 June 2020 referred to Spanish anti-Blackness and the death of African refugees in the Mediterranean. The solidarity with George Floyd would overlook the deaths of people of color in custody in Spain. An appendix pointed to the non-abolition of slavery by the Constitution of 1812, and to Cádiz as market of human trafficking until the mid-nineteenth century (Vera), proof that some knowledge circulated about Cádiz and enslavement beyond the academy. Precise proposals about what to do in Cádiz to commemorate slavery's past were not made.

Although Cádiz has been going through a process of renaming streets named after supporters of the dictator Franco (*Catálogo*), there was no debate comparable to the one in the French port towns (Schmieder, *Monuments*) about streets named after enslavers and defenders of slavery and colonialism in Cuba. Cádiz has still a calle Antonio López, and a calle O'Reilly paying tribute to Alejandro O'Reilly McDowel (1723–1794), a military commander in Cuba and governor of Louisiana before he became captain-general of Andalusia. The descendants of his Cuban marriage became members of the sugar aristocracy, and he carried on trade with enslaved persons (Maldonado; Franco 47). In 2021 the Alameda Marqués de Comillas (referring to Claudio López Bru), had been renamed to Alameda Hermanas Carvia Bernal celebrating Ana and Amalia Carvia Bernal, pioneers of the movement for the women's suffrage. The Alameda Apodaca had got the new name Calle Clara Campoamor, recognizing an important leftist and feminist politician of the Second Spanish Republic (*Repertorio*). It had honored Juan Ruiz de Apodaca y Eliza (1754–1835), Capitán General of Cuba (1812–1816), during the upswing of sugar production and slavery. He continued the reign of terror against Afro-Cubans begun by his predecessor Somoruelos after the anti-slavery, anti-colonial conspiracy led by Afro-Cuban militiaman José Antonio Aponte. Apodaca was connected

162 | Ulrike Schmieder

to his birth-town of Cádiz through leading positions at the port´s arsenal (Ortuño; Ferrer 325). Both rebaptisms cannot be considered as elements of a decolonization of the public space of Cádiz. They let fall the colonial past of the town into oblivion and reinforce the idea that only white people had done something worth to commemorate it. The choice of persons of color who had resisted enslavement and colonialism or had fought against the legacies in racism would have a decolonizing effect.

Nobody suggested adding commemorative plaques to the local monuments for Segismundo Moret (fig. 6.4), the author of the Free Womb Law in Cuba, 1870, and Emilio Castelar, the minister responsible for the

Figure 6.4. Monument for Segismundo Moret, honored as liberal, not abolitionist politician, Plaza San Juan de Dios, Cádiz, September 2018. *Source:* Photo by the author.

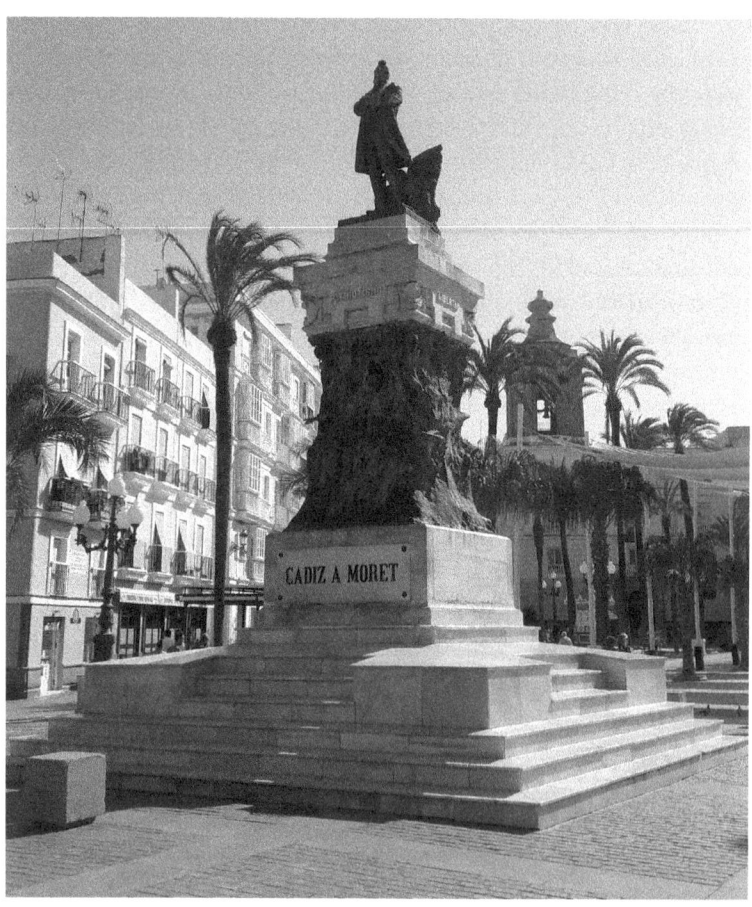

abolition of slavery in Puerto Rico, 1873 (Schmidt-Nowara 126–160), or to the bust of the abolitionist deputy from Ecuador in the Cortes of 1812, José Mejía Lequerica (García León 424–27).

The three are honored as liberal politicians without highlighting their abolitionism. Nobody asked for a critical commemorative plaque on the giant monument to the Constitution of 1812 that did not end the deportation of Africans to the Americas and gave free men of African descent citizenship only in exceptional cases (*Constitución*). Nobody thought of paying tribute to early abolitionists related to Cádiz. Isidoro de Antillón spoke out in favor of the abolition of traffic and slavery as early as 1802. He died of wounds inflicted by a counter-revolutionary mob on the streets of Cádiz in 1813. Antonio Argüelles and José Miguel Guridi Alcocer made abolitionist proposals in the Cortes of 1812. Argüelles referred to the human traffic only and later retracted his abolitionist ideas, whereas Guridi wanted to abolish the traffic of African captives and slavery in America (Sarriés Griñó 167; Vila Vilar 111–12, 120–24; Sanjurjo 8–9, 15–19, 72, 95). As the mentioned study of Christopher Schmidt-Nowara has never been translated to Spanish, most Spanish studies of Spanish abolitionism have been published very recently, and none of the authors is associated with the University of Cádiz, the sparse knowledge might not have reached a broader public. It is difficult to assess if this is the reason for the neglect of Spanish abolitionists, or if the problem is that their commemoration would destroy the broadly held idea that late enslavers cannot be condemned because slavery was accepted widely in Spanish society until its very end.[5]

Madrid: Total Colonial Amnesia

In 2020 the recent research by Lizbeth Chaviano on the traces of enslavers in Madrid had not yet been published (Chaviano, *Las huellas*). Thus, nobody could refer to it in the year of toppled statues. What could the protesters know about the roots of the colonial metropolis Madrid in slavery? In the school curriculum the topic has been and continues to be taboo. Not without reason, in 2018 the United Nations Human Rights Council recommended to Spain in a report noting the extremely high level of racial discrimination and human rights violations against people of African descent, "The Government should periodically review textbooks and other educational materials to ensure that they reflect historical facts accurately as they relate to past tragedies and atrocities, such as enslavement, the trade in enslaved Africans and colonialism" (UNHRC).

Demonstrators would find no serious and detailed information about slavery in the Museo de América, where the enslavement of Africans is addressed in only one display case under the heading "Emigración Africana" ("African emigration"). Aside from that single showcase, the Afro-Hispano-American population appears in demographic statistics and racist *casta* paintings without any critical comment. There is no reference to capital transfer from American slavery to the metropolis. The Museo de Arqueología presents the commerce of the colonial empire on the seldom-visited third floor without reference to Africa and the trade in human beings. The only mention of slavery is part of an explanation of porcelain figures representing domestics of African descent. Visitors learn, without any historical contextualization, that Black servants had been a sign of social distinction in aristocratic households in the eighteenth century. The Museo Africano Mundo Negro, operated by Combonian missionaries, has very limited opening hours, and therefore not much coverage. The trafficking of Africans is not denied in it, but it erroneously states that Spaniards only participated in that commerce through other nations. Captions contain many factual errors. Visualizations represent Africa as a continent without a history and urban culture, where people move half-naked and work in primitive agriculture.

Some anti-racist activists may have known Miguel Ángel Rosales's documentary *Gurumbé: Canciones de tu memoria negra* (*Gurumbé: Afro-Andalusian Memories*; 2016) about the African roots of Spanish culture, including interviews with pioneer researchers about the enslavement of Africans and Pan-African activists. If protesters had gone to a library it would have been difficult for non-historians among them to realize that a book entitled *Hacer las Américas* (Make/do the Americas) (Bahamonde and Cayuela) referred also to the buildings owned by enslavers in Madrid, or that a book entitled *Isabel II: Los espejos de la reina* (*Isabella II: Mirrors of the Queen*) included information about María Cristina de Borbón-Dos Sicilias (1806–1878, regent of Spain 1833–1840), a queen who benefited from the trafficking and exploitation of enslaved Africans on Cuban sugar plantations managed by her morganatic husband Agustín Fernando Muñoz y Sánchez, Duque de Riánsares (Piqueras 104–05).

Members of the Afro-Spanish community are better informed than most other people about Atlantic slavery through their own research (Toasije, "La memoria"), and they create their own temporary sites of memory of enslavement and colonialism in Equatorial Guinea and the Americas during their annual meeting Conciencia Afro (fig. 6.5).

Figure 6.5. Festival Conciencia Afro in Madrid-Matadero, Sept. 2018. *Source:* Photo by the author.

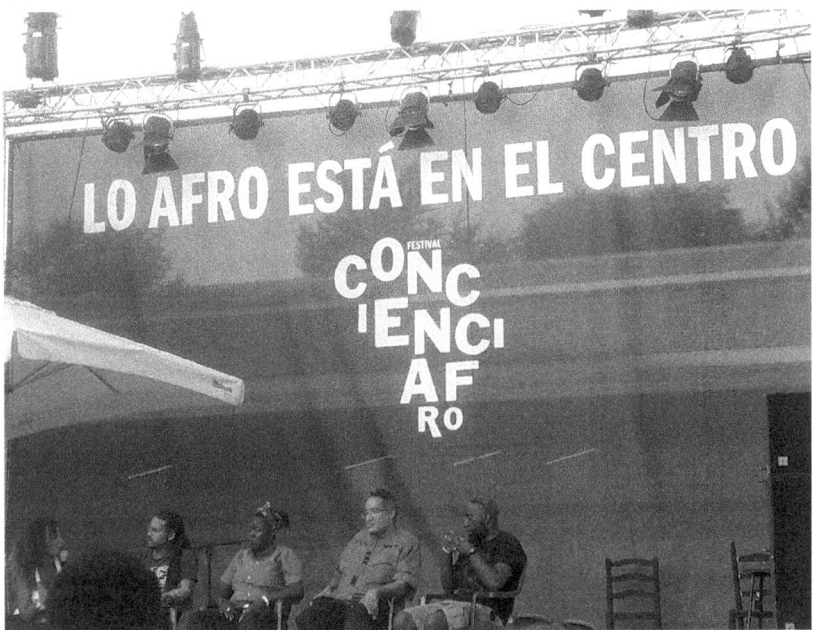

The historian Antumi Toasije, the founder of the Centro Panafricano and author of a doctoral thesis about the history of Africans and Afrodescendants in Spain, has developed a detailed plan on how to teach and remember enslavement in the Atlantic space, and the legacies of slavery in racism in schools and universities, through the removal of monuments to enslavers and colonizers, the establishment of new memorials, and the renaming of streets. Madrid, as the capital, should inaugurate a major center of commemoration that may function as a museum, cultural center, space for academic and educational events attracting international experts, also from Abya Yala, America (Toasije, personal interview, *Presencia*).

BLM activists may have come across the publications of José Miguel López about the enslaved in eighteenth-century Madrid—and kings and nobles as owners of the enslaved (López, "Los esclavos"). His book about slavery in Madrid 1701–1837 (*La esclavitud*) appeared in 2020 in the middle of the BLM movement and would not yet have arrived in libraries during the first demonstrations. Some of its content was distributed through online editions of newspapers: elDiario.es (Cruz), *El País* (López, "Los 20.000 esclavos").

The article in *El País* about vestiges of slavery in Spain (Hernando) mentions Madrilenian sites related to enslavement, such as monuments or street names of enslavers like Queen Regent María Cristina, the Count Peñalver, Cánovas del Castillo, Esquilache, Felipe V, Fernando VI, and Carlos III (whose monuments should be removed, José Miguel López argued in an interview for the article). It also mentioned sites connected with Black religious confraternities, the sign of slavery, the letter "S" impaled by a nail (*clavo* in Spanish, read as "es-clavo," "slave"), a marker of enslaved persons used for branding, carved next to the door of the parish church San Ginés.[6] The article also alluded to tableaux made by painters of African descent (Sebastian Gómez, Juan de Pareja). *El País* referred also to the Salamanca quarter, where profits from slavery were laundered, but without indicating buildings once owned by enslavers. A Google search for "esclavos Madrid" would find a reference to the book by López from June 5, 2020, onwards. Typing "esclavistas Madrid" ("enslavers Madrid") would have led to a newspaper article pointing to the royal enslavers (Hernando), but not to the enslavers of the nineteenth century who invested in real estate and resided in Madrid.[7]

Against which statues, street names, and place names could the activists have protested because the persons commemorated had been enslavers, defenders, or beneficiaries of slavery? They could have attacked the monuments of royal owners of enslaved Africans and profiteers of human trafficking in the eighteenth century, for instance the big equestrian statue in the Puerta del Sol for the enlightened King Carlos III (1993) (fig. 6.6).

He was the owner of 20,000 enslaved persons, 1,500 of whom were exploited in Spain (López, *La esclavitud* 80).[8] This is not mentioned in the inscriptions honoring him as the promoter of free trade with America and of scientific expeditions to America and Australia. There is also an older statue of this monarch in the Real Jardín Botánico in Madrid, founded under his auspices, near the Prado Museum.

BLM activists could have protested the statues of royal enslavers and defenders of slavery of the nineteenth century, for example the monument for the enslaver queen María Cristina (fig. 6.7), which was inaugurated in 1893 and is located in front of the Casón del Buen Retiro, also near the Prado Museum.[9]

The inscription on the pedestal honors her for the Decree of Amnesty (after the persecution of liberals under Fernando VII), the Statute of 1834 (a monarchical Constitution), and the promotion of science, arts, and crafts, among other achievements. Her daughter Isabel II (1830–1904, reigned 1843–1868) was not a trafficker of human beings, as far as we know. However, she supported slavery, preventing between 1843 and 1867 the

Figure 6.6. Plaza Puerta del Sol in Madrid, reformed in the 19th century by enslaver Juan Manuel Manzanedo, with the equestrian statue for King Carlos III, owner of 20,000 enslaved Africans, September 2018. *Source:* Photo by the author.

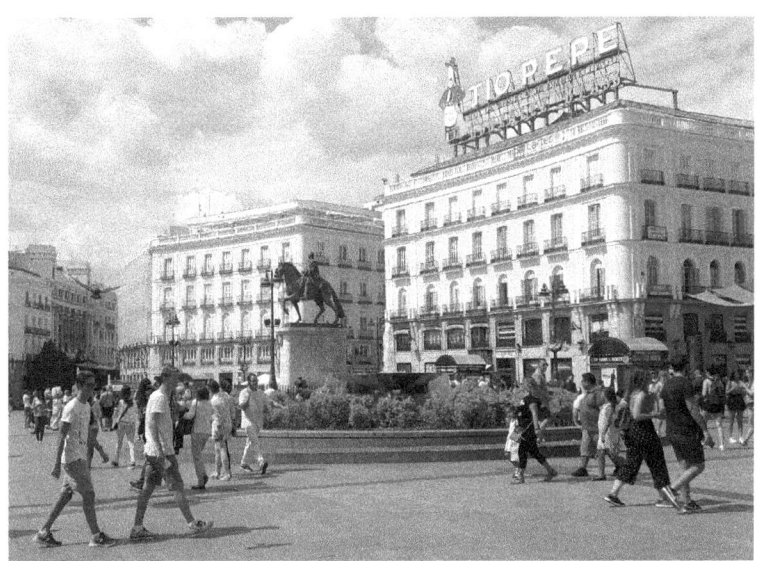

Figure 6.7. Statue of Regent Queen María Cristina, involved in trafficking African captives, in front of the Casón del Buen Retiro, Madrid, Sept. 2018. *Source:* Photo by the author.

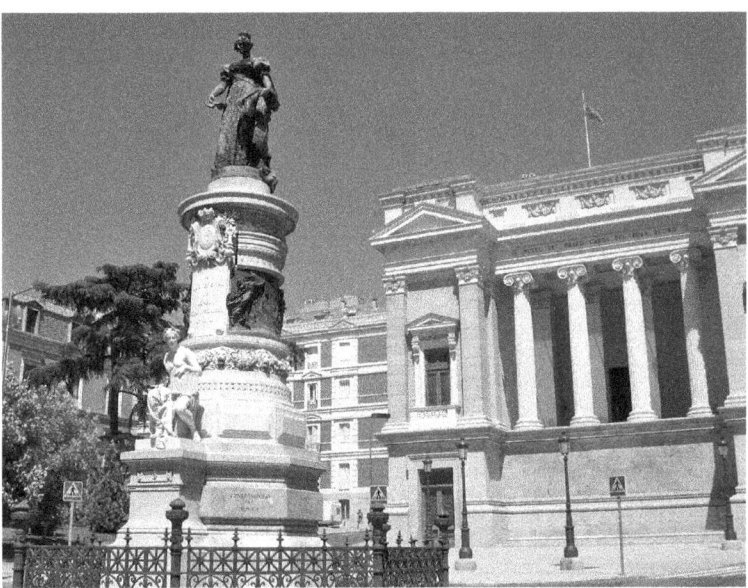

enforcement of treaties with the UK to end the human trafficking from the African coasts. She ennobled many enslavers or made them senators (Piqueras 97, 101–106; Chaviano, *Las huellas*).

María Cristina and Isabel were rewarded for their loyalty to the moderate liberals and their Constitution of 1837 (which excluded Cuba and the colonies from constitutional rule) with money from slavery-based revenues from the Havana exchequer, 121 million *reales* for the mother and 100 million *reales* for the daughter (Piqueras 95). Isabel's husband, Francisco de Asís de Borbón, whose father and sister were related to the Cuban enslaver oligarchy through marriage, was involved in the business of human trafficking (Piqueras 99; Moreno Fraginals 229). Isabel's son, Alfonso XII (1857–1885), king in 1874, continued the tradition of ennoblement of enslavers, usually conservatives who had backed the Restoration of the Bourbon monarchy after the Democratic Sexennium (Rodrigo, *Los Marqueses* 69, 75; Surwillo 149, 153), hoping for the maintenance of slavery in Cuba under monarchical rule.

Isabel II has various statues, one in the National Library, founded by her in 1866 (Burdiel, *Isabel II*, image 26), and another in front of the opera house, the Teatro Real (fig. 6.8), whose construction she had promoted.

Isabel II has often been judged according to her "loose" sexual morals, incompatible with the middle-class values of the liberals concerning appropriate female behavior, used to delegitimize monarchical rule, instead of being judged on her politics (Burdiel, *The Queen's Two Bodies*). The outcome of an evaluation of Isabel's role in history would be very different if it had considered her role as a patron of public institutions, arts, and sciences in Madrid or if it took into account how she plundered Cuba, amassing a fortune for her family, lovers, and camarilla. All her entourage benefited from exploiting enslaved Africans.

The BLM protesters in Madrid did not touch any of these monuments. Perhaps they did not connect these kings and queens with the history of colonialism and the enslavement of Africans, or they preferred to target a more emblematic site of colonial nostalgia. In July 2020, the activists daubed in red and put a placard with the text "Fuego al orden colonial" on the giant memorial to Columbus (fig. 6.9) at Plaza de Colón, where the Fiesta Nacional is celebrated every October 12.

The demonstration where these actions took place united persons of the *pueblos originarios* (original peoples) of Spanish America and persons of African descent. The manifesto of the activists referred to the trafficking of Africans, the colonialism in Abya Yala and Africa, and the recent racist murders in Spain of refugees from Africa (Maroto).

Figure 6.8. Statue of Queen Isabel II, profiteer from Caribbean colonial revenues, protectress of human trafficking and enslavers, in front of the Teatro Real, Sept. 2018. *Source:* Photo by the author.

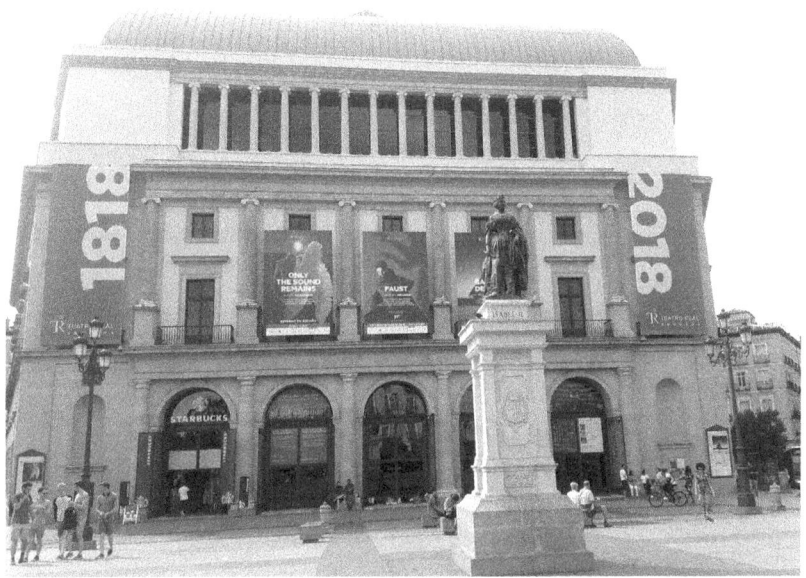

The renaming of streets could have been an aim of protesters, too. The Madrilenian calle Conde de Peñalver is named after the third Count of Peñalver, Nicolás de Peñalver y Zamora (1853–1916), a conservative politician, mayor of Madrid and promoter of the famous commercial avenue Gran Vía (*Diccionario Biográfico Español*). His political career was based on the fortunes amassed by his grandfather, Cuban enslaver in Matanzas and mayor of Havana, Nicolás de Peñalver y Cárdenas-Vélez de Guevara, given the title of count by Isabel II in 1836 (Bergad 111, 148, 161), and his father, Narciso José de Peñalver y Peñalver, inheritor of the Narciso sugar plantation in Banagüises with 400 enslaved workers. The latter had transferred the family fortune from Cuba to Spain and France ("Narciso José de Peñalver"). The Barrio Comillas with the Parque Comillas and Plaza Marqués de Comillas are named for the above-mentioned enslaver Antonio López, Marqués de Comillas. The metro station and the street called Serrano are named after the *capitán general* of Cuba (1859–1862) and defender of slavery Francisco Serrano y Domínguez (1810–1885), once the influential lover of Queen Isabel II. Later he married Antonia María Domínguez y Borrell, daughter of the governor of

Figure 6.9. Monument for Columbus, Plaza de Colón, Madrid, in September 2018; it was later attacked during BLM 2020. *Source:* Photo by the author.

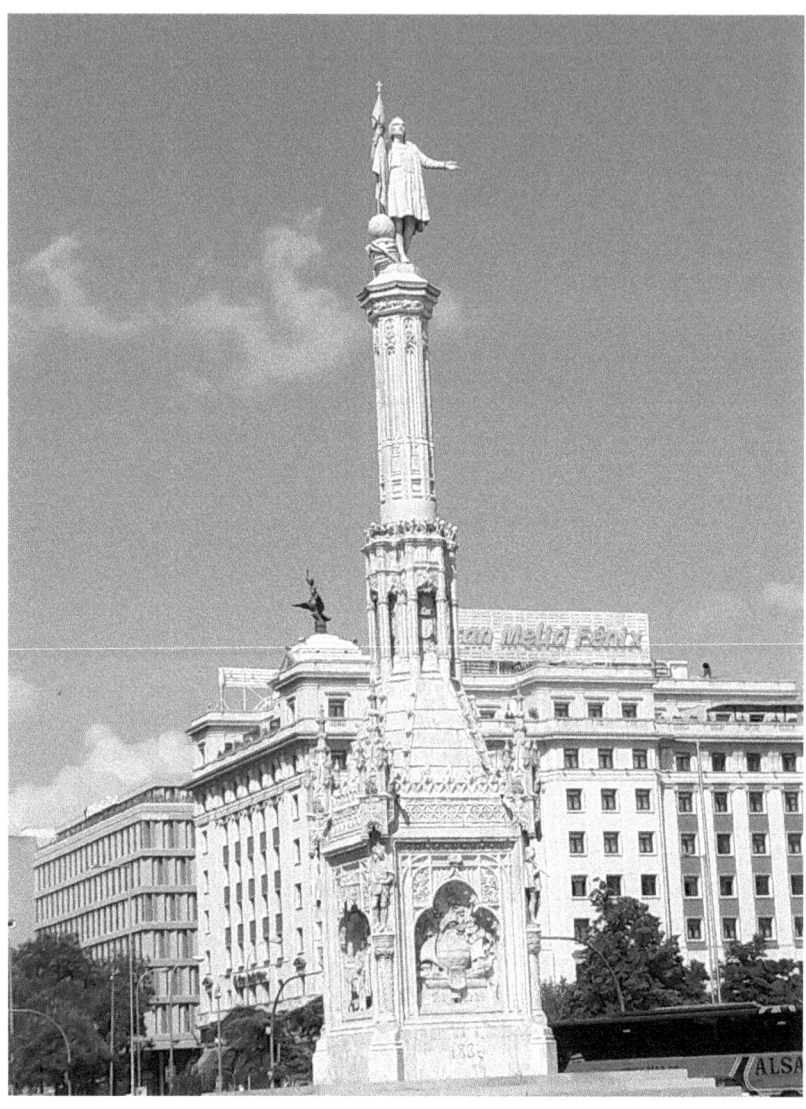

the Cuban province of Trinidad, Miguel Domínguez de Guevara, and Isabel Borrell Lemus from a notorious enslaver family in Trinidad (Bellido; Ortuzar; Burdiel, *Isabel II* 192–213; Piqueras 103). The proposal to change street names was made in an article in *El País* (Hernando). For a long time, associations of people of African descent have been asking for an apology for enslavement from the Spanish monarchy and government, the renaming of streets named after enslavers (without referring to the above-mentioned examples), and the installation of statues for enslaved fighters against enslavement (Toasije, *La memoria*), so far without success in Madrid.

The only monument to an abolitionist in Madrid is the *Glorieta de Emilio Castelar*, in a roundabout at Paseo de Castellana. As a minister, Emilio Castelar was responsible for the abolition of slavery in Puerto Rico. Later he became president of the ephemeral First Spanish Republic, 1873–1874 (Schmidt-Nowara 152–55). The giant monument from 1908 shows naked freed men, women, and children at the rear, with the inscription "Levantaos esclavos porque teneis patria" ("Stand up slaves as you have a fatherland") (fig. 6.10).

This representation reflects the racist-paternalistic attitude toward Africans of the early twentieth century. The statue for Agustín Argüelles at the Plaza Marqués de Cerralbo, Avenida de Francisco Pí y Margall, and the calle

Figure 6.10. The rear of the monument honoring Emilio Castelar, responsible for the abolition in Puerto Rico, Paseo de la Castellana, Madrid, Aug. 2011. *Source:* Photo by the author.

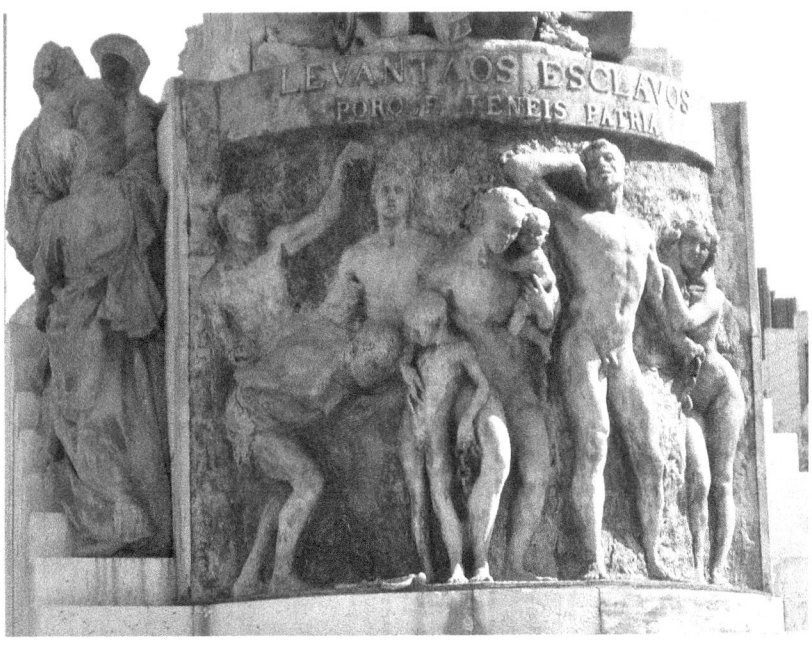

Concepción Arenal pay tribute to moderate and radical abolitionists without explaining that they had been abolitionists. Madrid not only continues to honor enslavers, but also lacks memorials to enslaved but resisting Africans and an adequate, de-colonized commemoration of white abolitionists. There were, of course, more than three Spanish abolitionists. No street or statue in Madrid pays homage to the leading personalities of that movement in the 1860s and 1870s, Rafael María de Labra, Julio Vizcarrondo, and Harriet Brewster de Vizcarrondo (Schmidt-Nowara 117–19, 136–37, 141–44).

The material vestiges of nineteenth-century slavery in Madrid were not assaulted in 2020. Juan Manuel Manzanedo, Marqués de Manzanedo, Duque de Santoña (1803–1882), had benefited from various enslavement expeditions to Cuba. He invested his fortune acquired in Cuba (more than 50 million *reales*) in Madrilenian real estate, in the historic city center and the Ensanche. He also traded in sugar, and acted as a *refaccionista*, a banker who gave credit to plantation owners who repaid it with the harvest or forfeited their property to the creditor. Manzanedo multiplied his fortune with investments in railways, capital stock in Paris, banking (as co-founder of the Banco de Fomento y Ultramar, Banco Hispano Colonial, and Banco de Santander and through business with Baring Brothers in London and Rothschild in Paris), ship insurance, the tobacco monopoly, agriculture, a bread factory, wash houses in Madrid and port warehouses in Santander. By 1875 he had amassed 200 million *reales*; he was as rich as the Duke of Alba and the House of Medinaceli, the highest ranks of the old nobility. As president of the Círculo Hispano-Ultramarino and the Banco Hispano Colonial he fought for the retention of Cuba and against the abolition of slavery (Cayuela and Bahamonde 138–45; Rodrigo, *Un hombre* 189–90).

Manzanedo bought an eighteenth-century mansion at the corner of 13 calle Huertas/28 calle Príncipe, currently the seat of the Chamber of Commerce and Industry of Madrid (fig. 6.11), and rebuilt it in neo-Baroque style as a morning gift for his wife.

It was re-inaugurated in 1876, in the presence of King Alfonso XII (Bahamonde and Cayuela 216, 213). Manzanedo commissioned the construction of a second mansion in 1878, completed in 1882, intended as the summer residence of the duchess (where she never lived): 12 calle de Montalbán, today the seat of the Museo de Artes Decorativas (Bahamonde and Cayuela 208; "Palacio de la Duquesa"). His wife, María del Carmen Hernández Espinosa (1828–1894), founded the Hospital del Niño Jesús, the first pediatric hospital in Madrid (Sazatornil 563, 565–66). Juan Manuel Manzanedo also financed the nineteenth-century renovation of the most

Figure 6.11. Palace Santoña at the corner of 13 calle Huertas/28 calle Príncipe, once owned by enslaver Juan Manuel Manzanedo, Duque de Santoña, Madrid, Sept. 2018. *Source:* Ulrike Schmieder. Photo by the author.

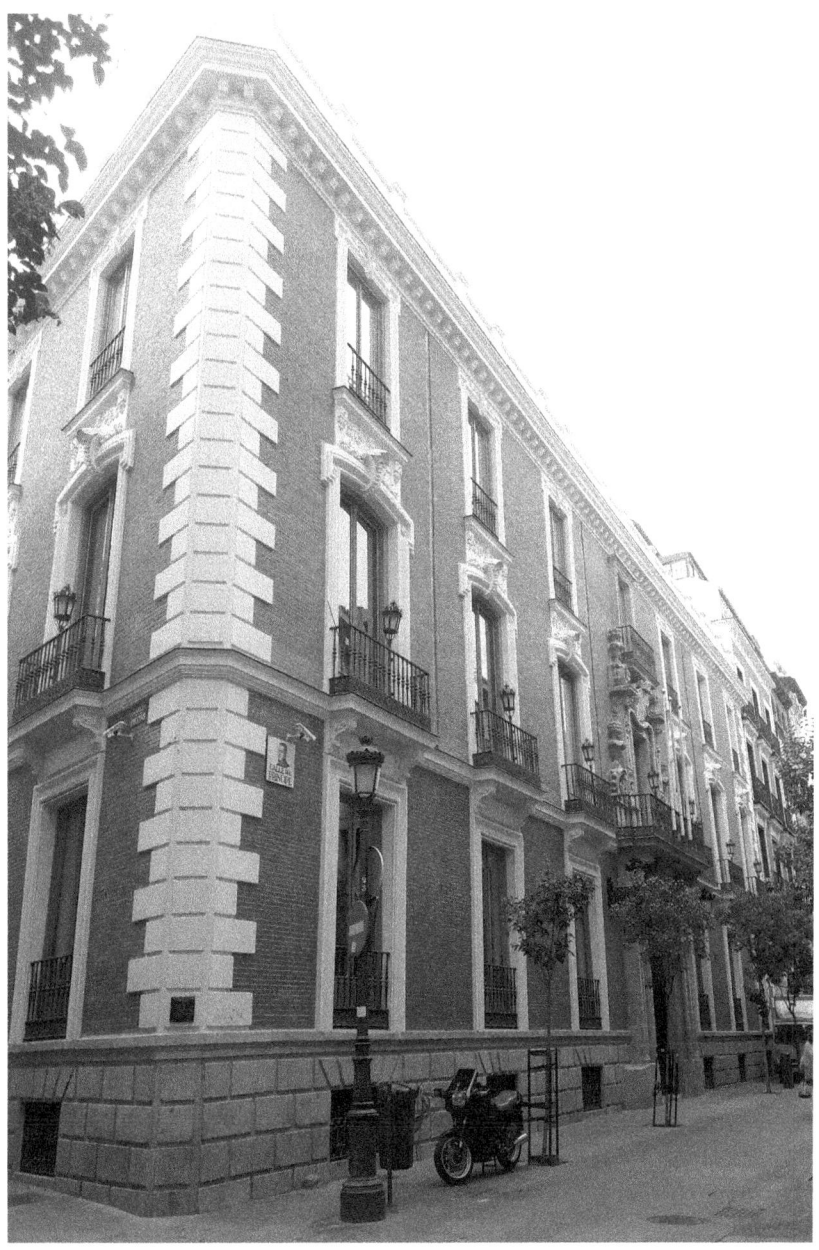

important square in Madrid, the Puerta del Sol, where he bought the giant building complex of the Casa Cordero from the banker Santiago Alonso Cordero, and four more properties where he raised new houses (Cayuela and Bahamonde; Chaviano, *Las huellas* 52; "The Stamp"). This means that the most emblematic square in Madrid took on its current appearance from profits from Cuban slavery.

The Black Lives Matter demonstration, organized by the Comunidad Negra Africana y Afrodescendiente de España, took place there on June 7, 2020 (Ramos). The protesters don't seem to have referred to the link of the Puerta del Sol to the enslaver, although the de-colonial politics of memory and the remembrance of enslavement are among the aims of the association (CNAAE). The disconnection between the protests and the historical significance of that central urban space probably has its origin in the information gap not only in schoolbooks but also in published academic research.[10]

Capital transfer from the Cuban slavery economy did not occur solely via merchants directly involved in the traffic of African captives. The Madrilenian banker Manuel de Gaviria Alcoba, Marqués de Gaviria (1794–1855), a friend of King Fernando VII and his wife, and intendant of the Royal House, had never been in the Caribbean, but he took part in the businesses of the enslaver queen María Cristina and her husband. He acted as a broker of Rothschild's loan to the General Treasury of the Royal Household to be repaid with revenues from Puerto Rico, Cuba, and the Philippines in 1837 (López-Morell 56–58). He was still profiting from investments in Cuba in 1857 (Bahamonde and Cayuela 178–79). Gaviria's opulent mansion, modeled on the Farnese Palace in Rome, at 9 calle Arenal is used today as an exhibition center. The ceiling frescos in the main hall depict the conquest and conquerors of America with colonial pride and nostalgia. The banker and his second wife were intimate friends of Isabel II. The Queen participated in the inauguration ball in 1851 and at various festivities. She made Gaviria gentleman-in-waiting and his widow a lady-in-waiting (Burdiel, *Isabel II* 151, 559; "Palacio de Gaviria"; Pérez-Olagüe). There is little public awareness of the traces of nineteenth-century connections to enslavement in the Madrilenian cityscape. The colonial pride and nostalgia demonstrated by Manuel Gaviria in the nineteenth century persist until now, as the celebrations of October 12 regularly demonstrate.

Apart from the events of 2020, there have been regular de-colonial protests at the Día de la Fiesta Nacional (National Holiday of Spain) on October 12, the date of the "discovery" of America. No other former

European colonial power has made the beginning of the annihilation and exploitation of colonized people into its national commemorative day. The official discourse that the close relations between Spain and Spanish America are celebrated (not conquest and colonial power) is not credible. Who needs a military parade when cultural ties are commemorated? In contrast to the masses of people participating in the parade in the presence of the royal family, the number of protesters is small. In 2018, during the march "Descolonicemos. 12 de Octubre: Nada que celebrar" ("Let's decolonize. October 12: Nothing to celebrate"), which I observed (fig. 6.12), most demonstrators were members of the Pueblos originarios from Spanish America. The descendants of the first victims of Spanish colonialism had been also the first protesters against pompous celebrations of colonial rule, particularly since 1992, and have launched a campaign against colonial monuments in 2014 (Bernecker and Jaffé 514–17; see also interview with Oriol López Badell and Celeste Muñoz Martínez in this book, Arellano 193–196).

Figure 6.12. Protest march on October 12, 2018, against the National Commemorative Day of Spain celebrating the "discovering" of America. *Source:* Photo by the author.

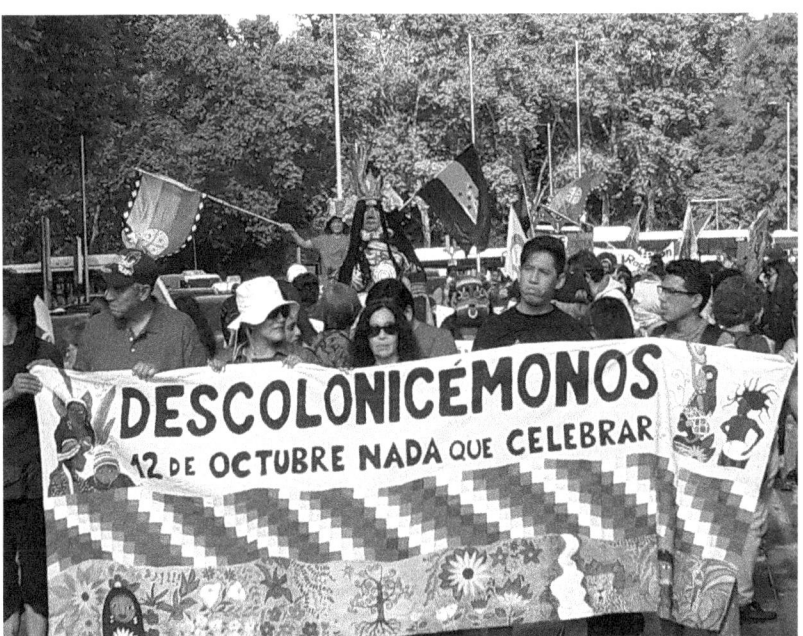

Persons of African descent and white Spaniards from leftist groups were also present in 2018. Instead of celebrating male conquerors, the protesters paid homage to female anti-colonial heroes such as Micaela Bastidas, the leader of the indigenous liberation war of 1780 in Peru with Tupac Amaru (Stavig and Schmidt); Queen Njinga of Ndongo-Matamba in Angola, who fought against Portuguese colonial rule from 1631 to 1656 (Heywood); and Dandara of Palmares, a warrior and the queen at Zumbi's side in the maroon kingdom in Alagoas, Brazil, 1612 to 1695 (Williams).

The conservatives (Partido Popular) and the extreme right (VOX) consider the expression of counter-memories of some hundred people a threat to the Spanish monarchy. In 2021 Isabel Díaz Ayuso, President of the Community of Madrid (Partido Popular), declared, "El indigenismo es el nuevo comunismo" ("Indigenism is the new Communism"; "Ayuso"). This verdict expresses anger not only about the Black Lives Matter demonstrations in Madrid but also about the toppling of statues of Spanish conquerors and missionaries in Latin America and the United States in 2019 and 2020 (Schmieder and Zeuske 299, 311). Commentators in the Spanish media, in their overwhelming majority, spoke out against the de-colonization of public space and presented the conquest of America as an endeavor aimed at evangelizing "pagans" and repeated the myth of "mild Iberian slavery."[11]

A step toward answering the urgent need to disseminate knowledge about this part of Spanish history was taken in October 2021, with the inauguration of the traveling exhibition *La esclavitud y el legado cultural de África en el Caribe*, curated by Consuelo Naranjo Orovio and Miguel Ángel Puig-Samper in the Museo de América, displayed until February 2022.[12] On the one hand this was a real achievement. Africa was described as a "rich and diverse continent" before the traffic of captives to the Americas. The enslaved were presented not solely as merchandise and a workforce, but also as victims and resisters with reference to the Haitian Revolution (1791–1804) and the insurrection on the slave ship *Amistad* (1839). On the other hand, entanglements with Madrilenian history and capital transfer from Cuban slavery to the metropolis of the empire were omitted. The notorious enslavers Pedro Blanco, discussed in Gustau Nerín's chapter, and Julián Zulueta, from the family studied by Kirsty Hooper, were mentioned, but not Manzanedo or others who have left traces in Madrid. Thus, the history of enslavement was presented as something that happened *elsewhere*, *overseas*, not as a past whose material vestiges have left their mark on Spanish cityscapes. If the protesters of 2020 could have seen the displays, they could not have deepened their knowledge about Madrilenian urban space and tangible cultural heritage with Atlantic slavery.

The exhibition depicted ethnobotanical heritage, culinary traditions, music, Carnival, *mestizaje*, religions, literature, and the visual arts, but not racialized inequality in Spain and Hispano-America as legacies of slavery. One could not listen to the voices of the enslaved, as they appear in petitions, juridical processes, testimonies, and notarial records (García Rodríguez; Schmieder, *Nach der Sklaverei*). The displays did not refer to the family memories of enslavement that still exist in the communities of descendants of the enslaved (Toutain). In the audio guides, new expressions like *esclavizados* ("enslaved") coexisted with racist generalizations about "the black slave" or "multiple tribes of Africa." The anonymity of the enslaved prevented the empathic engagement of visitors. Without reference to the legacies of slavery in Spain and Madrid, and the political relevance of the topic (BLM and destroyed statues were elided), the exhibition could not give rise to the necessary ground-breaking public debate on the new politics of memory.

Explanations for Colonial Nostalgia and Silence about Enslavement

For one who has studied museums in British or French port towns with permanent galleries dedicated to the enslavement past, monuments and renamed streets remembering slavery, abolition, or the enslaved as subjects of history, comments on street names with a de-colonial emphasis, and events commemorating emancipation, the profound silence in Cádiz's museums and public space and the occasional, perfunctory, often erroneous remembrance of enslavement in Madrilenian sites, are, to a certain degree, shocking. Tentative explanations for this silence given in interviews and discussions with colleagues refer to three points (Rodrigo and Schmieder):

1. The still unhealed traumas and legacies of the Second Republic, the Civil War, and Franco's dictatorship overlay the memories of colonialism. Left-wing city councils like that of Cádiz till 2023 aspired to remove Falange symbols, excavate corpses of unidentified victims of the Civil War, and establish sites of memory for murdered Republicans first. They postpone a de-colonial revision of the memorial sites in the urban space (Osuna; *Catálogo*; Tsuchiya on Catalonia in this volume). This prioritization of Civil

War victims should be contested because there was, at least in some cases, a continuity between the enslaver elites of the nineteenth century and the oligarchic and fascist elites of the twentieth century. Two descendants of the above-mentioned enslaver family Abárzuza carved out a career during the dictatorship of Franco: Felipe Abárzuza y Rodríguez was minister of the navy (1959–1964), and Fernando Abárzuza Oliva became in 1940 Deputy Chief of the General Staff of the Navy, and, in 1941–42, mayor of Cádiz (Madueño), at the height of fascist terror against Republicans. The politics of memory referring to the Franco dictatorship should look at these connections in search of the origin of dictatorial terror. Historians in Cádiz should find out if there is a clandestine influence on public opinion and political decisions by descendants of enslavers *today*, as Martín Rodrigo has proven for Catalonia and central Spanish governments (*Un hombre*, 9–26; Rodrigo and Chaviano 7–10).

2. Most of the Spanish population obviously does not want to challenge the image of Spain's glorious imperial past, related to the idea that Spaniards were and are less racist than other (post)colonial nations, that they treated colonized populations "better" than their northwest European neighbors, and that native populations should be grateful for having been freed from their despotic rulers and evangelized in the Catholic faith. Such worldviews were expressed in October 2021 by politicians who were supported by many voters, such as José María Aznar, Pablo Casado, Isabel Díaz Ayuso (PP), Toni Cantó (Ciudadanos, UPyD, PP), and Iván Espinosa de los Monteros (VOX) (Muñoz). Those politicians conceal the enslavement of Africans by Spaniards. The historical narrative of colonial pride is expressed in the book *Imperiofobia* by Elvira Roca Barea, a bestseller despite its many errors and infractions of basic academic standards (Straehle).

3. The Afro-Spanish movement in Spain is less influential than the Afro-Caribbean associations in the United Kingdom and France. The underdeveloped relations between critical historians studying the legacies of slavery on the Iberian Peninsula and the Afro-Spanish communities prevent effective lobbying for a de-colonial reform of memorial cityscapes. According to the UNCHR Report and interviews conducted with the Afro-Spanish community (Caballero, Romero, Rocabruno, Toasije, personal interviews), the exclusion of the Afro-Spanish community and associations from representation and power on all parliamentary and state governance levels, cultural institutions, the mainstream media, and academia, as well as the heterogeneity and internal conflicts in the Afro-Spanish movement, had impeded any significant influence on state politics of memory.

This conclusion shall not devalue the communal commemorative events and activities as expressions of counter-memories of the descendants of enslaved and colonized Africans as described above with respect to Conciencia Afro in Madrid. It is rather deplorable that Spanish politics and academia renounced the expertise on colonial and slavery history and their legacies acquired in the Afro-Spanish community when they shaped the politics of memory and history education. A first step to overcome this attitude might have been to appoint Antumi Toasije as President of the Consejo para la Eliminación de la Discriminación Racial o Étnica in October, 2020 ("El presidente").

Conclusion

Not only politicians and state functionaries in educational and cultural institutions are responsible for the lack of knowledge about the enslavement past and its poor representation in museums; academia has also played a part in this ignorance. This critique does not refer to the tiny minority of above-quoted scholars who study the topic *and* disseminate their knowledge to a broader public.[13] Mainstream academic scholarship on the Spanish Atlantic has played an important part in downplaying enslavement (García-Baquero, Bustos). A research group in the Instituto de Historia del Consejo Superior de Investigaciones Científicas in Madrid has studied Atlantic entanglements, including enslavement in the Spanish Caribbean, for many years (Grupo de Investigación; Naranjo and Puig-Samper), but it did not connect this history with material vestiges of enslavement in the capital city of Spain, or monuments in the Madrilenian public space. However, those most to blame are the countless historians who write and teach about Spanish history as if slavery had never existed, neither in Spain nor in Spanish America.[14]

Notes

1. This article presents results from the author's project *Memories of Atlantic Slavery*, which was funded by the German Research Foundation, project no. 393718958. The fieldwork in Madrid and Cádiz was carried out in September and October 2018.

2. I use the term "enslavement" for the violent and traumatizing process of reducing human beings to enslaved non-persons, "chattel slaves." I maintain the more

common expression "slavery" referring to the juridical institution once abolished, and the economic system narrowly related to capitalism.

3. Michel distinguishes the "régime mémoriel abolitionniste" (abolitionist memorial regime), the "régime mémoriel nationaliste" (nationalist memorial regime), and the "régime victimo-mémoriel" (victim's memorial regime) with respect to slavery past (230). For the Caribbean the resistance-focused memory regime must be added, expressed in statues of maroons and (once) enslaved warriors. Christine Chivallon, who studies Antillean memories, labels the memories of the descendants of the enslaved "mémoires minorées ("Rendre visible" 11–14). I discovered during my research in Cuba and Martinique in 2019 and 2022 that those memories focus on the suffering of the enslaved ancestors, not on armed rebellion. However, as descendants of the captives demonstrate high respect for the dignity and resilience of the enslaved forebearers, I would not qualify their memory regime as only "victim-centered."

4. *Las Murallas de Cádiz y el Comercio: 1717–2017* (Casa de las Américas, 2017).

5. This idea was propagated, for instance, in the Maritime Museum in Barcelona (2021) and was expressed by Madrilenian members of the research project ConnecCaribbean (see note 12), during academic events in 2019.

6. See, López García, *La esclavitud* (fig. 1); Fracchia 105 (about branding with S and nail).

7. This would refer to Juan Manuel Manzanedo, see below, Carlos Drake y Nuñez de Castillo, Conde de Vegamar, Manuel Pastor Fuentes, Conde de Bagaes, and Antonio Vinent y Vives, Marqués de Vinent, according to Chaviano ("Las huellas"). Cross-reading of the historiography on capital transfer from Cuba and on architectural history shows that at least ten mansions of enslavers or their immediate heirs still exist in the Spanish capital.

8. If the role of someone as prominent as King Carlos III as enslaver was not known, it is not surprising that there is less knowledge about his predecessors and did not refer to their statues. In the Jardines de la Plaza Oriente an equestrian statue of Felipe IV (1605–1665) is to be found. He was a profiteer from *asientos* and licences given to Portuguese and Genoese merchants of African captives (Thomas 166, 212). Felipe V (1683–1746), whose statue is situated in the attic of the Royal Palace, was a beneficiary of the French and British *asiento*s with the Compagnie Royale de Guinée and the South Sea Company. The statue of his successor Fernando VI (1713–1759), who profited from the British *asiento* (López García, "Los esclavos" 210), is to be found near to the Plaza de la Villa de París.

9. The Real Fábrica del Bueno Retiro (producing porcelain) was designed by enslaved, later manumitted Antonio Carlos de Borbón, once the property of Carlos III (López García, *La esclavitud* 83). Freedmen got the surname of their former owner, here de Borbón.

10. A map of traces of enslavers and enslaved in Madrid was published in 2023 context of the exposition *El gran experimento ¿El fin de la esclavitud?* by Miguel

Ángel García, in the Museo Nacional de Antropología (Pérez and Monteagudo), based on the work of José Miguel López.

11. See newspapers articles on the website of the Regidoria de Memòria Democràtica of Barcelona: *Memòria Col·lectiva*, nos. 194–198 (June–Sept. 2020). The idea that Ibero-American slavery had been milder, less harsh, than slavery in the United States derives from Frank Tannenbaum (1946). For a discussion and refutation see Schmieder (*Nach der Sklaverei* 37–38).

12. Documentation of the panels and audios of the exhibition by José Miguel López, November10, 2021, which he kindly made available to me. He considers that too much space was dedicated to remaining elements of African culture and not enough to the everyday life of the enslaved. The exhibition is part of the European Union project *Connected Worlds: The Caribbean, Origin of Modern World (ConnecCaribbean)*.

13. De-colonial historians form the network Memoria y lugares de memoria de la esclavitud y el comercio de esclavos en la España contemporánea and are to be found in the Universidad de Sevilla and Universitat Jaume I, Castellón de la Plana.

14. The website where most Spanish academic publications (books, articles, chapters, reviews, theses) in humanities and social sciences are to be found indicated in March 2022 6,817 items about "General Franco" (and 237 about "dictador Franco"), 15,026 about "conquistadores," 19,581 items about "Carlos III," 21,963 about "guerra civil," 24,264 items about "Isabel I," 463 issues concerning "esclavos América," 398 referring to "esclavos España," and 291 with reference to "esclavos Cuba," in the case of the latter more than one fifth written by foreign historians in Spanish reviews or collective books (*Dialnet*).

Works Cited

Araujo, Ana Lucia. *Shadows of the Slave Past: Memory, Heritage, and Slavery*. Routledge, 2014.

Arellano Cruz, Fabiola. "Decolonizing Colonial Monuments: Counter-Memory Activism in Madrid and Barcelona." *De-Commemoration: Removing Statues and Renaming Places*, edited by Sarah Gensburger and Jenny Wüstenberg, Berghahn Books, 2023, pp. 190–200. https://doi.org/10.1515/9781805391081-022.

"Ayuso, desde EEUU: 'El indigenismo es el nuevo comunismo.'" *Huffington Post*, 27 Sept. 2021, www.huffingtonpost.es/entry/ayuso-desde-eeuu-el-indigenismo-es-el-nuevo-comunismo_es_61517c8be4b0016411962b53.

Azarmandi, Mahdis. "Monumentos coloniales, migración y memoria en la Barcelona (post)colonial." *Rivista dell'Istituto di Storia dell'Europa Mediterránea*, vol. 7, no. 2, 2020, pp. 169–202.

Bahamonde, Ángel, and José Cayuela. *Hacer las Américas: Las élites españolas en el siglo XIX*. Alianza, 1992.

Bellido Andréu, Antonio. "Miguel Domínguez Guevara." *Diccionario Biográfico electrónico*, Real Academia de Historia, dbe.rah.es/biografias/69727/miguel-dominguez-guevara.

Bergad, Laird W. *Cuban Rural Society in the Nineteenth Century: The Social and Economic History of Monoculture in Matanzas*. Princeton UP, 1990.

Bernecker, Walther L., and Verónica Jaffé. "El aniversario del 'descubrimiento' de América en el conflicto de opiniones." *Ibero-Amerikanisches Archiv*, vol. 18, no. 3–4, 1992, pp. 501–20.

Burdiel, Isabel. *Isabel II: Una biografía (1830–1904)*, 3rd ed. Taurus, 2011.

———. "The Queen's Two Bodies: Beyond Private and Public in the Biography of Isabel II of Spain." *Life-Writing in Europe: Private Lives, Public Spheres and Biographical Interpretations*, 20–21 Apr. 2012, U of Oxford.

Bustos Rodríguez, Manuel. *Cádiz en el sistema atlántico: La ciudad, sus comerciantes y la actividad mercantil (1650–1830)*. Sílex, 2005.

Caballero, Clara. Personal interview. 2 and 8 Oct. 2018.

Caldeira, Arlindo Manoel. *Escravos e traficantes no império português: O comercio negreiro português no Atlântico durante os séculos XV a XIX*. Esfera dos Livros, 2013.

Catálogo para de la retirada de simbología franquista de la ciudad de Cádiz. Ayuntamiento de Cádiz, 2019. https://todoslosnombres.org/wp-content/uploads/2022/03/catalogo-para-la-retirada-de-simbologia-franquista-de-la-ciudad-de-cadiz.pdf.

Cayuela, José Gregorio, and Ángel Bahamonde. "Trasvase de capitales antillanos y estrategias inversoras: La fortuna del Marqués de Manzanedo (1823–1882)." *Revista internacional de sociología*, vol. 45, no. 1, 1987, pp. 125–47.

Chaviano Pérez, Lizbeth. "Cádiz, capital de la trata negrera." *Cádiz y el tráfico de esclavos: De la legalidad a la clandestinidad*, edited by María del Carmen Cózar Navarro and Martín Rodrigo y Alharilla, Sílex, 2018, pp. 163–93.

———. "Las huellas de la esclavitud en Madrid a través de los senadores." *Del olvido a la memoria: La esclavitud en la España contemporánea*, edited by Martín Rodrigo y Alharilla, Icaria, 2022, pp. 39–62.

———. "The Stamp of Slavery on Spanish Nineteenth-Century Urbanism." *Cultural Heritage and Slavery: Perspectives from Europe*, edited by Stephan Conermann, Claudia Rauhut, Ulrike Schmieder and Michael Zeuske, De Gruyter, pp. 203–22.

Chivallon, Christine. "Rendre visible l'esclavage : Muséographie et hiatus de la mémoire aux Antilles françaises." *L'Homme*, no. 180, 2006, pp. 7–42.

———. "L'usage de la mémoire de l'esclavage dans les anciens ports négriers de Bordeaux et Bristol." *L'esclavage, la colonisation, et après . . . , France, États-Unis, Grande-Bretagne*, edited by Patrick Weil and Stéphane Dufoix, Presses Universitaires de France, 2005, pp. 559–84.

Comunidad Negra Africana y Afrodescendiente de España (CNAAE). cnaae.org. Accessed 15 Feb. 2022.

Connected Worlds: The Caribbean, Origin of Modern World. conneccaribbean.com/?lang=en. Accessed 2 Mar. 2022.

Constitución política de la monarquía española. 1812. Congreso de los Diputados, Constituciones Españolas 1812–1978. www.congreso.es/docu/constituciones/1812/ce1812_cd.pdf.

Cózar Navarro, María del Carmen. "Entre Cádiz y La Habana, Pedro Martínez y Compañía: La Gran casa de comercio de esclavos en el reinado de Isabel II." *Cádiz y el tráfico de esclavos: De la legalidad a la clandestinidad*, edited by María del Carmen Cózar Navarro and Martín Rodrigo, y Alharilla, Sílex, 2018, pp. 229–62.

———. *La orca del Atlántico: Pedro Martínez y su clan en la trata de esclavos (1817–1867)*. Sílex, 2020.

Cózar Navarro, María del Carmen, and Martín Rodrigo y Alharilla, editors. *Cádiz y el tráfico de esclavos: De la legalidad a la clandestinidad*. Sílex, 2018.

Cruz, Luis de la. "Sí, Madrid fue una ciudad con esclavos." *elDiario.es*, 5 July 2020, www.eldiario.es/madrid/somos/malasana/si-madrid-fue-una-ciudad-con-esclavos_1_6412881.html.

Diakité, Tidiane. *Louis XIV et l'Afrique Noire*. Arléa, 2013.

Dialnet. dialnet.unirioja.es. Accessed 1 March 2022.

Diccionario Biográfico Español. "Nicolás de Peñalver y Zamora." *Diccionario Biográfico electrónico*, Real Academia de Historia, dbe.rah.es/biografias/4903/nicolas-penalver-y-zamora.

Ferrer, Ada. *Freedom's Mirror: Cuba and Haiti in the Age of Revolution*. Cambridge UP, 2014.

Fracchia, Carmen. *"Black but Human": Slavery and Visual Art in Hapsburg Spain, 1480–1700*. Oxford UP, 2019.

Franco, José Luciano. *Comercio clandestino de esclavos*. Ciencias Sociales, 1996 [1976].

García, Eduardo J. "Expertos internacionales analizan la relación de Cádiz con la esclavitud." *O Cádiz digital*, 10 Sept. 2017, ocadizdigital.es/noticia/c%C3%A1diz/expertos-internacionales-analizan-la-relaci%C3%B3n-de-c%C3%A1diz-con-la-esclavitu.

García-Baquero González, Antonio. *Cádiz y el Atlántico 1717–1778: El comercio colonial español bajo el monopolio gaditano*. 2 vols., Escuela de Estudios Hispanoamericanos, 1976.

García León, José María. *Los diputados doceañistas: Una aproximación al estudio de los diputados de las Cortes Generales y Extraordinarias (1810–1813)*. Quorum, 2012.

García Rodríguez, Gloria. *Voices of the Enslaved in Nineteenth-Century Cuba: A Documentary History*. U of North Carolina P, 2011.

González de Oleaga, Marisa, Ernesto Bohoslavsky and María Silvia Di Liscia. "Entre el desafío y el signo: Identidad y diferencia en el Museo de América de Madrid." *Alteridades*, vol. 21, no. 4, 2011, pp. 113–27.

Grupo de Investigación de Estudios Comparados del Caribe y Mundo Atlántico, Instituto de Historia-CCHS, CSIC. https://cchs.csic.es/es/org-structure/estudios-comparados-caribe-mundo-atlantico. Accessed 13 June 2024.

Guixé Coromines, Jordi, and Núria Ricart Ulldemolins. "A. López y López, quinto asalto. Memorias incómodas en el espacio público." *Rivista dell'Istituto di Storia dell'Europa mediterránea*, vol. 7, no. 2, 2020, pp. 139–67.

Hernando, Silvia. "Lo que queda de la esclavitud en España: estatuas, calles, pinturas y música." *El País*, 23 June 2020.

Heywood, Linda Marinda. *Njinga of Angola: Africa's Warrior Queen*. Harvard UP, 2017.

Hidalgo, José A. "Los monumentos no dan problemas en Cádiz." *El Diario de Cádiz*, 6 July 2020.

Hourcade, Renaud. *Les ports négriers face à leur histoire: politique de la mémoire à Nantes, Bordeaux et Liverpool*. Dalloz, 2014.

Jordá, Eduardo. "Dos mundos: Todo enfrentamiento civil ha sido alentado por unos medios de comunicación entregados sin escrúpulos a uno de los bandos." *Diario de Cádiz*, 29 Aug. 2020.

Ledoux, Sébastien. "Entre choix du passé et poids du présent : Les acteurs invisibles de l'enseignement de l'esclavage en France." *Enseigner les traites, les esclavages, les abolitions et leurs héritages*, edited by Marie-Albane de Suremain and Éric Mesnard, Karthala, 2021, pp. 275–88.

López, José Antonio. "Cuando Cádiz fue puerto esclavista: La Academia Hispano Americana presenta hoy en el Casino Gaditano el libro 'Cádiz y el tráfico de esclavos. De la legalidad a la clandestinidad,' de Carmen Cózar y Martín Rodrigo." *Diario de Cádiz*, 15 Nov. 2018.

López García, José Miguel. *La esclavitud a finales del Antiguo Régimen: Madrid, 1701–1837: De moros de presa a negros de nación*. Alianza, 2020.

———. "Los esclavos del Rey de España a finales del Antiguo Régimen. Un aspecto poco conocido de nuestro reformismo ilustrado." *La Corte de los Borbones: Crisis del modelo cortesano*, vol. 1, edited by José Martínez, Concepción Camarero and Marcela Luzzi, Poliferno, 2013, pp. 207–35.

———. Personal interview and guided tour on the traces of Africans in Madrid. 3 and 5 Oct. 2018.

———. "Los 20.000 esclavos de Carlos III: El soberano se convirtió en el mayor propietario de mano de obra cautiva de la Monarquía hispánica." *El País*, 25 July 2020.

López-Morell, Miguel A. *The House of Rothschild in Spain, 1812–1941*. Ashgate, 2016.

MacCreery, David Jameson. *The Sweat of their Brow: A History of Work in Latin America*. Sharpe, 2000.

Madueño Galán, José María. "Fernando Abárzuza Oliva." *Diccionario Biográfico electrónico*, Real Academia de Historia, dbe.rah.es/biografias/65615/fernando-abarzuza-oliva.

Maldonado de Arjona, Jesús. "Alejandro O'Reilly Mc Dowel." *Diccionario Biográfico electrónico*, Real Academia de Historia, dbe.rah.es/biografias/13705/alejandro-oreilly-mc-dowel.

Maroto, Marta. "Activistas antirracistas cuelgan una pancarta de la estatua de Colón de Madrid para pedir su derribo: 'Fuego al orden colonial.'" *elDiario.es*, 17 July 2020, www.eldiario.es/desalambre/activistas-antirracistas-cuelgan-pancarta-estatua-colon-madrid-fuego-orden-colonial_1_6112115.html.

Martino, Enrique. "Money, Indenture, and Neo-slavery in the Spanish Gulf of Guinea, 1820s to 1890s." *Comparativ*, vol. 30, nos. 5–6, 2020, pp. 560–80.

Memoria y lugares de memoria de la esclavitud y el comercio de esclavos en la España contemporánea. U Pompeu Fabra and U de Barcelona, 17–19 June 2021. cau.upf.edu/documents/7951176/8269683/Programa+simposio+17-19+junio+2021.pdf/bb134299-52be-f053-04bd-94c961b182e2.

Michel, Johann. *Devenir descendant d'esclave : Enquête sur les régimes mémoriels*. Presses Universitaires de Rennes, 2015.

Moreno Fraginals, Manuel. *Cuba/España, España: Historia común*. Crítica, 1996.

Morgado García, Arturo. *Una metrópoli esclavista: El Cádiz de la modernidad*. U de Granada, 2013.

———. Personal interview. 12 Sept. 2018.

Muñoz, Miguel. "La derecha española refuerza su discurso racista contra los pueblos indígenas latinoamericanos a las puertas del 12-O." *publico.es*, 12 Oct. 2021, www.publico.es/politica/12-octubre-derecha-refuerza-discurso-racista-pueblos-indigenas-latinoamericanos-12-o.html.

Naranjo Orovio, Consuelo, and Miguel Ángel Puig-Samper, editors. *La esclavitud y el legado cultural de África en el Caribe/Slavery and the African Cultural Legacy in the Caribbean*. Doce Calles, 2021.

"Narciso José de Peñalver y Peñalver." *EcuRed*, v https://www.ecured.cu/Narciso_Jos%C3%A9_de_Pe%C3%B1alver_y_Pe%C3%B1alver. Accessed 12 June 2024.

Nimako, Kwame, and Stephan A. Small. "Collective Memory of Slavery in Great Britain and The Netherlands." *New Perspectives on Slavery and Colonialism in the Caribbean*, edited by Marten Schalkwijk and Stephen A. Small, Amrit/Ninsee, 2012, pp. 92–115.

Nora, Pierre. "Entre mémoire et histoire : La problématique des lieux." *Les lieux de mémoire*, vol. 1, edited by Pierre Nora, Gallimard, 1984, pp. 17–42.

———, editor. *Les lieux de mémoire*. Vols. 1–3.3., Gallimard, 1984–1992.

Ortuño Martínez, Manuel. "Juan José Ruiz de Apodaca y Eliza." *Diccionario Biográfico electrónico*, Real Academia de Historia, dbe.rah.es/biografias/5424/juan-jose-ruiz-de-apodaca-y-eliza.

Ortuzar Castañer, Trinidad. Francisco Serrano Domínguez. *Diccionario Biográfico electrónico*, Real Academia de Historia, dbe.rah.es/biografias/8161/francisco-serrano-y-dominguez.

Osuna, Fernando. Personal interview. 18 Sept. 2018.

"Palacio de la Duquesa de Santoña." *Casas Selectas Madrid*. www.casaselectasdemadrid.es/blog/palacio-de-la-duquesa-de-santona/40. Accessed 15 Feb. 2022.

"Palacio de Gaviria: la historia." *Palacio de Gaviria Madrid*. palaciodegaviriamadrid.com/palacio/la-historia/. Accessed 15 Feb. 2022.

Pastrana Jiménez, Lydia. "El patrimonio inmueble de los protagonistas de la trata negrera en la Cádiz decimonónico." *Del olvido a la memoria: La esclavitud en la España contemporánea*, edited by Martín Rodrigo y Alharilla, Icaria, 2022, pp. 227–40.

———. Personal interviews. 19 Sept. 2018, 18 May 2021.

Pérez, Luis, and Raquel Monteagudo, editors. *Carabelas: Crónica de la esclavitud moderna en España*. Special edition on the occasion of the project *El gran experimento* by Miguel Ángel García, 2023.

Pérez-Olagüe, Carmen. "Manuel Gaviria Alcoba." *Diccionario Biográfico electrónico*, Real Academia de Historia, dbe.rah.es/biografias/57456/manuel-gaviria-alcoba.

Pettigrew, William A. "Free to Enslave: Politics and the Escalation of Britain's Transatlantic Slave Trade, 1688–1714." *William and Mary Quarterly*, vol. 64, no. 1, 2007, pp. 3–38.

Piqueras, José Antonio. "La reina, los esclavos y Cuba." *Isabel II: Los espejos de la reina*, edited by Juan S. Pérez Garzón, Marcial Pons, 2004, pp. 91–110.

Presencia e influencia africana y africano-descendiente denominada negra en la historia y prehistoria de España, frente a la desafricanización y ultraeuropeización en la construcción del pasado (Antumi Toasije, 2019), https://dialnet.unirioja.es/servlet/tesis?codigo=248618. Accessed 17 June 2024.

"El Presidente." *Consejo para la Eliminación de la Discriminación Racial o Étnica* (CEDRE), igualdadynodiscriminacion.igualdad.gob.es/elConsejo/elPresidente/home.htm. Accessed 2 Feb. 2024.

Racial Discrimination in the Context of the COVID-19 Crisis. United Nations Human Rights, Office of the High Commissioner, 22 June 2020, www.ohchr.org/Documents/Issues/Racism/COVID-19_and_Racial_Discrimination.pdf.

Ramos Aísa, Lucia. "Thousands Take to Madrid Streets to Protest against Racism." *El País*, 7 June 2020.

Repertorio de vías cuya denominación ha sido creada o modificada en 2021, Ayuntamiento de Cádiz, Alcaldía, https://institucional.cadiz.es/area/documento/repertorio-de-v%C3%ADas-con-denominaci%C3%B3n-modificada-en-2021. Accessed 17 June 2024.

Ribeiro da Silva, Filipa. "Le passé oublié: La traite, l'esclavage et leur abolition dans le programme national portugais de l'histoire." *Enseigner les traites, les esclavages, les abolitions et leurs héritages*, edited by Marie-Albane de Suremain and Éric Mesnard, Karthala, 2021, pp. 156–76.

Rodrigo y Alharilla, Martín. "Barcelona, capital del retorn." *Les bases colonials de Barcelona, 1765–1968*, edited by Martín Rodrigo y Alharilla, MUHBA, 2012, pp. 79–92.

———. "Cádiz y el tráfico ilegal de esclavos en el Atlántico (1817–1866)." *Cádiz y el tráfico de esclavos: De la legalidad a la clandestinidad*, edited by María del Carmen Cózar Navarro and Martín Rodrigo y Alharilla, Sílex, 2018, pp. 195–227.

———. "Entre Barcelona, Cádiz y América, Claudio López Bru, segundo marqués de Comillas, Conferencia impartida en la Real Academia Hispano Americana de Ciencias, Artes y Letras el 25 de marzo de 2010." *Revista Hispanoamericana*, no. 1, 2011, revista.raha.es/bru.html.

———. "From Slave Trade to Banking in Nineteenth-Century Spain." *Comparativ*, vol. 30, nos. 5–6, 2020, pp. 600–14.

———. *Un hombre, mil negocios: La controvertida historia de Antonio López, Marqués de Comillas*. Ariel, 2021.

———. *Los marqueses de Comillas, 1817–1925: Antonio y Claudio López*. Lid, 2000.

———. "Memories in Dispute: Statues in Honour of Enslavers and Conquerors in Barcelona." *Comparativ*, vol. 31, nos. 3–4, 2021, pp. 356–73.

Rodrigo y Alharilla, Martín, and Lizbeth Chaviano. "Introducción." *Negreros y esclavos. Barcelona y la esclavitud atlántica (siglo XVI–XIX)*, edited by Martín Rodrigo y Alharilla and Lizbeth Chaviano Pérez, Barcelona, Icaria, 2017, pp. 7–16.

Rodrigo y Alharilla, Martín, and Ulrike Schmieder. "Políticas de memoria sobre la esclavitud en España: Barcelona en perspectiva comparada." *Historia Social*, no. 105, 2023, pp. 87–104.

Roca Barea, María Elvira. *Imperiofobia: Roma, Rusia, Estados Unidos y el imperio español*. Siruela, 2016.

Rocabruno, Juan Carlos. Personal interview. 8 Oct. 2018.

Romero, Tony. Personal interview. 9 Oct. 2018.

Sanjurjo, José. *In the Blood of our Brothers: Abolitionism and the End of the Slave Trade in Spain's Atlantic Empire*. U of Alabama P, 2021.

Sarriés Griñó, Miguel. *Aniversario de la Abolición de la esclavitud en España el 7 de octubre de 1886*. A.bis, 2006.

Sazatornil Ruiz, Luis. "Arte y mecenazgo de los indianos montañeses: Santoña, Comillas, Valdecilla (1820–1930)." *Arte y mecenazgo indiano: Del Cantábrico al Caribe*, edited by Luis Sazatornil Ruiz, Trea 2007, pp. 543–612.

Schmidt-Nowara, Christopher. *Empire and Antislavery: Spain, Cuba, and Puerto Rico 1833–1874*. U of Pittsburgh P, 1999.

Schmieder, Ulrike. "Lugares de memoria, lugares de silencio: La esclavitud atlántica en museos españoles y cubanos desde una perspectiva comparada internacional." *Jangwa Pana*, vol. 20, no. 1, 2021, pp. 52–80.

———. "Monuments and Street Names: Conflicts about the Traces of Enslavers and Defenders of Slavery in French Cities." *Comparativ*, vol. 31, nos. 3–4, 2021, pp. 335–55.

———. *Nach der Sklaverei: Martinique und Kuba im Vergleich.* 2nd ed., Lit, 2017.

———. "Orte des Erinnerns und Vergessens: Denkmäler, Museen und historische Schauplätze von Sklaverei und Sklavenhandel." *Comparativ*, vol. 22, no. 2, 2012, pp. 60–94.

———. "Sites of Memory of Atlantic Slavery in European Towns with an Excursus on the Caribbean." *Cuadernos Inter.c.a.mbio sobre Centroamérica y el Caribe*, vol. 15, no. 1, 2018, pp. 29–75.

Schmieder, Ulrike, and Michael Zeuske. "Introduction: Falling Statues around the Atlantic: Colonizers, Enslavers and White Abolitionists as Targets of Anti-Racist Activism and the Historical Background of Not-decolonized Memorial Cityscapes." *Comparativ*, vol. 31, no. 3–4, 2021, pp. 297–313.

Soto, Fernando. "Cuando tuvimos bodegas. I. Bodegas Abárzuza." *Cádiz 3000*, 17 Dec. 2018. ocultismocadiz3000.blogspot.com/2018/12/cuando-tuvimos-bodegas-i-bodegas.html.

Stavig, Ward, and Ella Schmidt, editors. *The Tupac Amaru and Catarista Rebellions: An Anthology of Sources.* Hackett Publishing, 2008.

Straehle, Edgar. "Historia y leyenda de la Leyenda Negra: Reflexiones sobre Imperiofobia, de María Elvira Roca Barea." *Nuestra Historia*, no. 8, 2019, pp. 113–37.

Surwillo, Lisa. *Monsters by Trade: Slave Traffickers in Modern Spanish Literature and Culture.* Stanford UP, 2014.

Tannenbaum, Frank. *Slave and Citizen: The Negro in the Americas.* Vintage Books, 1946.

Thomas, Hugh. *The Slave Trade: The History of the Atlantic Slave Trade, 1440–1870.* Macmillan, 1998.

Toasije, Antumi. "La memoria y el reconocimiento de la comunidad africana y africano-descendiente negra en España: el papel de la vanguardia panafricanista." *Nómadas*, vol. 28, no. 4, 2014, pp. 277–316.

———. Personal interview. 29 Sept. 2018.

Torres Ramírez, Bibiano. *La Compañía Gaditana de Negros.* CSIC, 1973.

Toutain, Maxime. *Santos parados: Ethnohistoire et régimes mémoriels des maisons de culte du central Méjico (Matanzas, Cuba).* 2019. U Toulouse II, doctoral thesis.

Tsuchiya, Akiko. "Monuments and public memory: Antonio López y López, slavery, and the Cuban-Catalan connection." *Nineteenth-Century Contexts*, vol. 41, no. 5, 2019, pp. 479–500.

United Nations Human Rights Council (UNHRC). *Report of the Working Group of Experts on People of African Descent on Its Mission to Spain.* 14 Aug. 2018, A/HRC/39/69/ Add.2. ap.ohchr.org/documents/dpage_e.aspx?si=A/HRC/39/69/Add.2.

Vázquez-Fariñas, María. "Los legados de la esclavitud en Cádiz: el patrimonio inmobiliario de los hermanos Abarzuza en el siglo XIX." *Del olvido a la memoria: La esclavitud en la España contemporánea*, edited by Martín Rodrigo

y Alharilla, Icaria, 2022, pp. 197–225.
Vera, Pilar. "Minnesota, Almería, Cádiz." *Diario de Cádiz*, 14 June 2020.
Vila Vilar, Enriqueta. "Las Cortes de Cádiz y el problema de la esclavitud." *Cádiz y el tráfico de esclavos: De la legalidad a la clandestinidad*, edited by María del Carmen Cózar Navarro and Martín Rodrigo y Alharilla, Sílex, 2018, pp. 109–28.
Williams, Erica Lorraine. "Dandara of Palmares." *Dictionary of Caribbean and Afro-Latin American Biography*, edited by Franklin W. Knight and Henry Louis Gates, Oxford African American Studies Center, 2017.

Chapter 7

Memorialized Blackness

The Case of the Museo Atlántico

Jeffrey K. Coleman

In 2016, the Museo Atlántico opened off the coast of Lanzarote in the Canary Islands within a UNESCO World Biosphere Reserve. Designed by British-Guyanese sculptor Jason deCaires Taylor, this museum is part of his global collection of installations that touch on a wide range of sociopolitical issues including climate change, immigration, capitalist greed, and technological addiction, to name a few. The museum is a sculpture garden divided into ten installations, containing a total of more than three hundred life-size human statues placed fourteen meters underwater (see fig. 7.1). These sculptures are made of a special formulation of cement that allows for the growth of marine life such as coral. Thus, the museum helps to rebuild coral reefs and repopulates the area with fish and other marine creatures. My focus in this chapter will be on the third, fourth, and fifth of the ten installations, respectively entitled "The Raft of Lampedusa," "Disconnected," and "Crossing Rubicon." These three installations call attention to the precarity of the migrant crisis that has led to the death of thousands of migrants who have died trying to cross the ocean to reach Europe and the way those deaths have been ignored while ubiquitous in Western media discourse.

The mass deaths of African migrants in the Atlantic attempting to reach the Canary Islands over the last three decades create an interesting

Figure 7.1. Museo Atlántico Map. *Source:* Photo by the author.

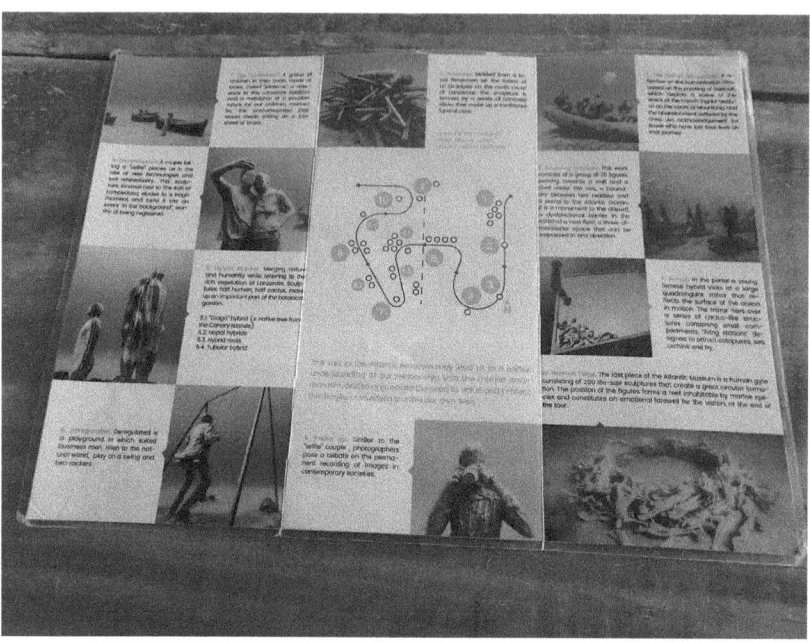

parallel to the transatlantic slave trade, since the ocean plays as a vehicle and location of death, ultimately serving as a cemetery in both cases. Since the early 1990s, the passage of migrants from the African continent to Europe has led to more than 33,000 deaths. In 2017, the German newspaper *Der Tagesspiegel* published a forty-eight-page table created by Turkish artist Banu Cennetoğlu that outlines all the known deaths that had been recorded since 1993.[1] Spain is referenced on almost every page of the document, with Lanzarote alone being referenced thirteen times. The long roster lists men, women, and children of all ages among the dead. As Lorenz Maroldt notes in the commentary that accompanies the list, "Es geht um Geflüchtete, aufgelistet, als Versuch, zehntausende Tote als menschliche Wesen kenntlich zu machen, mit einer Herkunft, einer Vergangenheit, einem Leben" ("It's about the refugees, listed, as an attempt to identify tens of thousands of dead people as human beings, with an origin, a past, a life"; Maroldt). Similarly, archeologists are working in the Caribbean and the Atlantic to uncover slave ships and learn about those who were forcibly carried aboard (see Chason; Roberts). Though this work may not be able to create a roster like Cennetoğlu's, it does help us as a society to recover the memory and recognize the magnitude of the atrocity that was the transatlantic slave trade. As Valérie Loichot notes, "Instead of receding, the memory of the drowned victims of the middle passage resurface at an alarming rate with the mass drownings of exiles and refugees" (6). The enslaved and contemporary migrants are both victims of captivity in which race plays a major role in their subjectivity. The enslaved were stolen from their homelands because their Blackness connoted strength and endurance for the manual labor that white colonial powers needed to develop the Americas. Migrants today are trapped within a racist, capitalist system that exploits their labor and their bodies. Many live in precarious conditions, working what Désirée Kleiner-Liebau refers to as "3-D jobs," (dirty, dangerous, and demeaning) (80). By linking these two phenomena, we can understand how the historical memory of slavery can manifest in contemporary contexts.

It is within this framework that this chapter aims to analyze the Museo Atlántico as a space that simultaneously memorializes and erases Blackness. I argue that despite the museum's admirable ecological mission, its location, aesthetic, and general inaccessibility obfuscate and undermine the purported purpose of these installations in which the Black body is observed at the location of its death. The financial capital required not only for the travel to Lanzarote, but also for the scuba training needed to safely access the museum, allows one to be a passive observer into the destruction of humanity, or specifically, in the case of the installations I will analyze, into the death and dehumanization of Black bodies. I will demonstrate how the Museo Atlántico undermines the commemoration of Black life/death through Valérie Loichot's concept of the unritual, which she defines as "the privation of ritual. . . . Unritual is a state more absolute even than desecration or defilement, since the latter implies the existence of a previous sacred state or object—a temple, a grave, a ceremonial" (7). Through a close reading of the statues (via photography, video, and fieldwork) and an understanding of their touristic impact, this chapter will delineate how the sculptures reify imagery that is later commodified and that further dehumanize those who have died by rendering their human image unrecognizable over time. As coral and marine life consume the statues, their humanity gradually deteriorates until they simply meld with the oceanscape, just as the bodies of the enslaved in centuries past and those of migrants today deteriorate to become part of the ocean. As N. Michelle

Murray states, the statues are "drowned to represent the thousands of deaths in the Mediterranean as migrants risk their lives in pursuit of a European dream" (297). The submersion of the statues, which mirrors the drowning of Black bodies, is critical to the mission of the artist, but begs to question to what extent can this be considered a museum given its limited access and ephemeral nature. Through the analysis of the Museo Atlántico, we can reach a critical reflection on the violence of commemoration through which a ritualized space—the museum—becomes an unritual. In doing so, the Museo Atlántico inadvertently becomes a commentary on the value of Black life in the artistic and touristic spheres.

Like the enslaved Africans whose bodies were dropped into the Atlantic centuries ago, the bodies of migrants who have died attempting to reach the Canary Islands in recent decades have created a cemetery that embodies "this paradox: that the extremely isolating submersion of objects and persons can produce precise, common, and recognizable sites of mourning. Watery realms of unritual graves are nowhere and everywhere at once, absolutely lost and omnipresent. Water is, by definition, the site where no grave can be had, but, at the same time, it is also a site that can be sacred everywhere" (Loichot 139). Given this paradox, we must understand that the location of the museum, off the coast of Lanzarote (the easternmost of the Canary Islands, and thus the closest to the African continent), cannot simply be read in the context of its popularity for scuba divers. Rather, the location also represents a probable site over which *cayucos* (rafts filled with migrants) have passed in the three decades since such migrations have been recorded by Spanish media. Thus, the creation of the museum on this site represents either an attempt to ritualize the death of said migrants who are often anonymized, or an attempt to erase the connotation of the seascape as a mournful space and reclaim its appeal to tourists.

Are Underwater Museums Even Museums at All?

The Museo Atlántico is the second of Taylor's five underwater museums to date. The other four are the Museo Subacuático de Arte (Cancún, Mexico; installed in 2009), The Coral Greenhouse (John Brewer Reef, Australia; installed in 2019), the Écomusée sous-marin (Cannes, France; installed in 2021), and the Museum of Underwater Sculpture Ayia Napa (Ayia Napa, Cyprus; installed in 2021). According to the International Council of Museums, "A museum is a not-for-profit, permanent institution in the service of society that researches, collects, conserves, interprets and exhibits tangible and intangible heritage. Open to the public, accessible and inclusive, museums foster diversity and sustainability. They operate and communicate ethically, professionally and with the participation of communities, offering varied experiences for education, enjoyment, reflection and knowledge sharing" ("Museum Definition"). Under this definition, Taylor's underwater museums do not entirely qualify as museums due to their lack of accessibility. In addition, inaccessibility also implies that the museums are not inclusive, as those with physical limitations are unable to descend to the installations. Finally, given the way marine life inhabits the sculptures, one could argue that the museums are not permanent, since their artistic value will eventually dissipate as coral reefs consume the installations. To maintain the installations in their human form requires the removal of the marine life, thus contradicting the ecological mission of the museum. To prioritize marine life (which symbolizes nature more broadly), the integrity of the sculptures must be sacrificed.

Classifying the Museo Atlántico as a museum is an interesting decision because, as Amy Sodaro notes in her book on memorial museums, "They are imbued with authority and widely considered to be trustworthy sources for information" (23). Though the museum is a didactic space in which knowledge is preserved and transmitted, in many cases they are also *public* sites of violence (be it epistemic or physical). This violence is particularly notable when looking through a racial lens, as there is a long history of racial violence in museums around the world, particularly in relation to the Black body. We must therefore ask, what information is being transmitted to visitors of the Museo Atlántico? The official story being told is about the dangers of climate change. The sculptor creates a dystopian rendering of what will happen to humanity in the future if we do not act soon. However, there are subtexts throughout the museum that consider the past and present, thus facilitating a space for remembrance. Given the subaquatic location of the Museo Atlántico and the limitations that such a location implies (physically and temporally), who is the target audience that is granted access to remember those whose lives have been lost?

Access and Mission

Though there are plenty of photos and videos of the museum, I found it paramount to visit the museum myself to understand the process through which one accesses the space. As mentioned previously, this museum is underwater and thus requires the ability to swim, snorkel, and/or scuba dive. As a result, visits to the museum are booked through diving schools. My visit was booked through Dive College Lanzarote, founded in Playa Blanca in 2001 by Bart Prinsen. The school's "friendly and qualified team of PADI instructors provides briefings and training in English, but also in German, Spanish, Dutch, French and Italian. They have all had a special training to become guides for Museo Atlántico" (Prinsen, "About Us").[2] My visit on February 23, 2022, consisted of the following: a refresher shore dive at twelve meters depth to ensure that I was comfortable with the scuba gear I rented and to review safety protocols, a break known as a surface interval during which the body releases nitrogen absorbed during the dive, a boat ride to the museum entrance, a forty-minute dive at fourteen meters depth to visit the museum, and the boat ride back to the Dive College Lanzarote. Of the thirty or so visitors at the school that day, none were Spaniards, and I was the only person of color. Many were not certified divers or had never dived before, and therefore they had to do the beginner program that includes a shallow shore dive, a scuba lesson in the pool, and a twelve-meter dive to the museum (i.e., swimming above the museum rather than through it). Although the museum is a tourist attraction, not everyone who came to the diving school was able to visit the museum. Several people in the beginner class were prohibited from diving down to the museum because they had difficulty equalizing the pressure in their ears while underwater. Only five, myself included, were PADI-certified divers, and thus allowed to dive the full fourteen meters to the museum. Therefore, access to the museum is not simply a matter of financial means but also one of physical ability. Furthermore, even those who can access the museum must do so fairly quickly, for safety concerns. It would thus require multiple dives down to the museum to capture every detail, which would be an additional cost for air tanks and boat trips from the dive college to the museum site and back. Hence, as my experience demonstrates, only a select few will have the chance to fully experience the museum in its totality.

    To swim among the sculptures highlighted the vast power of water as well as the funereal nature of the space. The sight of immobile human figures underwater was at first startling, but as they were covered in marine growth, there was an immense sense of natural beauty present as well. Loichot argues that "Taylor returns to the drowned their visibility and establishes their humanity, despite the corrosion, or rather, precisely thanks to this corrosion and new assemblages between the human and the nonhuman" (144). I would counter that in the case of the three installations I will detail in the chapter, their visibility and gradual corrosion rather dehumanize those who have already lost their lives. Consequently, "[t]he epistemic violence of representing the unritual kills a second time, desecrates once more what has already been deprived of a veil of decency in the first place" (Loichot 16). Migrants who are anonymized and erased in their oceanic deaths will experience the same underwater as they become part of the landscape of the Atlantic Ocean. This is strikingly similar to the experience of the enslaved in the Americas, because, as Ana Lucía Araujo notes, "In most cases, bondspeople were buried in unmarked graves, condemned to be forgotten even in death" (41). However, in the case of the ocean, there is no grave to mark. Bodies lost to the sea are simply erased beyond recognition, just as the sea will eventually overtake the humanity of Taylor's statues.

The erasure of the subjects' humanity constitutes not only a race critique of the museum but also one of class. As Yasmin Ibrahim observes regarding photography, "Bauman contends these attempts to leave traces can be class specific where the more affluent may have more recourse to leaving traces of mortality whether others may succumb to an anonymous presence" (11). The same may be said for the Museo Atlántico, as only those of a certain social class have access to the museum such as to create memories there by way of photography and social media, whereas the subjects of the museum are anonymized. However, Loichot claims that the sculptor's "website is widely accessible in the liquidity of its slideshow, in its interactive, criss-crossed, and non-linear construction, in its constant growth (the evolution of sculptures is meticulously documented and updated)" (175). I would argue that despite the ubiquity of the internet in today's society, it is unlikely that those making the treacherous journey to the Canary Islands or the families of those who have drowned are looking at this website or even know of the museum's existence. According to Bart Prinsen of Dive College Lanzarote, there are 15,000 to 20,000 visitors annually, so the question remains: The museum and its website are for whom? Only for those with the access and capital to submerge themselves into the ocean as a form of recreation. What is a source of death for some is a source of enjoyment for others.

Sculptures

A visit to the Museo Atlántico requires one to descend twelve to fourteen meters underwater and swim above or through the ten installations. Read as a unit, the museum tells the story of what will happen to human civilization if climate change is not taken seriously (i.e., we will all die). However, within the narrative of the museum, three sculptures point to a different motif: immigration. The first of the three sculptures is entitled "The Raft of Lampedusa" (see fig. 7.2). Taylor based this sculpture on Théodore Géricault's 1819 painting *The Raft of the Medusa*, which portrays the real-life chaos that took place among a group of French sailors when their frigate, the *Medusa*, ran aground off the coast of Mauritania on July 2, 1816 (see fig. 7.3). Due to a lack of lifeboats, 150 of the 400 aboard were forced to construct a makeshift raft to survive at sea, but conditions on the raft descended into chaos as many starved to death from a lack of provisions, which later devolved into murder and cannibalism. As a result, there were fewer than twenty survivors when the raft was rescued by a British ship called the *Argus* thirteen days later. As Murray asserts, "The painting depicts the types of transoceanic voyages that served to impoverish Africa for Europe's benefit, laying the socioeconomic and nationalist foundations that generate today's routes wherein African migrants travel to Europe in search of a brighter future" (296). The sculpture mimics the painting by

Figure 7.2. "The Raft of Lampedusa." *Source:* Photo by the author.

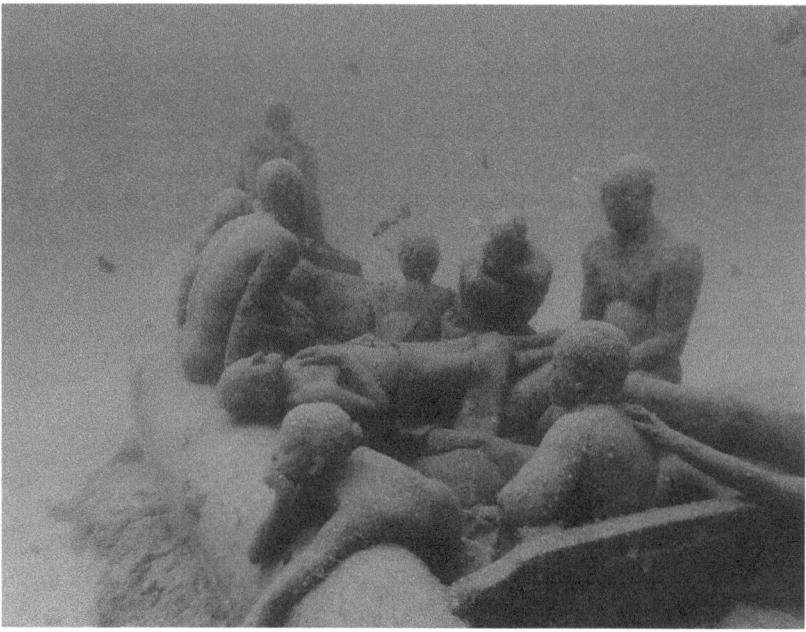

Figure 7.3. "The Raft of the Medusa" by Théodore Géricault (1819). *Source:* Wikimedia Commons. Public domain.

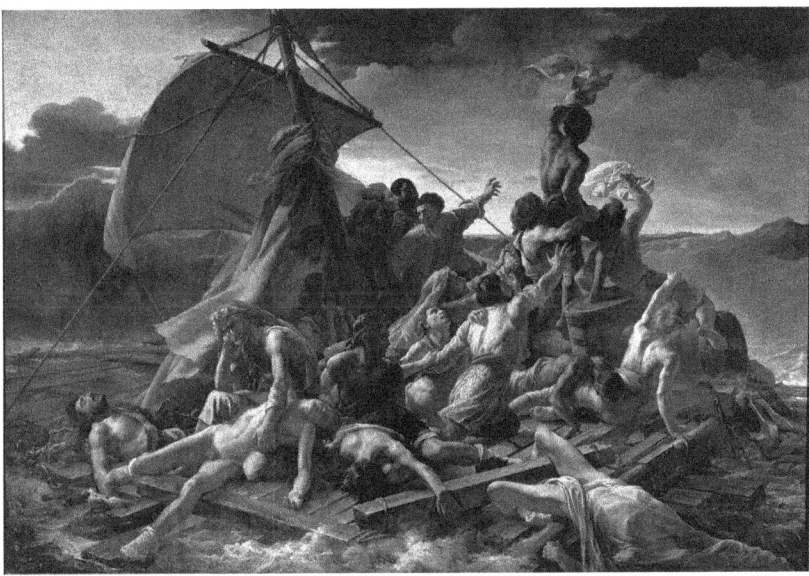

portraying thirteen figures on a raft, but instead of a group of French male sailors, there are migrants of different genders and ages on their way to Europe. Whereas Gericault's painting critiques the lack of humanity among the French sailors as a result of mismanagement, the sculpture highlights the humanity of migrants in the face of a continent that wishes not to receive them. The invocation of the Italian island of Lampedusa is in reference to the disastrous shipwreck off its coast on October 3, 2013, in which over 350 migrants died as their boat coming from Libya capsized in the middle of the night, leading to chaos as the passengers tried to save themselves. Given that this museum is in the Atlantic Ocean, the reference to Italy and the Mediterranean seems out of place and leads one to question why Lanzarote or Fuerteventura (the easternmost islands of the Canary Islands) were not invoked in the title of the sculpture instead.

These two inspirational sources converge to result in a sculpture that evokes a deep hopelessness, because, as Taylor notes, "[e]ven as raft after raft of refugees is lost beneath the waves of the Mediterranean, as the bodies of children wash up on European shores, Fortress Europe has withdrawn rescue operations, built barriers, turned away" (*The Underwater Museum*).

Spain plays a crucial role as a nation of Fortress Europe, as migrants can enter through three distinct routes: by land into Ceuta and Melilla, via the Mediterranean to the Iberian Peninsula and the Balearic Islands, and via the Atlantic to the Canary Islands (see Nair). This unique geographic position and the resulting migrant routes are what led Spain to having the world's second highest rate of immigration after the United States throughout the 2000s.[3] However, a high immigration rate also implied a higher number of migrant deaths as many like the figures on the raft tried to reach Spain.

As I have noted elsewhere, the sculpture inverts "the racial and (neo)colonial dynamics [in] order to commemorate those who have died and celebrate those who survived" (Coleman 192). This is achieved using some models who themselves made the perilous journey to Lanzarote and survived. Such is the case of the figure standing at the front of the raft, Abdel Kader, a Saharawi refugee who arrived to Lanzarote in 2000 at the age of thirteen. His inclusion in the creation of the sculpture implies a devotion to the humanity of those dead and alive. While this may appear to contradict my premise about the dehumanizing nature of the museum, as I will demonstrate later in this chapter, "The Raft of Lampedusa" serves as a ploy through which to attract visitors to the museum. Abdel Kader is only mentioned on the artist's website, but not in any of the materials one receives during the visit. Therefore, for the average museum visitor, his body is simply a representation of the anonymous migrant who died at sea. In this way, Abdel Kader's body is being used as a pawn through which to draw in the spectator to reflect on the death of migrants. We are not able to contemplate the life of survivors when fourteen meters under the sea. In its totality, this sculpture and the vastness of the surrounding seascape invoke the tragedy of Lampedusa, while also transmitting a universalized story about the tragedy of migration in Europe.

The museum pamphlet provides the following description of the subsequent sculpture, "Disconnected": "A couple taking a 'selfie' places us in the use of new technologies and self-referentiality. This sculpture, located next to The Raft of Lampedusa, [alludes] to a tragic moment and turns it into an event 'in the background,' worthy of being registered" ("Museo Atlántico"). What is not mentioned in this description is that the two figures are faceless (see fig. 7.4). This deliberate choice connotes the universality of selfie culture, such that this couple could be just about anyone. In addition, with their backs to the raft, the suffering of migrants abroad becomes a background in the couple's photo, and without facial expressions, it is impossible to determine whether the presence of the raft is desired or

Memorialized Blackness | 201

Figure 7.4. "Disconnected." *Source:* Photo by the author.

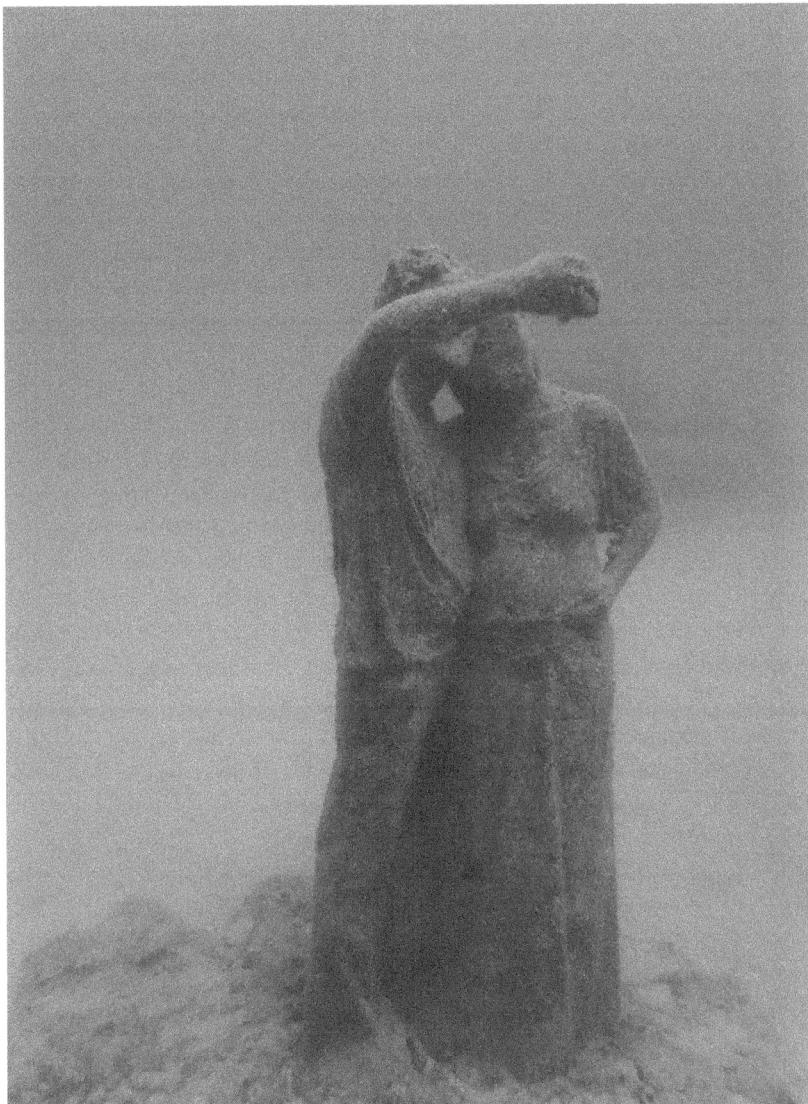

is an eyesore that ruins their romantic moment. In either case, the result is callous dehumanization.

Whereas the proliferation of migrant deaths in the media has inured Spaniards to the magnitude of the humanitarian crises that compel people to make the harrowing journey across the sea, this sculpture illustrates the way in which such selfie culture has compelled many to capture themselves in the midst of disaster and/or death. As Yasmin Ibrahim contends, "The juxtaposing of the living self against a site of death becomes a deliberate device to impress one's mortal presence and to equally capitalise on the residue of the media memory. This curation of the self into the media event and the production of the selfie as an aestheticised commodity of exchange raise further scrutiny into the ethics of visuality online. . . . The tragedy is intertextually referenced in the image but the self remains detached from it" (5–6). Furthermore, those of the Global North taking disaster selfies with those of the Global South in the background as auxiliary subjects are reifying neo-colonial racial dynamics mediated through technology that adds nuances of class as well.

"Disconnected" thus can be read as a commentary on the ethics of the selfie within the context of dark tourism, which Anthony Seaton defines as "travel to a location wholly, or partially, motivated by the desire for actual or symbolic encounters with death, particularly, but not exclusively, violent death" (15). As mentioned earlier, the site of the Museo Atlántico off the coast of Lanzarote is where many pateras have met a tragic fate. This macabre fact transforms the museum into a site of dark tourism. The selfie being taken in "Disconnected" then not only captures the plight of those on "The Raft of Lampedusa," but also the funereal space that is the ocean. In her canonical essay "On Photography," Susan Sontag notes that photography "is a social rite, a defense against anxiety, and a tool of power" (8). Therefore, the selfie in "Disconnected" can be interpreted as a hegemonic gesture aimed at distancing the statue's white European subjects from the racial anxieties of migration, further dehumanizing the migrant subjects in the raft.

"Crossing Rubicon" is the fifth installation in the museum: "This work consists of a group of thirty-five figures walking toward a wall and a door under the sea, a boundary between two realities and a portal to the Atlantic Ocean. It is a monument to the absurd, a dysfunctional barrier in the midst of a vast fluid, a three-dimensional space that can be surpassed in any direction" ("Museo Atlántico"; see fig. 7.5). The piece's title comes from the phrase "to cross the Rubicon," which signifies a figurative boundary that, once crossed, commits the person irrevocably to the decision—a point of no return. The phrase references Julius Caesar's crossing of the Rubicon River in 49 BC that sparked a long civil war that he eventually won. This war led to the end of the Roman Republic as Julius Caesar declared himself dictator

Figure 7.5. "Crossing Rubicon." *Source:* Photo by the author.

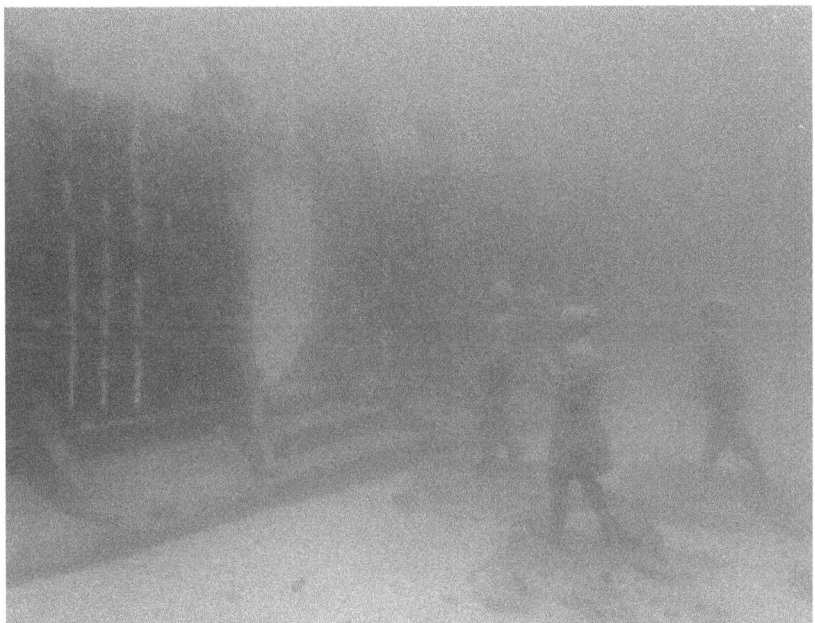

for life, paving the path for the creation of the Roman Empire, signaling a new world order.[4] Taylor's invocation of the Rubicon is deliberate, as the creation of the Roman Empire is one of the most important parts of world history. In a similar vein, once humanity crosses the point of no return with regard to climate change, a new environmental order will develop, resulting in the extinction of humanity as nature does its best to survive, which is demonstrated in the remainder of the museum's installations.

Although "Crossing Rubicon" is meant to mark the before and after of the point of no return regarding climate change, it relies on the imagery of the transatlantic slave trade. This installation mimics the dynamics of the "Door of No Return" found at many slave castles in Western Africa that established a boundary between being free and enslaved. This is made further evident by the fact that migrants who survive the sea journey to Spain may find themselves in conditions of modern slavery, working in horrendous conditions, such as those in the "Mar de plástico" (the industrial greenhouses in Almería that produce a large portion of Europe's produce). Therefore, upon leaving their homelands, migrants have crossed a Rubicon, taking on new identities that are imposed upon them by the receptor nation.

The wall is absurd and dysfunctional for its permeability and its location. Water can flow through and around the barrier in any direction, demonstrating that there is no Rubicon for the ocean. Water will continue to flow and circulate, yet humanity may not unless we act soon. Adding to the carnivalesque nature of this installation is the intercalation of another installation entitled "Photo Op," in which a photographer hidden between the grates of the Rubicon's wall takes photos of those walking toward the Rubicon. As the pamphlet notes, "Similar to the 'selfie' couple, photographers pose a debate on the permanent recording of images in contemporary societies" ("Museo Atlántico"). As Ibrahim asserts in reference to the disaster selfie, such photos serve "not to extend the project of empathy or solidarity with the fallen or the incapacitated but to capitalise on the media memory and the residual quality or aura of the place memory" (5). This museum simultaneously critiques and reifies the problematics of photography that sensationalize and later inure the public to the plight of migrants.

Artistic Intention versus Public Reception

In my conversations with Bart Prinsen (director of Dive College Lanzarote), I was told that "The Raft of Lampedusa" was a last-minute addition aimed at attracting attention from the media when the museum opened.[5] If this is indeed true, then migrant deaths serve as a pawn in the capitalist marketing of this museum, further exemplifying how Black bodies are used as entertainment. To capitalize on the tragedy of Lampedusa (as well as those occurring in the Canary Islands) as a way to promote the ecological mission of the museum and attract visitors leaves much to be desired. Indeed, "The Raft of Lampedusa" was a major draw when the museum first opened, as photos of it were spread through traditional and social media. This led many, myself included, to initially understand the entirety of the museum to be an artistic homage to migrants who have lost their lives on the journey to reach Europe.

However, this is not the first time that Taylor has encountered an incongruence between his artistic intention and the public reception of his pieces. The most notable example is his 2007 piece "Vicissitudes," submerged off the coast of Grenada. According to the original description of the piece, "'Vicissitudes' depicts a circle of figures, all linked through holding hands. These are life-size casts taken from a group of children of diverse ethnic backgrounds. Circular in structure . . . the work both withstands strong currents and replicates one of the primary geometric shapes, evoking ideas of unity and continuum" (Carozza).[6] Many interpreted the piece to be about the transatlantic slave trade as a result of the statue's structural supports near the clasped hands that resemble shackles. The artist, in a now-deleted statement, said, "It was never my intention to have any connection to the Middle passage. . . . Although it was not my intention from the outset I am very encouraged how it has resonated differently within various communities and feel it is working as an art piece by questioning our identity, history and stimulating debate" (Carozza). The deletion of both the original description and his statement illustrates a lack of awareness of how such a piece would be perceived given its location and composition. One could also interpret the deletion as a desire for the public to interpret it as they see fit, rather than to impose an artistic interpretation.

It is evident that in creating the Museo Atlántico, Taylor wanted to avoid interpretations of his work that would connect him to the legacies of the transatlantic slave trade, but once again the subjects and location dictate a social meaning larger than the artist because, as historian Jessica Millward points out, "Despite DeCaires Taylor's platitudes against naming the sculptures as a monument to the Atlantic slave trade, that so many make this connection speaks of a need to reconcile with the horror of chattel slavery. For many, the sculptures function as a way to make peace with the past." Given that the Atlantic is forever linked to the historical memory of slavery, the construction of an art piece featuring racialized figures in, on, near, or under the Atlantic is surely to provoke interpretations linked to the transatlantic slave trade. To ignore such a fact is to misunderstand the magnitude of the Middle Passage and to further dehumanize those who have lost their lives.

That said, must every art piece with racialized figures juxtaposed with or placed in the Atlantic Ocean connect to the transatlantic slave trade? Clearly not, but the public's need for such a hermeneutic connection speaks to the ways in which the legacy of slavery has been insufficiently engaged with, leaving millions of Afro-descendants with no cathartic experience through which to process their transgenerational trauma. This lack of catharsis is the core of the unritual, since the relationship between those lost lives and the art installations of the Museo Atlántico are an attempt to ritualize those who have passed that is ultimately deterred, in this case, by the ocean and the seascape. However, that privation of ritual is facilitated by the materials used to create these installations; thus, Taylor deprives us of the ability to ritualize those lives. We are therefore left with two questions: How can those who have been consumed by the sea be remembered when the ocean consumes all that it touches? If the ocean itself is a monument, then is an ecological approach the only way to honor those lives? Central to these questions is the fact that the majority of the installations of the Museo Atlántico have human form in order to be more realistic. Taylor creates many of his sculptures based on actual human beings, as in the case of Abdel Kader in "The Raft of Lampedusa." The realism of the sculptures adds to the morbid nature of their installation, as to submerge them is to submit these figures to the forces of the ocean to be gradually disappeared.

Conclusion

The installations of the Museo Atlántico create an echo of the transatlantic slave trade by means of their location, methodology, and subject matter. Despite the ecological mission of the museum, when examined through a racial lens, the discourse presented within these installations is that of an ephemeral memory that is gradually consumed by the sea. In this way, the museum constitutes an unritual, a space in which those lives lost are subjected to a second death and thus never able to be ritualized. This consumption of Blackness reifies the historical and contemporary violence that the Atlantic Ocean represents for Black people in Africa and in the diaspora. Although Taylor had no intention of linking his work to the slave trade, the memory of the atrocity overshadows his environmental mission both in Spain and in the Caribbean, because once the installations are in place, they take on new meanings. Furthermore, as he himself states on his website, "As soon as we sink them, they belong to the sea," and no grave is possible in the vastness of the ocean ("Museo Atlántico").

Notes

1. For the full table, visit www.tagesspiegel.de/politik/downloads/listeentire-berlinccbanu (Cennetoğlu).

2. Founded in 1966, PADI (Professional Association of Diving Instructors) is the world's largest ocean exploration and diver organization.

3. It is worth noting that these routes do not constitute the majority of Spanish immigration.

4. For more detail on Caesar's conquest of Rome, see Fezzi.

5. I was unable to meet with the artist to confirm this.

6. This description is no longer available on the artist's website.

Works Cited

Araujo, Ana Lucía. *Slavery in the Age of Memory: Engaging the Past*. Bloomsbury, 2020.

Carozza, Davide. "Jason De Caires Taylor, 'Vicissitudes.'" *Deeps*. sites.duke.edu/blackatlantic/sample-page/depictions-of-the-middle-passage-and-the-slave-trade-in-visual-art/levitate-windward-coast-and-vicissitudes-curatorial-statement/jason-de-caires-taylor-vicissitudes/#_ednref1. Accessed September 3, 2022.

Cennetoğlu, Banu. "Liste Von 33.293 registrierten Asylsuchenden, Geflüchteten und Migrant*Innen, die Aufgrund der restriktiven Politik der Festung Europas zu Tode kamen." *Der Tagesspiegel*, 9 Nov. 2017.

Chason, Rachel. "African Scuba Divers Rewrite a 'Settlers' Narrative' of the Slave Trade." *Washington Post*, 17 Nov. 2022.

Coleman, Jeffrey K. "From Racial Contaminant to Nutrient in Spain's Ecological Future." *A Companion to Spanish Environmental Cultural Studies*, edited by Luis I. Prádanos, Tamesis, 2022, pp. 188–92.

Fezzi, Luca. *Crossing the Rubicon: Caesar's Decision and the Fate of Rome*. Translated by Richard Dixon, Yale UP, 2017.

Géricault, Théodore. *Le Radeau de la Méduse*. 1819. Louvre, Paris.

Ibrahim, Yasmin. "Self-Representation and the Disaster Event: Self-Imaging, Morality and Immortality." *Journal of Media Practice*, vol. 16, no. 3, 2015, pp. 211–27.

Kleiner-Liebau, Désirée. *Migration and the Construction of National Identity in Spain*. Iberoamericana, 2009.

Loichot, Valérie. *Water Graves: The Art of the Unritual in the Greater Caribbean*. U of Virginia P, 2020.

Maroldt, Lorenz. ""Die Liste" von Banu Cennetoglu: Künstlerin dokumentiert das Sterben von 33.293 Geflüchteten." *Der Tagesspiegel*, 9 Nov. 2017.

Millward, Jessica. "From the Ocean Floor: Death, Memory and the Atlantic Slave Trade." *Black Perspectives*, 8 March 2017, www.aaihs.org/from-the-ocean-floor-death-memory-and-the-atlantic-slave-trade/.

Murray, N. Michelle. "Visualizing the Black Mediterranean." *Liquid Borders*, Routledge, 2021, pp. 289–302.

"Museum Definition." International Council of Museums, 25 Aug. 2022, icom.museum/en/resources/standards-guidelines/museum-definition/.

"Museo Atlántico." Centros de Arte Cultura y Turismo del Cabildo de Lanzarote, 2016.

Nair, Parvati. "Europe's "Last" Wall: Contiguity, Exchange, and Heterotopia in Ceuta, the Confluence of Spain and North Africa." *Border Interrogations: Questioning Spanish Frontiers*, edited by Benita Sampedro Vizcaya and Simon Doubleday, Berghahn Books, 2008, pp. 15–41.

Prinsen, Bart. "About Us." Museo Atlántico Lanzarote. underwatermuseumlanzarote.com/en/about-us/. Accessed August 15, 2022.

———. "Museo Atlántico Visitors." Email to Jeffrey K. Coleman, 22 Jan. 2023.

Roberts, Tara. "Hidden No More." *National Geographic*, March 2022, pp. 36–57.

Seaton, Anthony V. "Guided by the Dark: From Thanatopsis to Thanatourism." *International Journal of Heritage Studies*, vol. 2, no. 4, 1996, pp. 234–44.

Sodaro, Amy. *Exhibiting Atrocity: Memorial Museums and the Politics of Past Violence*. Rutgers UP, 2017.

Sontag, Susan. *On Photography*. Picador, 2001.

Taylor, Jason deCaires. "Museo Atlántico." www.underwatersculpture.com/projects/museo-atlantico-lanzarote/. Accessed 15 Aug. 2022.

———. "Underwater Gallery." underwatersculpture.com/works/underwater/. Accessed 15 Aug. 2022.

———. *The Underwater Museum: The Submerged Sculptures of Jason DeCaires Taylor*. Chronicle Books LLC, 2014.

Chapter 8

Public Memory Policies in Spain

How Is the Colonial Past Addressed?

Oriol López Badell and Celeste Muñoz Martínez,
interviewed by Akiko Tsuchiya and Aurélie Vialette,
translated by María Cristina Urruela

Oriol López Badell is a historian who has served as the coordinator of the European Observatory on Memories (EUROM) at the University of Barcelona Solidarity Foundation since 2012. He was also the international relations officer while working for the Memorial Democràtic, spearheading the promotion of memory policies for the Catalan government. As a member of the historical memory organization Associació Conèixer Història, he participated in presentations and guided tours aimed to interpret the traces of historical memory in Catalonia and Spain. He also coordinates the project www.memoriabcn.cat, a digital platform designed to disseminate information about sites of memory in the city of Barcelona.

Celeste Muñoz Martínez is a historian (PhD, University of Barcelona) at the National University of Distance Education in Madrid (UNED). Her research has focused on the study of Spanish colonialism in Equatorial Guinea, from a legal, political, and memorial perspective. Her doctoral thesis, situated at the intersections of history and anthropology, was titled "Law against Custom: Segregation, Legal Assimilation, and Punishment in Equatorial Guinea under Francoism (1936–1959)." With López Badell, she collaborates in the European Observatory on Memories, where she is the coordinator of the "colonial memories" line of research and the "online memories" project, which applies new digital methodologies to memory studies. Additionally, she coordinates the team in charge of the Spanish part of the Trans-Atlantic Redress Network project, which aims to map historical injustices related to racial discrimination.

Given their backgrounds in public history, López Badell and Muñoz Martínez are well positioned to reflect on the state of public memory policies in Catalonia and Spain.

This interview was conducted in January, 2023.

Could you tell us a little about your EUROM project and its objectives? How was the project conceived? What kind of institutional (and financial) support have you received? Who are the main participants in this initiative?

OLB: The European Observatory on Memories (EUROM) is an international network of institutions and organizations committed to the analysis and promotion of public policies on societal memory of historical events. It (EUROM) aims to consider the history of struggles for democracy and freedom in Europe and beyond, and to promote collective memories from a plural, diverse and multidisciplinary approach. The Observatory is led by the Fundació Solidaritat of the University of Barcelona and has the financial support of the European Commission, through the Citizens, Equality, Rights and Values program (CERV), and the Barcelona City Council. Among the diversity of topics that we have addressed with our partners since the creation of EUROM in 2012, the main historical episodes of the twentieth century highlighted are the consequences of Nazism, Fascism, and Stalinism; the Spanish Civil War and Franco's dictatorship; civil rights in Northern Ireland; pro-democratic movements in Eastern Europe during the Cold War; resistance against dictatorships in Greece and Portugal; and the transition processes in several countries. But since 2015 we have also continuously dealt with current memory of the colonial period to analyze what consequences this historical period has for today's societies, what symbols still link us to it, and what current responsibilities European countries (may) have.

Have you worked closely with the Spanish government or the local (Barcelona) government in your project? If so, what has your experience been?

OLB: Public policies regarding (historical) memories in Spain are very recent; the first Spanish Law of Historical Memory was approved in December 2007, and only two months before, the law of Democratic Memory was launched in Catalonia, which was the first Autonomous Community of the Spanish State to have one. But coincidentally when we created the Observatory in 2012, the first steps made in this field were sharply interrupted by the rise to power of conservative parties that saw in these laws a confrontation with a difficult past that "opened old wounds." In Spain the Popular Party government had left the implementation of the Law of Historical Memory without financial resources and, in Catalonia, the Christian Democrats of Convergència i Unió reduced its memory policies to a minimum expression. So, at first, we just received support from the European Union. It was not until 2015 that we began to collaborate, at the local level, with the Barcelona City Council, which had for the first time created an office for the planning and implementation of memory-related policies in the urban area. The aim of this collaboration is to promote activities related to memory among the citizens of the different neighborhoods of Barcelona, often adding other international perspectives. One of the first initiatives we developed with the city council was precisely in the field of colonial memory, to contribute to the debate on the future of the monument to Antonio López y López, a Spanish businessman who made his fortune in Cuba in the nineteenth century, in part by including in his business activities the trafficking of enslaved people.

Once work on memory policies was restarted at the state level with the creation of a Secretary of State for Democratic Memory in 2020, at EUROM we began in 2021 to collaborate with the Spanish government in a small project to identify and manage conflicts in different memory sites in the Spanish state. And in 2022 we jointly organized an international meeting in Barcelona to present good practices in the field of databases of victims in Spain and other countries.

To what extent do you think public awareness of Spain's colonial and slave-owning past has changed in recent years, especially since 2020? Do you think the silence has been broken?

CMM: It is important to point out the existence of different turning points that have characterized the proliferation of debates on Spain's colonial past, its legacies, and its historical responsibilities. Without this detailed perspective we can hardly understand what has happened since 2020. In my opinion, the first (turning point) was in 1992, during the sumptuous commemorations of the quincentenary of the arrival of Columbus in America. At that time, numerous indigenous and native peoples' movements raised their voices against the approving tone that characterized the October 12 celebrations, and the supposed feat of "discovery." As a result, a few years later, the proposal to commemorate the Day of Indigenous Resistance in Latin America emerged as a counterproposal to the historical memory in the Hispanic world. All these questions challenged historical thinking in Spain and marked, in my opinion, the beginning of a progressive change of views on this past. In addition, that same year saw the murder of Lucrecia Pérez, the first racially motivated hate crime recognized in Spain, which also led to a greater mobilization of the anti-racist movement in Spain. The second turning point would come in 2010. This new wave, however, was not driven by a specific event, but by a worldwide increase in the momentum of anti-colonial and anti-racist movements. A particular characteristic of these movements is that they went beyond a mere change of narratives about the past and aspired to reparations for African, Afro-descendant, and diasporic communities in general. In Spain, one of the most significant examples of this new phase is the debate on the removal of the monument to slave-owner Antonio López in Barcelona, initiated in 2010. Additionally, that same year the Proposal of Non-binding Resolution "on the memory of slavery, with the recognition and support of the black, African, and Afro-descendant community in Spain" was approved. This parliamentary initiative was neither binding nor legislative in nature, but it was the first time that a proposal of this type, promoted by African associations, was approved by Congress. Throughout the following decade, there was a sustained growth in this type of initiative. The year 2020 signifies a new momentum that could be attributed to a third turning point in the form of the Black Lives Matter movement. However, this is too recent an event to analyze the dynamics with sufficient historical perspective.

And have global movements like Black Lives Matter had an impact on the general public in Spain? Have these global movements helped to break the silence around colonialism (and racism) in Spain?

CMM: Despite the lack of historical perspective, it is clear that since Black Lives Matter there has been a greater social debate in Spain. And just as in previous decades, this debate has been driven primarily by anti-colonial movements, activists, and Afro-descendants in different fields. The political and institutional policy agenda has lagged far behind. In fact, it could be said that it is being dragged along. The difference in this new phase, in my perception, is that it is accompanied by a greater public recognition of the links between the past and the present. That is, a growing awareness that racism, immigration laws, and institutional violence against migrants, or racialized people, are strongly associated with the colonial past and modern-day processes reminiscent of slavery. Indeed, movements such as Black Lives Matter, born out of the murder of George Floyd at the hands of the police, ended up supporting actions against monuments of slaveholders and colonialists. This is a clear sign of connections between the symbols of the past and present events. A precedent, the Rhodes Must Fall movement, which occurred in South Africa in 2015, also points to this connection. In Spain, the mobilizations against monuments to Christopher Columbus, among others, have, since 2020, been more intense and numerous, accompanied by proclamations against racism and colonialism—understood as a structure that survives in time.

How can we explain the absence of an institutional politics of memory concerning monuments linked to colonialism and slavery in Spanish history, when there has been a broad and public debate (since 2007) on the historical memory of the Civil War? Why this selective amnesia precisely on colonial and racial issues?

CMM: I believe that the belated development of memory policies on the Civil War and Francoism, characteristic of a Spanish model of impunity, also helps us to understand better the difficulties in reckoning today with the past. The 2007 memory laws came more than thirty years after the death of the dictator and today the issue is far from resolved. In fact, it remains a tense political and social battlefield. This difficulty in dealing with the past is one element that explains the absence of memory policies on slavery and colonialism. However, there are other elements—for example, that of identity. The idea of the Spanish empire portrayed positively has been a significant part of the public identity of the Spanish state. To break with this reality means to demolish some very deep-rooted elements of national identity, and such a demolition has an enormous sociological impact. These impacts are often resisted because various political elements feel it is useful to appeal to the emotional part of the old memory. The intent is not a judgment of a guilty society, it is not an "us" to be redeemed, nor a dichotomy between "good" and "bad"; it cannot be presented in this way, since the intent is simply to critically review what happened in the past and shape present symbols that deal with historical events or personalities to build more just societies. Again, the difficulties of a change in historical memory are intricately involved with the concept that we have, in the past, benefited from certain discriminations and inequalities (regional, racial, and economic). Here in Catalonia, for example, the *indianos* (businessmen who settled between Cuba and Catalonia in the nineteenth century, such as Miquel Biada or the Güell family) have historically been associated with progress and occupy a privileged place in the public space. They have represented the bourgeois ideal of a universal modernity linked to the industrialization of our country. It matters little that their economic power resulted from the exploitation of enslaved people in the plantations, along with the Catalan industrial proletariat. Therefore, changing historical referents that do not represent the majority today should be understood as a collective benefit for all. But questioning all these foundations and replacing them with positive elements is not an easy task, especially with the appearance in the last decade of reactionary waves opposing these paradigm shifts.

What kind of cultural and political initiatives have there been to examine the legacies of colonialism and slavery in Spanish society and, more specifically, in Catalonia? Have there been movements for the recognition of the historical memory of Catalan colonialism?

CMM: Yes; recently, we can situate certain political initiatives such as the apologies for the crimes of colonialism by the Parliament of Catalonia in 2021, or the final removal of the monument of Antonio López y López by the city council of Barcelona in 2018. Political criticism has also begun concerning the "Firas d'Indians," commonly held in some towns of the Catalan coast, that portray a stereotyped way of life of the *indianos* in Cuba (through musical performances, representations, or other activities). Another initiative that is perhaps worth mentioning is the report done by the Observatorio de la Vida Cotidiana, commissioned by EUROM and the Barcelona City Council, on the Moroccan collections of the Museu Etnològic i de Cultures del Món in Barcelona, with the aim of identifying possible demands for patrimonial restitution (of artistic or handcrafted objects and images that were taken during the Spanish colonial experience in the Protectorate). Cultural reparations may also be an issue. This pioneering work at the national level was presented at the seminar "Repairing the Past: International Seminar on Justice and Colonialism" (October 2022). These types of seminars and debate forums in multiple contexts are very well received and allow us to connect academia, activists, the art world, etc. Even then, there is a long way to go in improving education and curricula on colonialism and slavery. Additional effort is needed for the revision of migration policies, for combating inequalities and racism, and for better political representation of the diversity in our society. In other words, to confront structural issues that propagate much of the ignorance and stereotypes that exist today.

What kind of activism and cultural initiatives have there been to create events to enhance commemorative justice? We are thinking, for example, of the artists and cultural activists who have addressed the places of colonial memory (monuments of Antonio López, Columbus, etc.), the photographic exhibition in MACBA by Daniela Ortiz on colonial memory, the mobilizations of October 12 (Day of *Hispanidad*).

CMM: It is important to insist that without the impulse of activism in the Afro-descendant communities (in all of their heterogeneity), the advancement of debates on historical justice would not have been possible. One example I would like to mention is the process following the renaming of the Antonio López square, which since 2021 bears the name of Idrissa Diallo. Anti-racist collectives and activists were the driving force behind this renaming after years of struggle and signature gathering. Idrissa Diallo died in 2012 in the Center for Internment of Foreigners (CIE) in Barcelona. The recovery of his memory, that of a victim of racism and institutional violence, in the place previously occupied by a slaver, is a very powerful message. These results of struggle are added to key cultural initiatives, such as those mentioned, by Daniela Ortiz. Other examples are the Radio Africa Magazine project for the dissemination of African arts and cultures, the recently inaugurated biennial of African photography, and many other actions and festivals that make visible the richness of African cultural productions. I consider that cultural initiatives are, in a broad sense, also acts of reparation that respond to stereotypes and invisibilization, even if they do not have as their main objective issues such as slavery or colonialism. In this sense, the list is very long and growing. However, I would like to emphasize that I believe it is a pending task. It is a matter not only of contesting memory of a past represented by its monuments, but also of generating new memories and spaces. In this sense, with the removal of symbology, we must add the filling of absences. There is no memorial, monument, or museum in Spain that seeks to remember and commemorate either colonialism or slavery (initiatives that we do find in other contexts such as the USA, the UK, France, or the Netherlands).

OLB: Precisely; given this lack of official recognition of Spanish responsibility in colonialism and the slave trade, in 2016 EUROM promoted a "public history" initiative (using this term born in the United States in the mid-1970s) that took the form of a guided tour of the traces left by colonial fortunes in Barcelona, such as buildings, monuments and streets named after distinguished individuals (see fig. 8.1). The tour addressed the role of Catalan and Spanish "entrepreneurs" in the slave trade in the eighteenth

Figure 8.1. Route of slavery, Barcelona (2017). *Source:* Photo by the author.

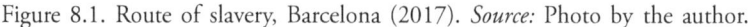

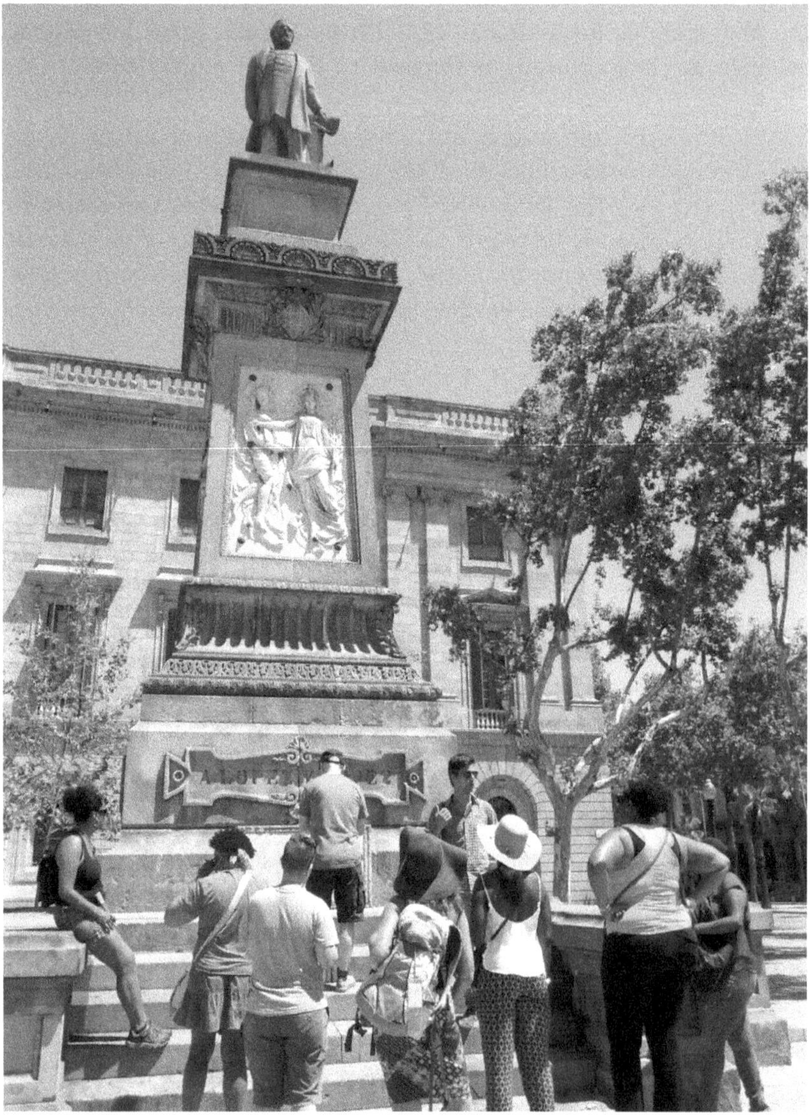

and nineteenth centuries, who made investments that helped shape modern Barcelona. The route clearly was intended to contribute to the debate about certain monuments and public sites of historical importance in the city, especially since the emergence of the Black Lives Matter movement. Conveying the necessary information for society to reflect on the meaning of certain monuments and street names, the guided tour contributes to the process of public recognition of the damages inflicted on peoples and communities by colonialism and slavery in the past. I see this as a modest form of reparation. The route was developed together with our colleagues from the Associació Conèixer Història (www.memoriabcn.cat/en/legacies-of-slavery/) and the Fundación Cipriano García (www.ccoo.cat/ciprianogarcia/), linked to the trade union Comisiones Obreras, and was offered until the arrival of the Covid-19 pandemic. Thanks to an article that appeared in the British newspaper *The Guardian* (Eilers), the route aroused much interest among foreign tourists visiting Barcelona, including many African Americans.

Have there been any conversations about possible acts of reparation (beyond mere acknowledgment) to the communities most directly affected by colonialism?

CMM: A big pending issue. The area of restitution has been the one that has recently advanced the most. There are some requests for the return of museum artifacts, an example being the return to Colombia of the Quimbaya Treasure from the Museum of America in Madrid. In October 2022, the Ministry of Culture announced the creation of a commission to study possible demands and procedures for the return of items taken during the colonial period. But a concrete initiative has not yet materialized. There are also requests from the CARICOM (Caribbean Reparations Commission), but none of these demands, not even that for public apologies, has been supported by the authorities. Another unsuccessful example is the compensation demanded by the Rif communities for the use of chemical weapons during the Rif War (1911–1927). This request was discussed in the Congress of Deputies in 2005 and was rejected by a very large majority of the members of the Parliament.

Perhaps one of the few cases that have been resolved favorably, in addition to the removal of the López monument, was the campaign initiated by the Haitian physician Alphonse Arcelin for the removal of a desiccated body, supposedly of a member of the San people, in the Darder Museum in Banyoles (Catalonia). In this case, after an intense political and judicial battle, the body was removed and repatriated to Botswana in 2000. But the general conclusion is that, for now, neither apologies, nor restitutions, nor museum and public space relabeling, nor financial compensations, is a reality.

OLB: In this sense, in 2021 EUROM promoted the European section of the African American Redress Network project, initiated by the Institute for the Study of Human Rights at Columbia University in New York and the Thurgood Marshall Civil Rights Center at Howard University, to identify instances of historical injustice for which there are feasible processes of reparation and memorialization. Under the name Trans-Atlantic Redress Network, we, together with colleagues from the NIOD Institute in Amsterdam, have initiated a mapping of reparations initiatives in our two countries, Spain and the Netherlands. So far, we have published two reports containing the findings of two-year research. The reports conclude that Spain is still at a very early stage compared to the magnitude of initiatives documented in the USA or the Netherlands. Nevertheless, we identified more than fifty actions among legislative initiatives, demonstrations, reparation for hate crimes, heritage restitution, removal of monuments or street names, and creation of exhibitions and memory sites.

What has been the biggest obstacle for Spain and Catalonia to confront their colonial and slave-owning past?

CMM: From my point of view, it has been a combination of the lack of political will and the rise of a reactionary movement against these types of claims. On the first issue, we can take for example the apology demanded by the president of Mexico, López Obrador, in the year 2021. The reaction of high-ranking political representatives was, for the most part, one of contempt and ridicule. Another example is the recent Law of Democratic Memory (2022), related to the Civil War and Franco's dictatorship. This law does not include the victims of colonial Francoism as subjects eligible for reparations, ignoring an important part of the victims of the dictatorship. On the second issue, there seems to be a revitalized interest in productions that seek to replay the thesis of the "black legend," in the book by Elvira Roca Barea, or the documentary *Spain: The First Globalization* (*España, la primera globalización*). These productions attempt to deny or relativize the violence and thereby generate a social discourse favorable to the Spanish empire, similar to what was previously described regarding the question of identity. The most worrying thing is the support they have received from some institutions. However, it is necessary that those of us in the academy be self-critical, because sometimes we have abandoned public dissemination to focus on publishing in specialized journals of little social impact. To mitigate this problem, the work of EUROM and other institutions or associations whose activities focus on public awareness and dissemination should be acknowledged and encouraged.

Works Cited

Eilers, Richard. "Barcelona's Slave Trade History Revealed on New Walking Tour." *Guardian*, 13 Apr. 2016.
European Observatory on Memories (EUROM). europeanmemories.net.
"Legacies of Slavery and Abolitionism." *Memòria Barcelona*. memoriabcn.cat/en/legacies-of-slavery/.
Report on Moroccan Collections (OVQ-EUROM). *EUROM*, 2022.
"Titulo X. De las proposicións no de ley" (Arts. 193–195). Congreso des los Diputados. www.congreso.es/ca/cem/t10.
"Trans-Atlantic Redress Network Project: Spanish Case." *EUROM*. europeanmemories.net/projects/african-american-redress-network-spanish-case/.

Part 3

Interpreting the Legacies of Slavery in Literature, Music, and Visual Culture

Chapter 9

Pedro Blanco, the Accursed Slave Driver
Literature and Historical Memory of Slavery in Spain

Gustau Nerín,
translated by María Cristina Urruela

This study focuses on the historical memory of slavery in Spain based on literary representations of the character of Pedro Blanco (1793–1856), a slave trader who was particularly prominent, and who was repeatedly featured as a character in literature. The first section of the essay analyzes the memory of the slave trade in Spanish society and highlights the role played by literature in this area. The second section deals with the figure of Pedro Blanco, reviewing his biography particularly in terms of what information about his personality and character circulated in his time, as well as how that information was circulated, both in Spain and in other countries. The third section analyzes the construction of the literary representations of Pedro Blanco and how this literary character contributed to the "whitewashing" and legitimization of the slave traders. The fourth section analyzes the differences between the previous representations of Blanco and how the character is portrayed in recent narrative. Finally, the literary treatment of Blanco is contextually evaluated as an example of the complexities of historical memory of Spanish participation in the slave trade.

Silenced History, Forgotten History

Throughout the twentieth century, there was very little awareness among Spaniards of Hispanic participation in the slave trade. This is no accident. Much of the Spanish slave traffic took place during the illegal period, at a time when participation in this business was condemned. More than 2,000 Spanish vessels were involved in clandestine trade between 1820 and 1866 (Piqueras 30). Most of those who practiced the slave trade at that time did not publicly admit their involvement in it. For example, it was a clandestine activity for Antonio López, Antoni Vinent, and the Marquis of Manzanedo. Although the Spanish press was generally fiercely anti-abolitionist ("Gacetilla"; "Causa notable"), it also largely avoided this issue. Even though Hispanic involvement in the trade was a burning issue between 1835 and 1844, it was not debated in the Cortes (Vila Vilar 576–81). After Atlantic transportations were ended, discussion of the slave trade was conveniently shelved. Silence gave way to oblivion and lasted for decades. For this extended period, historians did not examine the facts of the historical behavior. It was not until the 1970s that a few classic studies began to appear: those of Jordi Maluquer de Motes, Josep Maria Fradera, and Arturo Arnalte. The investigations carried out by scholars, such as those of Vilà i Galí on Captain Agustí Conill, went almost unnoticed. Substantive allegations of involvement in the slave trade by ancestors of some of Spain's great fortunes (or of the Royal House itself) have not been reflected in academic publications.

Only in the twenty-first century that trend has been reversed. Although the wave of reflections on the historical memory of slavery that has shaken the West in recent decades reached Spain only belatedly, it has begun to invigorate this field of study. Since 2012, scholarly studies on the Spanish slave trade have multiplied dramatically.[1] It seems that scholars are making up for lost time. Numerous books and articles have been published in recent years on certain characters involved in the slave trade; for example, Martín Rodrigo has produced works on Antonio López, the Goytisolo family, and Jaime Tintó (*Un hombre, mil negocios*; *Los Goytisolo*; "Comerciando con esclavos"); and Bahamonde and Cayuela researched the Zulueta family.

Despite these relatively recent studies, from 1860 until the end of the twentieth century the only Spanish slave trader who was well known as such in Spain was Pedro Blanco. Although there were some academic studies on him,[2] Spanish society knew Blanco mainly through literature, as he was a key character in some very successful novels, including *Barcelona y sus misterios* by Antonio Altadill and *Pedro Blanco, el negrero,* by Lino Novás Calvo. In fact, literary representations of Blanco have been widely studied by specialists in Spanish or Cuban literature since the 1970.³ The trafficker of the novels caused more rivers of blood to flow than the real Pedro Blanco, eventually becoming a symbol for the Spanish slave trade. And yet, while in Spain and Cuba the memory of Pedro Blanco has never disappeared, in Sierra Leone, where Pedro Blanco actually had his slave factories, it has vanished. Historian Adam Jones, who for years collected oral testimonies in the Gallinas region, did not find a single witness who had heard of Blanco's activities. In fact, many of the Vai even denied that their group had ever engaged in the slave trade in the past (Jones, "Some Reflections" 162). While the Spanish have opted for a selective memory on slavery, the Vai seem to have opted directly for dismemory. Literary works filled the void of memory of the Spanish slave trade for more than a century, and they did so precisely through portrayals of Pedro Blanco, who paradoxically was never well known in the Spain of his time.

Hated in the World, Ignored in Spain

Pedro Blanco was a very active slave trader, one of the most active in the Atlantic trade in the 1830s. But in Spain, while he was alive, there were never any explicit accusations against him. While the Spanish slave trader was criticized throughout the world, from the Portuguese senate to the British and Brazilian press, his prominent role in the Atlantic trade was systematically concealed in Spain. Pedro Blanco represents a special case among Spanish slave traders. Many of those who invested in the slave trade, and thereby enriched themselves, never set foot on a slave ship. Some did begin their careers as ship captains. However, it was much less frequent that they would settle in Africa. Pedro Blanco was very different in this regard, having spent a total of fifteen years as a trafficker in Rio Gallinas, in today's Sierra Leone, buying slaves from the coastal villages and selling them to ship captains or directly to Cuban planters. During this time, he became a very influential figure in the area. It is estimated that he eventually amassed a fortune worth a million dollars (Burgos Madroñero 37).

Blanco was born in 1793 in Malaga, Andalusia, and studied at the Marine School in that city. He sailed to America, and from 1816 on became involved in the slave trade as captain, but also as a shareholder in at least 26 slave expeditions (Burgos Madroñero 38; *SlaveVoyages*). We do not know for certain when he settled on the African coast of Gallinas, but he likely spent time there in 1824 (BPP [1825] 54). From 1825 onwards British abolitionists already began to cite Blanco as a "slave dealer" who was established on the coast at Gallinas (BPP [1842] 460). He married a daughter of King Siaka of the Vai and from their relationship had a daughter, Rosa, whom he adored. In Gallinas, Blanco gradually acquired a veritable harem, in which there were women belonging to the most prominent families of the area ("Historia colonial" 526). This was probably due to his need to establish family and commercial alliances with the local elites. The colonial officers were forced to adapt to local economic dynamics but, under the influence of literary representations, the Spaniards imagined that polygamy was attributed simply to the uncontrollable sexual desires of the officers. Pedro Blanco managed to consolidate an immense business with the collaboration of the chiefs of the area, and he also received the help of English and African officials from neighboring Sierra Leone and Liberia (Stebbins 163; Verger 555). In addition, Blanco had a wide network of associates around the world: Cape Verde, Puerto Rico, Baltimore, New York, London, Matanzas, and Havana. Blanco's slave quarters in Gallinas were immense, with the barracks housing up to 2,000 slaves. The Andalusian trafficker had a luxurious mansion, where he lived with his sister (Canot and Mayer 257–64, 278–85, 348; Nerín 135).

Blanco was a survivor at a time when Europeans tended to die soon after settling in Africa. But finally in 1839, Blanco left Gallinas, for health reasons, taking his daughter Rosa with him (García 252–55). He left his factories in the hands of his agent, or perhaps partner, Rodríguez Burón. On November 9, 1840, British forces led by Major Denman destroyed the Spanish slave factories at Gallinas and rescued 841 slaves (García 239). But in 1841 Blanco's factories were once again shipping slaves (Arnalte, *El tribunal mixto* 199). Blanco himself lived in luxury in Cuba, running his businesses, but he had many problems. In the first place, Cuban high society refused to accept his *mestiza* daughter Rosa, because of her skin color (*Pedro Blanco solicita*). The Andalusian slave dealer was also condemned for his scandalous behavior: he killed his rival in a tavern brawl; he had homosexual relations with Blacks and whites; he paid for private tutors and riding lessons for the slaves he slept with; he raped one of his nephews, a minor. And he suggested to his wife that she watch while he engaged in sexual activities with his bed partners (Barcia, *Pedro Blanco* 188). Finally, his wife sued him, asked for a separation, and threatened to make her accusations public. This situation led Blanco to leave Cuba, forever, with their daughter Rosa (García 257; Barcia, "Casinos españoles"; Barcia, *Pedro Blanco* 193–94).

In 1842 Blanco moved back to his birthplace, Malaga. He tried to become a senator but failed. He was very active fighting the abolitionist policies promoted by the regent Bartolomé Espartero and the captain general of Cuba, Gerónimo Valdés. In the face of Pedro Blanco's intrigues, Valdés dusted off the accusation that Blanco's wife had made and circulated it among the governors and high officials, which destroyed Blanco's reputation and his political ambitions (Burgos Madroñero 36–40; Barcia, *Pedro Blanco* 124). Blanco's slave businesses had been left in the hands of his nephews, who, with the complicity of his angry wife, organized a massive scam to dispossess him of his assets (Barcia, *Pedro Blanco* 137–40). In 1848 the nephews bankrupted Pedro Blanco's business and escaped to New Orleans (Arnalte, *El tribunal mixto* 179; Barcia, *Pedro Blanco* 146–47). There is little data on the last years of Pedro Blanco's life. On June 16, 1856, he died in Barcelona. According to the death certificate, his death was due to a "cerebral congestion caused by a dementia from which he had suffered for many years" (*Libro de defunciones*).

Pedro Blanco was not unknown in his time. His actions were closely followed by anti-slavery activists. Blanco is repeatedly mentioned in the correspondence of British diplomats and military officers devoted to the suppression of the slave trade. A review of the British digital newspaper archive shows that his name appeared with some frequency in UK newspapers as early as 1826 (*British Newspapers Archive*). The American press also actively denounced Blanco's illegal business dealings: it explained in detail the destruction of his factories, denounced his maneuvers to buy slave ships in Baltimore, brought to public light the complicity of Liberian leaders with his activities ("The Slave Trade"; "Revival of the African Slave Trade"; "From Trinidad"). Blanco's fame reached far and wide. In 1839 his illegal activities came to light in a session of the Portuguese Senate, which was reported on even in Brazilian newspapers ("Portugal"). The French press also echoed Blanco's role in the illegal traffic. In 1844 it described him as "one of the richest traffickers on the west coast of Africa" ("París, 27 Avril"). While other Spanish slavers remained anonymous, Blanco was well known abroad.

In contrast, the Spanish press systematically hid Pedro Blanco's slave-holding activities. In the Digital Newspaper Library of the Spanish National Library, there are almost no references to the man. Although the destruction of the Spanish slave factories of Gallinas and Corisco in 1840 raised a wave of media protests (there was talk that an "injustice" had been committed because "under the cloak of humanity, countless outrages and atrocities were covered up"), rarely were the owners of the facilities mentioned, and never Blanco ("Causa notable"). The Spanish colonial press even presented the famous slave trader as a benefactor of humanity ("Ministerio de Marina"). What is most surprising is that, although we know that Pedro Blanco settled in Barcelona in the last years of his life, no newspaper in the city included news about him. His death in 1856 went unnoticed by the Barcelona press. Blanco's tomb, today, is untraceable.

Although Pedro Blanco managed to remain in Spain inconspicuously while he was alive, he rose to literary prominence in 1860, four years after his death, with the novel *Barcelona y sus misterios* by the Catalan progressive Antonio Altadill. In the first part of the novel, Pedro Blanco is the main antagonist of Diego, the protagonist. Blanco, as captain of a slave ship, rescues Diego, who has survived a shipwreck, and then sells him as a slave to the king of Loango. Diego finally manages to return to Barcelona and, by threatening to reveal Blanco's secrets, forces him to make large donations to the poor and to free his slaves. At the end of the volume, Blanco dies, and Diego keeps the secret about his past. Altadill does not give the impression that he had a very accurate idea of Blanco's life; he portrays him more as a simple slave captain than as the owner of factories in Africa or as a shipowner of slave ships. In truth, Altadill's criticism of Blanco focuses less on his role as a slaveholder than on his role as a con man and his dirty dealings that ruined middle-class whites in Catalonia, probably because Altadill's main concern was to denounce the inequalities in Europe and not the relationships between whites and Blacks (Vialette 246–47). Altadill accurately places Blanco in Barcelona during his last days. However, his novel is not faithful to the historical character, even though it is a literary work that claims to reveal the type of hidden truths about the city that do not usually appear in the newspapers. It places Blanco in Barcelona in 1844, but at that time, he was in Cuba. And Diego's revenge against the trafficker takes place in 1857, when in fact Blanco had already died (and had previously been ruined and developed dementia). The factual errors offered by Altadill show to what extent Pedro Blanco went unnoticed in the Catalan capital. It appears that readers of the *folletín* were not even aware that he had developed dementia before he died.

Regardless of factual errors, *Los misterios de Barcelona* continued to transmit a memory of the slave traders, since Altadill's extensive work did not fall into oblivion: it was repeatedly republished (the last reprint and translation into Catalan dates from 2015). It was given a new life when in 1916 Alfredo Marro shot the film series *The Mysteries of Barcelona*. That film did not focus on the period of the decline of the slave trade, but rather on a half a century later, so the cinematic Pedro Blanco was no longer even presented as a slave trader (Cardona 67–70).

Altadill's criticism of slave traders was limited. The main accusation against Pedro Blanco, as a slaver, was that he had enslaved a white man and sold him to an African, something that the public might have found more scandalous than enslaving an African and selling him to a white plantation owner. In fact, the novel explains in detail the sufferings of a Catalan family who were the victims of Blanco's intrigues, but nothing about the misfortunes of the slaves held captive by him. It was probably easier for Catalan bourgeois readers to empathize with their countrymen than with the slaves (about whom many stereotypes prevailed). Moreover, while Altadill's work can be read as a critique of the slave traders, it also lends itself to a very different reading: to some extent, the work helped to conceal the Barcelona slave traders.

Blanco, in his last years of life, was an easy individual to stigmatize. After becoming extraordinarily wealthy, he lost most of his assets when his nephews defrauded him (Barcia, *Pedro Blanco* 136). His aggressive behavior, the recognition of his *mestiza* daughter, and his homosexual relationships with white and Black people, had already excluded him from Cuban high society and barred him from becoming a member of the Barcelona elite. Pedro Blanco did not come from marginal environments, as Lino Novás writes in his novel, but he was marginalized from the circles of power in his old age. During the last years of his life, he was diagnosed with dementia, which reinforced his exclusion. Unbalanced, ruined, and reviled for his sexual inclinations, he had no one to defend him.

For the reader of *Barcelona y sus misterios*, Pedro Blanco clearly played the role of scapegoat. He is the only slave trader mentioned by name. No other Barcelona slave trader is mentioned in the novel, even though in 1860 several people involved in slavery held prominent positions in the city, such as Antonio López, the Marquis of Comillas, or the Vidal i Ribas family. Altadill probably did not have the will, or the capacity, to openly confront Barcelona's high society. Blanco was clearly demonized, and with this the author succeeded in making the Spanish participation in the slave trade visible. But, at the same time, Altadill kept the slave-owning past of some

Spanish celebrities hidden. Blanco became the face of the evils of slavery, while other slave traders and slave plantation owners were enshrined as exemplary citizens. No one would reproach the "good families" of Barcelona for their involvement in the slave trade.[4]

Pedro Blanco was an important player in the Atlantic slave trade, but in Spain there were many more. Even the Duke of Riánsares, the husband of the regent María Cristina de Borbón, thanks to the support of the Crown, was involved in the illegal trade (Arnalte, "Riánsares y María Cristina" 68–77). Of the many who were involved in trafficking, it seems only Pedro Blanco remains infamous.

In Cuba, where Blanco and his accomplices in the slave trade were probably much better known than in Barcelona, literature treated him quite differently. In 1879 the Cuban Cirilo Villaverde, an active abolitionist and supporter of independence, published the novel *Cecilia Valdés*, a kind of portrait of Cuba in the 1830s. One of the characters, Leonardo Gamboa, was portrayed as the son of an associate of Pedro Blanco. In this work Blanco is only briefly mentioned, but he is presented as the tip of the iceberg of the evils of the slave trade. One of Villaverde's characters, in a conversation, makes it clear that by singling out the colonial officer from Gallinas, others involved in the slave business, such as the plantation owners, try to mask their guilt. By denouncing Blanco, the Cuban writer, unlike Altadill, intended to denounce all those involved in this activity. Villaverde's book became one of the greatest exponents of Cuban Romanticism. It gave rise to two *zarzuelas*: *María la O*, by Ernesto Lecuona, and *Cecilia Valdés*, by Gonzalo Roig. In these, Pedro Blanco was not even mentioned, nor did he appear in the various film adaptations of *Cecilia Valdés*. Criticism of the slave trade was diluted in the most popular versions of the novel. The attractive mulatta María ended up displacing the perfidious Pedro. The existence of the slave trade would be ignored for decades.

Both Altadill and Villaverde criticized Pedro Blanco, though Altadill did not couple it with direct criticism of other beneficiaries of this business. Literature played a positive role in the knowledge of the slave trade: it contributed to maintaining the knowledge of Spanish participation in it, but on occasions it did so by identifying the slave trade with a single isolated character, Pedro Blanco, and ignoring the fact that part of the local elites had participated as well. Moreover, in the most popularized versions of Altadill's and Villaverde's works (the films and the *zarzuelas*) the slave-owning aspect of the character ended up completely disappearing.

From Evil to Good: Whitewashing Blanco

Literature has not only served to portray the crimes of the protagonists of the slave trade but has in some cases also been used to legitimize them. Some traffickers were presented as heroic characters, whose positive characteristics would suffice to counteract their crimes, and some literary works involving Pedro Blanco have at times served to give a positive vision of him. During Blanco's lifetime, the French slave trader Theodore Canot provided the most information about Blanco's life in his memoirs, *Revelations of a Slave Trader; or Twenty Years' Adventures of Captain Canot*, a book published in 1854 that circulated widely at the time in English and in various translations, and is still reprinted. Canot's description of Blanco was not devoid of admiration. Although he told many stories about the Spaniard's cruelty (for instance, that he killed an African for refusing to light his cigar), he attributed them to Blanco's pride and arrogance, two characteristics that Canot admired. It was Canot who asserted that Blanco was "the Rothschild of slavery" who made a fortune, an ambiguous description that carries some positive connotations (Canot and Mayer 257–64, 278–85, 328, 348). Captain Richard Drake, himself a slave trader who worked for some time for Blanco and praised him in his memoirs, also contributed to this mythical vision of the Malagueño (72–96).

Novelists soon detected the literary possibilities of such an adventurous and extravagant character as Pedro Blanco. Even before his death, the Frenchman Gabriel de La Landelle included him in his popular novel *Les princes d'Ébène*, of the series *Les géants de la mer*, which was first published in 1852. Landelle used the slave trader in Gallinas as a secondary character (175–81, 278–85, 348). This novelist did not demean the trafficker, but rather turned him into a positive model through his courage, intelligence, and ability to conquer African societies. The Blanco of *Les princes d'Ébène* is a precursor of the heroes of colonial novels, ingenious and intrepid whites who prevail over the brutal inhabitants of a torrid and inhospitable Africa. Landelle participates in a literary genre, colonial literature, which was beginning to develop (Fanoudh-Siefer 47–48).

In Spain, the epic vision of the slave traders began to take shape during the period of the illegal slave trade, through works of nonfiction. The Spanish Vice-Admiral Baltasar Vallarino in 1844 published the essay *El marinero africano*, in which he praised the "genio vivo y travieso" ("lively and mischievous genius") of the crew of the slave ships, which would be "la flor y la nata de lo más perdido, de lo más desmoralizado de toda la marinería" ("the creme de la creme of the most outcast, of the most derelict of all the seamen"). This was essentially admitting that the crews of these slave ships were the most vile and degenerate scum of humanity, while at the same time trying to dress the admission in laudatory prose. Vallarino, who according to international treaties should have worked to repress the slave trade, glorified those who engaged in it (D.B.V. 79, 89). This mythologized vision would eventually find its way into fiction. Pío Baroja, for example, in his *Pilotos de altura*, praised the slave sailors.

In fact, it was the Spanish-Cuban Lino Novás Calvo who brought Blanco to fame in Spain with *Pedro Blanco, el negrero*, a book that was published in 1933 and has never gone out of print (Chouciño). Its influence on the Spanish and Cuban imagination regarding the slave trade was immense: even historians used it as a source.[5] Novás had read the memoirs of many slave traders and had quite reliable information, especially that provided by Canot. But he subtitled his work *Vida novelada de Pedro Blanco Fernández de Trava*; the key to the success of this text is that it combined accurate historical documentation with extraordinary literary talent and boundless imagination (Barcia, *Pedro Blanco* 9). In the plot of *Pedro Blanco, el negrero*, fantastic elements abound, such as Blanco's passionate incestuous relationship with his sister (with an added lurid element: he travels the world with her embalmed corpse hidden in a chest). Novás, regardless of Blanco's actual experiences, takes advantage of the wealth of orally transmitted seafaring anecdotes to place his protagonist in extreme situations (such as a slave voyage with no potable water) and to describe the different stages of trafficking. Although some authors have defended the biographical character of Novás's work, the author himself affirmed that he did not intend "hacer historia propiamente, ni menos de tierra—sino novela de mar" ("to strictly write history, much less land history—but a novel of the sea"; Gómez de Tejada 70).

Novás does not use the episodes of Blanco's life that created the most scandal in his time (such as Blanco's homosexual relations with Black servants and with his nephews) in his novel. It is most likely that Novás did not know about them, because they circulated among high officials of the administration, but were not made public; it is also possible that he preferred to censor them, because they did not fit with the heroic nature he wanted to attribute to the character. Novás Calvo portrayed Blanco as a slave trader capable of great cruelties, but at the same time, he highly valued his courage, his insight, and his intelligence, fully accepting the heroic vision of Canot (Daroqui). Moreover, he portrayed him as an individual capable of great acts of generosity, even toward his enemies. The author actually acknowledged a certain degree of sympathy for the character (Tejada). This was possible because, in the novel, slaves were made invisible, as were Africans as a whole. Their sufferings and thoughts were completely ignored. No wonder that the press that discussed the publication of Novás's work also reproduced racist stereotypes, as shown by Martín Rodrigo and Juliana Naleiro's chapter in this book.

To a certain extent, Novás Calvo's Pedro Blanco is associated with the protagonists of militaristic works of his time, such as *La bandera*, by Pierre Mac Orlan (1931); *Tras el águila del César: Elegía del Tercio*, by Luys Santa Marina (1924); or even Franco's own *Marruecos: Diario de una bandera* (1922). All of them presented marginal individuals who acted with great brutality against non-European populations and managed to prevail over them with positive characteristics (racism helped to normalize their brutalities). Their courage or their patriotism would serve to redeem them and allow their actions to be described as exemplary. Politically, these latter authors, fascists or reactionaries, were far from Novás Calvo, who defended the Republic in 1936. But the characters in *La bandera* or *Diario de una bandera* were not so different from the literary Pedro Blanco. In fact, these types of protagonists were made possible by the colonial perception of the Black man as a brutal and intellectually and spiritually limited being, a stereotype that contributed to the dehumanization of Africans. Lino Novás's novel offers, in fact, a strikingly colonial vision of the slave-holding period.

Pedro Blanco, el negrero had great impact, both in Spain and in Cuba. Cordero Torres, one of the ideologists of Franco's Africanism, even defended Blanco as a Spanish colonial hero. He did so in 1943, when the dictatorship still dreamed of expanding its African empire through its alliance with Nazism. Cordero asserted, against all evidence, that Blanco had been the sovereign of a great kingdom reaching as far as the Niger River, which would give "rights" to Spain over this area (Cordero; Nerín and Bosch). Franco's irredentism considered Blanco's slave-holding activities unimportant in the face of his supposed colonial values.

The influence of Novás is also evident in several novels in which the slave trader appears as a character. And, following the steps of Novás, the slave trader is ultimately glorified. The real Pedro Blanco was watered down to the literary Pedro Blanco. An example of Novás's inspiration can be found in the novel *La hora de las anclas*, by Juan Cepas, published in 1965. The protagonist of the novel, Pedro Salazar, is a Malagueño (like Cepas himself and Pedro Blanco), who deeply admires the famous slave trader. Salazar, somewhat younger than Blanco, dreams of meeting the slave trader. At the end of the novel, he ends up working in the slave trade himself and encounters Blanco in Gallinas. No doubt, Cepas was inspired by Novás in describing Blanco: he accepted the anecdotes told by Novás (such as the one about incest with his sister) and endowed Blanco with a heroic aura: "es un hombre como pocos. Yo lo he visto hacer cosas increíbles" ("he is a man like few others. I have seen him do incredible things"), declared one of the characters (Cepas 75).

Cepas showed no empathy for the Africans (although the protagonist of *La hora de las anclas* felt a great attraction to Black women's bodies). As an officer of a slave ship, Salazar allows Blanco to massacre a cargo of slaves; the author did not present this action as a criminal act, but as a feat, a great show of fidelity to his captain, the mythologized Pedro Blanco. The Africans are shown as individuals ruled by absurd rituals and prey to an irrational fear of the unknown. Cepas offered a horribly racist vision of the slave-owning world, indebted in part to the works of Novás and Canot, but also to the colonial literature in vogue. The Malaga-born Cepas admired the bravery, intelligence, and promiscuity of Pedro Blanco, without questioning the consequences of his actions. In *La hora de las anclas*, the slave trade became normalized: it would be nothing more than a demonstration of the natural dominion of the always superior white men over savage Blacks. Literature, in this case, served to justify not only Blanco's actions, but those of all Westerners involved in the slave trade.

The Cinematic Turn: From Hollywood to the Dustbin of History

The days were numbered for this complacent view of slaveholders' activities, because attitudes were changing. In 1987, a historical novel, *Amistad*, by David Pesci, was published in the United States. It was a strong denunciation of the slave trade, based on an actual historical case of a rebellion on a ship carrying captives from Blanco's factories and on the trial in the United States that resulted from those events. Pesci briefly mentioned Blanco and described his activities in very harsh terms. Three years later, the Cuban Lisandro Otero published *El árbol de la vida*, a novel that was a journey through the history of the island of Cuba, in which he made a harsh criticism of those involved in the slave trade and in which Blanco appeared as a secondary character.

Although Pesci's novel became a best-seller, it was Steven Spielberg's 1997 film *Amistad* that brought Blanco's character back into the spotlight, both in the world of literature and in the world of historical studies. This film was a harsh critique of the slave trade, albeit from the point of view of the white savior, and coincided with a worldwide shift in the understanding of the history of slavery. Criticism of the historical facts proliferated, especially from initiatives by African American groups (who, for example, pushed for the inscription of archaeological remains of slavery on UNESCO's World Heritage List). This attitude change caused a substantial shift in the narratives about Blanco. In fact, Pedro Blanco is not even mentioned in the film *Amistad*, although in the footage of the Lomboko factory from which the slaves departed there is a brief glimpse of an elegant trafficker who could be Blanco (since the *Amistad*'s slaves had been purchased from his establishments in Gallinas). The impeccably dressed slaver standing at the gates of the fort as the shipment takes place is the only iconic image of Blanco, beyond Cobos's engravings for the Francoist article by Cordero Torres: not a single portrait of Blanco is preserved.

Following the release of *Amistad*, academic and literary works on Blanco multiplied. In the field of history, the works of Michael Zeuske, Iyonolu Folayan Osagie, Markus Rediker, and Howard Jones, as well as Tony Buba's documentary, stand out. All these studies move away from Novás's epic vision and integrate Blanco into the global mechanism of the Atlantic slave trade. They focus not so much on his exceptional nature, but rather on the role he played in a large international structure. The impact of Spielberg's work and the relentless passage of time also had an impact on literature, which significantly changed the image of the slave trader. In 2007 Gonzalo Guijarro won the XI Nostromo Prize, dedicated to maritime narrative, with *Memorias difusas de Isidro Blanco*, a novel in which the protagonist, Isidro, is a younger cousin of Pedro Blanco. In the novel, the former is an exact counterpoint to the slave trader. Guijarro, while criticizing Blanco's slave-trading "exploits," highlights the complicities of this marginal character with businessmen who have been dedicated to the slave trade and who maintain a position of power in Spain. Much more than Altadill or Novás Calvo, Guijarro uses Blanco to shape an overall critique of Spanish involvement in the slave trade, and he does so without a hint of ambiguity (111, 228–30).

Toni de la Rosa also portrayed Pedro Blanco as a character in *Lomboko*, a novel published in Catalan in 2010, which offers a vision of the trafficker similar to that provided by Guijarro. In the early stages of this novel, Blanco is presented as absolutely evil: a slave trader who murders, rapes, mutilates, and personally mistreats slaves. But in his old age, he repents of his past behaviors. De la Rosa contrasts the figure of Blanco with that of Antonio López y López, a man who enriched himself with slaves and who, according to the novel, continued to maintain racist and immoral behavior throughout his life. López, the Marquis of Comillas, unlike Pedro Blanco, became a pillar of Catalan society. In *Lomboko*, paradoxically, Blanco is the human and positive opposite of Antonio López (when this work was written, there was already controversy over whether to remove a statue dedicated to him near the port of Barcelona). De la Rosa, unlike Altadill, uses Blanco to highlight the complicity of the Barcelona elite with the slave trade.

Blanco's character also made it into American literature after the success of *Amistad*. Alan Ryall's 2018 *Set a Thief to Catch a Thief* is a novel about Gallinas based on American abolitionist sources and not on Novás's book; Ryall does not cite any of the latter's apocryphal anecdotes. The protagonist of *Set a Thief to Catch a Thief*, Tom, is a young white American who by chance ends up in the slave trade. When his ship is loading slaves in Gallinas, Tom falls ill and Pedro Blanco saves Tom's life when he offers to take him into his factory and let his African wives take care of him. Nevertheless, Tom offers a terribly crude portrait of Blanco, predictably repeating Canot's anecdote in which the slave-trading colonial officer kills a man because he won't give him a match to light his cigar. But he does so not to praise Blanco's concept of honor, but to enhance his brutality. In this novel, Blanco embodies absolute horror. Contrary to historical evidence, Ryall's Pedro Blanco organizes expeditions to capture slaves, and his men travel thousands of miles inland to buy slaves from Arab merchants. Thanks to these inaccuracies, Blanco is presented as solely responsible for the slave trade, along with the evil Arabs, and the Black Africans are mere victims—ignoring the essential role of the Vai mediators in all trafficking networks. Nor did Ryall explore Blanco's connections with Spanish, Cuban, or American business circles. Thus, the singling out of Blanco in *Set a Thief to Catch a Thief* was not associated with a global critique of the slave trade phenomenon, but rather attributed the evils of the trade to the sick personality of the Malaga slaver.

Pedro Blanco jumped back into the media in 2019 with the publication of *Mongo Blanco*, by actor and screenwriter Carlos Bardem, a novel also born in the wake of Novás. Bardem, who is a historian and who did extensive research for the work, incorporated very relevant historical data about the character, such as pertaining to sexual relations with his nephews. In his final narrative twist, he completely breaks with Novás's romantic vision (which showed a hero whose uncivil acts were offset by his greatness) to present us with the crudest Blanco, a monster without any justification who deserves no admiration. In *Mongo Blanco*, the trafficker himself, aged and crazed, presents the reader with a cynical and stark vision of his life, and includes Spanish society's complicity with the slave trade. But Bardem does not omit some of the fantastic elements invented by Novás, such as the incestuous relationship of the slaver with his sister or the existence of an abusive stepfather. To these he adds a large number of invented scandalous scenes. And he does inherit some of the distorted perceptions of Novás and Cordero Torres. He presents us with a white man turned "King of Gallinas," who rules over a savage and fanatical Africa. There is not much difference between Bardem's Africans and those in the novels of Verne or Alfred E. W. Mason. Bardem's Africa is a continent of witches, of absurd rituals, of tribal wars. And this, even though the Vai, among whom Blanco lived during this period, had even developed their own writing, and although their leaders were praised by even the British officers who fought against the trade (Nerín 120). Bardem's novel argues that Blanco adopted brutal behaviors because "África se le metió dentro" ("Africa got inside him"; 484). In the end, Bardem attributes the brutality of trafficking not to the violence inherent in the trafficking phenomenon, but to the savagery of the Africans.

In spite of the continuities between Bardem and colonial literature's vision of African cultures, the truth is that after the film *Amistad,* the narrative changed its vision of Blanco and stopped offering a heroic image of his performance in Gallinas. The publications of the late twentieth and early twenty-first centuries reject any praise of Pedro Blanco and in no way justify his practices, although in some cases criticism of Spanish participation in the slave trade or of African participation in the slave trade is avoided.

Conclusion

For a very long time in Spain, when newspapers, legislators, and textbooks were silent about the Spanish slave trade, the memory of Spanish participation in the slave trade was preserved thanks only to adventure novels. Through the literary works of Altadill and Novás, Pedro Blanco became the embodiment of the slave trade in Spain. Novels about this character forced Spaniards to confront their slave-owning past.

Nevertheless, throughout the twentieth century the literary character of Pedro Blanco was presented with some ambiguity. Although the cruder aspects of his slavery activities and cruelty were mentioned, he was also presented as a character who was exceptional for his intelligence, courage, and firmness. Some novels, such as Novás Calvo's or Juan Cepas's, reduced the brutality of the slave trade by glorifying one of its main promoters. But this vision disappeared at the end of the twentieth century. Since the release of the film *Amistad* and the worldwide revisions in views of the history of slavery and the slave trade in Europe, Pedro Blanco has regained prominence, both in literary and historical terms. At the literary level there has been a significant change in the treatment of the slaver: the most recent works that feature him as a character openly condemn him. Nonetheless, Blanco is still the only slaver included in the collective memory of the Spanish participation in the slave trade. In the end, his considerable presence in literary works allows the many other individuals who also participated in slave activities to remain in the shadows.

Notes

1. See, for example, Piqueras, Rodrigo and Chaviano, Nerín, and Arnalte ("Riánsares y María Cristina").

2. Mainly, the small biographical study by Manuel Burgos Madroñero in 1989 and a chapter in Dolores García Cantús's 2004 doctoral thesis on Fernando Poo (197–259). More recently, an extensive study by Maria del Carmen Barcia has delved into his trajectory. The role of the Spanish slaver was also highlighted in works on the history of the Gallinas area, such as those of Christopher H. Fyfe or Adam Jones.

3. The studies of Rosa María Cabrera, Ignacio Galbis, Jesús Gómez de Tejada, Hedy Habra, Xiomara Francisca Núñez García, and Lisa Surwillo, among many others, are worth mentioning.

4. Co-founder of Barcelona's Banco Hispano-Colonial, Antonio Vinent, from Menorca, obtained the designation of senator for life, and was named Gentilhombre de Cámara de S.M. con ejercicio, Caballero Gran Cruz y Collar de la Real y Distinguida Orden de Carlos III y Gran Cruz de Isabel la Católica (Gentleman of the Chamber of S.M., with exercise, Knight Grand Cross and Collar of the Royal and Distinguished Order of Charles III and Grand Cross of Isabella the Catholic); the Barcelona family Vidal y Ribas was defended by all the Spanish forces when

the English captured their slave schooner *Conchita*; and the Marquis of Comillas, Antonio López, had monuments built in Barcelona, Comillas, and Cádiz (Nerín 220–31; Sanjuan 131–58; Rodrigo, *Un hombre*).

5. For example, the Cuban historian José Luciano Franco asserted, following Novás, that Blanco had married a daughter of the Brazilian trafficker Chachá (190).

Works Cited

Altadill, Antonio. *Barcelona y sus misterios*. Viuda e Hijos de J. Torrens, 1886.
Arnalte, Arturo. "Riánsares y María Cristina de Borbón: Una merienda de negros." *La Aventura de la Historia,* no. 265, 2020, pp. 68–77.
———. *El tribunal mixto anglo-español de Sierra Leona (1819–1874)*. 1992. U Complutense de Madrid, PhD dissertation.
Bahamonde, Ángel, and José Gregorio Cayuela. *Hacer las Américas: Las élites coloniales españolas en el siglo XIX*. Alianza, 1992.
Barcia, María del Carmen. "Casinos españoles ¿de color?." *SEMATA: Ciencias Sociais e Humanidades*, vol. 24, 2012, pp. 351–74.
———. *Pedro Blanco, el negrero: Mito, realidad y espacios*. Ed. Boloña, 2018.
Bardem, Carlos. *Mongo Blanco*. Plaza & Janés, 2019.
Baroja, Pío. *Pilotos de altura*. Espasa-Calpe, 1931.
British Newspapers Archive. www.britishnewspapersarchive.co.uk. Accessed 13 June 2024.
British Parliamentary Papers (BPP). *Class A*. 1825–1842.
Buba, Tony, director. *Ghosts of Amistad: In the Foosteps of the Rebels*. Braddock Films, 2014.
Burgos Madroñero, Manuel. "De negrero a intendente de la marina española: Pedro Blanco." *Jabega*, no. 66, 1989, pp. 36–44.
Cabrera, Rosa María. "Aproximación al tema de la esclavitud en *Pedro Blanco, el negrero*, de Lino Novás Calvo." *Actas del VIII Congreso de la Asociación Internacional de Hispanistas*, vol. 1, Istmo, 1986, pp. 293–99.
Canot, Theodore (Theophilus Conneau), and B. Mayer. *Revelations of a Slave Trader; or Twenty Years' Adventures of Captain Canot*. Richard Bentley, 1854.
Cardona, Rosa. "La recuperación para el mercado alemán de 'La secta de los misteriosos.'" *Secuencias: Revista de Historia de Cine*, no. 27, 2007, pp. 66–80.
"Causa notable." *Diario constitucional de Palma*, 7 Apr. 1848, p. 3.
Cepas, Juan. *La hora de las anclas*. Luis de Caralt, 1965.
Chouciño Fernández, Ana. "Lino Novás Calvo: Autor transatlántico." *Symposium*, vol. 69, no. 3, 2015, pp. 119–30.
Cordero Torres, José María. "Pedro Blanco, negrero y colonizador." *África: Revista de Acción Española*, no. 18, 1943, pp. 29–30.
Daroqui, María Julia. "Escribir el sujeto anómalo: (Des) leer *El negrero* de Novás Calvo." *Revista Iberoamericana*, vol. 67, no. 194–95, 2001, pp. 191–200.

D.B.V. (Don Baltasar Vallarino). *El marinero africano, vida marítima del día.* Imprenta de Agustín Gaspar, 1844.
Drake, Capt. Richard. *Revelations of a Slave Smuggler.* Robert M. De Witt, 1850.
Fanoudh-Siefer, Léon. *Le mythe du nègre et de l'Afrique Noire dans la littérature Française de 1800 à la 2ᵉ Guerre Mondiale.* Les Nouvelles Éditions Africaines, 1980.
Fradera, Josep Maria. "La participació catalana en el el tràfic d'esclaus (1789–1845)." *Recerques* no. 6, 1984, pp. 119–39.
Franco, Comandante. *Marruecos: Diario de una bandera.* 1922.
Franco, José Luciano. *Comercio clandestino de esclavos.* Ed. Ciencias Sociales, 1975.
"From Trinidad." *New York Herald*, 7 Aug. 1843, p. 2.
Fyfe, Christopher H. *A History of Sierra Leone.* Oxford UP, 1962.
"Gacetilla. Fisonomía de las sesiones." *El Balear: Periódico de la tarde*, 4 Jan. 1855, p. 2.
Galbis, Ignacio, RM. "Tanatología en la obra de Lino Novás Calvo." *Symposium: A Quarterly Journal in Modern Literatures*, vol. 29, no. 3, 1975, pp. 229–42.
García Cantús, Dolores. *Fernando Poo, una aventura colonial española en el África Occidental (1778–1800).* 2004. U de València, PhD dissertation.
Gómez de Tejada, Jesús. "Biografía y autobiografía en Lino Novás Calvo: Pulsión por lo extraordinario." *Lino Novás Calvo: "Ese lugar de donde me llaman,"* edited by Ramón Villares. Consello da Cultura Galega, 2019, pp. 55–81.
Guijarro, Gonzalo. *Memorias difusas de Isidro Blanco.* Juventud, 2007.
Habra, Hedy. "El negrero como personaje romántico en *Pedro Blanco, el negrero* de Lino Novás Calvo." *Afro-Hispanic Review*, no. 18, 1999, pp. 46–52.
"Historia colonial: Un negrero español en el Río Gallinas." *Revista de Geografía Comercial*, vol. 2, no. 147, 1887, p. 526.
Jones, Adam. *From Slaves to Palm Kernels: A History of the Galinhas Country (West Africa) 1730–1890.* Franz Steiner Verlag, 1983.
———. "Some Reflections on the Oral Traditions of the Galinhas Country, Sierra Leone." *History in Africa*, vol. 12, 1985, pp. 151–65.
Jones, Howard. "Cinqué of the Amistad a Slave Trader? Perpetuating a Myth." *Journal of American History*, vol. 87, no. 3, 2000, pp. 923–39.
Landelle, Gabriel de La. *Les géants de la mer.* Decorce-Cadot, 1852.
Libro de defunciones de 1856, nº 2. Arxiu Històric de la Ciutat de Barcelona, Arxiu administratiu.
Mac Orlan, Pierre. *La bandera.* Orbis, 1985.
Maluquer de Motes, Jordi. "La burgesia catalana i l'esclavitud colonial: Modes de producció i pràctica política." *Recerques*, no. 3, 1974, pp. 83–136.
"Ministerio de Marina, Comercio y Gobernación de Ultramar." *Gazeta del Gobierno de Puerto Rico*, 20 Apr. 1843, p. 1.
Nerín, Gustau. *Traficants d'ànimes: Els negrers espanyols a l'Àfrica.* Proa, 2015.
Nerín, Gustau, and Alfred Bosch. *El imperio que nunca existió: La aventura colonial discutida en Hendaya.* Plaza & Janés, 2001.
Novás Calvo, Lino. *Pedro Blanco, el negrero.* Colección Austral, 1933.

Núñez García, Xiomara Francisca. "El negro en la narrativa cubana: La obra de Lino Novás Calvo y Alejo Carpentier." *Islas: Revista de Humanidades y Ciencias Sociales,* vol. 47, no. 143, 2005, pp. 62–75.

Osagie, Iyonolu Folayan. *The Amistad Revolt: Memory, Slavery, and the Politics of Identity in the United States and Sierra Leone.* U of Georgia P, 2003.

Otero, Lisandro. *El árbol de la vida.* Siglo XXI, 1990.

"París, 27 Avril." *Le Constitutionnel,* 28 Apr. 1844, p. 1.

Pedro Blanco solicita la legitimación de su hija Rosa sin perjuicio de su hijo habido en legítimo matrimonio con Rosalía Pérez, 1840. Archivo Histórico Nacional, Ultramar, 1626, exp. 27.

Pesci, David. *Amistad.* Marlowe & Company, 1987.

Piqueras, Antonio. *Negreros españoles en el tráfico y en los capitales esclavistas.* Los Libros de la Catarata, 2021.

"Portugal. Discussão do tráfico da escravatura." *Correio Mercantil: Jornal Político, Commercial e Literário,* 22 May 1839, p. 2.

Rediker, Markus. *The Amistad Rebellion: An Atlantic Odyssey of Slavery and Freedom.* Penguin, 2012.

"Revival of the African Slave Trade." *New York Herald,* 13 Mar. 1843, p. 2.

Rodrigo y Alharilla, Martín. "Comerciando con esclavos africanos desde Barcelona: Jaime Tintó Miralles (1770–1839)." *Hispania,* vol. 81, no. 267, 2021, pp. 73–100.

———. *Los Goytisolo: Una próspera familia de indianos.* Marcial Pons, 2016.

———. *Un hombre, mil negocios: La controvertida historia de Antonio López, Marqués de Comillas.* Ariel, 2021.

———. *Los marqueses de Comillas: Antonio y Claudio López.* Lid, 2000.

Rodrigo y Alharilla, Martín, and Lizbeth Chaviano Pérez, editors. *Negreros y esclavos: Barcelona y la esclavitud atlántica (siglos XVI–XIX).* Icaria, 2017.

Rosa, Toni de la, *Lomboko.* Carena, 2010.

Ryall, Alan. *Set a Thief to Catch a Thief: Story of a Baltimore Schooner/Slaver.* S.e., 2018.

Sanjuan, José Miguel, "El tráfico de esclavos y la élite barcelonesa: Los negocios de la Casa Vidal Ribas." *Negreros y esclavos: Barcelona y la esclavitud atlàntica (siglos XVI–XIX),* edited by Martín Rodrigo y Alharilla and Lizbeth Chaviano Pérez, Icaria, 2017, pp. 131–58.

Santa Marina, Luys. *Tras el águila del César: Elegía del tercio (1921–1922).* Yunque, 1939.

"The Slave Trade." *New York Tribune,* 25 Dec. 1841, p. 1.

SlaveVoyages. www.slavevoyages.org. Accessed 13 June 2024.

Stebbins, G. B. *Facts and Opinions Touching the Real Origin, Character, and Influence of the American Colonization Society.* John P. Jewett and Company, 1853.

Surwillo, Lisa. "Transatlantic Currents: Oceanic Crossings in Novás Calvo's *El negrero.*" *Transatlantic Studies: Latin America, Iberia and Africa,* edited by C. Enjuto-Rangel et al., Oxford UP, 2019.

Tejada, Jesús Gómez. "Lino Novás Calvo: Narrativa antiesclavista y afrocubanismo en la biografía del negrero Pedro Blanco." *Afro-Hispanic Review*, vol. 31, no. 1, 2012, pp. 73–86.
Verger, Pierre. *Flux et reflux de la traite des nègres entre le golfe de Bénin et Bahia de Todos os Santos du dix-septième au dix-neuvième siècle.* Mouton, 1968.
Vialette, Aurélie Mireille. *Espacios para la cultura obrera en el siglo XIX español: Literatura, música, representación.* 2009. UC Berkeley, PhD dissertation.
Vilà i Galí, Agustí Maria. *Navegants i mercaders: Una nissaga marinera de Lloret.* Club Marina "Casinet," 1989.
Vila Vilar, Enriqueta. "La esclavitud americana en la política española del siglo XIX." *Anuario de Estudios Americanos*, no. 34, 1977, pp. 563–88.
Villaverde, Cirilo. *Cecilia Valdés o La loma del ángel.* Proyecto Gutenberg, 2009 [1879].
Zeuske, Michael. *Amistad: A Hidden Network of Slaves and Merchants.* Markus Wiener, 2014.

Chapter 10

Searching for Cayetana's Daughter
From Goya to Carmen Posadas

Rosalía Cornejo-Parriego

> Ella bailaba, o reía, o echaba las cartas, o jugaba con un perrillo de lanas, y todo se oscurecía alrededor. La luz se iba hacía ella y allí quedaba vibrando. Podría recordarla una mañana cualquiera en Sanlúcar de Barrameda, aquel verano de 1796, chapoteando en la alberca con la chiquilla negra que había ahijado, riendo las dos niñas, la negra y la blanca, igualadas en edad y en rango por el regocijo del desnudo y del agua fresca . . .
>
> —Antonio Larreta, *Volavérunt*[1]

> Damián—dijo este con la mayor naturalidad—es un esclavo de Mozambique. Me lo obsequió hace cinco años el conde de Ribadavia. Lo mismo pudo regalarme un morisco pero hubiese sido una vulgaridad. El favor era demasiado alto para una atención tan mezquina. Hoy en día, un esclavo de Mozambique es un lujo propio de la aristocracia.
>
> —Miguel Delibes, *El hereje*[2]

In October 2021 several media reported on the questions raised by a disturbing eighteenth-century portrait of Yale University's namesake, Elihu Yale.

The painting depicts four white men (with Yale at the center), a group of white children playing in the background, and in the right margin, next to the men, a Black child. The boy wears fine clothes, but the locked collar around his neck is a visible sign of his enslavement. As is the case with most Black figures in Western art, he has no name (Joseph; Kenney). In this particular instance, historians have begun to research the identity of this child, while artist Titus Kaphar has created in *Enough About You* a new version of the original painting with the boy framed in gold at center stage and without the collar (McGreevy). However, many Black children remain anonymous, without history or story. This void is not limited to art; it extends to their representation across a range of different media and discourses.

This paper will focus on an eighteenth-century enslaved Black child in Spain who, unlike the one shown in Yale's portrait, does have a name: she is María de la Luz (Luz), the little girl that Cayetana, the thirteenth Duchess of Alba, adopted (*prohijar* or *ahijar* were the Spanish terms used at the time), emancipated, and bequeathed a pension for life in her last will.[3] On the other hand, information about her family's enslavement is scarce and her fate after her adoptive mother's early demise is not known. My study does not have a historical goal in mind and, therefore, will not address the matter of factual accuracy per se; nor will it speculate on the maternal feelings of the duchess toward Luz. Instead, my aim is to analyze the depiction of the child in several visual and literary texts and the discourses that surround her representation. While her significance in the social and historical landscape has been largely forgotten, and her pre- and post-Cayetana history remains a mystery, Luz, even though relegated to the margins in most cases, has not been absent from representation.

A widow without biological children, Cayetana died at the age of forty. Her unconventional personality, her rivalry with Queen María Luisa de Parma over the powerful politician Manuel Godoy, the conjectures about the true nature of her relationship with Francisco de Goya and whether or not she was the model for his *Maja Desnuda*, not to mention the suspicious circumstances of her death, are certainly more than enough elements to captivate the imagination. Cultural texts about Goya also abound and are inevitably tied to the duchess. The fictionalized autobiography *La duquesa de Alba* (1995) by Carmen Barberá, the novel *Volavérunt* (1980) by Uruguayan author Antonio Larreta, which inspired Bigas Luna's homonymous film (1999), as well as *Goya in Burdeos* (1999), a movie directed by Carlos Saura, are only a few examples that attest to the enduring allure of this couple. This fascination extends beyond the borders of Spain, as the opera *Goya* (1986) by Italian composer Gian Carlo Menotti and the Italian American movie *The Naked Maja* (1959), directed by Henry Koster and starring Ava Gardner, confirm.[4] In these examples, Luz makes only a minor appearance. Larreta refers to her in a footnote (114) and only once in the body of the text (see epigraph); Barberá incorporates a few brief mentions, always racializing her as "la negrita María Luz" ("the little Black girl María Luz"; 271, 278, 280, 286, 297); Bigas Luna introduces a Black girl, presumably Luz, in a single moment; and Koster creates a few scenes where Luz interacts (without talking) with her adoptive mother and Goya (see Appendix).[5] However, Luz does appear prominently during the eighteenth century in two of Goya's artworks and in a poem that the *ilustrado* Manuel José Quintana dedicated to her, and finally, in 2016, in Carmen Posadas's novel *La hija de Cayetana* (*Cayetana's Daughter*). Despite the chronological distance between these works, I focus on them because the eighteenth-century creations have left their imprint on later representations of Luz and Cayetana, including on Posadas's novel.

Goya and Quintana: Enlightened Gazes

Luz makes her first appearances in two of Goya's works, both of which depict her in a domestic setting. In the painting *"La Beata" with Luis de Berganza and María de la Luz* (1795; fig. 10.1) we see two children, one Black and one white, identified by their names. Luz and Luis, who is the son of steward Tomás de Berganza, are shown tugging at an elderly woman's clothing. This lady is the chambermaid Rafaela Luisa Velázquez, known as la Beata.

While the painting represents, at first glance, a simple scene, it is quite unique. Reflecting in *Slavery and the Culture of Taste* on the African image in the European imagination, Simon Gikandi praises Rembrandt's *Two Negroes* (1659) for avoiding the stereotype, painting the individuality of each man, and using "his genius to reclaim the human from the detritus of enslavement" (1).[6] Although his is a very different kind of painting, Goya has also avoided the stereotype. With the slave trade flourishing, European portraits of Black children as objects of luxury and distinction began to proliferate. In these works, they are, with few exceptions, anonymous shadows confined to the margins: rendered as servants or mere props, and, above all, graphically robbed of their childhood. The Spanish painter,

Figure 10.1. *"La Beata" with Luis de Berganza and María de la Luz* (1795). *Source:* Wikimedia Commons, public domain.

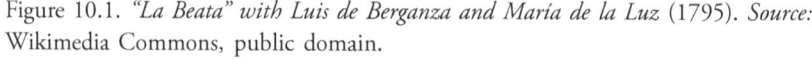

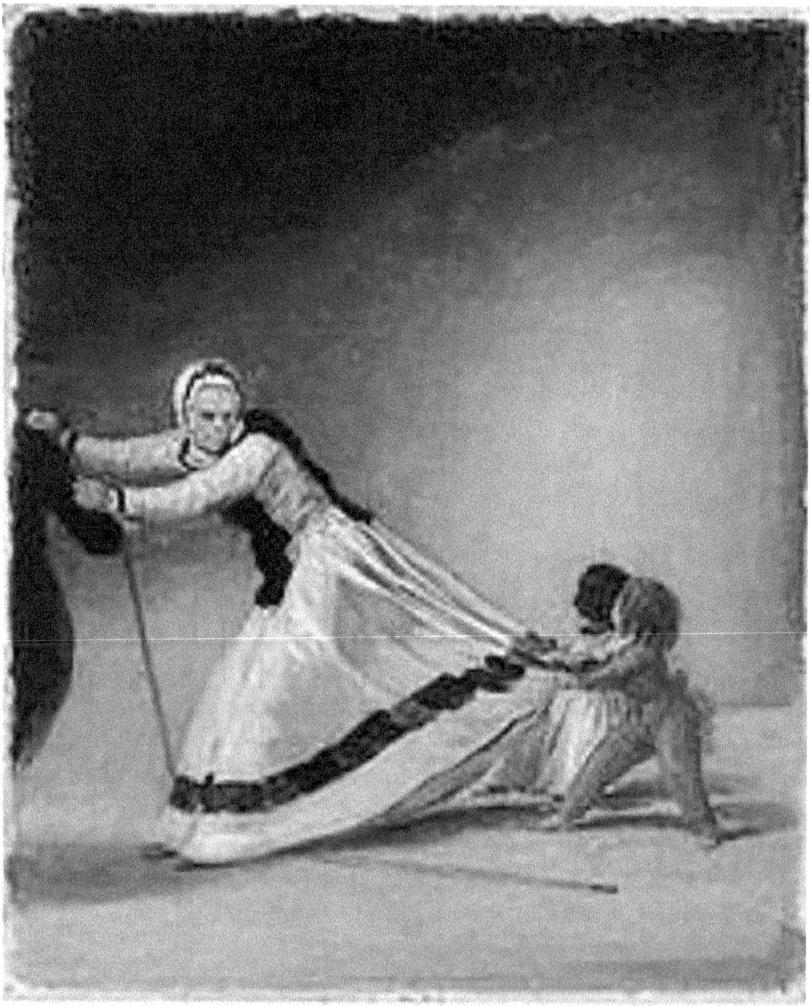

however, "surrounds the children with plentiful and warm light, suggesting the happiness apparent in their game. With total success Goya portrays, in this incident, childhood as a joyous and playful moment" (Tomlinson 220). Faced with a long history of visual imagery that seems only capable of reflecting the impossibility of the Black child experience, Goya departs from the dominant paradigm depicting two mischievous youngsters, granting Luz the right to childhood.[7]

Searching for Cayetana's Daughter | 247

The drawing *The Duchess of Alba with María de la Luz in Her Arms* (1794–1795; fig. 10.2), which belongs to Goya's album *Sanlúcar de Barrameda*, conveys a warm depiction of motherhood in which Cayetana is holding Luz in a quasi-nursing position. The two look lovingly at each other. It is evident that Goya wanted to capture the duchess in a private, intimate setting, "in a moment of maternal tenderness toward her adopted daughter, as if little María—in an age when the slavery of black Africans was commonplace in Spain and the Spanish colonies—were her biological

Figure 10.2. *The Duchess of Alba with María de la Luz in Her Arms* (1794–1795). *Source:* Wikimedia Commons, public domain.

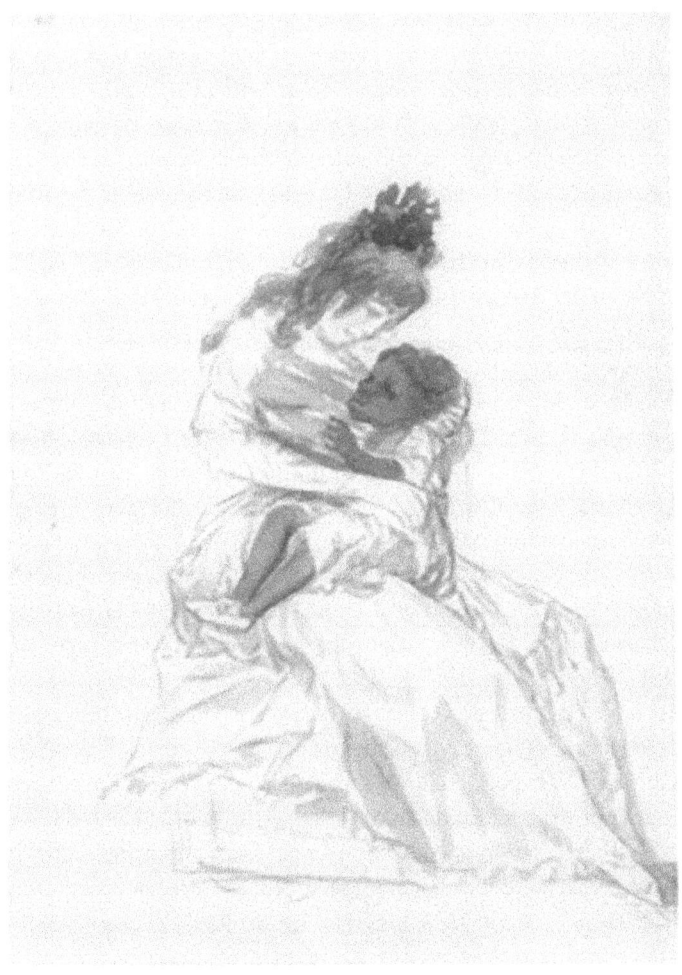

daughter. She almost seems to be breastfeeding the child in the touching scene, in which the contrasts between the two figures—black-white, child-adult—are juxtaposed with the union of mother and daughter, both physically and emotionally" (Lewis 275). There is no doubt that this maternal painting has left its imprint on subsequent representations of Cayetana and Luz. In fact, framing the narrative, it is reproduced on the first page of *La hija de Cayetana*; the film *The Naked Maja* includes an image of the duchess with Luz in a rocking chair that seems inspired by Goya's drawing (see the appendix of this chapter), and Larreta's *Volavérunt* refers to it in a footnote, while in Barberá's fictionalized autobiography Cayetana wonders about the painter's underlying intentions.[8]

A few years after Goya's representations, the *ilustrado* Manuel José Quintana (1772–1857) dedicated a poem to Luz, although without naming her explicitly, and only referring to her as "una negrita": "A una negrita, protegida por la duquesa de Alba" ("To a Little Black Girl Protected by the Duchess of Alba"; 1802). Quintana's poem consists of three parts and reproduces a dialogue between the voice of the male poet, we assume, and the nameless child. In the first part, the poet addresses the little girl directly and begins by juxtaposing her skin color and hair texture with that of the "graciosas europeas" ("graceful Europeans"), accentuating the well-known aesthetic hierarchy that associates whiteness with beauty and Blackness with ugliness. This hierarchy, as we see later in the poem, has been internalized by the child herself. Her skin, metaphorically depicted as ebony and linked to the darkness of night ("Tu tierno cutis la noche / Vistió de sus sombras negras" ["Your tender complexion the night / Dressed in its black shadows"]) differs radically from that of the European women, which is covered by snow. Likewise, the Europeans' "cabello ondulado" ("wavy hair") stands in sharp contrast with her "crespas vedijas," a term associated with animals and disheveled hair.[9] This recurring discursive positioning of the Black body against the white body, emphasizing the absence or presence of beauty, continues, as Debbie Olson observes, "the Western myth of white superiority" (65).

Nevertheless, the poem cannot conceal its paradoxes, because, despite a gaze that affirms white aesthetic superiority, as a product of the Enlightenment, Quintana does condemn Luz's enslavement. He denounces her violent uprooting from her land and family ("Allí vivió tu familia, / Allí crecer tú debieras" ["There your family lived / There you should have grown up"]) and the undeniable economic interests ("sed del oro" ["thirst for gold"]) that fuel the slave trade, labeling it a "peste fatal" ("fatal plague") that leads "padres viles" ("vile parents") to sell their own children. In addition, he reverses the dichotomy civilization/barbarism that traditionally connects barbarism and primitivism with Africa and he reconceptualizes Europe as the barbaric locus ("Bárbara Europa"). Given the traumatic events that Luz has experienced, the poet, in what almost constitutes a verbal depiction of the girl with her playmate in Goya's painting, questions how she can be so oblivious, joyful and even mischievous ("Desenfadada y contenta, / Con dulce gracejo ríes / Y festiva traveseas. ¿Cómo así?" ["Carefree and happy, / With sweet grace you laugh / And you happily frolic. How so?"]). He wonders if divine intervention has allowed her to erase the memories of her suffering. However, in her response, contrary to what her interlocutor might be expecting, Luz surprisingly proclaims her happiness after the journey that led her from slavery to freedom thanks to the "hand" of the duchess, who, horrified by her predicament, liberated her: "Y quebrantó mis cadenas" ("And broke my chains").

The poem transitions, then, from the physical enslavement of Africans to the symbolic enslavement in courtly love, where unrequited lovers become slaves of a cruel beloved. In this case, the person responsible for Luz's freedom, Cayetana, has paradoxically enslaved many others through her beauty. Nevertheless, the most significant aspect is that the little girl emphatically declares with a chiasm that "she" has restored everything that her forced abduction had taken away from her:

>Patria, familia y cariños
>Me robó la suerte adversa;
>Cariños, familia y patria
>Todo lo he encontrado en ella.

>Homeland, family and love
>Adverse luck robbed me;
>Love, family and country
>In her, I have found everything.

Luz proceeds to deliver an ode to her benefactor that, through a series of anaphors, emphasizes her maternal qualities and tenderness. Furthermore, as an indication of her own internalization of white superiority and as the most convincing proof of Cayetana's moral stature, generosity and love for her, the little girl affirms that her protector would, without hesitation, exchange her beautiful whiteness for her "atezada sombra" ("dark shadow"):

Mira el maternal esmero
Con que ampara mi flaqueza,
Y la incansable ternura
Con que mi ventura anhela.
Cuando risueña me llama,
Cuando consigo me lleva,
Cuando en su falda me halaga,
Cuando amorosa me besa,
. . .
Y por mi atezada sombra
Sus bellos colores diera.

Look at the maternal care
With which she protects my frailty,
And the tireless tenderness
With which she longs for my happiness.
When she calls me smiling,
When she takes me with her,
When she cuddles me on her lap,
When she lovingly kisses me,
. . .
For my dark shadow
Her beautiful colors she would trade.

Being near Cayetana, the girl concludes, nobody could be unhappy. Following this unqualified praise of her benefactor, the male poetic voice encourages Luz to become a living monument, hyperbolically superior to magnificent obelisks and pyramids, in order to bear witness to the goodness of the Duchess of Alba.

Crece, dulce criatura,
Vive, y monumento seas
Donde de tu amable dueño
Las alabanzas se extiendan;
Monumento más hermoso
. . .
[que] Los soberbios obeliscos,
Las pirámides eternas.

> Grow up, sweet creature,
> Live, and be a monument
> From which, of your kind owner
> Praises spread;
> A more beautiful monument
> . . .
> [than] The superb obelisks,
> The eternal pyramids.

As readers, we realize, then, that the title of the poem is misleading: while it suggests that it is dedicated to the "negrita," in reality, it is meant to praise the duchess. Luz becomes a monument to honor Cayetana and to pay tribute to a maternal figure who is also the "amable dueño" ("kind mistress") and who has more than demonstrated her moral virtues.

In her study of the feminization of charity in eighteenth-century Spain, Elizabeth Lewis argues that "ideas regarding the feminine nature of sensibility and sentimentality . . . increasingly assigned women an innate 'charitableness'" (269). Furthermore, she explains that charity became an acceptable way for women of the upper classes to participate in Enlightened social reform (267). These women, she adds, quoting Carolyn Williams, found pleasure in the "luxury of doing good" (274). Quintana's poem and even Goya's maternal scene certainly reflect the discourses on womanhood that Lewis examines. In fact, the critic specifically refers in this context to Cayetana's adoption of Luz and to Goya and Quintana's admiration for her: "The sentimental image of this wealthy, powerful and sexy white woman, who treats a small, motherless, black child as her own, is a powerful testimony to the valorization of feminine virtue in 'doing good,' especially to other, less powerful women (or girls in this case)" (275–76). However, if we add to this feminization of charity and sentimentality the question of race, Quintana's poem raises crucial questions regarding its racial and gendered ventriloquism that evokes the hagiography of Chicaba, the eighteenth-century African slave who became a nun in Spain (Pan y Agua).[10] Quintana, the white male poet, creates the voice of the "negrita" who apparently has erased and forgotten the trauma associated with her capture, enslavement, and violent separation from her family. Her suffering is made invisible, absent, negligible. Cayetana's extraordinary generosity overshadows the child's pain in a poem that undoubtedly constitutes a manifestation of the white savior trope.

La hija de Cayetana or All About My Mother(s)

The Uruguayan-Spanish writer Carmen Posadas (1953–) acknowledged in an interview that it was Goya's drawing of the Duchess of Alba holding a Black child in her arms that piqued her curiosity and inspired *La hija de Cayetana* (Drake). In fact, as mentioned, the scene appears in the first page of the novel. In her article "De lo que aprendí en Sevilla persiguiendo sombras" ("What I learned in Seville Chasing Shadows"), Posadas confesses her ignorance of the presence of African slaves in the Iberian Peninsula, having wrongly assumed that slavery was limited to the Americas. She is certainly not alone in her obliviousness, considering Spain's erasure of the historical memory of slavery. For Arlindo Caldeira and Antonio Feros, this amnesia has achieved "the status of a national myth: the belief that the enslavement and exploitation of thousands of black Africans had been an exclusively colonial problem, and never one of the metropolis" (261). Moreover, Posadas describes her journey to Seville searching for the shadows of the duchess and her husband, José Álvarez de Toledo, the embodiment, respectively, of the *castizos* and the *afrancesados*, the two sociopolitical factions that defined eighteenth-century Spain. The author adds, however, that she was searching for a third shadow:

> Pero había otra sombra, mucho más desconocida y esquiva que yo deseaba perseguir en la parte antigua de la ciudad, la de la tercera protagonista de mi novela. . . . Una esclavita que, según costumbre de la época, le regalaron como quien regala un perrito o un guacamayo, pero que María del Pilar Teresa Cayetana no solo aprendió a amar como a una hija, sino que, tras su temprana (y misteriosa) muerte, se convirtió en una de sus herederas y en una mujer muy rica. Me interesó bucear en esta historia sobre todo por el ejemplo de generosidad y tolerancia que supone en un tiempo tan lejano como el siglo XVIII.

> But there was another shadow, much more unknown and elusive, that I wanted to pursue in the old part of the city, that of the third protagonist of my novel. . . . A slave girl who, according to the custom of the time, was gifted, like you would gift a puppy or a macaw, but whom María del Pilar Teresa Cayetana not only learned to love like a daughter but who also, after her early (and mysterious) death, became one of her heirs and a very

rich woman. I was interested in delving into this story above all because of the example of generosity and tolerance it represents in a time as distant as the eighteenth century.

Her search resulted in a historical novel that focuses on two distinct but intertwined worlds: the world of the aristocrats of *la Corte* and that of the slaves. Despite a, once again, deceptive title, the main protagonists of the novel are Cayetana, the historical adoptive mother, and Trinidad, the fictional biological mother of Luz.[11] Contrary to Quintana's poem, which points toward Africa as Luz's origin, in Posadas's novel her biological mother is a Cuban slave who arrives in Spain with her *ama* (mistress) Lucila Manzaneda and a child fathered by her master, Lucila's significantly younger husband Juan. Posadas places this child in the context of slavery in the Iberian Peninsula, but also reflects on its transnational nature (Rodrigo y Alharilla 301) and the diasporic circulation of slaves from Africa to Spain, from Africa to the Americas or, as in the case of Trinidad, from the Americas to Spain. Furthermore, the novel addresses with notable irony the thirst for exoticism and commodification of Black bodies among the European elites, which turned these bodies not only into objects of distinction and taste but also into victims of tragic and dangerous experiments. Notwithstanding the underlying critique of this commodification, the story created for Luz and her mothers is unable to completely escape either Africanist and Orientalizing representational practices or the white savior narrative allied with the persistent discourse of Spain's exceptionalism.

After her arrival in Spain, Lucila Manzaneda writes a letter to her father relating her greatest surprise about life in Madrid: "Parece ser que, acá en la metrópoli y entre personas de calidad, tener un criado negro y vestirlo como un duque con su peluca . . . o bien adoptar una niñita negra y llenarla de lazos y de bodoques es muy *dernier cri*." ("It seems that, here in the metropolis and among people of high standing, to have a black servant and dress him like a duke with his wig . . . or to adopt a little black girl and filling her with ribbons and bows is very *dernier cri*"; 28). She adds that "people of colour" are also in high demand in the world of theater, and while male slaves are sought after for strenuous physical labor, female slaves have a reputation for being competent hairdressers and seamstresses (29). Coming from Cuba, Lucila's astonishment is understandable, considering the differences between slavery and the slave conditions in the colonies and in the metropolis. There are no plantations on the Peninsula and slaves are mainly employed as domestic servants or as wage-earners in a variety of trades (Caldeira and Feros 269). But Lucila's words also point toward the fascination with Blackness (according to some characters, due to Spain's *afrancesamiento*), and Blacks becoming a sign of prestige and/or luxury objects that serve ornamental purposes. As Celeste, the other Cuban slave who accompanied Lucila on her voyage, explains to Trinidad: "¿No ves que los morenos empezamos a ser moda en la metrópoli y eso hace que cada vez traigan *pacá* más y mejores ejemplares. Como cocineros, mozos de cuadra . . . y luego, los que son más vistosos o raros los traen *pa* simple adorno. El otro día oí de una señora que se había comprado un niñito negro especialmente lindo como si fuera un tití." ("Don't you see that we Black people are starting to become fashionable in the metropolis, and that is why they bring more and better specimens here. As cooks, stable boys . . . and then, those who are more eye-catching or rare, they bring them for simple decoration. The other day, I heard about a lady who had bought a particularly cute little black boy as if he were a marmoset"; 78). Consequently, Black slaves turn into "elegant gifts" for friends and benefactors, which is clearly how Martínez views Trinidad and her daughter when he purchases them (330).[12] Furthermore, Black people leave their mark even as exotic trendsetters, which some aristocrats like the Duchess Amaranta readily embrace, as evidenced by her choice of a turban (212). Gikandi very graphically highlights the tragic irony underlying the impact of Blackness and Black bodies on European culture: "a new global economy that revolved around the sale of Black bodies on the West African coast, their enforced labor in the Americas, and their use in the production of the goods—primarily tobacco, coffee, and sugar—that were to epitomize luxurious living and the culture of taste . . . the age of reason, enlightenment, and civility, which was also the time of slavery" (54). Aristocrats and upper classes in *La hija de Cayetana* are oblivious to these ironies, embodying instead the silence of the culture of taste vis-à-vis the "[t]he material conditions that enabled it" (Gikandi 63).

In conjunction with this objectification of Black bodies is the Enlightenment's interest in human nature. As Julia V. Douthwaite examines in *The Wild Girl, Natural Man, and the Monster: Dangerous Experiments in the Age of Enlightenment*, in the eighteenth and early nineteenth centuries this attention to the nature of human beings was accompanied by the proliferation of amateur experiments (1–2). Scientific societies multiplied and numerous new publications popularized science, making experimentation "an accessible and popular pastime for many middle- and upper-class people in England and France" (6). Furthermore, this amateur scientism was linked to the discourse on perfecting mankind and its assumption that other people should emulate European culture, the epitome of social and intellectual progress (1–2; 6). Nevertheless, in her case studies, Douthwaite explores the "sinister implications" of experimentalism, which could create "full-fledged dystopias" (4).[13] Amaranta's Corte de los Milagros in *La hija de Cayetana* constitutes a tragic parody of these experiments, also influenced by Jean-Jacques Rousseau's ideas, particularly his concept of the noble savage.

Caragatos, one of Amaranta's white servants, sarcastically introduces Trinidad to their mistress's Corte de los Milagros, inspired, in her opinion, by the French philosopher and his incitement to return to the natural world (162–63).[14] As an Enlightened woman, Amaranta's intent was to undertake a Rousseauian experiment with a group of noble savages and non-normative bodies that would make her famous in Europe (164). This is not a completely original project, since, as Olson reminds us, "The practice of putting people from different cultures on display for white visual consumption has a long history in Europe" (63), as the ethnographic exhibits that were popular at the height of colonialism (from the seventeenth to the mid-nineteenth centuries) reveal. Recalling José Moreno Villa's study of the "gente de placer" (pleasure people) during the Habsburg dynasty in his *Locos, enanos, negros y niños palaciegos* (*Madmen, Dwarfs, Blacks and Palace Children*, 1939), Izaskun Álvarez Cuartero confirms that this fascination with the body of Others (racialized, disabled, and "freak" bodies) was present early on in Europe (even to a certain extent in medieval times).[15] The non-normative bodies of "pleasure people" became collectibles that European monarchs exchanged as a sign of courtesy. The eighteenth century witnessed an increased interest and a very illuminating parallelism between the collection of exotic (or curious) objects and animals from distant places and the collection of exotic human beings among artists, scientists and travelers (Álvarez Cuartero 464–65).[16] All these discourses converge in the Corte de los Milagros.

This profoundly disturbing court is composed of disabled, Roma, and Black individuals whom Amaranta has tried to "amaestrar" (train), teaching them reading and writing, music and languages (164). But the court has evolved from an intended utopia and Arcadia into a monstrous dystopia where the "noble savages" live in subhuman conditions: abandoned in filthy cages, they are given laudanum to deprive them of agency (173–75; 194–95). Amaranta's experiment at her property El Olvido is fictional, but it replicates the European desire for this type of natural experiment, as other examples included in the novel indicate (176–79). In fact, Amaranta and her Corte de los Milagros can also be read as a caricature of Rousseau's pedagogical prescriptions (the members of the court start their day with a nutritious breakfast, they engage in healthy physical activity and various cultured and educational activities, etc.; 178) and of the Enlightened white savior narrative:

> ¿qué puede haber más gratificante que cambiar el futuro de otro ser humano, arrancarlo del mísero destino que la suerte le deparaba, convertirlo en un ser ilustrado, con dotes para la música, para las lenguas, para el baile? . . . Tengo un gitanillo de seis años que toca el violín mejor que Mozart a su edad y una negrita saladísima, que me han regalado no hace mucho y a la que estoy amaestrando para que recite Racine en francés. (178)

> What could be more gratifying than changing the future of another human being, tearing them away from the miserable destiny that luck had in store for them, turning them into enlightened beings, with talents for music, for languages, for dancing? . . . I have a little six-year-old gypsy who plays the violin better than Mozart at his age and a very charming black girl who was given to me not long ago and who I am training to recite Racine in French.

At some point, the aristocrat loses interest in her experiment, and ennui sets in (194). Bored and frustrated with not seeing the expected results, her projected utopia metamorphoses into the dystopia that Caragatos and Trinidad encounter.

While parodying the effects of Rousseau's pedagogical and philosophical ideas, as well as the experiments with exotic Others and their exhibition for European consumption, *La hija de Cayetana* itself cannot completely escape an exoticizing, or what Toni Morrison calls an Africanist representation (6–7). An almost ethnographic gaze upon a subaltern Other is very noticeable in the depiction of Afro-Cuban cultural practices in Madrid, particularly in "Una noche con los orishas" ("A Night with the Orishas"). The *babalawo* Gran Damián with his *santería* rituals, his syncretic altar that unites orishas and Catholic saints, the animal sacrifices, his readings of the *caracoles* (84–87) that will allow him later even to predict Cayetana and Manuel Godoy's future (154), provides an excellent opportunity for a racialized *costumbrista* gaze. But nothing like the images that decorate his luxurious house for a perfect display of Orientalism:

"El Gran Damián sobrevuela Bagdad," rezaba el primero, en el que podía verse a un gigante negro de lustrosos bíceps sentado sobre una alfombra voladora. En otro cartel, el Gran Damián, vestido solo con unos bombachos rojos, lanzaba cuchillos silueteando a una mujer. Y más allá, Damián rompiendo unas cadenas bajo el agua; y Damián luchando contra un cocodrilo; y Damián hipnotizando a una cobra . . . (80)

"The Great Damián flies over Baghdad," read the first, in which a black giant with shiny biceps could be seen sitting on a flying carpet. In another poster, Grand Damián, dressed only in red baggy trousers, threw knives silhouetting a woman. And beyond, Damián breaking some chains underwater; and Damián fighting a crocodile; and Damián hypnotizing a cobra . . .

If we add to the above Celeste's knowledge of herbs and roots, which is emphasized on several occasions (even to try to save Cayetana at the end; 507), we can argue that the novel recycles the recurring historical association of Black people with the natural world and the irrational.

Cayetana herself cannot escape an Africanist framework when she takes Luz to the *campamento de negros*, which provides an opportunity to reconnect with N'huongo, a former Cuban slave who managed to escape to Spain, and whom she had befriended in one of her escapadas as a thirteen-year-old. The duchess remembers the day that he tried to teach her to dance and how she looked at his body: "Cayetana había observado fascinada cómo sus músculos perfectos se contraían o estiraban bajo su piel lustrosa y oscura. Incluso olvidaba que era rengo cuando lo veía moverse como un animal salvaje taimado, lento, insinuante" ("Cayetana had watched in fascination as his perfect muscles contracted or stretched beneath his shiny, dark skin. She even forgot that he limped when she saw him move like a sly, slow, insinuating wild animal"; 400). Cayetana views N'huongo through a lens that reproduces tropes of the threatening savage and animalized Black body. She also clearly remembers through an essentializing Us/Them dichotomy that N'huongo taught her "cómo sienten y aman los morenos" ("how Black people feel and love") (424). As George Yancy asserts in *Black Bodies, White Gazes*, "The white gaze, as a ritual performance . . . is inextricably bound with objectifying, exoticizing, and sexualizing the Black body, inscribing it with myths and codes that function to ontologize it, thus returning it as that which it is not" (192). Furthermore, the description of the camp focusing on the miserable living conditions of its inhabitants has much in common with what is now characterized as "poverty porn" or the reduction of Black people to precariousness (Lissner): "Esos niños en harapos . . . La precariedad de las tiendas de lona, el vientre hinchado de los niños, las caras resignadas de los hombres y desafiantes las de las mujeres" ("Those children in rags . . . The precariousness of the canvas tents, the swollen bellies of the children, the men's resigned faces and the women's defiant ones"; 422–23).

Posadas has undoubtedly done extensive research to write her historical novel. She has captured vividly and with a great deal of irony the political intrigues of the Spanish court, the amorous triangles that put Godoy at the center, the customs (from the coded language of the fake *lunares* and the design of dentures [50, 62] to the figure of the cortejo, thoroughly analyzed in Carmen Martín Gaite's *Usos amorosos del dieciocho en España*), and Spain's, and particularly its aristocrats' relationship with French culture and Blackness. However, when the novel turns to the world of the enslaved men and women, the ironic gaze becomes exoticizing, and the weight of the regime of representation of Afro-descendants in the Western imagination seems very palpable and especially problematic in the juxtaposition of the two mothers in the novel.

The story of Trinidad begins by borrowing from the genres of the maternal melodrama and the folletinesque. The biological mother endures having her daughter Marina Amalalá Umbé (31) taken from her. As a slave, she lacks the power to prevent this abduction, although the narrator does not depict her as completely devoid of agency, since she is described as determined to find her daughter. But, interestingly, most of the action surrounding Trinidad is devoted to her search (with questionable verisimilitude) for her former master, Juan, who fathered her child. From the beginning, we know that she understands their relationship as a true love story and not just one more example of the sexual abuse of female slaves (18). Without denying the complex ambiguous feelings that might characterize some master-slave relationships (the novel portrays Juan and Trinidad as two children who grew up together), as Cuban author Nancy Morejón explores so well in her poem "Amo a mi amo" ("I Love My Master") (1986), in *La hija de Cayetana*, we are presented with an extremely idealized vision of Trinidad and Juan that downplays or outright denies the unequal power dynamics. We see Trinidad embark on a voyage that echoes adventure stories or even Byzantine novels: an implausible maritime journey that takes her from Spain to Madeira, during which she endures sexual abuse at the hands of the repugnant señor de Santolín; is employed by Elisa, a mysterious sex worker originally from the Philippines who seems to fulfill men's pedophile fantasies; finds Juan, who is one of Elisa's clients; and discovers that he has changed and is now trapped in a marriage with a calculating and vindictive woman whose accusations land Trinidad and Elisa in prison, where the former is subjected to further sexual and physical abuse. Finally, Trinidad manages to return to Spain, acknowledging that Juan is dead to her (453). In short, all of Trinidad's tribulations that would define a mother's search for her daughter in the maternal melodrama are very problematically redirected in Posadas's novel toward her master. Furthermore, while Juan is presented as a morally failed individual, slavery and the power dynamics that define the couple's relationship are ignored.

If we remember that the first page of the novel includes a reproduction of Goya's drawing of a maternal Duchess of Alba, it is clear that Cayetana-as-mother frames the narrative and is the point of departure, in spite of the first chapters being dedicated to Trinidad and the birth of Luz during a voyage from Cuba to Spain. Luz is gifted to Cayetana as an infant, and the novel captures their tender mother-daughter interactions (the baby reaching out to Cayetana, Cayetana giving her the bottle and personally taking care of her; Cayetana frantically trying to rescue her adopted daughter when the flames engulf the Palacio de Benavente), as well as Luz interacting with Goya as if she were a true family member (445–46). We also know that she is tutored in French and music. Contrary to what some might believe, the narrative makes it clear that for Cayetana, this is not a Rousseauian experiment but rather a response to her loneliness and the impossibility of having her own biological children (181). The presence of Luz in her household becomes, for the duchess, a genuine experience in mothering, even an experience in transracial adoption.

In fact, the novel attempts to explore, albeit in a rather superficial way, this aspect at a late point in the novel. When Luz is approximately ten years old, she begins asking questions about her origins and identity. She tries to extract information about her biological mother from Martínez, who, she knows, had bought her from the widowed Lucila and later offered her as a present to the duchess (329). She is also depicted as being very upset after receiving a blond doll with which she cannot identify (324–25); she starts chanting a Black lullaby in an "idioma ininteligible" ("unintelligible language") that one of the servants, a former Cuban slave, has taught her (375); she immerses herself in the library to look at the colonial "pinturas de casta" that portrayed the offspring of different racial mixtures and were very popular during the Enlightenment (376). Cayetana observes changes in the child's personality and even in the way she arranges her hair, and she laments their distancing: "Todo lo que hace y dice últimamente está dictado por una parte de su forma de ser, que me es completamente ajena" ("Everything she does and says lately is dictated by a part of her way of being, which is completely foreign to me"; 422). In an apparent effort to connect her with her roots, Cayetana takes Luz to the *campamento de negros*, where she tells her childhood friend N'huongo that her daughter is obsessed with finding her mother, a common issue in adoption (424). Finally, when Hugo de Santillán, the Dominican mixed-race "abogado de pobres" ("lawyer for the poor") who will become Trinidad's husband, writes to the duchess explaining who the biological mother is, the circumstances under which she lost her daughter, and her desire to see her, even without unveiling her identity, Cayetana has a revelation: she decides to offer Trinidad work in her household so that she can be close to Luz. Moreover, she responds positively to the letter by inviting Trinidad to visit, which, undoubtedly, as she puts it, will be the best gift for her daughter's tenth birthday (473–74). Furthermore, at that point in the novel, we already know that Cayetana has bequeathed Luz (and her future caregiver, Trinidad) a pension for life that will allow her to become a wealthy Black woman. It is evident that Posadas, like Quintana, chose the white savior narrative to tell the story of Cayetana's daughter.

When *La hija de Cayetana* reaches its final chapter, the narrative shifts. Writing from Havana in 1845, Luz becomes a first-person narrator, disclosing that she was the author all along, but had preferred to use the third person because, for her, this is the story of her two mothers, and she wanted to capture their points of view. It is only after the lives of both women converge (in the chapter specifically titled "Dos madres" ["Two Mothers"]) that she turns to the first person to write the conclusion. She informs the reader of the death of Cayetana, the return to Cuba of her biological mother, and the passing of Rafaela, Celeste, and N'huongo. The final chapter provides a reassuring and comforting ending that shows a desire to establish a racial balance and to embrace the dual heritage, where one might even perceive echoes of Nicolás Guillén's 1934 poem "Balada de los dos abuelos" ("Ballad of the Two Grandfathers").[17] Through the voice of Luz, Posadas's novel portrays the embrace of the white adoptive mother and the Black biological mother, as clearly demonstrated by the names that Luz chooses for her two daughters: Cayetana and Trinidad. Yet this conclusion overshadows and dismisses the profound disparities between both mothers: the slave condition of Trinidad opposed to Cayetana's racial and socioeconomic privilege to free a person, to bequeath a pension and, ultimately, as we saw in Quintana's poem, to do good.

In *Unthinking Eurocentrism*, Ella Shohat and Robert Stam discuss the concept of "anthropocentric moralism" or "the treatment of complex political issues as if they were matters of individual ethics" (201). Narratives of white saviors, they contend, are an expression of this phenomenon: the altruism of the "hero," rather than the larger configurations of power or the urgent systemic or structural changes, lies at the center of these narratives. Moreover, the Others saved, even if they presumably constitute the thematic focus, play a "subsidiary function" and become "a trampoline for personal sacrifice and redemption" (206). *La hija de Cayetana* describes the duchess's unconventional personality, her liberal sexual life, her desire to scandalize, her fearlessness, and her association with bullfighters, *majas*, and other individuals, such as N'huongo, not belonging to her social milieu. To what extent, we might wonder, does Posadas use Luz as a springboard to emphasize Cayetana's transgressive personality and generosity in a way that recalls Quintana's poem? Moreover, we might ask if even the racist attacks directed at the little girl (for example, during her father's funeral [434–35]) ultimately serve to accentuate Cayetana's moral stature and confirm her uniqueness. In accordance with the white savior script, the adoption of a little slave girl places the duchess on the right side ethically, but at no point does she question the institution of slavery itself.

Supported by some of Posadas's writings in the press, there is one more relevant component in *La hija de Cayetana* that must be highlighted: the discourse of exceptionalism that defends the relative benevolence of the Iberian system of slavery and colonialism.[18] Early on, the novel presents a significant conversation between an English overseer and the chaplain of the Garcías in Cuba. They talk about a widower who has decided to free his enslaved son and is even considering marrying his son's mother. While the overseer finds this preposterous, the chaplain seizes the occasion to assert the difference between the Spanish and British colonial models and to defend the Iberian one as rooted in Christianity and, therefore, in the belief in racial equality that leads to *mestizaje*: "Vuestras leyes no sólo prohíben los matrimonios, sino que castigan con dureza todo trato carnal con negros. Las nuestras, en cambio, están basadas en los preceptos de la Santa Madre Iglesia" ("Your laws not only prohibit marriages, but harshly punish any carnal relations with blacks. Ours, on the other hand, are based on the precepts of Holy Mother Church"; 19). In "De lo que aprendí en Sevilla," referring to Cayetana's love for Luz, Posadas writes that she felt intrigued by this story of (white) generosity and tolerance. Furthermore, recalling (thanks to Cervantes) that Seville was known as "el damero de Europa por el crisol de culturas que en ella se daba cita" ("the checkerboard of Europe for the melting pot of cultures that gathered there"), she adds that "no era raro ver en sus calles a gentes de todas las razas convivir en perfecta armonía" ("it was not unusual to see on its streets people of all races living together in perfect harmony"). Warning against the current rise of xenophobia and racism, Posadas encourages readers to remember that centuries ago, Seville practiced tolerance and taught solidarity to the world. While such an optimistic and harmonious vision is difficult to sustain, bearing in mind that part of the population was enslaved, it is a clear manifestation of the belief in Spain's difference with regard to slavery and colonialism.[19] Moreover, this affirmation of exceptionalism, which has prevailed for centuries, has been recently revitalized in the public sphere, and Posadas inscribes her novel within this contemporary discourse.[20]

La hija de Cayetana ends with the following words from Luz: "Para poner fin a este relato solo me falta dar respuesta a una pregunta: ¿murió Cayetana de Alba envenenada? Espero que Dios me dé vida suficiente para un día resolver el enigma" ("To end this story I only need to answer one question: did Cayetana de Alba die from poison? I hope God gives me enough life to one day solve the enigma"; 509). From this response, it is easy to conclude that, despite the title, the novel is all about Cayetana. In addition to the title, the cover of *La hija de Cayetana*, which combines a photograph of a little girl and Goya's 1795 portrait of the Duchess of Alba, is equally deceptive (fig. 10.3). The face of Cayetana is not visible and we only see part of her body and face. Luz occupies the center wearing a beautiful dress and a red bow in her hair that closely resemble those of her adoptive mother.[21] While these similarities constitute an attempt to underline the strong mother-daughter bond, they also erase the power relations at play in the adoption of the child of a slave. This essay started by recalling Titus Kaphar's painting *Enough About You* and his recovery of the anonymous enslaved child from the margins, placing him at the center of a portrait dedicated entirely to him. The title and cover of Posadas's novel point initially toward a similar strategy, yet the narrative and a closer look at the cover betray it, much as the title of Quintana's poem deceives readers.

Without denying the progress made in representational terms (giving voice to Luz, creating a story for her and her biological mother), *La hija de Cayetana* is still very much about a superior being, the Duchess of Alba, who eclipses everyone else, as Larreta's epigraph indicates. While it

Figure 10.3. Cover of *La hija de Cayetana.* *Source:* Courtesy of Espasa, an imprint of Editorial Planeta, S.A.

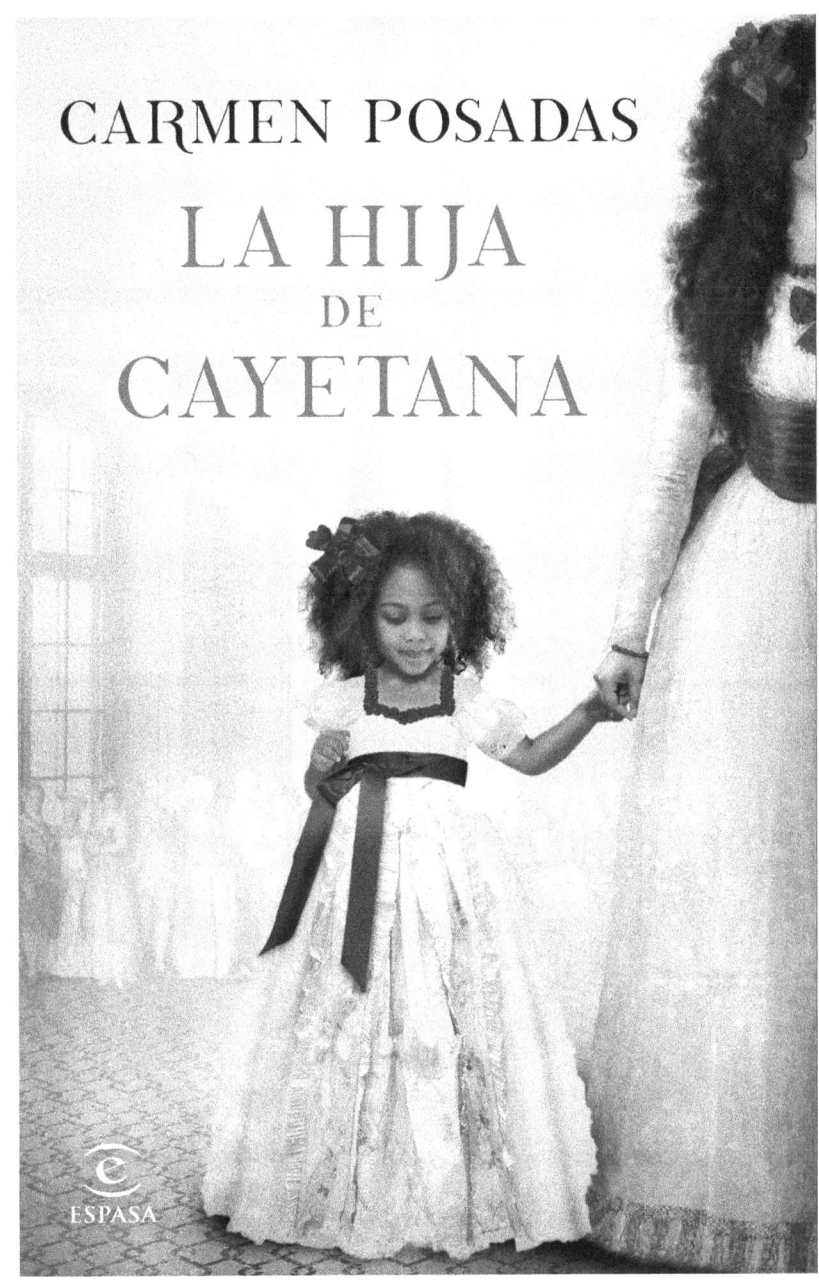

is undisputable that the relationship between Cayetana and Luz is inspired by real events, it is also true that artists and writers choose not only the stories they want to fictionalize, but also the perspective from which to tell them. Following in Quintana's footsteps, Posadas inserts her novel into a long tradition of narratives of white women as saviors of Black children, while Luz still waits for her own *Enough About You*.

Notes

1. "She danced, or laughed, or played cards, or played with a little poodle, and everything around her went dark. The light went towards here and there it remained vibrating. I could remember her on any given morning in Sanlúcar de Barrameda, that summer of 1796, splashing in the pool with the little black girl she had adopted, the two girls laughing, the black one and the white one, equal in age and rank thanks to the joy of the nakedness and the fresh water. . ." All translations are mine, unless otherwise indicated.

2. "Damian—he said matter-of-factly—is a slave from Mozambique. The Count of Ribadavia gifted him to me five years ago. He could have given me a Moorish man but that would have been too ordinary. The favor was too high for such measly attention. Nowadays, a slave from Mozambique is a luxury typical of the aristocracy."

3. For information regarding the duchess's will and Luz, see Mühler-Maurer (226–28; 237–38). According to unpublished documents, Luz was born in June 1793 in Havana. Her parents, Domingo Escobar and María Josefa Dávalos y Zinoco, were slaves of Antonio Dávalos y Zinoco. Don Manuel María de Ampudia bought Luz, and his wife Manuela Joaquina de Alcázar gifted her to the Duchess of Alba, who later freed her. Mühler-Maurer also refers to another 15-year-old slave she received, had baptized, and emancipated (238).

4. For more on audiovisual productions about Goya, see Lázaro Sebastián and Sanz Ferreruela.

5. *The Naked Maja* deserves a more nuanced analysis, which, due to space constraints, I am unable to undertake here. In spite of its mediocrity, the film generated significant controversy, including the opposition of the Alba family and Franco to its filming in Spain, and the US marketing of the film using a reproduction of Goya's *Maja desnuda*. See Salas y Guirior's article published following its premiere in Cape Town, South Africa. It is accompanied by a photo of Ava Gardner with Yemiko Fullwood, the actress who plays Luz.

6. Gikandi refers to Velázquez and Rubens as two other artists who place Africans at the center of their works and do not confine them to the margins, as court painters such as van Dyck had previously done (3). According to Gikandi,

"the recognition of the African as a figure worthy of representation in painting was often at odds with the perception of Africans as objects of trade" (3).

7. Commenting on Hollywood practices, Olson refers to the ritual exclusion of Black children from the "larger cultural politics of innocence" (70), the result of a long history of representing them as uncivilized, uncultured, and animalistic. For Olson, "This racialization of the discourse of childhood was a construction that served to enforce, and naturalize, existing social relations of inequality" (23).

8. "Nunca creí estar maternalmente herida, pero tú me has mostrado la cicatriz. Al cabo de los años es una crueldad desvelar esta carencia mía. ¿Tan evidente resulta? ¿O tan profunda es tu intuición?" ("I never thought I was maternally wounded, but you have shown me the scar. After so many years it is cruel to reveal this lack of mine. Is it so obvious? Or is your intuition that deep?"; Barberá 283).

9. The *Diccionario de la lengua española* defines "vedija" as: "1. mechón de lana, 2. Pelo enredado de cualquier parte del cuerpo del animal, 3. Mata de pelo enredada y ensortijada" ("1. lock of wool, 2. Tangled hair from any part of the animal's body, 3. Tangled and curly hair").

10. In *Black Bride of Christ*, the hagiographer Juan Carlos Miguel de Pan y Agua transcribes Chicaba's voice, but the trauma of her capture and enslavement are obliterated and explained as the path to Christian redemption and holiness. Contrary to Quintana's poem, it does not condemn slavery.

11. It is interesting to note that item 8 in Cayetana's will reads, "A la Trinidad que cuida á la negrita a ella y a sus hijos también se les otorga una pensión vitalicia" ("To the Trinity that cares for the black girl, she and her children are also granted a pension for life"; Mühler-Maurer 228). This was likely the inspiration for the name of the fictional mother.

12. In Seville, Trinidad confirms that "tal como ocurría en Madrid, pero con mayor incidencia, tener un esclavo en Sevilla y vestirlo de modo llamativo era un signo de estatus, de distinción" ("just as it happened in Madrid, but with greater incidence, having a slave in Seville and dressing him in a striking way was a sign of status, of distinction"; 245).

13. Douthwaite examines the cases of three famous "wild children" who, in spite of being subjected to different educational methods, never lost what was considered their monstruous attributes. Electrical experiments that used the human body as a conductor were very popular and a clear example of amateur scientism (7–8).

14. Caragatos's familiarity with Rousseau might seem implausible, but she is an illegitimate child in Amaranta's family who was close to her aristocratic grandfather, with whom she spent a lot of time in his library.

15. For more on the cultural construction and exhibit of the freak body, see Garland-Thomson.

16. The words of sixteenth-century Italian humanist Francesco Matarazzo are revealing: "La magnificencia de un gran señor ha de verse tam bién en sus caballos, en sus perros, en sus halcones y demás aves, como en sus bufones, sus músicos y

en los animales extraños que posee" ("The magnificence of a great lord must also be seen in his horses, in his dogs, in his falcons and other birds, as well as in his jesters, his musicians and in the strange animals he owns"; qtd. in Gómez-Centurión Jiménez 160). Regarding exotic animals, see Sánchez Espinosa's chronicle of the arrival of the elephant in Madrid and Gómez-Centurión's article on the royal camels in Aranjuez in the eighteenth century. As European colonial expansion intensified, more "pleasure animals" were brought to Europe and exhibited in brutal entertainments for the upper classes (Gómez-Centurión Jiménez 164).

17. In "Balada," the Cuban poet tries to reconcile his European and African heritage represented by his two grandfathers: "Los dos se abrazan / . . . los dos del mismo tamaño, / ansia negra y ansia blanca, / los dos del mismo tamaño" ("The two embrace / . . . both the same size, / black anguish, white anguish, / both the same size"; Guillén and Netchinsky 186, 187).

18. As Caldeira and Feros explain, this occurs in spite of numerous studies that point out the "no less insidious nature in terms of blocking avenues to freedom and impeding the integration of freedmen and their descendants" (262). In "De lo que aprendí en Sevilla," Posadas also presents a quite patronizing, simplistic and idealized view of Black *cofradías*, and again as part of a white savior narrative. Historical studies present a less idealized view (see Bravo Caro; Martín Casares and Delaigue).

19. In her article "Soñar en español" ("Dreaming in Spanish"), Posadas expresses an equally problematic view of the *reducciones*: "Años más tarde, y siempre con la música por cómplice, nativos y misioneros crearían una de las experiencias de igualdad social y convivencia más interesantes y vanguardistas que se conocen en la Historia, las llamadas 'reducciones'" ("Years later, and always with music as an accomplice, natives and missionaries would create one of the most interesting and avant-garde experiences of social equality and coexistence known in history, the so-called 'reductions'"). This belief constitutes the core of the ideology of Hispanidad and Hispanotropicalism, Gustau Nerín's term for Spain's official discourse on colonial matters (Cornejo-Parriego 205–06).

20. The best example are some statements made by Isabel Díaz Ayuso, president of the Comunidad de Madrid, during her visit to the United States in September 2021 in which she condemned *indigenismo* as an attack against Spain's leadership (Di Liscia; "Madrid Leader"). See "Ayuso es la nueva colonialidad de siempre" ("Ayuso Is the New Everlasting Coloniality"), by Peruvian author Gabriela Wiener, and the excellent satire, "Imperialista" ("Imperialist") by Spanish novelist Marta Sanz comparing Ayuso's adventures in the United States with Tintin's in the Congo. Nor should we forget that King Felipe VI, during his visit to Puerto Rico in January 2022, defended Spain's colonial model and encouraged pride in its legacy (González).

21. Álvarez Cuartero, among others, points out the similarities between Cayetana and Luz in regard to dress and adornments in some of Goya's painting (459).

Works Cited

Álvarez Cuartero, Izaskun. "*Gentes de color, gentes de placer y otras rarezas:* Una aproximación a su estudio en la pintura europea y americana de los siglos XVII y XVIII." *En torno a las Antillas hispánicas: Ensayos en homenaje al profesor Paul Estrade*, Archivo Histórico Insular de Fuerteventura, 2004, pp. 458–72.

Barberá, Carmen. *La duquesa de Alba*. Planeta, 1995.

Bravo Caro, Juan Jesús. "Los esclavos de Málaga a mediados del siglo XVIII, una minoría en extinción." *Baética: Estudios de arte, geografía e historia*, vol. 19, no. 2, 1997, 83–108.

Caldeira, Arlindo, and Antonio Feros. "Black Africans in the Iberian Peninsula (1400–1820)." *The Iberian World 1450–1820*, edited by Fernando Bouza et al., Routledge, 2019, pp. 261–80.

Cornejo-Parriego, Rosalía. "*Arriba* and the Black Civil Rights Movement: Time to Mend Fences or Time for Revenge?" *Black USA and Spain: Shared Memories in the 20th Century*, edited by Rosalía Cornejo-Parriego, Routledge, 2019, pp. 194–215.

Delibes, Miguel. *El hereje*. Cátedra, 2020.

Di Liscia, Valentina. "At New York's Hispanic Society, Leader of Madrid Laments Indigenous Movements as an 'Attack Against Spain.'" *Hyperallergic*, 30 Sept. 2021.

Douthwaite, Julia V. *The Wild Girl, Natural Man, and the Monster: Dangerous Experiments in the Age of Enlightenment*. U of Chicago P, 2002.

Drake, Virginia. "Carmen Posadas: 'Me tuve que tomar un "gin-tonic" para escribir una escena de mi nueva novela.'" *XLSemanal*, 26 Oct. 2016.

Diccionario de la lengua española. Real Academia Española, 2022. dle.rae.es.

Garland-Thomson, Rosemarie, editor. *Freakery: Cultural Spectacles of the Extraordinary Body*. New York UP, 1996.

Gikandi, Simon. *Slavery and the Culture of Taste*. Princeton UP, 2011.

Gómez-Centurión Jiménez, Carlos. "Exóticos pero útiles: Los camellos reales de Aranjuez durante el siglo XVIII." *Cuadernos dieciochistas*, vol. 9, 2008, pp. 155–80.

González, Miguel. "El Rey reivindica en Puerto Rico el 'modelo español' de colonización de América." *El País*, 25 Jan. 2022.

Goya, Francisco. "*La beata*" *with Luis de Berganza and María de la Luz*. 1795. Private collection.

———. *The Duchess of Alba with María de la Luz in Her Arms*. 1794–1795. Museo del Prado.

Guillén, Nicolás, and Jill Netchinsky. "Balada de los dos abuelos / Ballad of the Two Grandfathers." *Nicolás Guillén*, special issue of *Callaloo*, no. 31, 1987, pp. 184–87.

Joseph, Paterson. "The Outrageous Neglect of African Figures in Art History." *Art UK*, 31 Oct. 2019.

Kaphar, Titus. *Enough About You*. 2016, Yale Center for British Art.

Kenney, Nancy. "Art Historians Try to Identify Enslaved Black Child in an 18th-century portrait." *CNN Style*, 12 Oct. 2021.

Koster, Henry, director. *The Naked Maja*. S.G.C/Titanus, 1959.

Larreta, Antonio. *Volavérunt*. Planeta, 1980.

Lázaro Sebastián, Francisco Javier, and Fernando Sanz Ferreruela. *Goya en el audiovisual: Aproximación a sus constantes narrativas y estéticas en el ámbito cinematográfico y televisivo*. Prensas de la U de Zaragoza, 2017.

Lewis, Elizabeth F. "*Actos de caridad*: Women's Charitable Work in Eighteenth-Century Spain." *Dieciocho: Hispanic Enlightenment*, vol. 31, no. 2, 2008, pp. 267–82.

Lissner, Jorgen. "Merchants of Misery." *New Internationalist*, 1 June 1981.

Luna, Bigas, director. *Volavérunt*. Mate Production/MDA Films, 1999.

"Madrid Leader Takes Issue with Pope's Apology for 'Painful Errors' in Mexico." *The Guardian*, 29 Sept. 2021.

Martín Casares, Aurelia, and Christine Delaigue. "The Evangelization of Freed and Slave Black Africans in Renaissance Spain: Baptism, Marriage and Ethnic Brotherhoods." *History of Religions*, vol. 52, no. 3, 2013, pp. 214–35.

Martín Gaite, Carmen. *Usos amorosos del dieciocho en España*. Anagrama, 1987.

McGreevy, Nora. "Who Is the Enslaved Child in This Portrait of Yale University's Namesake?" *Smithsonian Magazine*, 15 Oct. 2021.

Morrison, Toni. *Playing in the Dark: Whiteness and the Literary Imagination*. Vintage, 1993.

Mühler-Maurer, Gudrun. "Biografías enlazadas: Goya y los duques de Alba." *La duquesa de Alba "musa" de Goya: El mito y la historia*, by Manuela B. Mena Marqués and Gudrun Mühler-Maurer, Museo Nacional del Prado, 2006, pp. 165–259.

Olson, Debbie. *Black Children in Hollywood Cinema*. Springer International Publishing, 2017.

Pan y Agua, Juan Carlos. *Black Bride of Christ: Chicaba, an African Nun in Eighteenth-Century Spain*. Edited, translated, and with an introduction by Sue E. Houchins and Baltasar Fra-Molinero, Vanderbilt UP, 2018.

Posadas, Carmen. "De lo que aprendí en Sevilla persiguiendo sombras." *XL Semanal*, 21 Nov. 2016, www.elcorreo.com/xlsemanal/firmas/carmen-posadas/lo-aprendi-sevilla-persiguiendo-sombras.html.

———. *La hija de Cayetana*. Espasa Libros, 2016

———. "Soñar en español." *XLSemanal*, 7 May 2016, www.elcorreo.com/xlsemanal/firmas/carmen-posadas/sonar-espanol-9758.html.

Quintana, Manuel José. "A una negrita protegida por la duquesa de Alba." Biblioteca Virtual Cervantes, 1999 [1802].

Rodrigo y Alharilla, Martín. "The Legacies of Atlantic Slavery in Nineteenth-Century Spain." *The Routledge Hispanic Studies Companion to Nineteenth-Century Spain*, edited by Elisa Martí López, Routledge, 2021, pp. 295–306.
Salas y Guirior, José. "España sí, España no," *ABC Sevilla*, 8 Oct. 1959, pp. 11, 13.
Sanz, Marta. "Imperialista." *El País*, 3 Oct. 2021.
Sánchez Espinosa, Gabriel. "Un episodio en la recepción cultural dieciochesca de lo exótico: La llegada del elefante a Madrid en 1773." *Goya: Revista de arte*, nos. 295–96, 2003, pp. 269–86.
Shohat, Ella, and Robert Stam. *Unthinking Eurocentrism: Multiculturalism and the Media*. 2nd ed., Routledge, 2014.
Tomlinson, Janis A., ed. *Goya: Images of Women*. National Gallery of Art Washington/Yale UP, 2002.
Wiener, Gabriela. "Ayuso es la nueva colonialidad de siempre." *elDiario.es*, 29 Sept. 2021, www.eldiario.es/opinion/zona-critica/ayuso-nueva-colonialidad_129_8350554.html.
Yancy, George. *Black Bodies, White Gazes: The Continuing Significance of Race*. Rowman and Littlefield, 2008.

Appendix

Scenes from *The Naked Maja*

Figure 10.4. Image from *The Naked Maja*. Dir. Henry Koster, 1958.

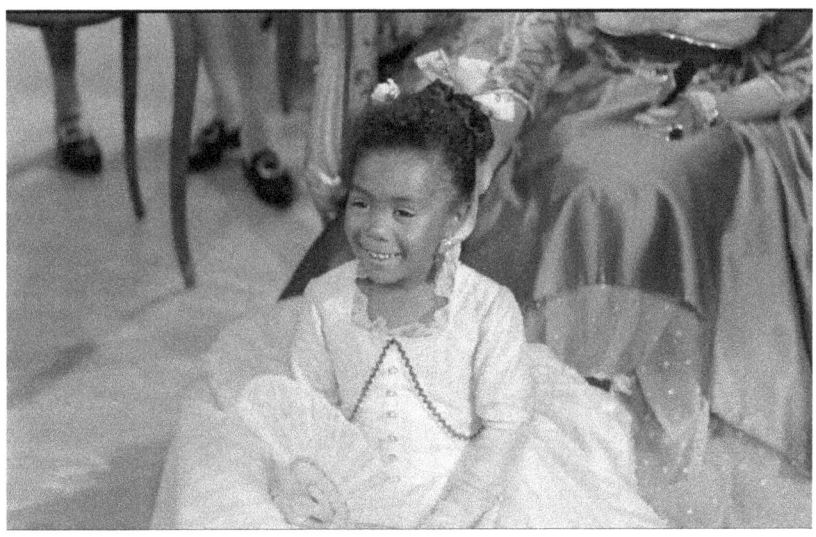

Figure 10.5 Image from *The Naked Maja*. Dir. Henry Koster, 1958.

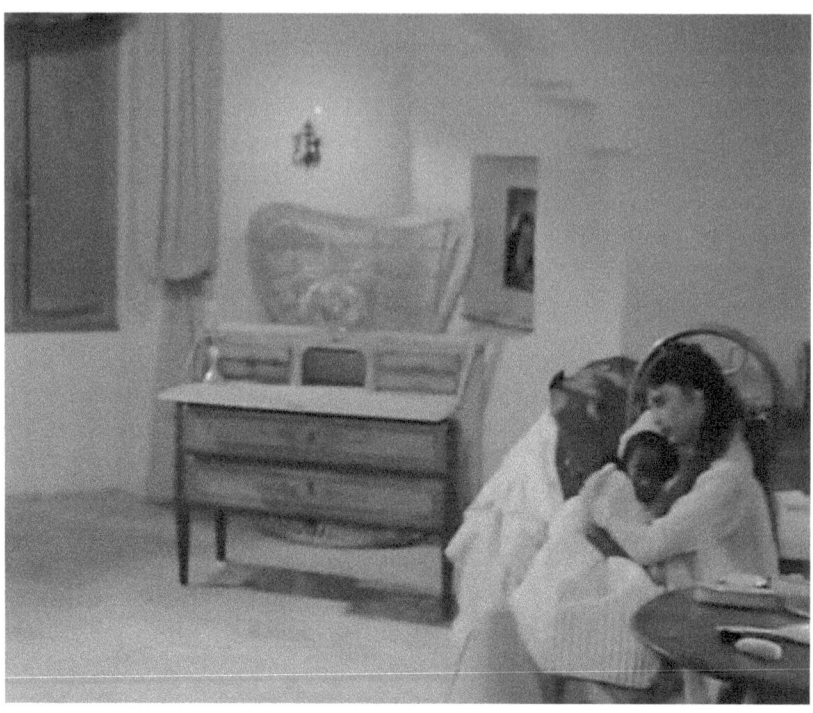

Figure 10.6. Image from *The Naked Maja*. Dir. Henry Koster, 1958.

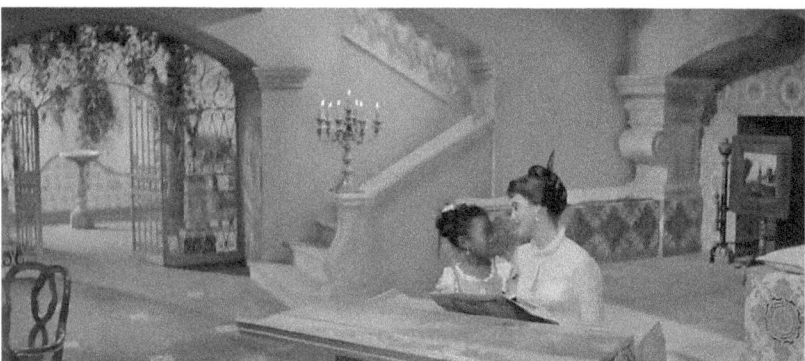

Figure 10.7. Image from *The Naked Maja*. Dir. Henry Koster, 1958.

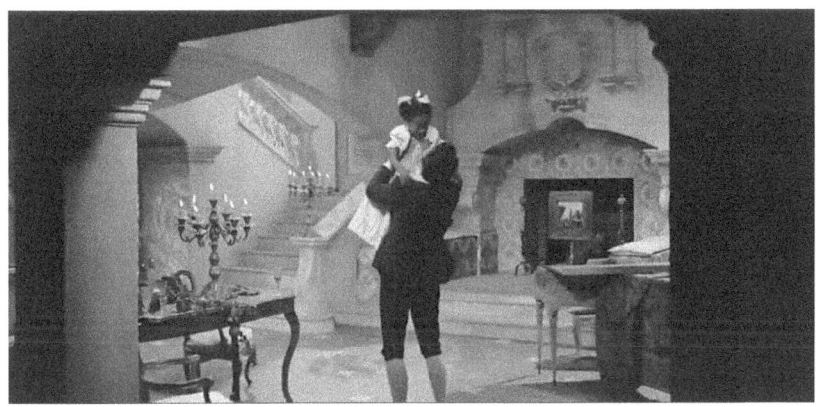

SCENE FROM *VOLAVÉRUNT*

Figure 10.8. Image from *Volavérunt*. Dir. Bigas Lunas, 1999.

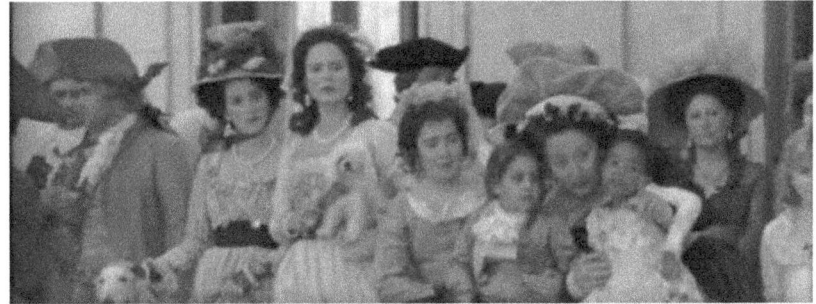

Chapter 11

The Urgency of a Black Iberian Thought

TANIA SAFURA ADAM,
INTERVIEWED BY AKIKO TSUCHIYA AND AURÉLIE VIALETTE,
TRANSLATED BY MARÍA CRISTINA URRUELA

Tania Safura Adam is a journalist and cultural producer based in Barcelona, and the founder of Radio Africa Magazine. *Her work explores migrations, Black diasporas (with a special emphasis on women), and African music throughout the Black Atlantic. She has curated many exhibits, including* Microhistories of the Diaspora: "Embodied" Experiences of Female Dispersion *(La Virreina, 2018–19),* Making Africa: A Continent of Contemporary Design *(CCCB, 2016), and* Blue Black Futures *(MACBA, 2022), among others. Since 2018 she is also the director and presenter of Radio Africa on beteví radio. She has contributed to various media outlets and regularly participates in debates and conferences at venues such as the Contemporary Art Museum of Barcelona (MACBA), Center of Contemporary Culture in Barcelona (CCCB), Born Cultural Center, and the Museum of Reina Sofía (Madrid), among others. In this interview, conducted on February 27, 2023, she reflects on her various cultural projects that center on Black subjectivity, while confronting the challenges of negotiating her place as a Black intellectual within the cultural institutions of Spain.*

What has been your trajectory, how did you come to the *Radio Africa Magazine* project?

Radio Africa was born out of a personal and collective need and a sense of urgency to have a space to think about a condition and to understand what you are from a political perspective. This need comes from a sense of discomfort: in Barcelona, where I live (but it can be said for all of Spain), African, Black sounds were conceived from a very simplistic and folkloric point of view, which had nothing to do with what I experienced or knew.

That commitment first took shape through music, with a monthly podcast in 2012 that was called *Radio Africa Urban Sounds*. The intention was to show, by way of different musical groups, what was happening in African cities. Gradually, it morphed into *Radio Africa Magazine*. In the *Magazine*, the perspective I adopt is that of cultural democracy. I understood that music and photography could establish a cultural dialogue between the African continent and Spain because they were spaces of democratization for the creators themselves.

Little by little, the narrative that I had proposed fell short, because in a way it was very aesthetic, and I began to feel the need to go deeper. This need became a research project: *Microhistories of the Diaspora: Stories of Female Dispersion*. In that project, I invite different women, not only African but also from Latin America, to think together about what the diasporic condition is. In Spain, there were African studies, which, basically, are Africanist studies that appropriated a series of discourses connected by the idea of development, not creation. What Black intellectuals from the African continent and other places of the diaspora thought was not contemplated within African studies. Then, I began to approach a whole range of thought, a whole series of intellectuals who gave me a totally different view from that proposed by the Spanish intellectual sphere. So, the process became more complex. My own development and evolution as a person began to take shape in *Radio Africa*, or it could be said that *Radio Africa* began to nurture me.

What is your relationship with the art world?

At one point, I was invited to curate an exhibition on Black futurisms. This allowed me to delve into Black thought in the United States and Latin America, and to contrast it with what was happening on the African continent. The research done for the exhibit wanted to focus on Black futurisms from different diasporic places. I began to see a series of cultural connections, encounters, and trains of thought that had occurred throughout the twentieth century all over the world. But when I looked at Spain, I found nothing. And I said to myself, it can't be that nothing exists here in Spain. In Europe, I was looking at France, Germany, the United Kingdom, even

Portugal, and I was finding research and information. On the other hand, when I looked at Spain, it was very difficult for me to find any configuration of Black thought. My starting thesis of the exhibition was: In the face of an oppressive present, if Black subjects wanted to transform their social space, they had to project themselves into a future to transform the present. They had to appeal to the radical imagination. Therefore, what we were looking for were people, initiatives, cultural, artistic, and musical projects in which this relationship was present. I needed to figure out how to transfer that idea of utopia to transform society.

But I finally withdrew from the exhibition on Black futurisms because I didn't like the way it was being presented; I felt that the Black subject and I were being instrumentalized. I felt very uncomfortable with the museum's approach, and I resigned from the curatorship, and in the end, the museum gave up on the exhibition.

Does this also indicate an inability on the part of the museum to give you the creative freedom to do the very thing they asked you to do?

They did not allow me creative freedom, because what they wanted was a very visual, very superficial exhibition and I was proposing a revision of all forms. That is, how do you negotiate oppression as a Black person: from the abolitionist movements to the use of literature and creativity to make individual thought become something collective. These are processes that appeal to futurisms beyond a project that is called futurist, or Afrofuturist. I wanted to prove that Afrofuturism is not only a contemporary issue but that it even predates Italian futurism itself. It is a way of approaching the future by breaking the barriers of time, wanting to move toward a specific place, either a future without race, or a future in which there is equality. The premise I was putting on the table was the question of humanity itself. That is, given a problem that Black subjects were not considered human, the issue is how to break free from that non-humanity. I was putting forward a very complex thesis that took time and was going to get to a much more interesting place than putting up a big installation by an artist who has a fantastic studio in the center of Paris, and who thereby defines what Afrofuturism is. So, we clashed there.

Can you explain what *Radio Africa Magazine* is all about?

The *Magazine* and *Radio Africa* allow me to experiment. The *Magazine* is a space for thinking, a space for slow journalism, as I call it, in the sense that whoever writes an article must research and write about a topic that really affects them.

How often does the *Magazine* come out?

Once a week or every two weeks. Parallel to the *Magazine* are the radio programs, which deal with more local issues. They are made from the platform Barcelona Televisió (betevé), which also has FM.

The radio program explains context through music. It does not have the ambitious goal of explaining technical details of the musical formations or the sound, but how various kinds of music are conceived, how social contexts absorb music, and vice versa. From this idea, we pivot to consideration of the African continent and the whole diaspora. We talk about both Black sounds and the people who make these sounds.

What kind of unique work is done with radio compared to other media?

Working with radio is unique, yes. I interviewed Danielle Almeida, who is in Brazil doing research on Black female singers in the Latin American context. The program was nice because she explained how research connected to a Yoruba context, Orishas, and then we went into each of these women singers, with a specific song. We delved into the social context of each song, we listened to the song, which is often an interpretation, because they are not composed by the women themselves. Music is a vehicle to explain many situations. With music, you talk about ways of survival, of life, which are not always visible when you talk; for example, immigration is usually approached from a victimization point of view, yet it also implies a great creation. In the end, human beings are carriers of sounds, and as we mix them with our thoughts, our legacies: sounds are mixtures, they are not pure. Music allows me to work on all this.

What is the backbone of the project?

There is a section called *Diaspora Lab*, which is a research endeavor; *Black Spain: Journey towards Negritude in Space-Time* is born from this. *Radio Africa* is a space of thought or recovery of alternative thinking. It thinks through music, photography, or a work of art. Our motto is to displace the center, appealing to the thought of Kenyan writer Ngugi wa Thiong'o. There is no pretension to create another center to replace the hegemonic center, in this case European or Eurocentric. The bet is that societies are plural and that people need diverse inputs. *Radio Africa* is a space where other epistemologies are experimented with, which allows us to understand society and look for solutions in other places.

What does *Black Spain* consist of? Who collaborates in the project?

It is a space to think about what the Black experience is like and what it has been like, and if there has been a Black thought. It opens a search for something that is not visible. We cannot resort to the reproduction of centrality because the relationship with Blackness in the territorial space of Spain and in time is different. Therefore, we must pay attention to this starting point. That is why it is called *Black Spain*; it is a journey in which the Black person goes from being an object to being a subject, in the past and in the present and in the future. The subject is central and becomes a human being. And here I am appealing to Sylvia Wynter's reflections on what is human, what is not human.

Slavery studies, in the end, are looking for the slave, the enslaved person. In that search, we needed different approaches to the work, and we needed to find places where they could accept our way of working and finance it. This first phase are different investigations located in the Basque Country with Artium, here in Barcelona is the CCCB, the IVAM in Valencia, and in Madrid is the Reina Sofía. In this first phase, we are going to address these four areas. The idea is that in the second phase, we will go to the Canary Islands and Andalusia. You can't even imagine how tiring it is to manage the different museums, but if you really want something to happen, you have to roll up your sleeves, you have to put yourself out there.

In the summer we made an open call because we wanted to have Black women researchers. We wanted to give an opportunity to those who want to go deeper, who are transfixed by their condition as Black people, who can contribute a specific legacy. It seemed important to us to push the button of opportunity, because there are no spaces in the public sphere, neither in the academy nor in museums, where Black thought can be explored in depth.

We found it interesting to work with oral history, as part of the embodied experience, which does not touch so much on the legacy of slavery, but more on the legacy of colonization and immigration. When we talk about the Black subject becoming a subject of research, we are also appealing to this idea. The team is made up of two people in the Basque Country, two people here in Catalonia, two people in Valencia, and in Madrid we have one person. With the Reina Sofía we have created the Iberian Black Studies group, where we do a series of sessions on topics of interest for this research. There is a pedagogical aspect, but it is not a traditional paternalistic pedagogy, but a self-taught pedagogy. This is a platform, and this platform allows you to find a way out yourself. In the sessions we do at the Reina Sofía, we are self-training, and getting to know each other; the self-taught pedagogy is a very African pedagogy.

We wanted to ask you about institutional support. Institutional support is basically, above all, museums and radio in Barcelona?

Betevé is not institutional support per se; it is where the radio is located. The institutional support is with the *España Negra* project. That is to say, you offer a specific investigation and research on the genealogy of negritude to a museum, and the funds they give you are to carry out this research.

Are there decolonization projects in museums?

I was just interviewed for *El Salto Diario* (a report on decolonization in museums). Honestly, I think that decolonization is a slogan, basically, it is not a reality. If you take decolonization only as a process in the program domain, but don't make an in-depth revision of your existing structures, it's simply a way of appearing to respond to current trends. A large part of the people who work in museums are from a specific social class and cultural background.

I could say that the phrase "decolonize museums" makes me a little angry. I have worked in immigration, with people in the social field, and I can say that in the artistic fields, more words are used than facts. It's true that this need to open up makes it possible for projects like *España Negra* to take place, something that maybe two years ago didn't happen. The problem is that sometimes museums hire people to say they are doing something, but in the end what they propose is hogwash. You claim you want a program by someone who is Black, but you actually don't care about that, and when you have to give artistic residencies, you don't give them to these people.

Museographic structures are plural; there are museums that have heritage that comes from colonial plundering or are the fruit of the colonial era. So, the idea of decolonization will be a little different. The Museum of Anthropology in Madrid has now started to do public programs that reflect on slavery, and immigration, but I ask, when are they going to go through their collection? When are they going to return their collection?

When we talk about considering the plurality of a territory, this plurality crosses the different museographic structures. That is, in how they treat their workers. What kind of workers do you have on staff? How do you do the sessions? It is something that is much more plural. The workers have always had not only diversity of culture but also diversity of gender, a series of diversities so that you can fashion a real transformation of the museological space so that it ceases to be a hegemonic space. Decolonization is a part of everything, but it is not the panacea; I have great doubts regarding the use and abuse of the word "decolonization." I don't buy the vocabularies and grammars of the present because they drag you into absolute starvation.

What other cultural projects, besides yours, have emerged in recent years to foster greater awareness in Spain about issues of race, racism, and colonialism?

I started *Radio Africa* in 2012. I was swimming alone for a long time. Then there was suddenly a kind of boom of Black consciousness; it started as a resurgence of meetings of and with different Black people, young people, who lived here. In 2016 we did all the programming from *Radio Africa*, for the exhibition *Making Africa* in the Civic Centers. What we proposed was to unite a little bit the diaspora, the Afro-descendency; from then on, projects started to emerge, and people joined, to create, to think, and to be together. It was the seed of many projects that have been running in Barcelona for some time now.

There are certain parallels in other cities: there are projects in Valencia, in Madrid, projects in different places. I would say that the difference—and this is not very well received by many people—is that *Radio Africa* is not an identity project, nor does it pretend to be. This does not go down very well in many spheres, because there is no defense of Black identity. We take Blackness as a political project, as a space from which to transform the mechanisms of social thinking, not only focusing on the Black subject. We live in a diasporic space, and we are not in a context of absolute Blackness in which you can work only for the benefit of Black people. Working at the political level only with the Black community is like working on feminism only with women. What we propose is a social epistemic transformation that considers other spaces.

Do you use the word *activist*?

No, we don't use the word *activist*, because we consider that what we do is to analyze society and propose transformations according to the analysis. The word *activism* has been used so much and in such a banal way that one way of resisting banality is to say that we are not activists.

How do you see the impact that these projects have had on the general public? Do you see a change in terms of the general public's attitude toward these issues? Is there a greater awareness of these issues?

Yes, it has had a real impact, to the point where my ten-year-old children are starting to question racist attitudes. For me, the activist, or the colonization of the word *activist*, has gone toward the idea of the military trench; you must be all the time looking about, if the other has said this, if you have said that, if it is politically correct, what is said or not said. I am bored by all this world of political correctness, the world where everything must be according to the established social premises of that moment, of people who question a word you say, and depending on a word you say, they are already against you. It is important that it exists . . . but I don't want to be part of that. There's a rearguard that's in the trenches, projects of questioning, of confrontation, of victimization, identity projects. But I believe that, if there is nothing behind the rearguard, all this is thrown away, it is not sustainable, and all this energy is useless. It is the people who are in the trenches who promote the transformation, and therefore I see it as a collective work, although it is not recognized as such. I recognize the trench, but the trench does not recognize the positions we take because it considers them to be elitist, and they do not take into account the grassroots.

Another thing we wanted to ask you about is the question of education. What has been the role of education? Here in the US, many states are censoring materials related to the history of slavery and colonialism. In Spain, are materials on these topics included in the curriculum? What is the place of Black studies in the curriculum? In the schools? In the universities?

No, one of the things we are trying to implement is home Black studies. There are people who are fighting for that to be possible at the political level, to have a curriculum in which they take colonization and slavery into account. This is not our case. In *Radio Africa* we enter a voluntary space; that is to say, the curriculum is a space of obligation, you have to enter and make it political, you have to enter to create a series of movements, to drag people along. I do not have that capacity with *Radio Africa*, that is why we work in other spaces.

Chapter 12

On Making Art from Hidden Places

Yinka Esi Graves,
interviewed by Akiko Tsuchiya and Aurélie Vialette

Yinka Esi Graves is a British Flamenco dancer and practitioner whose choreographic work explores the links between Flamenco and other forms of corporeal expression from an African diasporic and contemporary perspective. She is featured in Miguel Ángel Rosales's documentary film, Gurumbé: Canciones de tu memoria negra *(2016), the first Spanish film to highlight the influence Spain's African population had on Spanish culture, particularly Flamenco. In the summer of 2023, she debuted* The Disappearing Act, *her first solo creation, which combines dance, live music, and text to explore how Black women articulate their resistance to erasure. In this interview, conducted in August 2023, she addresses the ways in which her artistic practice engages with the history and experiences of those who belong to the Afro-diasporic community.*

Can you tell us a bit about your personal background and history? What kind of impact has it had on your artistic trajectory, as a dancer and choreographer (of Flamenco in particular)?

My name, while just a name, says quite a bit about my personal background and history, the family I was born into, and our aspirations. *Yinka* is the Yoruba name my mother (of Ghanaian descent) and father (born in London

Figure 12.1. *The Disappearing Act. Source:* Miguel Ángel Rosales. Used with permission.

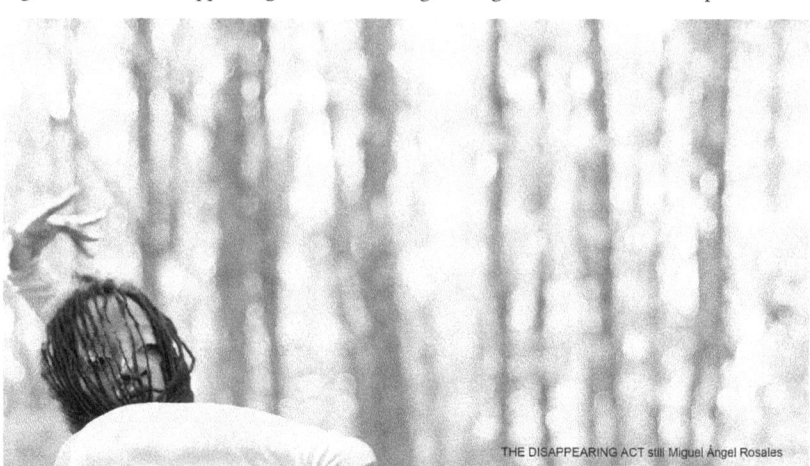

to Jamaican parents) wanted to give me to honor our African descendance, given they both have European first names and surnames.

Esi is my Fanti day name rooting me to my maternal Ghanaian heritage, despite my mother not speaking her mother's language. *Graves* is the colonial surname that has run in my maternal grandfather's family for at least a century.

I was born in London in 1983 and, for me, these three names reveal a tug between celebrating yourself as you long to be and the impossibility of escaping colonialism and slavery. So embedded are they in both my Caribbean and West African ancestry, my family endeavored to reverse and remedy the ills of colonialism and slavery to understand ourselves beyond it. While I consider myself to be British, my experience growing up in Nicaragua and Guadeloupe as a child has also shaped my sense of connectedness to ways of doing, living, and being south of northern Europe!

Dance has perhaps been the way in which I have most directly expressed and investigated this sense of connectedness. Flamenco, which I discovered in my early twenties, after a childhood and young adulthood of doing ballet, jazz, modern and Afro-Cuban dancing, has been the form that has prompted me to give up all my other aspirations; it took me from Brighton, where I was studying history of art at Sussex University, to Barcelona, Madrid, and then Seville, where I have been based since 2013. I took my very first classes with great innocence. I had no expectations and certainly didn't intend on Flamenco becoming my life and work. What I never could have imagined is that in following Flamenco and moving to southern Spain, where the form originates, I would come face to face with the legacy of a historical Afro-Andalusian population who have been forgotten and erased from the national collective memory. In hindsight and particularly in the process of developing my latest work, *The Disappearing Act*, I have come to believe that perhaps my body intuited this presence from the very beginning.

My love of Flamenco developed by doing it, engaging with the *cante* and the guitar. An internal push from the body is what has guided my need to keep going, not to accomplish anything, but simply to understand more fully and to be more comfortable in my interpretation of the form. A push, despite the general sense that no one really understood or even believed in a Black woman learning Flamenco! As I moved through my learning (an endless journey!) it quite soon became clear to me that I had things to say, to investigate, to explore. The schism between my internal push, which constantly alluded to a connection between my Blackness and Flamenco, and a subtle but persistent external gaze that reminded me to what extent I perturbed people's expectations of who a Flamenco dancer should be, is the space that has inspired my work and has taken me to the world of choreography.

In 2014 I co-founded a contemporary Flamenco dance company with two other British Flamenco dancers, which was a first step in defining my voice as a Flamenco dancer who is not Spanish. Together we made *No Frills*, a piece that invited viewers to engage with Flamenco beyond its aesthetic stereotypes. In 2016, I collaborated with ex–Alvin Ailey dancer Asha Thomas to create *Clay*. This experience was central for me. Working with Asha opened a new door in allowing me to create directly from my experience as a Black woman and through improvisation, as a way of trusting and valuing my body and its movements. Since then, I have had the privilege of working and collaborating with a number of artists, within and outside of the Flamenco genre, who have taught and inspired me to be brave and continue working to find my own voice. I'd like to acknowledge Mbulelo Ndabeni, Chloé Brulé and Marco Vargas, Dorothée Munyaneza, Qudus Onikeku, Nora Chipaumire, and Dr. S. Ama Wray. In early 2023, I premiered my first solo work, *The Disappearing Act*. I do not think I would have come to this work had I not experienced working with them.

Can you tell us a bit about your current project, *The Disappearing Act*? How does it engage with the history and experiences of those who belong to the Afro-diasporic community? How does it connect you to others who share your history in some way?

The Disappearing Act started as an inquiry, a desire to explore a sensation that has haunted me since I was a child. This awareness became accentuated in my professional and adult life. As Black people in the diaspora, in places where we are a minority, we are more times than not forced to take part in an unspoken dance in which the degree of our (in)visibility is at play.

Connecting my personal experience as a Flamenco dancer to how African peoples have been erased from the history of Spain, it was easy to understand the small and big ways in which Black presence is being constantly managed and imagined. In this context, invisibility felt like something almost material, thick, pathological. For me, it is an omnipresent force in our experiences in the diaspora, a common denominator floating through our diverse realities across class, gender, and religion.

Living in a city like Seville, where this history has been erased, our invisibility nevertheless felt tangible to me, long before I even understood what I was perceiving. On my daily trips to a dance class in Triana, I would cross a bridge known as El Puente de San Telmo. Every time I walked across this bridge, I felt myself being drawn to the river below and I repeatedly thought: my people are in this water. I didn't really think anything of it until a few years later when I found out that this bridge stood on what was once the "Port of the Indies," the very place where ships involved in the transatlantic trade of enslaved African people, as well as goods from the Americas, disembarked. As is the case in much of Spain, there is no mention of this part of the city's history. Yet, somehow, despite being omitted, erased, and made invisible, something of this history was totally present to me on a sensory level. This bridge became a symbolic tie between the personal and the historical in the early development of the work, between my individual experiences as a Black person living and working in Spain, and our collective (historical) reality.

My interest in developing my work from here was not so much about speaking to the depravity of chattel slavery and its atrocities, but about revealing the ways in which we are still swimming in its many consequences. I engage with the normalization of the violence of constantly erasing, literally and metaphorically, an entire continent and its people. From here, I am interested in showing through my work how those of us of African descent continue to make space for our freedom despite the violence, overt and subtle. In this way, I am never only speaking about myself.

The starting point for the development of *The Disappearing Act*, choreographically speaking, was to explore the aspect of invisibility that I perceived when crossing the Puente San Telmo and other sites that had historically been points of entry during the transatlantic slave trade. Those spaces in Spain and Portugal bear no visible trace or recognition of the violence and trauma to which they were witness. In Ghana, there are spaces of no return, long forgotten by the descendants of those forced to leave as enslaved people. These sites became spaces for creation, embodying what is left of history, despite the violence that once took place there.

I collaborated with my husband and filmmaker Miguel Ángel Rosales to archive these improvisations. Together we have made six short films: *The Coast*, *The Coast II*, *The Bridge*, *The Forest*, *The Island*, and *The Door*. I started to work on *The Disappearing Act* in 2019, and since then, Covid-19 has impacted the process of artistic creation and the consequent paralysis (which gave us time to produce the films that were not initially intended to be shared), as well as my pregnancy and becoming a mother. The creative process made space for a dialogue between the personal and the global.

Dr. Wray's Embodiology and Nora Chipaumire's *nhaka* were the practices that supported in-situ improvisations. Both engage the breath in a very intentional way. The Covid-19 pandemic, the murder of George Floyd, and the sudden global impact of the Black Lives Matter movement made the right to breathe and live a political question. This made my work feel even more relevant; it made sense to engage with historical sites and breathe them in to get the body to react to these sites and the forgotten peoples in them. Having developed a specific physical language through which I could address invisibility in these historical sites, in the stage piece I embody and reimagine the nineteenth-century acrobat Olga Brown depicted in Edgar Degas's 1879 painting *Miss Lala at Le Cirque Fernando*. Engaging with her legacy through this painting was a way of discussing the problematics of how Black women are viewed, never fully seen; she was at once all of us and none of us. As she is only partially visible to the viewer, her strength and performative prowess take center stage over her face, her eyes, and her personhood.

The Disappearing Act is an experiment in how best to protect our inner lives. I use aesthetics and the idea of camouflage to explore how we play with modes of invisibility, since our very existence in the diaspora is so intertwined with it.

Dance, as an embodied art form, is often seen as distinct from other forms of creative expression, such as literature, instrumental music, or visual art. Or is it different? What possibilities does this art form offer that makes it unique and particularly appropriate as a medium of expression/communication for you?

In 2017, I met Dr. S. Ama Wray and learned about the comprehensive system she has created, based on her research with Ghanaian Ewe communities. Her praxis, called Embodiology, centers on knowledge and creativity held in the body. Through its six-tier transdisciplinary methodology, Embodiology lays out a value system that can be perceived throughout African diasporic performance practices. Dr. Wray's work spoke directly to me when working with the fundamental components of the social aspect of Flamenco performance, how it is lived and created. Like Flamenco, her work is based on the interconnectedness of music and dance, the deep listening required by all participants, and creates a space for individual expression despite shared vocabulary, codes, and cues. Becoming a student of Embodiology has greatly shaped my practice and my understanding of why I am drawn to move. It offered me a new lens through which to give value to tools that I was already employing in Flamenco, but that I had never articulated from a place of knowing. As an improvisation technique, it allowed me to explore outside a traditional Flamenco aesthetic.

Nora Chipaumire, choreographer and challenger of all misconceptions placed on Black beingness, also became an inspiration over the past six years, as I engaged with her practice of *nhaka*. Both Wray and Chipaumire have practices entirely rooted in Africana understandings of the expressive, receptive, communicative body. Both of their disciplines helped me to use my embodied experience as a source for choreographing, as another way of knowing.

As I think through all the different forms *The Disappearing Act* has taken—including online and live film screenings, shared short residencies, interventions in gallery spaces, an exhibition of the visual elements of the work, a live illustrated conference, and a written publication on the way—the work for me takes real shape in the stage piece. It is a way of going beyond ideas and engaging with a lived, vibrant, sensory experience. In that sense, dance for me exists at an experiential level, not merely an aesthetic one.

While this piece is conceived of as a dance solo, it is a collaboration with three other artists without whom I could not have created the work.

I first started experimenting with Flamenco guitarist Raúl Cantizano, a pioneer in improvisation. Then I brought in the drummer and poet Remi Graves, my sibling. Their connection to the themes in the work and their experience playing other genres of music aside from Flamenco were vital. Flamenco singer Rosa de Algeciras was the last to join in the development of the piece. She has a rich voice and a willingness to try different ways of interpreting traditional Flamenco songs and has composed lyrics specifically for the piece. Together, through this live collaboration, slightly different each time, we hope to create an imagined space that goes beyond the real, where agency is articulated. For me, dance is the medium that best allows us to discover the unknown.

How do you make explicit the cultural connections (with slavery) found in dance when you perform? For instance, when you dance Flamenco, do you think it is necessary to inform the public or is dance its own medium?

I don't think I make anything explicit in my performative work. My investigative and ideological positioning is very clear; it forms the background of my work. My research process is meant, above all, to nurture my body/being and dance. I have been interested in exploring different aspects of the experience of enslaved African people(s) and their descendants, as I am one of them. I am reluctant to say I am interested in slavery itself; it is too great a disgrace. I am, however, intrigued and fascinated by how we have found joy, love, and beauty despite such horror.

When I am on stage, engaging with an audience, I am interested in arousing a sensation or a question as opposed to telling a specific story. My dance is very explorative. I believe I am searching, and I hope to bring (some) people with me! I am always dealing with ideas, questions, images, and feelings that are rarely conclusive. I believe this is possibly at the root of my deep love for traditional Flamenco. For to me, Flamenco dance is abstract in many ways. It is really about energy, and that is what I am most interested in communicating when I dance. In the last few years, as people have come to accept that the historical Afro-Spanish population played an important role in creating the popular music that would later be absorbed into what in the late nineteenth century became Flamenco, there has been a desire (by some) to label me and/or my dancing as Afro-Flamenco. I have insisted and, at times, have had to argue that Flamenco is intrinsically African in its values, in its way of coming to the body, in the relationship between music and movement, the ground and the body, percussion, and syncopation.

As in so many countries across the Americas that have had sizable African diasporas (as certain cities in southern Spain had), what is African or of African descent is rarely considered to be of value. Music and dance are probably the clearest examples of this, but I'm also thinking of clothes and hairstyles, language, food, and religion (if we think of the influence of Yoruban religious beliefs practiced by large parts of the general population in Cuba and Brazil). Once the African elements have been absorbed into popular culture, they become easier to divorce from their origins.

With this in mind, over the last few years, I have tried to clarify for myself what in Flamenco's core values connects to forms of performative expression across the African diaspora. This was, first and foremost, to enhance my own experience of dancing Flamenco. However, I am also interested in knowing how this focus resonates in the imaginary of my audiences. I dream that a space where Afro-Spaniards are included as one of five cultural or ethnic columns to Flamenco's foundations, alongside the Gitano, Andalusian, Moorish, and Jewish ones. Ultimately, I am interested in challenging the ways in which people, myself included, have been made to conceive of what it is to be African, as a consequence of the systematic erasure of their contributions to the rest of the world.

How was your experience with the cinema industry through your participation in the film *Gurumbé: Canciones de tu memoria negra*?

I am forever thankful to Miguel Ángel Rosales and his work *Gurumbé: Canciones de tu memoria negra* for a number of reasons. This film redresses the official history of Spain and its long involvement in the transatlantic trade of enslaved Africans. It also brings to light the importance of the historical African diaspora in Spain, Spanish culture, and Flamenco. When the film was released in 2016, it was an issue that was not discussed at all, outside very small academic or political circles. It has caused a real shift in what was possible for so many of us. It has really marked a before and after for me.

This seminal piece, in so many ways, confirmed what I was feeling on an intuitive level, as I was learning and dancing Flamenco. The process of making the film made me understand there was nothing strange about my interest in Flamenco! It answered so many questions for me. In terms of my career, it exposed me to audiences across the world. We have subsequently traveled to the USA, Senegal, Nigeria, and Panama with the film on various occasions.

I can't speak of a particular relationship to the film industry. This documentary was made with a very limited budget and was produced thanks to Intermedia and Miguel Ángel's persistent vision and extensive work with the artists and academics who inspired his research. While the film has taken part in many international festivals, I don't think it has been adequately recognized in Spain or in the film industry for the shift it has helped create, by making possible a conversation on the historical African, Black presence in Spain well into the nineteenth century.

Is there a new project you are working on and that you would like to share with us?

I feel very privileged to be involved in several new projects with international collaborators for 2024–25. I am in the very early stages of composing another stage piece, but first I want to tour with *The Disappearing Act*, as much possible, if we are afforded the opportunity.

I am also now in a life-long project of motherhood. At the moment, this is the project that most consumes me, as I navigate creating, touring, and performing in a number of works. I feel it is important to share that I haven't yet found the way to continue my creative endeavors while tending to the development of a little one. Becoming a mother has completely shifted my relationship with my work, which used to be all-consuming. So, as I move onto a new project, I must find new parameters and methods of work. I believe this will take me a while to achieve!

Chapter 13

Hispano-tropicalism

Flamencology and the Denial of Black Presence in Spain

Miguel Ángel Rosales,
translated by María Cristina Urruela

The South (the Souths) is (are) constructed by a hegemonic North. They are always places located "below . . . ," symbolic places created by a hierarchical relationship. As so often happens in this relationship between North and South, the creations that appear to have been made far from the centers of power are loaded with identity and symbolic value and lead to appropriation processes that use these elements to symbolically sustain their political and economic hegemony. In the case of Spain with respect to its south, Andalusia, this appropriation has been evident, and many Andalusian cultural elements have been used to represent the idiosyncrasies of Spain. Flamenco, with its entire aesthetic and expressive universe, is perhaps the most significant of these.

About eight years ago I started researching the possible influences of some African music on Flamenco for a documentary film I wanted to call *Gurumbé. Afro-Andalusian Memories*. I didn't want to write a thesis, nor approach the subject as extractive research, but to put into practice some form of creative archaeology that would help to understand certain connections. It was clear to me from the beginning that approaching the subject of

African traces in the expressive foundations of Flamenco—precisely because of its identity and symbolic value and because of what Flamenco represents for the Spanish national culture—could be quite problematic, given that Spanish individuality had been built on the desire to distance itself from its relationship with the African continent, even though it is separated by barely 15 km.

I had many doubts about the version that most scholars and aficionados had about the relationship between Flamenco and American and African music. According to the most common version, Flamenco could have been influenced in the nineteenth century by some Black rhythms through the connection of the ports of southern Spain (Andalusia) to the American ports (especially Havana) and their high population of African descendants, a phenomenon that was known as *ida y vuelta* ("round trip"). The "ida y vuelta" was that of certain songs and dances that left the Iberian Peninsula with the Spanish colonists and returned transformed ("contaminated" for some) by Caribbean rhythms and repertoires that when "*properly* flamencoized" (Núñez) brought to the Andalusian ports exotic features yielding new repertoires.

This idea, deeply rooted in popular knowledge, is reflected in Flamenco literature from way back: Hipólito Rossy's *Teoría del Cante Jondo*, González Climent's *Flamencología,* Jorge Ordóñez Sierra's writings on Flamenco, or the influential *Mundo y forma del Cante Flamenco* by the *cantaor* Antonio Mairena. Although some of these writings do not specifically mention the *ida y vuelta* as a concept, all of them at least reflect this idea of Spanish repertoires that cross the Atlantic to return influenced by American elements. According to the Flamencopolis website[1] it was the writer Fernando Quiñones who extended the term by applying it to *palos* (Flamenco sounds and rhythms) with "Hispano-American ancestry." The difficulty of tracing a concept so widely used by flamencology and the lack of criticism around it tells us about the way in which Flamenco history has been put together, based on non-contrasted fragments sometimes created from popular imagination. Thus, we could say that a great part of this literature becomes almost mythological, where legend is more relevant than historical data.

Seen from a critical point of view, the *ida y vuelta* of flamencology proposes a single direction to the movement of musical exchanges that, of course, have Spain and its musical repertoire as the original starting point, a central foundation to which everything else is indisputably attracted. On the other hand, this fiction depletes and limits to the short period of the nineteenth century, and exclusively to its contact with the American continent, the influence that Black music of the African continent had on Flamenco (of course filtered and mediated by the colonial relationship).

Imbued with a kind of Hispano-tropicalism (Nerín 10), these ideas ignore the slave system on which the Spanish Empire was based; from the end of the fifteenth century, thousands of enslaved Africans were brought not only to its colonies and overseas territories but also to the Iberian Peninsula, over time giving rise to one of the largest Black populations in the history of Europe. The concept of Hispano-tropicalism is borrowed from the Catalan anthropologist and historian Gustau Nerín, just as the Portuguese Gilberto Freyre used the concept of Luso-tropicalism to erase the Black-African elements in Brazilian culture through an idealized image of racial mixture and to justify Portuguese imperial domination in its former colonies.

This framework ignores the relationships produced by class, gender, and race in the contexts where the exchanges that gave rise to these new musical expressions took place. Likewise, the radical inequality imposed by the fact that Black men and women were mostly enslaved (or at least in a subordinate position) in societies that were mainly structured by race and the social hierarchy was ignored:

> Es la mulata un terrón
> Es mi mulata un terrón de azúcar canela hecho
> que arrimándoselo al pecho
> quita el mal de corazón
> ella vive con el don y a ningún hombre maltrata
> y si le llaman ingrata es más dulce que la uva;
> del azúcar que hay en Cuba es la mejor la mulata.

> A mulatta is a spoonful of sugar
> My mulatta is a spoonful of cinnamon-sugar
> that when held against my breast
> cures heartache
> she has a gift and mistreats no man
> and if called unkind is sweeter than a grape;
> The mulatta is the best kind of sugar in Cuba.[2]

Today, in very recent publications on the relationship of Flamenco with America,[3] we see how "the American," a concept that simplifies an infinite number of exchanges and complex relationships, is used to reduce and hide the main element, which is none other than the African element and its new forms created by the Afro-diaspora. It also insists on the total acculturation of the Africans brought to Cuba, as a consequence of the practice of dispersion applied to slaves once they arrived in the colonies, and their total integration into a system dominated by the Spanish culture.

For most of these researchers there is no agency in what is Black; Black equals a passive element that can only interpret what it finds and is denied any creative and transformative power. These ideas are at their core as loaded with ethnocentrism and cultural superiority as those of years ago. Wouldn't it be more enriching to abandon that image of the *ida y vuelta*, and begin to imagine a richer dynamic—the *Caribbean-Afro-Andalusian interaction* of Antonio García de León—where, over several centuries, exchanges will take place in all directions, even though hegemonic narratives have described them until today as limited to one?

Nothing I say in this brief text will fully explain the complexity behind the origins of something we conceive of today as a homogeneous aesthetic universe: Flamenco. But I think there is a need to open the capacity to imagine other possible ways to think about it. And this goes through two fundamental steps: deconstructing the history of Spain and stripping it of its ethnocentric nationalism and demystifying our idea of Africa (as a whole) while ceasing to look at it as an empty continent without history.

I would like to propose here the idea that the historical and theoretical writing on the origins and forms of Flamenco has been one of the areas from which the history of the Afro-descendant presence in Spain and its legacy in Spanish society and culture has been erased. This narrative is based on a broader story that, while denying the existence of this Black-Andalusian population, perpetrates what I call a *memoricide*, intended to not recognize that a large part of Andalusian and Spanish society is made up of a population with a deep history of racial mixture. The traces of this Afro-descendant population have been hidden beneath the "great History" of the Spanish nation. However, these stories have survived and can be heard when we listen to sounds from the margins to the sources from which other ways of telling and interpreting history emerge.

Today we know that from the fifteenth century onwards, in the main Spanish ports, mainly Seville and Cádiz, and along the imaginary axis that links these two cities, a Black-African population was formed that would have a very important social and cultural presence. Numerous documents of all kinds, notaries, records of the Inquisition, parish and ecclesiastical archives, and commercial documents, among others, tell us of a number that could reach ten or fifteen percent of the population at some points in the history of cities like Seville or Cádiz.[4] These Black Andalusians will be mentioned until the year 1812, in the minutes of the Constitution of Cádiz, or in the *Asta Regia Magazine* of Jerez until 1880. On the other hand, numerous references in literature and art tell us of an active presence in Spanish society, of a transforming agency, and of a voice that managed to stand out against the dehumanization imposed by a society strongly marked by racism and blood purity.

The Black people of Andalusia were the performers of many of the dances and popular songs of the streets of Seville's Golden Age or eighteenth-century Cádiz. Vélez de Guevara, a great observer, and connoisseur of the underworld of the Seville of the Golden Age, left us in his novel *El diablo cojuelo* (Vélez de Guevara 14) a long list of creations related to the Black people of Spain who danced and sang at that time in the streets of Spanish cities. At the beginning of the story the protagonist, who is none other than the devil, introduces himself as follows:

> yo traje al mundo la zarabanda, el déligo, la chacona, el bullicuzcuz, las cosquillas de la capona, el guiriguirigay, el zambapalo, la mariona, el avilipinti, el pollo, la carretería, el hermano Bartolo, el carcañal, el guineo, el colorín colorado; yo inventé las pandorgas, las jácaras, las papalatas, los comos, las mortecinas, los títeres, los volatines, los saltambancos, los maesecorales . . .

> I brought to the world the zarabanda, the déligo, the chacona, the bullicuzcuz, the cosquillas de la capona, the guiriguirigay, the zambapalo, the mariona, the avilipinti, the pollo, the carretería, brother Bartolo, the carcañal, the guineo, the colorín colorado; I invented the pandorgas, the jácaras, the papalatas, the comos, the mortecinas, the puppets, the volatines, the saltambancos, the maesecorales . . .

This is just one example of many that we can observe in numerous works of Spanish literature in the eighteenth century, along with the presence of Black dances: the Guineo, the Cumbé, the Cucumbé, the Gurumbé, the Fandango, the Jácara, the Zarabanda, or the Chacona, all popular dances attributed to Black people in Spain. They were created and evolved over more than five centuries, conveying a unique expressiveness. They include their own body movements and language that are used in gestures, practices, melodies, and rhythms up to the present day.

I believe that Flamenco and its entire expressive universe is a place where the deep imprint of an ancient Andalusian Afro-diaspora remains, like a shred torn away from the dizzying passage of history and time. But to approach this hidden story, it is necessary to unravel a whole skein of myths, appropriations, re-appropriations, and political determinations. These explain its ontology today. They help us to search Flamenco and its history, not for the origin of something that was created in one day, but for the forces that from very ancient times created a deep expression that is continually mutating and being reborn. This African source theory does not explain in totality the complex origins where so many voices have spoken. But we must try to fit this piece into an inexplicable gap, without which much of the Andalusian and Spanish popular culture cannot be understood.

History and memory are two different forms of transmission of the past and human practices. History is a story that arises from the interpretation of records and is transmitted more or less intact through writing, while memory arises from collective participation in a process of constant creation. While the former is guided by the academies and the institutions from which it arises, memory is a collective recollection that contains heterogeneous elements that often lose their temporal references and their original meaning when integrated into new narratives. By losing their original references, these elements, embodied in the performance, camouflage presences that were visible in another time. We would have to combine history and memory to be able to read in the performativity of Flamenco the traces of the Afro-descendant Spanish population. These traces are not only in rhythmic structures and musical and dance forms (as has with difficulty been admitted), but in the very performance of the celebration, embodied in Flamenco.

As we began to talk about Flamenco in the middle of the nineteenth century, we find there are common historical similarities between Andalusia and the American Afro-diaspora that must be understood in order to see the point from which the desire and rebelliousness that nourish Flamenco arise. First, as in the Caribbean, there was an enslaved Black population from the fifteenth to the seventeenth centuries in the axis that linked the ports of Cádiz and Seville and passed through Utrera, Lebrija, or Jerez. This population has a fundamental role in the music and the popular inventiveness and, through them, affirms their political subjectivity. In addition, we can see some logistics of human exploitation and some commercial structures that show there are many things in common between Cuba and Andalusia in the nineteenth century. The country house and the plantation are architecturally and symbolically similar.

As on the American shore of the Afro-Andalusian Caribbean, in Andalusia new relationships with and from the body will emerge, creating a language of gestures, a new orality that speaks to us today of the desire to possess life, of nostalgia for the lost land, of weeping for broken ties. To quote feminist thinker Seyla Benhabib, "new modes of association appear in a community of needs and solidarity that becomes magically audible in the music itself and palpable in social relations . . . a desire to invoke new modes of friendship, happiness, and solidarity to overcome social oppression" (qtd. in Gilroy 37). In his chapter in *The Black Atlantic*, "Jewels Brought from Bondage: Black Music and the Politics of Authenticity," Paul Gilroy shows the ambivalence toward modernity manifested in much of Black cultural expression, including music, even as it partakes in modernist aesthetics (73). Flamenco, like other music of the Afro-diaspora and like other music born in the fractures of globalizing modernity, emerges from the most marginal classes, as an expression that finds its foundations in pre-modern elements and is configured as a discourse confronting modernity and the destructive processes modernity imposes on peoples and communities: displacement, rupture of social ties, theft of their territories or the transformation of their bodies into work machines. Citing Gilroy, we could say that Flamenco is, in part, another of those "jewels brought from bondage" (72–110).

> A clavito y canelita
> Me hueles tú a mí
> El que no huele a clavo y canela
> No sabe distinguir.
>
> To me you smell
> Of cloves and cinnamon
> One that can't smell cloves and cinnamon
> Cannot distinguish.

This lyric, recorded for the first time in the voice of the gypsy singer Tomás Pavón in 1928, speaks of smell and taste, two senses deeply linked to memory and remembrance. Those who smelled of "cloves and cinnamon" (spices linked to the Moorish, Black, Gitano, and Jewish world, smells representative of Otherness) lived in those margins where they were able to distinguish, to recognize certain hidden codes, in a world of persecution for what was considered strange.

Despite the denial, the traces of these almost-erased codes still reach us today. So subtle and light, so indescribable, but as present as the smell of a spice. People without history, as the anthropologist Eric Wolf would say (I would add dispossessed of their history), continue to speak to us from the depths of gesture, from the surviving word that seemed to have lost its meaning, from the bodies where their stories have left us. A new grammar is needed for these hidden stories that resonated and spoke from the skin of the drums and the bare feet that called to the earth, and today sound in the resonance boxes of guitars and the rhythmic clapping of the Flamencos.

Notes

1. flamenco.plus/flamencopolis/pagina/terminologia/.
2. These lyrics belong to a Flamenco song (palo) called "Guajira." It is precisely one of those songs included in the repertoire of *ida y vuelta*. The lyrics attributed to Hermenegildo Montes were popularized by the singer Pepe Marchena in the 1930s. The exoticized and sexualized vision of the Black and *mestiza* woman from the perspective of the colonizer has recently had a critical review from the dance and stage works of the dancer Yinka Esi Graves.
3. I refer especially to Faustino Núñez's *América en el Flamenco*.
4. Studies by Jesús Cosano, Manuel F. Fernández Chaves and Rafael M. Pérez García, Antonio Domínguez Ortiz, Baltasar Fra Molinero, Carmen Fracchia, Chloe Irenton, Nicholas R. Jones, Aurelia Martín Casares, Luis Méndez Rodríguez, Isidoro Moreno, Alessandro Stella, Rocío Periáñez, and José Antonio Piqueras, among many others, attest to the presence of Afro-descendants in Andalusia.

Works Cited

Benhabib, Seyla. *Critique, Norm and Utopia: A Study of the Foundations of Critical Theory*. Columbia UP, 1986.

Cosano, Jesús. *Hechos y cosas de los negros de Sevilla*. 2nd ed., Colección Los Invisibles, 2023.

Domínguez Ortiz, Antonio. "La esclavitud en Castilla durante la Edad Moderna." *Estudios de Historia Social de España*, Madrid, 1952, pp. 369–428.

Fernández Chaves, Manuel F., and Rafael M. Pérez García. *La esclavitud en el sur de la península ibérica: Siglos XV al XVII. Demografía e historia social.* Catarata, 2021.

Fracchia, Carmen. *"Black but Human": Slavery and Visual Arts in Hapsburg Spain, 1480–1700.* Oxford UP, 2019.

Fra Molinero, Baltasar. *La imagen de los negros en el teatro del Siglo de Oro.* Siglo XXI Editores España, 1995.

Freyre, Gilberto. "Alguns aspectos da cultura ibérica, principalmente da portuguesa, projetada nos trópicos." *Boletim da Academia das Ciências de Lisboa,* no. 39, 1967, pp. 220–339.

García de León, Antonio. *El mar de los deseos: El Caribe afroandaluz, historia y contrapunto.* Fondo de Cultura Económica de México, 2016.

Gilroy, Paul. *The Black Atlantic: Modernity and Double Consciousness.* Harvard UP, 1993.

González Climent, Anselmo. *Flamencología.* Escelicer, 1964.

Irenton, Chloe. "Black Africans' Freedom Litigation Suits to Define Just War and Just Slavery in the Early Spanish Empire." *Renaissance Quarterly,* vol. 73, no. 4, 2020, pp. 1277–1319.

Jones, Nicholas R. *Staging Habla de Negros: Radical Performances of the African Diaspora in Early Modern Spain.* Pennsylvania State UP, 2021.

Martín Casares, Aurelia. *La esclavitud en la Granada del siglo XVI.* Editorial U de Granada, 2000.

Méndez Rodríguez, L. "Bailes y fiestas de negros: Un estudio de su representación artística." *Archivo Hispalense,* vol. 90, no. 273–75, 2007, pp. 397–412.

Molina, Ricardo, and Antonio Mairena. *Mundo y forma del Cante Flamenco.* Revista de Occidente, 1963.

Moreno, Isidoro. *La antigua hermandad de los negros de Sevilla: Etnicidad, poder y sociedad en 600 años de historia.* Editorial U de Sevilla, 1982.

Nerín, Gustau. "Mito franquista y realidad de la colonización de la Guinea española." *Estudios de Asia y África,* vol. 32, no. 1, 1997, pp. 9–30.

Núñez, Faustino. *América en el Flamenco.* Flamencópolis Ediciones, 2021.

Ordóñez Sierra, Jorge. "Apéndice." *Cante en Córdoba,* by Anselmo González Climent, Ayuntamiento de Córdoba, 1957.

Pérez García, Rafael M., Manuel Fernández Chaves, and José Luis Belmonte Postigo, editors. *Los negocios de la esclavitud: Tratantes y mercados de esclavos en el Atlántico Ibérico, siglos XV–XVIII.* Editorial U de Sevilla, 2019.

Periáñez Gómez, Rocío. *La esclavitud en Extremadura (siglos XVI–XVIII).* 2008. U de Extremadura, Cáceres, PhD dissertation.

Piqueras, José Antonio. *La esclavitud en las Españas: Un lazo transatlántico.* Los libros de la Catarata (Madrid), 2012.

Rosales, Miguel Ángel, director. *Gurumbé. Canciones de tu Memoria Negra.* Intermedia Producciones, 2016.

Rossy, Hipólito. *Teoría del Cante Jondo*. Credsa, 1966.
Stella, Alessandro. *Ser esclavo y negro en Andalucía occidental (siglos XVII y XVIII): Documentos de archivo*. 2005. core.ac.uk/download/pdf/71612602.pdf.
Vélez de Guevara, L. *El diablo cojuelo*. Biblioteca Virtual Miguel de Cervantes, 2022.
Wolf, Eric R. *Europe and the People Without History*. U of California P, 2010.

Contributors

Tania Safura Adam is a curator, researcher, and founder and editor of *Radio Africa*, a platform for critical thinking and dissemination of black arts and cultures. Her research explores black diasporas, their movements and resistances, and African popular music. She curated *Microhistories of the Diaspora: Embodied Experiences of Female Dispersion* (La Virreina, 2018–2019), *Blue Black Futures* (MACBA, 2021–2022), and *Requiem for Humanity* (La Casa Encendida, 2023–2024). She was responsible for the program of activities *Making Africa: A Continent of Contemporary Design* (CCCB, 2016). She writes in different media and has published the essay "Black Voices: An Oral History of African Popular Music Vol. 1." She also presented the talk show *Terrícoles betevé* (2017–2019) and *African Bubblegum Music* on Radio Primavera Sound (2019). She is currently directing the research *España Negra: Viaje hacia la negritud en el espacio-tiempo* (Museo Reina Sofía, MACBA, Artium, CCCB, IVAM), the Iberian Black Studies seminar of the Museo Reina Sofía's Own Studies Program. She presents the program *Radio Africa* on betevé.

Jeffrey K. Coleman is Associate Professor of Iberian Studies at Northwestern University. He specializes in Contemporary Iberian Spanish and Catalan theater and popular culture. His first book, *The Necropolitical Theater: Race and Immigration on the Contemporary Spanish Stage*, explores how the intersections of race and immigration manifest in Spanish theater from 1991 to 2016. He is currently working on two book projects. The first is tentatively titled *España Negra: The Consumption and Rejection of Blackness in Contemporary Spain*, which explores the ways in which Spanish media, popular culture, and literature have portrayed and appropriated Blackness from the early twentieth century to the present, leading to the creation of a Black Spain. The second is *Liquid Identities: Bottling the Nation*, which explores wine as an avenue through which to understand the complexities of Spanish history and culture. He is the co-founder of TRECE (Taller de Raza, Etnicidad y Ciudadanía en España), a research group that actively theorizes and conceptualizes race in contemporary Spain.

Rosalía Cornejo-Parriego is Professor of Hispanic Studies at the University of Ottawa, Canada. She is the author of *Entre mujeres: Política de la amistad y el deseo en la narrativa española contemporánea* (2008) and the editor of the collections of essays, *Black USA and Spain: Shared Memories in the 20th Century* (2021) and *Memoria colonial e inmigración: La negritud en la España posfranquista* (2008). In addition, she has co-edited special issues of *Romance Notes* ("The Rosalía Effect: Popular Music and Culture in Contemporary Spain," with N. Michelle Murray, 2023) and of *Revista Canadiense de Estudios Hispánicos* ("Queer Space," with K. Sibbald, 2011), and the collection of essays *Un hispanismo para el siglo XXI: Ensayos de crítica cultural* (with A. Villamandos, 2011). Her research project on women intellectuals in the press during Spain's Transition to democracy was funded by the Social Sciences and Humanities Research Council of Canada. Part of that research resulted in the edition of Ana María Moix's journalistic writings: *Ana María Moix: Semblanzas e impertinencias* (2016). Furthermore, she is the former editor-in-chief of the *Revista canadiense de estudios hispánicos* and has published numerous book chapters and essays on gender and race.

Yinka Esi Graves is a British Flamenco dancer and practitioner whose choreographic work explores the links between Flamenco and other forms of corporeal expression from an African diasporic and contemporary perspective. She is featured in Miguel Ángel Rosales's documentary film *Gurumbé: Canciones de tu memoria negra* (2016), the first Spanish film to highlight the influence Spain's African population had on Spanish culture, particularly Flamenco. In the summer of 2023, she debuted *The Disappearing Act*, her first solo creation, which combines dance, live music, and text to explore how Black women articulate their resistance to erasure.

Kirsty Hooper is Professor of Hispanic Studies at Warwick University in the United Kingdom and a specialist in Spanish, Anglo-Spanish, and Galician cultural history since 1800. Her books include *Writing Galicia into the World: New Cartographies, New Poetics* (2011), *The Edwardians and the Making of a Modern Spanish Obsession* (2020), and *Modern Literatures in*

Spain: A Cultural History (2022; co-authored with Jo Labanyi, Elena Delgado, Helena Buffery, and Mari José Olaziregi). From 2020 to 2023 she held a Leverhulme Major Research Fellowship for the project *Hispanic London: Culture, Commerce and Community in the Nineteenth-Century City*. She is a Fellow of the Royal Historical Society and a Corresponding Member of the Real Academia Galega.

Oriol Lopez-Badell is a historian and international relations officer, working as coordinator of the European Observatory on Memories (EUROM) at the University of Barcelona Solidarity Foundation. He has a long trajectory in promoting international networking in the academic and institutional fields. He has been in charge of designing and implementing projects to raise awareness of the legacies of the colonial past, both in the local and international spheres. Oriol is also active in research and dissemination of cultural and memorial heritage, having curated several exhibitions, guided tours and public events linked to the history of the city of Barcelona in recent years. He obtained a graduate degree in History and postgraduate studies in History and Communication from the University of Barcelona; he was also visiting scholar at the Alliance for Historical Dialogue and Accountability program at Columbia University in New York.

Celeste Muñoz Martínez is a historian at the National University of Distance Education in Madrid (UNED). Her research has focused on the study of Spanish colonialism in Equatorial Guinea, from a legal, political, and memorial perspective. Her doctoral thesis for the University of Barcelona, situated at the intersections of history and anthropology, was titled *Law against Custom: Segregation, Legal Assimilation, and Punishment in Equatorial Guinea under Francoism (1936–1959)*. At the European Observatory on Memories, she is the coordinator of the "colonial memories" line of research and the "online memories" project, which applies new digital methodologies to memory studies. Additionally, she coordinates the team in charge of the Spanish part of the *Trans-Atlantic Redress Network* project, which aims to map historical injustices related to racial discrimination.

Juliana Nalerio's research explores the legacy of literature in history and history in literature, and the moral and political implications of both. In her scholarly work, she reads and teaches Critical Race Theory, literature, history, visual arts, and performance as text. She earned her PhD from Stanford University's program in Modern Thought and Literature and prior to this held a Fellowship predoctoral (Mineco-FPI) at the University of Valladolid and Salamanca. She was a visiting scholar in humanities at the Universitat Pompeu Fabra (Barcelona, Spain). Juliana has taught in the History department of the City University of New York and her writing has appeared in *CAMINO REAL: Estudios de las hispanidades norteamericanas*, *Miscelánea: A Journal of English and American Studies*, and *Remezcla*. She is a proud Latine from Florida.

Gustau Nerín is Professor of History of Africa at the University of Barcelona. His research focuses on Spanish presence on the African continent and, especially, on the colonization of Equatorial Guinea. He has published the following books on Spanish colonialism in Africa: *Guinea Equatorial: Història en blanc i negre* (1998), *El imperio que nunca existió* (co-authored with Alfred Bosch, 2001), *La guerra que vino de África* (2005), *Un guardia civil a la selva* (2005), *La última selva de España* (2010), and *Corisco y el estuario del Muni (1470–1931)* (2015). He is also the author of a study on the presence of Spanish slave traffickers on the African coast in the nineteenth century: *Traficants d'ànimes: Els negrers espanyols a l'Àfrica* (2016). His recent research has centered on Spanish memory of slavery and colonialism. He has been professor at the Université Paul Valéry in Montpellier (France), Universidad Nacional de Educación a Distancia, Universidad Nacional de Guinea Ecuatorial, Universidad Federal de la Integración Latinoamericana at Foz do Iguaçú (Brazil), and Universitat Pompeu Fabra (Barcelona).

Martín Rodrigo-Alharilla is Associate Professor of Modern History in the Department of Humanities at the Universitat Pompeu Fabra (UPF) in Barcelona. He is a corresponding foreign member of the Cuban Academy of History, a member of the Associated Unit of the Asia-Pacific Studies Group (of the Consejo Superior de Investigaciones Científicas, CSIC), coordinator of GRIMSE (Research Group on Empires, Metropolis and Extra-European Societies) and of the Master in World History, both at the UPF, and director of the *Esclavitudes* (Slavery) collection of the Icaria publishing house. Among his many single-authored books on the study of slavery and the Atlantic slave trade are *Los Goytisolo: Una próspera familia de esclavos* (2016) and *Un hombre, mil negocios: La controvertida historia de Antonio López, Marqués de Comillas* (2021); and as co-author and co-editor, *Negreros y esclavos: Barcelona y la esclavitud atlántica, siglos XVI–XIX* (2017), *Cádiz y el tráfico de esclavos: De la legalidad a la clandestinidad* (2018), and *Del olvido a la memoria: La esclavitud en la España contemporánea* (2022).

Contributors | 305

Miguel Ángel Rosales is an anthropologist, documentary film director, and scriptwriter. He has written and directed several short films such as *Luz en los Márgenes* (2013), *Atrapados al Vuelo* (2012), and *La Maroma* (2010). His first feature film, *Gurumbé: Canciones de tu memoria negra* (2016), has had wide international recognition. It is the first Spanish film to shine light on the historical presence of African descendants in Spain and their legacy in flamenco and Andalusian culture. Miguel Ángel has received awards at the São Paulo Festival, SEMINCI, Festival Cine Latino de Minneapolis and Festival Cine Documental de Barcelona L'Alternativa, among others. He is currently working on various audiovisual and film projects related to the memory of Afro-descendants in Spain. Presently, he is working on two different films about the only remaining community in Spain known to be the direct descendants of the historical Afro-Andalusians and the first repatriation of human remains from Europe to the African continent. He is also collaborating with choreographer and dancer Yinka Esi Graves in her latest work, *The Disappearing Act*, presented at the Flamenco Festival Nimes 2022 and Africa Moment in Barcelona. He was invited as professor-in-residence at Smith College, Massachusetts, in 2022.

Benita Sampedro Vizcaya is Professor of Spanish Colonial Studies at Hofstra University. Her research engages with Spanish colonial pasts and presents, archives and legacies, in Africa and in Latin America and the Caribbean. She is invested in revisiting colonial links within and beyond the frame of the multiple Spanish imperial Atlantic and global networks and has written on colonial medicine, colonial carceral systems, colonial archives, borders and mobility, and the ruins of late colonial modernity. Her recent publications include the journal articles "Islands of the Global Hispanophone: Islands of Empire" (2023), "*Houseboys*: Domestic Labour Practices in Spanish Settlers' Homes in Colonial West Africa" (2022), and "Transiting Western Sahara" (2019); the book chapters "Inscribing Islands: From Cuba to Fernando Poo and Back" (2019) and "The Colonial Politics of Meteorology: The West African Expedition of the Urquiola Sisters" (2019); she coedited a special issue of the *Journal of Spanish Cultural Studies* entitled "Entering the Global Hispanophone" (2019) and the book *Re-routing Galician Studies: Multidisciplinary Interventions* (2017). She is currently completing two book manuscripts, *Racismo científico y prácticas biopolíticas: El proyecto colonial español en África como laboratorio de experimentación bajo el franquismo* and *Caribbean Deportee Narratives and African Presidios: Carceral Systems of the Late Spanish Empire*.

Ulrike Schmieder is Lecturer and Researcher in Latin America history and Manager of the Centre for Atlantic and Global Studies at the Leibniz University Hanover in Germany. She has taught Iberian, West European, Latin American, and Caribbean history at the Universities of Leipzig, Cologne, Zacatecas, Hanover, Heidelberg, and Bremen with a focus on gender, (post)slavery history, and memories of enslavement, focusing on comparisons and entanglements in the Atlantic space. Schmieder's most recent book (*Nach der Sklaverei: Martinique und Kuba im Vergleich*, 2017) treats Martinique and Cuba, after emancipation of the once-enslaved, within the wider debate on post-slavery societies. She has published *The End of Slavery in Africa and the Americas: A Comparative Approach* (2011) with K. Füllberg-Stolberg and M. Zeuske, the special issue *Falling Statues Around the Atlantic* in *Comparativ*, vol. 31, no. 3–4 (2021), with M. Zeuske, and *Cultural Heritage and Slavery: Perspectives from Europe* (2023) with S. Conermann, C. Rauhut, and M. Zeuske, with her chapter on "Dealing with Dissonant Cultural Heritage: Traces of Enslavers in European Cityscapes." Finally, she has written a series of articles and book chapters about sites of memory of enslavement in France and Spain, as well as in Martinique and Cuba. The results of this research will be published in a forthcoming book on the subject of sites of memory and sites of silence associated with the transatlantic slave trade, scheduled for release in August 2024 by De Gruyter.

Akiko Tsuchiya is Professor of Spanish and Affiliate in Women, Gender, and Sexuality Studies and the Center for the Study of Race, Ethnicity and Equity at Washington University in St. Louis. She received her PhD in Hispanic Literatures from Cornell University. Her areas of specialization include nineteenth- and twentieth-century Iberian literatures and cultures, with a focus on gender studies. She is the author of a book on Galdós and has published extensively on the nineteenth-century narrative and on women writers of contemporary Spain. Her other books include *Marginal Subjects: Gender and Deviance in Fin-de-siècle Spain* (2011) and two co-edited volumes: *Empire's End: Transnational Connections in the Hispanic World* (2016) and *Unsettling Colonialism: Gender and Race in the Nineteenth-Century Global Hispanic World* (2019). She is currently working on a new book, tentatively titled *Spanish Women in the Nineteenth-Century Antislavery Movement: Transnational Networks and Exchanges*.

Aurélie Vialette is an Associate Professor at Yale University in the Department of Spanish and Portuguese. She previously held appointments at Stony

Brook University, The Ohio State University, Cornell University, and The University of Texas at Austin. She earned her PhD from the University of California, Berkeley. Her research areas are working-class culture, popular music, social movements, gender studies, prison reform, slavery networks, Filipino studies, and disability studies. Her first book, *Intellectual Philanthropy: The Seduction of the Masses* (2018), is the recipient of the 2019 North American Catalan Society book award. Her co-edited volume on *Dissonances of Modernity: Music, Text, and Performance in Modern Spain* was published in March 2021. Her new book manuscript analyzes penal colonies in the Philippines and is titled *The Trial Run: Gender, Disability and Penal Colonies in the Philippines in the Nineteenth Century*. She is the director of www.clave.cat, a Digital Humanities project on music and politics. She is preparing a special issue on Disability Studies and Iberian Studies for *Hispanic Review*. Vialette has been invited professor at the École Normale Supérieure in Lyon, France.

Index

Abárzuza Hermanos, family and company, 156, 157, 178; Abárzuza y Rodríguez, Felipe, 178
Abárzuza Oliva, Fernando, 178
abolition, of slavery, 4, 14n2, 49, 62–63, 79, 82, 85, 86, 89, 99, 100, 101, 102, 104, 105, 113 156, 161, 163, 171, 172, 177
Abya Yala, 165, 168
activism, 4, 10, 12, 132, 215, 279
Adam, Tania Safura, 7, 9, 12, 113, 273–80; *Radio Africa* 9, 12, 276–77, 279, 280; *Radio Africa Magazine* 9, 12, 215, 273–74, 275; *España Negra* 9, 12, 278
African sound (or Black sound), 274, 276
African workers, 141, 158
Afro-Andalusian (or Black Andalusian), 283, 291, 294–95, 296, 297
Afro-descendants, 5, 8, 10, 13, 14, 98, 100, 101, 103, 104, 174, 205, 212, 258, 292, 294, 296, 298n4
Afro-diaspora (or African Diaspora), 11, 13, 15n7, 98, 288, 294, 296, 297
Afro-Spanish associations, community and movement, 11, 113, 164, 178, 179, 287

Alameda Apodaca, today *calle Clara Campoamor*, Cádiz, 161
Alameda Marqués de Comillas, today *alameda Hermanas Carvia Bernal*, Cádiz, 161
Albiach, Jéssica, 141
Alphonse XII (Alfonso XII), King of Spain, 60, 126, 129, 168, 172
Altadill, Antonio, 225, 228–30, 235, 236, 237
Amadeo, King, 59, 67
Amaru, Tupac, 176
Amistad, ship and insurrection of African captives, 89, 176; historical novel (David Pesci) 234; film (Steven Spielberg), 235, 236, 237, 238
anthropocentric moralism, 261
Antillón, Isidoro de, 163
anti-racism, 6, 10, 113; anti-racist groups, activists or movement, 2, 5, 8, 126, 132, 142, 143, 164, 212, 215. *See also* SOS Racisme
anti-Slavery Society, 54
Apodaca y Eliza, Juan Ruiz de, 161
Aponte, José Antonio, 161
Araujo, Ana Lucia, 3, 7, 14n1, 14n3, 144n3, 144n5, 154, 197; *Politics of Memory*, 2–3; *Slavery in the Age of Memory* 2

Arcelin, Alphonse, 130, 217
archive, 5, 9, 10, 21, 23, 37, 43n9, 73–91, 227; colonial archive, 41, 78, 305
Arenal, Concepción, 172
Argüelles, Antonio de, 163
Arnalte, Arturo, 224, 226–27, 230
art activism, activist, 132, 135, 139
Artigas, Xavier, 146n19; Idrissa, *Chronicle of an Ordinary Death* (documentary), 146n19
asiento, 156, 180n8
Asociación de Hacendados y Propietarios de Esclavos (Landowners' and Slave Owners's Association), 86
Asociación para la Recuperación de la Memoria Histórica, 145n10
Assemblea Nacional Catalana (ANC), 6
Atlantic slave trade, 2, 10, 89, 113, 205, 230, 235
Augusta, ship 53
Avenida de Francisco Pí y Margall, Madrid, 171
Azarmandi, Mahdis, 130, 138, 147n29, 147n30, 148n32, 148n34, 155. See also Roberto Hernández

Balangingi, 81, 83
Baldwin, James, 1, 9
Banco de Barcelona 85
Banco de España in Santander, 85
La Barcelona incòmoda, 7–8
Barcia, Manuel, 3
Bardem, Carlos, 236–37
Baró, José, 79
Baroja, Pío, 232
Basque merchants, 51, 87, 92n8
Bastidas, Micaela, 176
Beetham, Sarah, 143
Benhabib, Seyla, 297

Bernault, Florence, 22
Bernecker, Walther L., 175
Berquist, Emily, 3
Betevé, 273, 276, 278
Biardeau, Captain, 124
Bioko, 22, 112. See also Fernando Poo
Black Africans, 5, 212, 236, 247, 252, 293, 294
Black bodies, 9, 11, 12, 91, 193, 194, 204, 253, 254, 257, 283, 301
Black children, 12, 244, 245, 246, 265n7
Black consciousness, 279
Black dance, 295
Black futurism (or Afrofuturism), 274–75
Black Lives Matter, 11, 146n19, 132, 146n19, 153, 161, 168, 174, 176, 212, 213, 217, 285
Black Spain, 276, 277
Black thought, 274, 275, 277
Blackness, 11, 12, 99, 100, 103, 104, 114, 191, 193, 206, 248, 254, 258, 277, 279; anti-Blackness, 98, 113, 161
Blanco, Pedro, 12, 53, 55, 112, 176, 223–38; *Pedro Blanco, el negrero*, novel by Lino Novás Calvo, 112
Boabí, 23, 28, 29, 30, 31, 33, 34, 35, 44
Bodies, non-normative, 255, 256; freak body, 265n15. See also black bodies
Boil, Bernardo (Father), 140
Borbón, Antonio Carlos de, 180n9
Borbón, Francisco de Asís de, 168
Borrell Lemus, Isabel, 170
Boys, 21, 26, 31, 32, 33, 42. See also *Houseboys*
Brazil, 153, 154, 176, 276, 288, 293
Brewster de Vizcarrondo, Harriet, 172
Bristol, 14n3, 155
Britain's Slavery Abolition Act, 89

Brown, Olga, 285
Bullangues, 146n20; Plaza de les Bullangues, 130
Burdiel, Isabel, 168, 174
Burton, Antoinette, 3
Butler, Judith, 148n39

Cabreras of Ponce family, 50, 62, 64–67
Cádiz, 11, 51, 52, 56, 60, 88, 101, 153, 155, 156–63, 177, 178, 239n4, 294, 295, 296
Caldeira, Arlindo Manuel, 154, 252, 266n18
Calle Antonio López (Cádiz), 161
Calle Clara Campoamor (Cádiz), 161
Calle Conde de Peñalver (Madrid), 169
Calle O'Reilly (Cádiz), 161
Canal Historia; *Encadenados,* 8
Cantó, Toni, 178
capitalism, 75, 76, 180
Caribbean, 88, 104, 147n26, 169, 174, 178, 179, 180n3, 192, 206, 217, 282, 292, 294, 296, 297
Carreras y Xuriach, José, 85
Casado, Pablo, 178
Castelar, Emilio, 162; Glorieta de, 171
Catalonia, 6, 7, 10, 95, 96, 100, 101, 102, 104, 107, 114, 121–24, 126, 130, 131, 132, 136, 138, 139, 141, 142, 143, 156, 177, 178, 209, 210, 211, 214, 217, 218, 228, 277; empire (Medieval), 136, 147n28; immigration policies in, 142; industrial revolution, 6; Modernism 6, nationalism, 6, 131, 139, 142, 145n15
Catalonia in Common (political platform), 141, 148n36
Catedral de las Américas (Cádiz), 157

Cayetana, thirteenth Duchess of Alba, 12, 243, 244, 245, 247–51, 252–64, 266n21
Cayuela, José, 49
Centro Cultural El Doce (Cádiz), 157
Cepas, Juan, 233–34, 238
charity, 66, 105, 155; feminization of, 251
Chaviano Pérez, Lizbeth, 123, 155, 163, 168, 174, 178, 180n7
Chicaba, 251; *Black Bride of Christ,* 265n10
Chipaumire, Nora, 283, 285, 286
Círculo Hispano Ultramarino, 138, 172
climate change, 191, 195, 198, 203
Colau, Ada, 126, 130, 139, 141–42, 145n11, 148n36
Coleman, Jeffrey K., 11
Colomé, Francisco F., 86
Colomina, James, 133; "Humanity," 133
colonialism, 3, 4, 5, 10, 14, 126, 130, 138, 139, 141, 145n15, 147n29, 148n36. *See also* Spanish colonialism
colonofilia, 147n26
Colston, Edward, 155
Columbus, Christopher, 129, 136, 138, 142, 147n27, 211; Columbus monument. *See* monument
commemoration, 3, 11, 122, 138, 146n18, 147n27, 155, 158, 163, 165, 172, 193, 194, 211; of Columbus, 138, 147n27
commodification (objectification) of Black bodies, 11, 12, 253, 254
Compañía de los Caminos del Hierro del Norte de España, 86
Compañía Gaditana de Negros, 156, 158
Compañía Trasatlántica Española, 86, 158

Comunidad Negra Africana y Afrodescendiente de España (CNAAE), 174
Conill, Agusti, 224
Connected Worlds: The Caribbean, Origin of Modern World (project and network), 181n12
Consejo para la Eliminación de la Discriminación Racial o Étnica, 179
Constitution of Spain, or Constitution of Cádiz (1812), 161, 163, 295
Constitution of Spain (1837), 168
Cordero Torres, José María, 233, 235, 237
Corisco, 227
Cornejo-Parriego, Rosalía, 12, 243–71
counter-monument, 132
Crédito Mercantil, 85, 158
Cuba, 4, 10, 25, 49, 50, 53, 57–61, 79, 83, 85, 86, 87, 88, 89, 95–114, 123, 145n15, 153, 154, 155, 157, 158, 161, 162, 168, 169, 172, 174, 180n3, 211, 214, 225, 226, 227, 228, 229, 230, 233, 234, 253, 254, 259, 260, 261, 288, 293, 294, 297
Cuban import trade, 58
CUP, Popular Unity Candidacy (political party), 126, 141

dance, 12, 281, 282, 283, 284, 286, 287, 288, 292, 295, 296, 298n2
decolonial initiative (activism), 6, 16n10, 132, 139, 143
decolonization, 12, 34, 35, 162, 278–79
Democratic Memory, 9, 126, 142, 146n20, 211; Law of, 3, 15, 210, 218; Office of 7
Día de la Raza (Día de la Hispanidad), 138–39

Diallo, Idrissa, 126, 130, 146n19; Plaça Idrissa Diallo, 126, 128, 131, 135, 142, 143, 215
Díaz Ayuso, Isabel, 176, 178, 266n20
domestic service (work), vii, 9, 21, 22, 24, 25, 26, 27, 28, 31, 39, 41, 42, 43n4
Domínguez y Borrell, Antonia María, 169
Domínguez de Guevara, Miguel, 170
Douglass, Frederick, 121
Drake, Richard, 231

Eizaguirre, Joaquín, 87
Embodiology, 285, 286
empire, Spanish, 3, 30, 74, 87, 96, 124, 129, 139, 147n26, 154, 176, 213, 218, 293; transatlantic, 138. *See also* imperialism
Enlightenment, 248, 254, 259
enslaved, enslaved Africans, 1, 5, 12, 14n1, 14n2, 43n5, 59, 62, 89, 90, 96, 97, 98, 99, 100, 101, 102, 103, 105, 106, 107, 113, 130, 144n2, 154, 155, 156, 157, 158, 161, 163, 164, 165, 166, 167, 168, 169, 171, 172, 176, 177, 179, 179n2, 180n3, 180n9, 180n10, 181n12, 193, 194, 197, 203, 211, 214, 229, 244, 249, 258, 261, 262, 277, 284, 285, 287, 288, 293, 296
enslavement, 8, 11, 98, 103, 148n32, 153, 154, 155, 156, 157, 161, 162, 163, 164, 165, 166, 168, 171, 172, 174, 176, 177, 178, 179, 179n2, 244, 245, 248, 249, 251, 252, 265n10. *See also* enslaver
enslaver, 11, 106, 153, 154, 155, 156, 157, 161, 163, 164, 165, 166, 167, 168, 170, 171, 172, 173, 174m, 176, 178, 180n7, 180n8, 180n10

Equatorial Guinea, 21, 23, 158, 164, 209. *See also* Bioko and Fernando Poo
#EsclavitudSinComillas, 146n22
Espejo público (TV program), 142
Espinosa de los Monteros, Iván, 178
ethnographic exhibits, 255
European Observatory on Memories (EUROM), 6, 7, 8, 9, 16n14, 127–28, 132, 145n13, 209, 210, 211, 214, 215, 218, 219
exhibits on slavery. La esclavitud y el legado cultural de África en el Caribe, Madrid, Museo de América (2021–22), 176; El gran experimento ¿El fin de la esclavitud?, Madrid, Museo Nacional de Antropología (2023), 180n10; Las Murallas de Cádiz y el Comercio; 1717–2017, Cádiz, Casa de las Américas (2017), 180n4. *See also* museums

fascism (fascists), 124, 126, 130, 131, 139, 140, 161, 178, 210, 233
Ferdinand VI (Fernando VI), King of Spain, 166
Ferdinand VII (Fernando VII), King of Spain, 166, 174
Fernando Poo, vii, 9, 21, 22, 23, 24, 25, 26, 27, 28, 29, 30, 34, 35, 36, 37, 39, 41, 42, 43n5, 44n11, 112, 238n2. *See also* Bioko
Ferrer, Arnús, 82
Ferrer y Vidal, José, 79, 85
Festival Conciencia Afro (Madrid), 165
Flamenco, 9, 12, 13, 281–83, 284, 286–88, 291–94, 296–98
flamencology, 13, 291, 292
Floyd, George, 153, 161, 213, 285

Fracchia, Carmen, "*Black but Human*," 3, 5
Fradera, Josep María, 4, 16n12, 224
France, 3, 153, 154, 155, 169, 178, 194, 215, 254, 274
Franco, Francisco, 3, 124, 161, 181n14, 233; dictatorship 3, 76, 77, 124, 125, 126, 139, 145n10, 145n12, 177, 178, 210, 213, 218, 233, 264n5
freak body, 255, 265n15
Front Nacional de Catalunya (FNC), 6
"Fuck the Fascism" (organization), 140–41, 148n34

García-Boente, Xose Quiroga, 132, 139. *See also* Daniela Ortiz
García Cantús, Dolores, 25, 42n1, 45, 238n2
Gaviria Alcoba, Manuel de (Marqués de Gaviria), 174
General Tobacco Company of the Philippines (Compañía General de Tabacos de Filipinas), 10, 73–91, 123
Gheme, Linus N., 23, 35, 36, 37, 39, 40, 41, 44n17
Gilroy, Paul, 96, 98, 297; *The Black Atlantic*, 15n7, 297
Glorieta de Emilio Castelar (Madrid), 171
González, Felipe, 139
Goya, Franciso de, 12, 244, 245–49, 251, 252, 259, 262, 264n4, 264n5, 266n21; "*La Beata*" *with Luis de Berganza and María de la Luz,* 245, 246; *The Duchess of Alba with María de la Luz in Her Arms,* 247
Granja de San Saturnino, Marqués de la, 50, 59, 61

grass-roots activists (groups, initiatives), 6, 7, 8, 140
Graves, Yinka Esi, 9, 12, 281–89, 298n2; *The Disappearing Act*, 13, 281, 283, 284–85, 286, 289
Great Britain, 3, 49, 57, 61, 89, 153
Gue, 30, 31
Güell, Eusebi, 79, 85, 86, 138
Güell, Joan, 86, 138, 145n9
Guijarro, Gonzalo, 235, 236
Guillén, Nicolás, 260, 266n17
Guixé Coromines, Jordi 7, 127, 129, 132–33. *See also* Núria Ricart
Guridi Alcocer, José Miguel, 163
Gurumbé: Canciones de tu memoria negra (film), 9, 13, 164, 281, 288, 291

Haiti, 96, 104; Haitian Revolution, 96, 176
Hall, Stuart, 121
Harmony, Peter, 156
Hartman, Saidiya, 1
Havana, 50, 56, 57, 58, 60, 61, 67n3, 87, 97, 103, 106, 110, 112, 157, 168, 169, 226, 260, 264n3, 292
Hérnandez, Roberto, 130. *See also* Mahdis Azarmandi
Hernández Espinosa, María del Carmen, 172
"Hidden Atlantic," 4, 90
Hispanidad, 138, 139, 148n31, 215, 266n19
Hispanism. *See* panhispanism
Hispano-Colonial Bank (Banco Hispano Colonial), 79, 80, 85, 86, 87, 90, 92n4, 123, 158, 172, 238n4
Hispano-tropicalism, 13, 66n19, 213, 291, 293
Hooper, Kirsty, 9, 49–71, 176
Hospital del Niño Jesús (Madrid), 172

Huyssen, Andreas, 15n4, 132, 144n4, 147n23

Iberian Atlantic, 3, 4
Iberian Black Studies group, 277
Iberian studies, 3, 4
ida y vuelta ("round trip"), 292, 294, 298n2
immigrant, 5, 8, 83, 92n2, 126, 130, 132, 133, 135, 143, 146n19, 147n25
immigration, 131, 191, 198, 200, 276, 277, 278; laws (policies), 8, 142, 146–47n22, 212
imperialism, 3, 15n6, 141; imperial nostalgia, 143
indiano, 86, 96, 102, 103, 124, 129, 214
invisibility, 8, 129, 284, 285
Isabella II (Isabel II), Queen of Spain, 54, 164, 166, 168, 169, 174

Jiménez family, 50, 57–62, 64, 66, 67n3
Jones, Adam, 225, 238n2
Jones Mathama, Daniel, 22, 23, 28, 30, 31, 34, 35, 43, 44, 45; *Houseboys*, vii, 21, 22, 23, 24, 25, 26, 27, 28, 30, 31, 32, 33, 39, 41, 42, 43, 44, 46
Jones, Maximiliano Cipriano, 29, 30, 43, 44
Jones, Nicholas (Nick), *Staging* Habla de negros, 5, 298n4

Kaphar, Titus, 244, 262
kinship 86, 87, 91
Knauer, Lisa; *Contested Histories in Public Spaces*, 122, 144n4. *See also* Daniel Walkowitz
Knowing History Association (Associació Conèixer Història), 9, 209, 217

Labra, Rafael María de, 172
Landelle, Gabriel de la, 231
Una lanza por el Boabí, 23, 28, 30, 32, 34, 35, 43n6
Larrinaga, José de, 88, 89
Larrinaga, Ramón de, 87, 92
Law of Democratic Memory, Catalonia (2022), 3, 11, 15n5, 144n6, 218
Law of Historical Memory (2007), 3, 11, 126, 145n14, 210, 211
Lecuona, Ernesto, 230
Ley de Extranjería (immigration law), 141, 146–47n22
Lomboko, 235; novel, 236
London, 9, 14n3, 49–67, 75, 79, 81, 226
López Badell, Oriol, 9, 11, 15n4, 16n15, 175, 209–11, 215–17
López Bru, Claudio (Marqués de Comillas II), 87, 158, 160, 161
López García, José Miguel, 3, 100, 180n6
López y López, Antonio (Marqués de Comillas), 10, 73, 74, 76, 79, 80, 85, 86, 87, 90, 103, 122, 123, 141, 142, 146n21, 211, 214, 236
Luba, 22

Mac Orlan, Pierre, 233
MACBA (Museum of Contemporary Art in Barcelona). *See* museums
Madrid, 11, 54, 59, 75, 79, 91, 139, 153, 155, 156, 163–79, 180n10, 217, 253, 256, 277, 278, 279, 282
Maeztu, Ramiro de, 148n31; "Defensa de la Hispanidad," 148n31
Malabo, 22
Maluquer de Motes, Jordi, 224
Mandela, Nelson, 130
Manzanedo y González de la Teja, Juan Manuel de (Marqués de Manzanedo), 172, 173, 176, 180n7, 224
María Cristina de Borbón, Queen Regent of Spain, 164, 166, 167, 168, 174, 230
María de la Luz (Luz), 12, 244, 245–51, 253, 257, 259–63, 264, 264n3, 266–67n21
Marro, Alfredo, 229
Martín Casares, Aurelia, 4, 5, 298n4; *Mujeres esclavas y abolicionistas*, 5. *See also* Rocío Periáñez Gómez
Martin-Márquez, Susan, 15n6, 42n1, 146n17
Martínez, Pedro, 53, 156, 157
Martínez Valdivieso, Nicolás, 86
Martinique, 153, 154, 180n3
Martino, Enrique, 25, 26, 42n1, 44n11, 158
Mbembe, Achille, 21, 41
Mejía Lequerica, José, 163
Memoria y lugares de memoria de la esclavitud y el comercio de esclavos en la España contemporánea (project), 181n13
memorialization. *See* commemoration
memory, 73, 91, 123, 124, 141, 143, 193, 206, 210, 211, 212, 215, 296, 297; collective memory, 2, 3, 7, 8, 90, 121–22, 142, 143, 144n3, 238, 283, 296; colonial memory, 133, 211, 215; cultural memory, 16n7; democratic memory, 3, 7, 9, 15n5, 126, 142, 146n20, 210, 211, 218; historical memory, 3, 11, 12, 112, 126, 141, 145n14, 193, 205, 210, 211, 212, 213, 214, 223, 224, 252; local memory, 7; media memory, 202, 204; memory policies (politics of), 4, 11, 15n4, 154, 155, 174, 177, 178, 179, 209–19; memory programs (initiatives), 126, 145n13;

memory *(continued)*
  memory sites, 2, 3, 5, 10, 11, 122, 143, 153, 154, 155, 164, 211, 218; public memory, 2, 3, 11, 57, 74, 121, 124, 130, 144n5, 209; of slave trade (or slavery), 2, 3, 12, 14n3, 16n7, 112, 193, 205, 212, 223, 224, 225, 228, 237, 238, 252
Michonneau, Stéphane, 136, 138, 147n26
migrant, 23, 25–28, 35, 37, 43n5, 81–83, 146n19, 191, 200–202, 204
migration, 3, 5, 25, 28, 194, 200, 202, 214, 273
Modernism (Catalan), 6, 110
modernity, 95, 96, 98, 138, 214, 297
monument (memorial), 2, 4, 5, 8, 11, 14n3, 73, 74, 75, 121, 122, 136, 144n5, 147n23, 153, 154, 155, 165, 166, 168, 177, 179, 206, 213, 215, 216; to Antonio López y López (Barcelona), 10, 14n1, 122–36, 211, 212, 214, 217, 218, 239n4, 250–51; to Christopher Columbus (Barcelona), 10, 136–43, 147n30, 147n26, 147n30; to Charles III, King (Madrid), 166; to Claudio López Brú (Cádiz), 158, 160; Confederate, 74, 121; "Crossing Rubicon" (Museo Atlántico, Canary Islands); 202; Francoist, 140, 144n6, 145n14; to Isabel II, Queen (Madrid); to María Cristina; Regent Queen (Madrid), 166; Segismundo Moret (Cádiz), 162
Morejón, Nancy, 258
Moret, Segismundo, 162
Morrison, Toni, 114; Africanist representation, 256; Africanist framework, 258
Motoboys, vii, 22, 42

Muñoz Martínez, Celeste, 6, 7, 9, 11, 15n4, 16n15, 143, 175, 209, 211–15, 217–19
Muñoz y Sánchez, Agustín Fernando (Duque de Riánsares), 164, 230
Murray, N. Michelle, 3, 15n6, 193–94, 198
Museo Atlántico (Lanzarote, Canary Islands). *See* museums
museums, 10, 11, 14n3, 165, 275, 278–79; Darder Museum of Natural History, 130, 217; MACBA (Barcelona), 132, 142, 215, 273; Museo Africano Mundo Negro (Madrid), 164; Museo de América (Madrid), 164, 176, 217; Museo Atlántico (Canary Islands), 11, 191–207; Museo de Cádiz, 157; Museo de las Cortes (Cádiz), 157; Museum of Anthropology (Madrid), 180–81n10; 278; National Archaeological Museum (Madrid), 164; Prado Museum (Madrid), 166
music, 11, 12, 13, 56, 65, 110, 112, 127, 177, 256, 273, 274, 275, 276, 281, 286, 287, 288, 291, 292, 293, 296, 297; black music, 293, 297

The Naked Maja (film), 245, 248, 264n5, 269–71
Nalerio, Juliana, 10, 95–117
Naranjo y Orovio, Consuelo, 176, 179
National Day of Catalonia (September 11), 114, 139
National Day of Spain (October 12), 138, 139, 140, 141. *See also* Día de la Raza
Ndongo-Bidyogo, Donato, 30, 44n14
negrada, 95, 99, 106–108, 109–10, 112–13

Negrers: La Catalunya esclavista (documentary), 6, 143
negro/a, negrito/a, 95, 96–98, 99, 100–104, 105, 106, 107, 109, 110, 112, 130, 254, 257
Nerín, Gustau, 12, 112, 176, 223–42, 266n19, 293
Ngom, Mbare, 30, 43n7, 44n14
Nguji wa Thiong'o 277
Nigeria(n), 21, 23, 26, 28, 31, 35, 36, 37, 40, 41, 44n11, 45n17, 289
Nimako, Queen of Ndongo-Matamba (Angola), 176
Nora, Pierre, 3, 155
Novás Calvo, Lino, 112, 225, 232, 233, 235, 238

Olano e Oriondo, José Antonio de, 87, 88, 92
O'Reilly McDowel, Alejandro, 161
Orientalism, 12, 256
Ortiz, Daniela, 132, 139, 142, 215; *Estat Nació* 132. *See also* Xose Quiroga García-Boente
Osuna García, Fernando, 158
Otero, Lisandro, 234
Oyono, Ferdinand, 21, 28, 34

Palacio de Gaviria (Madrid), 174
palimpsest, 81, 122, 141, 144n4
Pan-Africanist groups (activists), 130, 132, 143, 164
Pan-Hispanism (Hispanism), 139
Pareja, Juan de, 166
Parque Comillas (Madrid), 169
Peninsular Steam Navigation Company, 52, 53
Peñalver y Cárdenas-Vélez de Guevara, Nicolás de, Conde de Peñalver, I
Peñalver y Peñalver, Narciso José de, Conde de Peñalver, II, 1, 169

Peñalver y Zamora, Nicolás de, Conde de Peñalver, III, 169
Pérez, Angel Bernardo, 85, 87, 92
performance, 13, 112, 127, 140, 214, 237, 257, 286, 296
Periáñez Gómez, Rocío, 5, 298n4
Pesci, David, 234, 235
philanthropy 51, 55, 56, 59, 60, 66, 67, 73, 105
Philip IV (Felipe IV), King of Spain, 180n8
Philip V (Felipe V), King of Spain, 166, 180n8
Philippines, 10, 73, 74, 81, 83, 85, 87, 88, 89, 91, 92n8, 92n9, 174, 259
Piqueras, José Antonio, 98, 123, 154, 164, 168, 170, 224, 238n1, 298n4
Pisarello, Gerardo, 146n18
plantation, 21, 22, 25–27, 30, 31, 34–36, 44n11, 96, 97, 155, 158, 214, 253, 297; Boca Chica 62, 64, 66; cocoa 158; coffee 97, 106; owner 29, 62, 172, 229, 230; sugar 57, 62, 64, 164, 169; tobacco 83–85
Plaza de Colón (Madrid), 168, 170
Plaza Marqués de Comillas (Madrid), 169
Posadas, Carmen, 12, 243, 245, 252, 253, 259, 260, 261, 262, 264, 266n18, 266n19; *La hija de Cayetana*, 12, 245, 248, 252, 254, 255, 256, 258, 260, 261, 262, 263
post-emancipation, 9, 22, 24, 25, 27, 28, 34, 42, 154
presentism, 14n1
Prim, Juan, 59, 145n9
Protestantism 62, 64, 66, 67
public art, 133, 142
public debate, 7, 15n3, 74, 122, 126, 136, 141, 143, 177, 213

public history, 8, 10, 11, 210, 216
public space, 2, 7, 8, 10, 73, 74, 121, 122, 123, 126, 131, 132, 133, 143, 148n39, 154, 158, 162, 176, 177, 179, 214, 218
Puerta del Sol (Madrid), 166
Puerto Rico, 25, 49, 50, 59, 62, 63, 88, 89, 104, 105, 108, 145n9, 163, 171, 174, 226, 266
Puig-Samper, Miguel Ángel, 176, 179
"purity of blood," 98, 139, 295

Quintana, Manuel José, 12, 245, 248, 251, 253, 260, 261, 262, 264, 265n10; "A una negrita, protegida por la duquesa de Alba," 248

race, 39, 95–101, 107, 131, 139, 193, 197, 251, 260, 275, 279, 293
racial justice, 4
racial thought, 10
racism, 2, 8, 10, 14n1, 16n15, 95, 98, 99, 103, 130, 136, 141, 146n22, 153, 162, 165, 212, 213, 215, 233, 262, 279, 295; anti-Black racism, 10, 95, 98, 103, 108–13
redress, 16n15, 147n23, 210, 218
reparation, 6, 15n5, 16n15, 126, 130, 143, 146n18, 146n19, 212, 214, 215, 217, 218
Republic of Spain, First, 50, 58, 62, 171
Republic of Spain, Second, 161, 177, 233
revisionism, historical, 15n4
Ricart Ulldemolins, Núria 128, 132, 144n6, 155. *See also* Jordi Guixé Coromines
Rio Gallinas, 225
Roca Barea, María Elvira, 178
Rocabruno, Juan Carlos, 178
Rodrigo-Alharilla, Martín (Martín Rodrigo y Alharilla or Martín Rodrigo), 4, 10, 15n4, 16n12, 74, 75, 76, 79, 80, 82, 85, 87, 89, 92n4, 95–117, 123, 124, 136, 144n7, 154, 155, 156, 157, 158, 168, 172, 178, 224, 233, 253
Rodríguez Burón, Tomás, 226
Roig, Gonzalo, 230
Roman Catholicism, 51, 55, 56, 58, 61, 66
Rosa, Toni de la, 236
Rosales, Miguel Ángel, 9, 13, 164, 281, 285, 288, 291–300; See also *Gurumbé*, 9, 13, 164, 281, 288, 291
Rousseau, Jean-Jacques, 255, 256, 259, 265n14
Ruiz, Carrie, 145n14
Ruta de los Cargadores a Indias (Cádiz), 158
Ryall, Alan, 236

Sampedro Vizcaya, Benita, 9, 16n10, 21, 43, 44n12
San Carlos, 22, 23, 28, 29, 30, 32, 33, 35, 37. *See also* Luba
Sánchez, Pedro, 139
Santa Isabel, 22, 23, 30, 37, 40. *See also* Malabo
Santa Marina, Luys, 233
Schmidt-Nowara, Christopher, 4, 62, 147n26, 147n27, 155, 163, 171, 172
Schmieder, Ulrike, 10–11, 153–89
Scott, Joan, 2
Seaton, Anthony, 202
selfie, 200, 202, 204
Sense ficció, 6
Serrano y Domínguez, Francisco, 169
Seville, 157, 252, 262, 265n12, 282, 284, 294, 295, 296
Siaka, King, 226
slave. *See* enslaved

Index | 319

slave trade, 2, 4, 6, 9, 10, 11, 14n2, 14n3, 15n7, 16n11, 16n12, 44n11, 49–51, 53, 61, 67, 74, 75, 76, 79–83, 85–87, 89–91, 92n3, 95, 96, 100, 107, 109, 113, 123, 130, 132, 143, 144n7, 155, 156, 192, 193, 203, 205, 206, 215–16, 223, 224–25, 227, 229, 230, 231, 232, 234–38, 245, 248, 285. *See also* Atlantic slave trade & transatlantic slave trade
slave trader, 5, 9, 10, 12, 53, 55, 73, 74, 75, 82, 86, 87, 89, 97, 109, 112, 113, 122, 123, 129, 145n8, 223, 224, 225, 228, 229, 231–36
slave-trafficking. *See* slave trade
slave voyages, 57, 198, 225
slavery route, 2, 8, 10
SOS Racisme, 8, 113, 114, 126, 132
Sotolongo y Alcántara, Pedro de (and Samá Sotolongo y Cía), 79, 85, 86, 87
Spanish Civil War, 15n5, 76, 77, 78, 124, 126, 145n10; anarchists in, 177, 210, 213
Spanish colonial Africa, 9, 21
Spanish colonial history, 10, 11, 139
Spanish colonialism, 3, 4, 5, 10, 12, 14, 16n15, 123, 138, 142, 161, 162, 175, 177, 209, 212, 213, 214, 215, 217, 261, 262, 279, 303
Spanish exceptionalism, 12, 253, 261, 262
Spanish Guinea, 26, 28
Spanish merchants, 9, 50, 54, 57, 60, 61, 136
Spielberg, Steven, 235. *See also* Amistad (film)
statue. *See* monument
Stoler, Ann, xii, 30, 78, 80, 82, 85, 89, 91
Sundiata, Ibrahim K., 42n1, 43n5

Surwillo, Lisa, 5, 15n6, 86, 104, 129, 130, 155, 168; *Monsters by Trade* 5, 15n6

Tabacalera, 74–81
Tannenbaum, Frank, 181n11
Tanquem els CIE, 8, 130, 132, 135, 146n19, 147n25
Taylor, Jason DeCaires, 191, 194, 195, 196, 197, 198, 199, 203, 204, 205, 206; "Crossing Rubicon" 191, 202–204; "Disconnected" 191, 200–202; "The Raft of Lampedusa" 191, 198–200, 202, 204, 206
Thomas, Hugh, 53
Tintó, JaimeTintó, 224
Toasije, Antumi, 164, 165, 171, 178, 179
Tofiño, Iñaki, 3
Torre Diaz, Count and Countess 50, 54–56, 61
Torre Tavira (Cádiz), 158
tours: historical, 9, 216, 217
Trans-Atlantic Redress Network, 16n15, 210, 218
Transatlantic Shipping Company (Compañía Trasatlántica Española), 86, 123, 145n15, 158
transatlantic slave trade, 11, 82, 91, 192, 193, 203, 205, 206, 285. *See also* slave trade
transatlantic studies, 3
transnational workers, 24, 26, 28, 42
Tsuchiya, Akiko, 1, 10, 14n1, 15n6, 74, 113, 121–52, 155, 177

"Undefined Territories: The Colonial Legacy in Art" (MACBA exhibit), 142
UNESCO slave route project (Routes of Enslaved Peoples), 2, 14n2

United Nations Human Rights Council (UNHRC), 163
Universal Exposition, Barcelona (1888), 136, 138
Universidad Pontificia de Comillas, 158
University of Barcelona Solidarity Foundation (Fundació Solidaritat), 9, 209, 210
unritual, 193–94, 197, 205, 206

Valdés, Gerónimo, 227
Valenciano-Mañé, Alba, 7, 143
Vallarino, Baltasar, 231–32
Verdaguer, Jacinto (Jacint), 74, 129, 145n15; *L'Atlàntida* 129, 147n24
Vialette, Aurélie, 1, 5, 10, 73–94, 228
"Vicissitudes" (sculpture). *See also* Taylor, Jason DeCaires
Vidal y Ribas, José, 229
Vilà i Galí, Agustí, 224
Vila Vilar, Enriqueta, 4, 156, 163
Villaverde, Cirilo, 230; *Cecilia Valdés*, 230
Vinent Vives, Antoni (Marqués de Vinent), 156
violence, 13, 15n5, 23, 34, 41, 76, 90, 130, 140, 141, 147n25, 147n29, 147n30, 194, 195, 197, 206, 212, 215, 218, 237, 284–85; colonial, 130, 140, 141
visual culture, 11, 12, 143
Vizcarrondo, Julio, 172

Walkowitz, Daniel, 122, 144n4. *See also* Lisa Knauer
Ward, Geoff, 136
West Central Africa, 25, 27, 34, 41, 42n1
white savior, 235; narrative, 12, 253, 256, 260, 261, 266n18; trope, 251
white supremacy, 5, 95, 96, 122, 130, 153
Wray, Amy, 283, 285, 286. *See also* Embodiology

Yancy, George, 257

Zeuske, Michael, 4, 80, 89, 90, 92n3, 96, 97, 103, 153, 154, 176, 235. *See also* "Hidden Atlantic"
Zulueta family, 50, 51–57, 60, 86, 224; Zulueta, Julián de, 79, 176; Zulueta, Pedro Juan and Antonio, 51, 53, 61, 62, 64, 66, 67, 156

www.ingramcontent.com/pod-product-compliance
Ingram Content Group UK Ltd.
Pitfield, Milton Keynes, MK11 3LW, UK
UKHW041923140426
5217IPUK00014B/287